THE
PERSONAL SESSIONS
Book 2 of
The Deleted Seth Material

Sessions
12/8/71– 11/27/73

THE EARLY SESSIONS

The Early Sessions consist of the first 510 sessions dictated by Seth through Jane Roberts. There are 9 books in *The Early Sessions* series.

THE PERSONAL SESSIONS

The Personal Sessions, often referred to as "the deleted sessions", are Seth sessions that Jane Roberts and Rob Butts considered to be of a highly personal nature and were therefore kept in separate notebooks from the main body of the Seth material. *The Personal Sessions* are expected to be published in 6 to 9 volumes.

"The great value I see now in the many deleted or private sessions is that they have the potential to help others, just as they helped Jane and me over the years. I feel that it's very important to have these sessions added to Jane's fine creative body of work for all to see." –Rob Butts

THE SETH AUDIO COLLECTION

Rare recordings of Seth speaking through Jane Roberts are available on audiocassette and CD. For a complete description of The Seth Audio Collection, request our free catalogue.. (Further information is supplied at the back of this book.)

For information on expected publication dates and how to order, write to New Awareness Network at the following address and request the latest catalogue. Also, please visit us on the Internet at www.sethcenter.com

New Awareness Network Inc.
P.O. BOX 192
Manhasset, N.Y. 11030

www.sethcenter.com

THE
PERSONAL SESSIONS
Book 2 of
The Deleted Seth Material
Sessions
12/8/71– 11/27/73

©2003 by Robert Butts

Published by New Awareness Network Inc.

New Awareness Network Inc.
P.O. Box 192
Manhasset, New York 11030

Opinions and statements on health and medical matters expressed in this book are those of the author and are not necessarily those of or endorsed by the publisher. Those opinions and statements should not be taken as a substitute for consultation with a duly licensed physician.

Cover Design: Michael Goode
Photography: Cover photos by Rich Conz and Robert F. Butts, Sr.
Editorial: Rick Stack
Typography: Raymond Todd, Michael Goode

All rights reserved. This book may not be reproduced in whole or in part, without written permission from the publisher, except by a reviewer who may quote brief passages in a review; nor may any part of this book be reproduced, stored in a retrieval system, or transmitted in any form or by any means electronic, mechanical, photocopying, recording, or other, without written permission from the publisher.

ISBN 0-9711198-5-6
Printed in U.S.A. on acid-free paper

I dedicate The Personal Sessions
to my wife, Jane Roberts,
who lived her 55 years
with the greatest creativity
and the most valiant courage.
-Rob

A NOTE ON THE COVER DESIGN PHOTOGRAPHS

June 2003. A note about the photographs Michael Goode used in his striking cover design for The Personal Sessions *series.*

The central colored photograph of Jane and the lower right and left-hand shots of her and myself were taken by my father, Robert F. Butts, Sr., in Sayre, PA a year or so after our marriage in December 1954. The upper right one of Jane in trance for Seth was taken (among many others) by Rich Conz, a photographer for the Elmira, NY Star-Gazette, while he witnessed Session 508 on November 20, 1969. (See Volume 9 of The Early Sessions.*)*

I don't know who photographed the young Jane shown on the upper left, but she saved that picture all of those years for me to inherit upon her death in September 1984, when she was 55.

My inventive and versatile father had always taken photographs, and in his later years turned professional, photographing many weddings and other events in the Sayre area (and also Jane's and my wedding at the home of my younger brother Loren and his wife Betts in Tunkhannock, PA). To help my father, my mother Estelle trained herself to hand-color his black and white photographs, for color film was not available then—and so she colored Jane's portrait. Now I wonder: do my long-deceased parents, and Rich and the unknown photographer of the young Jane, all know that their creativity will grace the covers of a series of books that I so lovingly dedicate to them, as well as to Jane and each reader? I believe that they do, each in his or her own way.

—Rob

SESSION 599 (DELETED PORTION)
DECEMBER 8, 1971

(This material is deleted from the 599th session for December 8, 1971.)

Now. We will divide the session into two parts, although they may or may not be equal parts.

We may do this presently for some sessions. I am taking it for granted that you are both determined to clear the air and set yourselves to a new level of achievement and freedom. Therefore I will make whatever comments I can on your progress.

First of all, this evening's small chat: it was a beginning. You should freely encourage each other however to express feelings. Those mentioned tonight on Ruburt's part were "negative" ones precisely because they were so strongly inhibited. He tossed them out cautiously, watching for their effect upon you.

You reacted cautiously. It was like the beginning of a dance. When Ruburt got a real touch of inhibited feeling he automatically translated it to the leg, and only by a strong exertion of will managed to get the <u>feeling</u> behind the words out at all. Nor did you freely encourage him to do so.

(These feelings involved unexpressed emotions stemming from several years ago, on Jane's part. When she became aware of them, she got a pain in a leg, but a little later did tell me about them.)

He worried about the effect of such expressed feeling on you, and both of you intellectualized, as is often your wont. This does not mean that a series of crying jags, explosive ones, need be in order, as Ruburt fears, and fears that you fear.

("I wasn't concerned about that.")

They would be well worth the while, however. This is the kind of thing I have been speaking of—the avoidance of a direct confrontation with those (in quotes) "negative emotions" blocks out the one emotional (in quotes) "solution": an emotional statement on your part that counters it—a meeting of emotions.

The <u>expressed</u> (underlined) emotional anger, accusation or hurt on Ruburt's part would automatically, or should, bring out in you an answering emotional statement. Answering in that any hurts or reasons on your part would be expressed with feeling, and the way cleared for an emotional statement of love, regret, or on both of your parts an emotional expression of sorrow for having hurt the other.

Instead you get to the point where the emotion barely surfaces and you say "Oh, yes, that came from such and such." This applies now to both of you.

Now you both handled emotional situations involving you both more or less in the same manner. You still do not want to feel and counter the emotions on their level.

This clears the emotions, the spirit and the mind as well as the body. This is what I meant by not moving each other to tears or laughter. By this small encounter this evening you showed your willingness to proceed, and also clearly showed how little you understood about what I really meant.

You want to do anything with the emotions but feel them. Write about them, paint them, talk about them, anything but feel them. Do you see the difference now?

("Yes.")

I want to get around your basic fears that emotional freedom is automatically the feeling of negative emotions, though you may initially begin there. Arguments between you for example would have been far healthier. Then you could have kissed and made up, and meant it.

This operates as strongly for you as Ruburt. You have seen him in a very few honest expressions of anger, once when he tried to throw a chair, and felt the suddenly released energy that he usually does not channel physically. That same unexpressed energy is present within you, but it must be felt first, and acknowledged. If you have questions ask them. Now. I mentioned, and you realize the significance of Ruburt turning down the radio when you enter the room. He tried to turn his emotions down in the same way. He felt you equated noise, period, with emotional behavior.

There is a rich bed of energy and emotions for you both. You were afraid to approach it. I will make the practice with your approval of commenting more or less regularly for a while.

("Okay.")

Do you have questions?

("No.")

Make it a point then to encourage your own expression of emotion, and Ruburt's. Do you want a break?

("How about a very short one?")

Then we will return to other material. *(9:35.)* Let me add, before your break, a few other remarks to this portion. The very fact that you now must take time out for the clear expression of emotion is telling, in itself. Once you learn, you will express your emotions freely as you go about your day.

(9:36. Jane's trance had been good. She said, regarding her leg pain, that when she got it just before the session she felt like crying, but didn't want to interrupt the session. She was afraid I'd be bothered, also.

(I told her in turn, and believe she agreed, that all phases of our lives were changing, that it was vital that they do so, since the way of life we had worked out was doing so poorly. This included my painting, my job at Artistic, my attitudes about money, classes—in short everything I could think of, I guess. I'm not so sure Jane would lump all of her activities together in the same way, though — she may not feel the need. I strongly suspected my days at Artistic were numbered; especially so since we now planned a long trip early next year, after taking care of checking the copyreading Prentice-Hall is now doing on Seth Speaks; *we are due to get the script back in January.)*

(9:50.)

Now. In our sessions and in your work with me, various kinds of teaching methods have been used, and will be. Steps and bridges will be provided.

It is senseless to ask whether or not a bridge is true. It exists. It gets you somewhere. A bridge is a valid reality, regardless of its architecture or the type of symbols that may be written upon it, or its color, or the material from which it is made.

The Sumari language is a bridge, and valid in those terms. It will lead you into the use of the inner senses, away from the confining nature of pet phrases and familiar language that is already loaded with its own connotations.

The Sumari language <u>is</u> a language then in those terms, a method of communication. It is the beginning of a logically unstructured vehicle that will carry you hopefully further into the inner heart of perception. I hope that eventually it will allow you to experience more fully the inner cognizance that is beneath physical perception and physical translation.

A bridge serves those both coming and going, and carries goods in both directions. The Sumari language in those terms will be used as a method of carrying you further into the nature of inner cognizance, and then allowing you to return again, retranslating what you have learned, not automatically into the stereotyped verbal pattern.

The language will effectively block the automatic translation of inner experience into stereotypes, therefore. This is a very simple explanation. The bridge in our case will be a multidimensional one, serving therefore other purposes also. It will be (in quotes) "constructed" in such a fashion that it allows the exploration of many different levels of reality. Some method was needed to prevent this translation of inner data from becoming too distorted by the verbal forms that so readily awaited it. Do you follow me?

("Yes.")

This is but one method. *(Pause.)* In following this particular line of development, Ruburt for example will be taught to free inner cognition from the recognized verbal patterns enough so that any future work with speakers manuscripts will not be stereotyped out of all proportion. A recognizable verbal pattern must of course result, but use of the language itself will break up these personal associative processes that cling to recognized language symbols.

Therefore clear perception of inner data can freely use the whole structure of your own language for its flow if need be, but the stereotyped patterns will be broken.

The practice with the language, and other practices that will be connected to it, will serve other purposes also. *(Pause.)* A certain amount of mental and psychic alertness is required on the one hand, and on the other alertness itself changes brain patterns in a most effective manner.

Other physical manipulations may also be involved, as Ruburt suspected this afternoon. The word cordella, now for example, was used instead of alphabet to break your ordinary conceptions of alphabet while conveying an idea of symbols closely allied, and upon which alphabets are based.

(Here Seth refers to Jane discussing Sumari in writing class this afternoon.)

There are, then, cordellas beneath the sensations of hearing, smelling, touching, seeing. If I told you that the skin had its own alphabet without what I have already explained, it would not have been nearly as clear. The word cordella, used in the same fashion, frees you from limiting conceptions of what an alphabet is.

Then, and only then, can you project this understanding or insight onto the word alphabet, and sense how the skin does have its own alphabet. The word alphabet itself becomes changed for you. Do you follow me?

("Yes.")

Do you want a break?

("Yes."

(10:17—10:35.)

Now. Do you remember the word given for painting?

(As Seth, Jane referred now to the Sumari language session we held on Wednesday, December 1, in place of the regular session. As I sat on the couch in our living room, my oil painting of Ianodiala, the 14th century Turkish clairvoyant, hung on the wall behind me. This is the painting Jane had used as a teaching instrument on Dec. 1, and referred to again now.

(The December 1 session had been recorded, and is extremely interesting. I ended up speaking some Sumari myself. Jane advanced to the point where she was able to translate some of this as we went along and the end product, in part, was some excellent poetry.

("No. It began with an M, though."

It was montella. *(My phonetic interpretation.)* Montellas are the end products of cordellas, arranged not only in a certain <u>fashion</u>, but congregated or placed within a certain rich sphere of dyniad activity.

("Wait—can you help me with that spelling? No. I've got it," I said, writing it out. Phonetically I spelled it out in my notes as den-i-ad. As it turned out, I wasn't quite correct after all. Reading these notes over, Jane told me I had spelled the word incorrectly, that it should be dyniad. This is the way she wrote it out herself. She saw the y, she said.

(We straightened out the spelling before I resumed typing these notes on Saturday evening, December 11.)

The word dyniah connotes an apparent boundary that serves to define that which lies within by acting upon it. dyniah, the word itself without the "d" ending, you see, while never appearing within the montella, defines its activity, reinforces its identity, and is as much a part of it as the hidden cordella that gives it form. *(Pause.)* From the outside the dyniah seems to bring the montella to an end. *(Long pause.)* Give us a moment here.

As you know, there is constant interaction going on within all portions of the montella, these possible because of the defining boundary (in quotes) "barrier."

I am using the different terms simply to give you an idea of how the language can be used to free your ideas about familiar things. The most (in quotes) "objective" montella is a symbol of course. The more true to life the montella is the less apt you are to realize its symbolic qualities on a conscious level.

Think in terms of impressionism and its values, then switch to the idea of a Sumari language and see the connection, and the purposes that can be served. The language is fluid. All of the words need not be defined, though key ones will be. It will be used as a method of <u>expanding</u> your concepts, not of teaching you to translate experience into just another but different stereotyped form that happens to be more exclusive.

Now our sessions have always involved methods of perception, and the translation of inner experience. The sessions themselves deal with experiences that are basically not verbal but must be physically translated. Translations go on of which you are not aware whether or not you perceive them, and whether or not you are affected. They are simply the results of such activity intruding into a physical montella.

Now do you see how the word used in that manner tells you something different?

("I think so. I just want a chance to think about it." Actually I did see, but still wanted time to think.)

I simply want to clue you into what I am doing as I do it.

If new ambrya—think of embryo now—(in parentheses now:) data were to be inserted into a painting, a completed painting, from the inside, then all the relationships within the painting would change. If new ambrya is inserted into a physical montella then all the relationships within it must change. *(Pause.)*

Everything within any given plane must follow the laws of the plane. A new sketch of a house, say, could not suddenly appear within a physical painting—the new data could not be given that way.

The new data emerging within your physical reality would have to appear in a way that was congruous with its surroundings, and adopt then some acceptable representation. To follow it back to its source however you would have to keep sight of it as it gradually was divested of these recognizable patterns. The language gives you a thread, then, to follow it backward. You may take a break or end the session as you prefer.

(I asked for a break at 11:05. Both of us were bleary, however, so the break turned into the end of the session.)

SESSION 600 (DELETED PORTION)
DECEMBER 13, 1971

(This material is deleted from the 600th session for December, 13, 1971.
Now, Good evening.

("Good evening, Seth.")

First we will have our fireside chat.

You have made a good beginning. Ruburt has noticed several occasions when he projected negatively in your direction. In other words, instances where he misinterpreted your meaning, or anticipated a negative reaction.

Your remark earlier to him to relax in the moment is indeed an important key, and he needs that reminder. The kitten was a way of bringing attitudes and problems to the surface, while incidentally helping a young animal. Your plans are good ones and I will have more to say in that area.

The trip is also advantageous, and it would not hurt you to keep your eyes and ears open during that journey.

There have always been possibilities for you, for example, in Florida, that you may or may not want to take advantage of. Your lines of communication are improving. Ruburt has greatly appreciated your efforts.

You may feel free to ask me about your plans, and I will give you what help I can. The emotional basis of your relationship is beginning to take its proper balance and direction. Now: Do you have any questions on the material just given?

("No, I guess not. Things seem to be going well.")

Then give us a moment.

(Pause at 9:27. This is the end of the deleted material. Now I present the restt of the session in its regular form.)

Consider again, for the sake of analogy, the Sumari language as compared to impressionism. At its <u>best</u> (underlined) impressionism achieved a certain focus unknown to <u>Western</u> art up to that time, in your terms, offering a breakthrough from cohesive objective form into the moving vitality that gives objects, say, their durability and shapes their images.

Using the art form, the artist in a strange way broke through line, destroyed what would seem to be the literal continuity of the objective shape. At the same time a few lines were used to hint at a variety of unseen, apparently unstructured objects, so that in that regard the line became in the hands of a master a strong symbol, hinting at other realities that lay within the seemingly distorted portrayal of objects.

Do you follow me?

("Yes.")

At its poorest, communication between the viewer and the painting was lost, for a poor artist could not work that magic with lines or colors. A thorough knowledge of form was needed so that it could be represented by line or color. At its best, impressionistic art by its very lack of indelible, delineated form, suggested all form and the vitality that gave it force.

Now the Sumari language will avoid specific, indelible, rigid pattern in much the same way. *(Pause.)* By changing the names of objects you automatically look at them in a new fashion, yet certainly all objects will not be given names, for this would defeat our purpose.

Instead the relationship between objects will be stressed through sound. The emphasis will be on an object's "placement," (in quotes) in title and space as you think of it, and on the ever-changing pattern of force that constantly alter relationships of any kind.

(9:39.) There will be words for example for feelings that you will be asked to imaginatively change into objects and back again, to project into time as you think of it, and sense the differences in the feeling's relationship to yourself. This can be compared in quite other terms to taking an object from one table and placing it in another room, and trying it out in various locations; but we will be working instead with feelings instead of vases, and psychological locations.

The sounds used in the language have their own importance, and will be in their own way representative or suggestive of feelings that have been largely unconscious, generally speaking. The feelings however are the tail end of inner cognizance, and we will use the sounds to carry us further and further into those inner landscapes where both objects and their representatives must finally desert us.

We will initially be using the language so that we can finally cease using it, in other words. These will be the beginnings of somewhat more profound methods of working through the inner senses.

Now you may take your break.

(9:45—10:00.)

Now. Our use of the language will not be heavy-handed. Use of it however will allow you to more clearly perceived your own inner reality, your physical and psychic experience. You will no longer translate inner experience with the same automatic glibness into stereotyped verbal patterns of images, but will be far better able to experience it for itself.

The language will be a necessary aid in the physical statement that must of course finally be made, but the final statement then, or physical interpretation, will be far truer to your original experience.

Now you almost automatically translate a feeling into a definite rigid word and image. The two go hand in hand. For physical reasons of course you need that camouflage interpretation, but you also need to learn the difference between it and inner cognizance.

(10:05.) You will also become far more aware of the actual processes of perception. There are many inner experiences, obviously, that cannot be expressed clearly or with any justice through even the combined use of words or images.

Use of the language, utilizing sound but not recognizable word symbols, will allow you to understand and express some of these. Doing so will enable you to express far more physically also. There are, to say the least, multitudinous levels of feelings that merge to form what you would call a given experience.

Alphabets can hardly hope to give you more than, if you will forgive me *(humorously)* lip services to these. Each symbol in an alphabet stands for therefore unutterable symbols beneath it. Now the human voice, as singers know, can be used to express far more qualities of feeling than the normal unadorned speaking voice. Sound itself, even without recognizable words, carries meaning. Oddly enough, sometimes the given meaning of a word does battle with the psychic and physical meaning of the <u>sounds</u> that compose it.

(10:11. Pause.) As I have said often, language is used as often to distort as it is to clearly communicate. There is a structure within the Sumari language, but it is not one based upon logic. Some of its effectiveness has to do with the synchronization of its rhythms with bodily rhythm. The sounds themselves activate portions of the brain not usually used in any conscious manner. It is a disciplined language in that spontaneity has a far greater order than any you recognize.

Now give us a moment. *(Pause at 10:16.)*

The word shambalina *(spelled by Seth at my request)* connotes the changing faces that the inner self adopts through its various experiences. Now this is a word that hints of relationships for which you have no word. *(Pause.)*

Shambalina garapharti *(spelled)*, or the changing faces of the soul, smile and laugh at each other. Now all of that is in one phrase. By saying the words and opening your perception the meaning becomes clear in a way that cannot be stated in verbal terms, using your recognizable but rigid language pattern; so we will be dealing then with concepts as well as feelings, but seeking them through the use of a new method, and sometimes translating them back and forth for practice.

(Long pause at 10:24.) Cordellas are invisible symbols that surface. As they surface they show the universe in a new light by the very nature of their relationships. In a very limited fashion alphabets do the same thing, for once you have accepted certain basic verbal symbols they impose their discipline even upon your thoughts, obviously since you think in words so often.

They throw their particular light upon the reality that you perceive, as for example you name objects. Alphabets are nevertheless tools that shape and direct perception. They are groups of relationships that are then transposed upon (in quotes) "reality." To this extent they shape your conceptions of the world that you know.

Their discipline and rigidity is considerable. Once you think of a "tree" (in quotes) as a tree, it takes great effort before you can see it freshly ever again, as a living individual entity. Cordellas do not have the same rigidity. Far greater, immensely greater fluidity operates. Inner invisible relationships are allowed to rise, the acknowledged recognized reality viewed through the lenses of these emerging relationships. Then the cordella changes its nature, becomes another new emerging group of relationships, another lens in other words. Do you follow the connections?

("Not too well, because I was busy writing. I think I understand what you mean. I have it all down all right."

(10:33.) Give us a moment.

It is as if, then, you had alphabets that worked for the other senses, for touch, and smell. Meanings are allowed to rise and fall where, when using your established ideas of language, meanings are instead rigidly attached to given experiences so that perception must be held within certain well-defined limits.

Now I will let you take your break.

(10:35. Jane's trance had been good, her pace mostly fast. She said she had felt Seth trying to get some "new concepts" across—trying very hard to make it clear to us. I said it was clear enough, but that I was so busy writing that eventually I lost all sense of the meaning of the words. Jane also had images, but Seth never vocalized what they meant. She knew they applied to cordellas and paintings.

(We talked it over. Jane had visualized a painting of houses and trees. She said Seth had considered that an artist could do, say, five paintings; each with different symbols but all with the same basic meaning. Resume in the same manner at 10:55.)

Now. In your terms the Sumari language is not a language, since it was not spoken verbally by arty particular group of people living in your history.

In quite different terms however it is a language that is at the base of all languages, and from which all languages spring in your terms. Alphabets do not change, or you would consider them relatively useless. Cordellas, as I told you, do change. Alphabets are the physical aspect of cordellas. One very small aspect of a cordella is sized upon and (in quotes) "frozen," so to speak, its ordinary motion and the rhythm of its changes therefore unrecognized. *(Long pause at 11 PM.)*

The living vitality of a cordella rises out of the universe's need to express and understand itself, to form in ever-changing patterns and take itself by surprise. Patterned language allows for no such surprises. The Sumari language has been used in the dream state.

(Jane's pace had slowed up. Now the phone began to ring in Jane's workroom, across the hall. I could hear it even through two closed doors. Presumably Jane could too, but she appeared to be not bothered as she sat in trance.)

The language itself <u>seeks out</u> meanings. It is hidden within all languages, whether or not they sound at all similar, for it is based upon the immaculate integrity of feeling, for which sound is only a dim representation.

It builds up from feelings that are by their nature denied clear expression through the specific but therefore limiting alphabet systems. *(Pause at 11:06.)* It allows the perceiver to face experience much more closely, and once having done this to some extent he is free in other areas also. If you were an accomplished artist in many fields, you could translate a given feeling into a painting. A poem, a musical masterpiece, a sculpture, a novel, an opera, into a great piece of architecture. You would be able to perceive and feel the experience with greater dimension, for your expression would not be limited to translating it <u>automatically</u>, without choice, into any one specific area. Its dimensions would be greater to you then. So a cordella as opposed to an alphabet opens up greater varieties of experience and expression.

(*11:11.*) As basic creativeness is behind all art forms, so cordellas are behind and within alphabets. Cordellas represent the ever-changing unfinished relationships that can never be fully expressed, and that constantly seek expression.

Through this session and the last I have tried to show you through some examples the different ways in which the word cordella can be used, and by inference the ways in which the use of this method will enrich your understanding and perception. Your closer relationship will have its effects upon our sessions also, for your energies are at peace *(louder:)*—and now I bid you a fond good evening, cordella and all.

(*Laugh. "Thank you very much, Seth. Good night."*)
(*11:16.*)

DELETED SESSION
DECEMBER 20, 1971

(*This is the regularly scheduled session for December 20, 1971. It is deleted from the record.*

Jane was quite relaxed this evening, hence our late start. We had gone Christmas shopping this afternoon, etc.)

Now—is it all right for me to come in now?

(*"Yes."*)

Dare I make a few comments about yesterday and today?

(*"Sure."*)

I will make the remarks concerning yesterday first. Ruburt was in poor shape yesterday. You helped him because he was <u>aware</u> of your love and concern. You <u>did</u> (underlined) make that obvious. He knew you were making every effort to provide your end of a merry Christmas, with the tree, etc.

His condition was the result of denying feelings and trying to hold them back again, so as not to upset the apple cart. The feelings were told to shut up. They were not intelligent. They were beneath consideration. They were not approved of, and intellectually Ruburt silenced them, <u>before</u> giving them adequate voice or expression.

The feelings can be adequately handled through reason and emotion <u>after</u>

(underlined) they are allowed expression.

Now your remark, not verbatim, "Come on, Hon, get with it," worked to some extent, for it roused his desire to give you a good day, not to spoil it, and his spirits rose to some degree. But you did not encourage him to express the feelings. Both of you dealt with the matter in the old way, to some extent.

He told himself he understood what the feelings were, and did not approve of them, but he did not allow them expression at all.

In the past a whole series of counterimpressions would have occurred. Your love and concern would not have been so apparent, you would have become dejected as a result of his condition, he would have interpreted that as disapproval and rejection, and a good week's time might have been spent under the same conditions, so you have improved.

But see what should have been done. You should have encouraged him to release the feelings and the two of you faced them together. They were not that terrible, you see.

("I didn't think of it.")

Now. What Ruburt said about the beloved monster *(Willy, our cat)* is true.

(This afternoon Jane had some very good insights as to why we had taken in the kitten, Parmesan – who, incidentally, is now gone to the parents of friends, etc.)

The loving encounter of this evening was extremely beneficial, and I mentioned the value right after the last such episode. The combination of love and physical touch, and the inner intent, is highly important. Reread what I told you, it will save us time, regarding the way in which emotions are buried within the body, and at your loving touch given release.

This is also of additional benefit to you, as you see that Ruburt responds to you and is not beyond your reach. Do you follow me?

("Yes.")

I want Ruburt to discuss those feelings with you also of yesterday. He thinks, simply because he knows them and disapproves of them, that thinking alone removes them.

Now your relationship, as I told you, is a creative springboard for you both. The Sumari development would not have occurred until your relationship had a revival, and further creative developments have already been sparked for the same reason.

You may take a break and we will resume with other material, unless of course you have questions on the above material.

("No, I guess not.")

(10:31. Jane's trance had been good. We discussed the events of yesterday, and the fact that my mother is due to return to Sayre on Sunday, December 26. Jane and

I are to spend Christmas in Rochester with brother Dick and family, and bring mother back with us, etc. 10:37.)

Now. I fear I am needed. I told you that in the past a week might have gone on with yesterday's conditions, plus the fact that I would not have been permitted to give you information, or feedback—and certainly a day such as today would not have followed.

A day like today is extremely significant to both of you, for it builds up inner confidence, particularly on Ruburt's part. Even your (underlined) behavior yesterday, while not what it might have been, was supportive enough to keep the situation from getting out of hand, and the memory of your night's dancing was also supportive, so that you have more supportive elements to cushion various situations.

In fact, your behavior yesterday was so appreciated that it led to the creative inspiration of your Christmas present, which is an exciting creative endeavor. I dare not say more. *(Humorously.*

(This was Jane's inspiration to write a series of songs for me in Sumari. This development promises many excellent ramifications.)

Your visit to class *(Tuesday, December 14)* meant much to Ruburt, and to the other students. By your complete absence, you see, you also led them to suspect that you disapproved, for they knew that in your other activities psychically you worked together. It was a symbolic gesture then of importance. You also did not attend until the Sumari development.

Now a small note: Your poor, misguided, unjolly bachelor friend downstairs did you a service many times, in complementing your wife when you were unable to do so, in giving her a sense or a glimmer of female pride or appreciation when you were unable to communicate, and you knew this.

You were partially grateful for it, and partially angry, but at yourself. Now that Ruburt is coming to you more fully again, and your neighbor's compliments and flirtations are no longer needed, you are ready to jump on him, both of you.

Ruburt was glad many times that a man found her attractive when she did not see that answering glimmer in your eye—not that it was entirely your fault, now.

He tries to be gallant. He is also worried because of his own nature that women find him unattractive, because of age, and because of a feeling for the other sex. He wants to feel that he is not so much a homosexual as that he leaves women unaffected. For this reason his comments and manner grow more "out of bounds" as he grows older and becomes more frightened.

I wanted to give you insight on that, however. Now take a break. Today can be considered a touchstone. Both of you did things right.

(*10:52. Ordinarily we have been getting some personal material, to be followed by theoretical data for the balance of the session. I now said I'd rather learn something about why Jane wasn't putting on weight, rather than get something on Sumari, for instance. 11:05.*)

Now. We will continue then along present lines.

I told you, in the context given, that Ruburt was emotionally deprived, this showing in the physical condition. That you were also to some extent, this showing in your work.

The beloved monster lost weight, looked neglected, lost his luster, became listless unless forced into activity, looked older. Now, he was <u>suddenly</u> deprived of his position. The emotional energy usually given him automatically was transferred elsewhere. You saw the sudden change. He also became in his own way obstinate.

He carries no grudges. When the condition was arighted he began miraculously springing back to normal.

(*Although as of this writing I don't think Willy has fully recovered as yet. There has been a very marked improvement, however.*)

Now Ruburt's weight is a part of the whole picture. Added to this are certain attitudes of your own, that is attitudes both of you <u>have</u>. Both of you have the same attitude, which means that they are magnified, doing double duty.

These are emotional. You may make intellectual adjustments <u>yourself</u>, but Ruburt has not made them. The emotional attitudes are: weight is bad. Whenever you speak of weight yourself it is with that connotation. People are overweight. The good word does not have the word weight in it. It is slim. It is the word weight, now, that is loaded—forgive my pun.

Whenever the word is used it has a negative connotation to you both. To put on weight is not desirable. Your diet has been geared with that in mind. Granted Ruburt exaggerated where you made adjustments, but both of your emotional attitudes are the same at that level.

Eating is more a gluttonous endeavor to you in that regard. The preparation of food is a waste of time. It takes time away from more valuable things, both in its preparation and cleanup later. It is too sensuous. Those are your attitudes emotionally. Food must be kept as simple as possible, as <u>unobtrusive</u>.

There is little fun connected with it. Now you do vary in your attitudes, but only in degree. You will be more adventurous or inventive perhaps at this time, but the strict emotional attitude remains the same. The kitchen is the least important part of your house. These attitudes, then, do not help. To some extent Ruburt is in a quandary, for the idea of gaining weight seems to contradict other deeply-buried feelings.

These feelings have much to do with the conflicts Ruburt feels with your friends Claire and Bob, for they go to the opposite extreme, where life revolves around nourishment. Give us time. You both often criticize those who are overweight, emphasizing in your minds and feelings the lack of control this implies to you, the overindulgence. This brings up those ideas of discipline, of giving into feeling, by implication.

Ruburt considers it in very poor taste *(humorously)* to 'oh' and 'ah' over food. Both of you enjoy a sense of moral superiority in the presence of your brothers' families, that they eat so heartily while you refrain. <u>Both</u> of you now prove that you are not sunken in materialism by being thin. Ruburt simply carries this further than you do, rigidly holding his ground despite all entreaties to the contrary.

("Will knowing all of this do him any good?")

It will indeed. But other steps should be taken.

The phrase, "giving into your appetites," is important here. It is one of the reasons for example why he does not like to eat, generally, in front of others. It is a moral principle to him, but also applies privately. It involves not being fleshy in voluptuous terms, a kind of esthetic discipline that morally disapproves of others. The sexual connotations are obvious, and added on. When he did not feel loved he would not eat—the two appetites, you see.

He did not, in the past now, feel nourished. When your intimate situation improves, so will his eating habits. But oddly enough the reverse also applies—when his eating habits improve so will your intimate lives. Your <u>tempting</u> him to eat, for example, and underline tempting, has strong sexual connotations to which he will respond, both sexually and through eating more.

Both of you also have emotional ideas, now being tempered I hope, emotional feelings, that to deny sex or minimize it is to improve your creative capacity. Instead you squeeze yourselves dry.

Philosophically and practically there are many ramifications on this subject that I hope to cover, but what I have said for now applies. The word tempt is important, for it implies on you part a willingness to have him taste and share with you both through food and sexual enjoyment. Telling him to eat without understanding your own emotional attitude is useless, for he picks up and exaggerates the Puritan-like feelings toward food. Your preparing food for him now and then as a counterpoint can help.

("I usually cook breakfast now.")

He does have, as you do, buried sensuous tastes that can be cultivated: his buried far more than yours. Your combined emotional feelings toward food have been exaggerated by him. He thinks you disapprove for example of the very foods you tell him to eat, the sugars and starches. You condemn them except when mentioning them to him.

Do you want a break?

("Yes.")

You may end the session if you prefer.

("I think we'd better. It's been very helpful.")

(Louder:) My heartiest regards.

("Thank you, Seth. Good night.

(11:33.)

SESSION 601
DECEMBER 22, 1971 9:25 PM WEDNESDAY

(From 6-7 PM this evening Jane and I attended a cocktail party given by Leonard Yaudes in his apartment downstairs. Afterward Jane, Shirley Bickford—one of Jane's ESP class members - and I listened to the tape of ESP class, made last night. The tape contained some of the Sumari chants Jane has been giving in class recently. They are extremely interesting. I told Jane before the session tonight that I couldn't give her much of any sort of answer to her questions about the chants or the Sumari development in general. I didn't have enough information, etc.

Are you ready?

("Yes. Good evening.")

If I go too fast slow me down.

("Okay.")

There are several issues I would like to discuss, and several angles from which I would like to view them for you. Let us begin with the voices, the tape.

First of all, before we get to the meaning or import of the tapes, let me say that Ruburt is learning to handle energy in other fashions. The experience itself, the voice demonstration, is highly therapeutic physically. Energy is received and discharged wholeheartedly, exuberantly and spontaneously through sound. This involves certain inner muscular coordinations and releases.

The sounds themselves are also therapeutic in this particular regard, the different pitches like a tuning fork having certain effects on the physical system. The use of breathing in itself is therapeutic under those conditions.

Now this is quite apart front anything else. The demonstrations involve an expansion of abilities and of methods, methods of teaching and methods of involving others also.

(9:30.) The chants set up deep emotional responses in listeners and in those involved. The emotional, responses then are used as departure points for other experiences. The music, the chants, are richly endowed with what you might call for now racial memory, striking psychic as well as biological chords, and thereby releasing certain inner mechanisms and memories.

Hopefully the memories will later become memories of the future as well as the past. While the chants are indeed seeped in ancient knowledge inherent in the race, the knowledge itself when intuitively felt brings forth an experience of timelessness. This will make it possible for some to obtain a clear vision of their timelessness of the self, existing in future as well as past terms.

(Pause at 9:34.) The actions that arise out of the chanting—as the circle arrangement of students—these are all deeply buried psychically and psychologically pertinent actions that have been a part of your race from its earliest times. The chanting and the action are physical keys or symbols that open up the doors to a nonphysical state of existence before those of your race entered history. *(Pause.)* They were significant then, and evocative. They reminded man of his past. They were ancient the first time the first man chanted, or the first circle was formed.

Ruburt never would have been free enough in the past for such a development to occur, and it was of course, again, no coincidence that you attended class the night the chanting began in earnest.

He wanted you there, both because he so trusts your judgment and because you <u>belonged</u> there. These developments are at their early stages.

(9:40.) The chants vary also in intent, purpose and meaning.

They will be used in different ways. The "language" (in quotes) bridges the gap between languages. It can convey the unique individuality of many different ceremonies, held by different nationalities through the centuries. The language <u>is</u> structured, but in such a way that it is loose enough to be highly flexible and elastic, and only tight enough to retain the sense or feeling of the kind of language you are used to.

Now the Sumari do not exist as I exist. As my name basically makes little difference, so does the name Sumari basically make little difference. But the names signify an independent, unique kind of consciousness that makes use of certain boundaries.

Your Sumari consciousness is that kind of consciousness, and so is mine, except that my boundaries are far less limited than your own, and I recognize them not as boundaries but as directions in which recognition of myself must grow. The same applies to the Sumari as such. This is not an undifferentiated consciousness, in other words, that addresses you now, but one that recognizes the nature of its own identity.

(9:49.) It is a personal consciousness. The difference in degree however between my recognition of my identity and your recognition of your own identity is vast. Do you follow me?

("Yes," I said.)

The point is that I am not impersonal any more than you are, in those terms, and the Sumari in those terms are also individual and to that extent personal. You are a part of the Sumari. You have certain characteristics, in simple terms, as a family might have certain characteristics, or the members of a nation.

They are recognizable, though as members of a family often emphasize their own individuality rather than family likenesses, so can the Sumari. The connection, the conscious connection, is important, for in that regard you are not alone. Others are working with you, and there are bonds that are held and honored. You may take your break.

(9:54 —10:01.)

Now. I will not keep you. There are some further points however I want to make, and I will try to make them briefly.

The Sumari songs are many things. They are training for later work on the speakers' manuscripts.

("I wondered about that.")

The Sumari language itself will help Ruburt by freeing his concepts, and release him from the almost automatic process of translating data into stereotyped English terms. The thought patterns beneath various languages are different, and he has been trained in the Western tradition. This is not enough.

The translations when they come must make sense to the Western mind. But they must not be limited by the nature of its stereotypes. The new songs are the first step in this procedure. The ancient songs will follow when the practice of the new ones is complete.

As you know there are complicated reasons why he began this at this time again. Your own relationship is closely involved. There will be much more I want to tell you. I am giving you some highlights this evening, but not having a long session. There are important healing aspects connected with the Sumari development, as Ruburt is beginning to suspect—a different kind of breakthrough, or easy access to energy.

(10:17.) This bypasses certain aspects that could act as impediments. I am speaking generally here now. He still feels badly because he does not have your card, but your card will be two books.

("That's very good."

(Here Seth means books on the ancient Sumari songs and on the new.)

The morning session involving the songs led him into a new kind of perceptive experience or trance state, in which he has not been before involved, and that will serve most beneficially in this and other areas and developments in the future.

You have begun highly significant new endeavors, under my auspices *(smile)*, and that auspices will continue. I add again that your relationship to each other itself is meant to reach certain levels, and when it does it triggers the psychic developments that both of you planned well ahead of time would occur. *(Emphatically.)*

You planned to work together. That is all I will give you for this evening, and that again is a bare outline of what is available and present to you now, were the mechanics of delivery effective enough now to give you the material all at once.

The Sumari dreams of Ruburt all involve training of the type I have mentioned. Some of the songs are given to him when he sleeps. They are also now available. Only the mechanics of delivery remain, in your terms. Tell him the same applies to complete health. And now I bid you a merry Christmas *(louder)* and a fond good evening.

("Thank you, Seth. The same to you.")

And you can have private sessions whenever you want, and you can know they are always available.

("I understand. Thank you very much. Good night." 10:27.)

DELETED SESSION
DECEMBER 27, 1971

(This is the regularly-scheduled session for December 27, 1971. It is deleted from the record.

(The session began at 9:13 PM. At 9:11, as Jane and I sat talking and waiting, I wrote the following lines in Sumari:

E pato um topagon ne mu noni ra tum de.
Or efuge rambo arghde re mu non de gor se to.
Ne ra mena do te dore gee portog po.

(I showed them to Jane after the session and asked her to translate them, as she has done with the Christmas card I made for her, but she hasn't had time to do so as I begin typing this the next evening. The translation will be added to the end of the session, presumably.)

Now, good evening.

("Good evening, Seth.")

I arrived somewhat earlier, as you have heard.

("Yes." At suppertime, Seth spoke to Jane rather harshly as she worked in the kitchen. His data concerned her symptoms, and evidently continued material we had been discussing ourselves the last day or two on our own. I asked that tonight's session deal only with personal material, so we were fairly well prepared. Jane shed a few tears when she came to the studio to tell me that she had heard from Seth late this afternoon. She also remarked that she wished she hadn't heard from him. However, I considered the insights she gained to be very valuable indeed.)

Now: Ruburt may sometimes object to the terms used to describe his work. On a surface level the seeming shift from writer to psychic annoyed and bothered him, but it was <u>always</u> the same work, and he knew it. And he was always driven to do whatever must be done in order to produce it.

In terms of this life, the justification of existence entered in, as I told you; the tale that he told himself in other words to see that he did his work.

He is magnificently intent, persistent and determined. When the situation allowed him to do so, he immediately began to pare down all activities not directly connected with his work, to shake them off, to force himself to be disciplined, to cut distractions to a minimum and thus avoid conflict, to his way of thinking.

He did this quite wholeheartedly, and with a vengeance. He would not have an ordinary job. He would force himself into a position where he must indeed make good through his work, financially and otherwise. He tried to emulate what he thought your actions would be in the same circumstances at the time this began.

You had the discipline by nature, he thought. He did not: therefore the enforced solitude, the narrowing of other interests until his vitality was forced in one direction, the inner direction. He gave stimulus to his mind with coffee and cigarettes, whipping it to make it go faster and faster.

At the same time he gave less and less nourishment to the body, denied it exercise until it began to wither from disuse. He goes inward then with great applied focus, but held the body in such tight reins that he denied it both energy and attention.

Now you, particularly earlier, acquiesced in this. Neither of you saw anything wrong with the basic ideas behind it. You would have only quarreled with the results. I outlined your joint ideas about food. In the same way your joint ideas about your work and the world in general were taken and put into literal action by our friend.

You had a history of bodily achievement in terms of sports, that led you to take an additional joy in the body that tempered the basic concepts you held. Ruburt did not.

The tendencies to so withdraw and deny the body were early obvious, but unrecognized. In college only the body's miraculous youth protected it when Ruburt did not eat properly, subsisted mainly on coffee and cigarettes, and went without proper sleep for months at a time.

He often hid from fellow students out of shyness and fear of confronting them. He would hide in his poetry. The tendency then was there. He had no great faith in the body because he saw how his mother's behaved, without any knowledge of the reasons. The body was not strong, therefore. He did not trust it. He trusted his mind, so the idea of retreating from the body into the mind was quite logical to <u>him</u> when this began. *(The sessions or the symptoms?)*

For reasons given much earlier, you both worried about the body mechanism in terms of childbirth, and it suited both of your purposes to minimize the possibilities in that direction, and to save yourselves from the monthly fear that a birth might have resulted.

Ruburt put his body on a strict survival level, giving it the barest of attention. He is in the habit of ignoring its feelings, attitudes or desires, so that he is quite numb to some of them.

("Well, I hear him do enough complaining about it." Meaning the symptoms.)

Numb to the body's desires for exercise, motion, air. Do you follow me?

("Yes.")

Again however understand that both of your attitudes worked here, though he exaggerated some indeed. You both considered the world in many respects as distracting, stupid, its people beneath your notice, and your work the only thing of importance. Given the opportunity *(when I obtained steady employment)* and as soon as he was able, Ruburt then retreated from it, and gave himself the excuse for doing so—your attitudes made flesh.

Before, <u>necessity</u> would not allow it. He leaped over that barrier, and when you thought you had given him the opportunity to be free, he was not about to misuse it. He would force himself to devote all his energies in that direction, to silence for example any stray temptations to go out into the yard in working time, to visit friends. He would see to it that he could not give in to such temptations.

Now the body quickly made its protests known, and Ruburt squelched them whenever possible. The body was not important except as it supported his ideas. His will would drive it.

A good number of his depressions were body depressions. The body was de-pressed, pressed down, and this of course affected the psychic state. He hides his body in his dress. His face is in good condition because he considers that the mirror of his soul, and allows it therefore free-enough expression. He trusts his head.

("How about the teeth?")

He has been satisfied with the bargain. He felt it was <u>necessary</u> (underlined) to inhibit physical expression in order to concentrate all of his energies inward into his work. He felt it was necessary to inhibit physical mobility in order to facilitate deeper penetration into inner reality.

He was trying to sublimate the energy, to take it away from the physical so that it could be used more productively, to his way of thinking. Now, this is <u>not</u> necessary. He was afraid of frittering away his energy. This was his idea of conserving it.

Do you want a break?

("Yes."

(9:45. The pace had been good. My hand was tired. I was absolutely appalled by the material. It was an extension of insights we had been discussing lately, but to see it all neatly arrayed together was devastating. I sat in silence for several minutes because I didn't know what to do; I seemed to be neutralized by the conflicting feelings washing over me. Nor did Jane say anything.)

(We have been recently planning that I am to leave my job at Artistic at the end of January, and take at least a year to paint, etc., after a month's trip to Florida in February. This after we have finished with Seth's book early in January. In a strange way I now felt that I had the freedom to do anything I wanted to, whereas before I had been worrying considerably about the financial effects of my leaving the job. Suddenly I viewed it in other ways.)

(I asked Jane why she was allowing this material to come through now, but she didn't know. I had been getting very angry lately however so I felt this was a prime reason. I was terribly depressed, at least briefly. I grimly promised Jane that there were going to be changes; and this was to not at all minimize my own role in this problem—it was merely my stated vehement desire that this madness come to an end, that I was ready for a change, and demanded one.)

(The strange thing in this is that this session contains <u>new</u> material, after all of the private ones we've had. And it deals with causes in a way that makes sense out of all that has gone by; especially does it explain our repeated failures to break out of the vicious circle that has imprisoned us for the last five years.

(10:05.) Now. You both said from your earliest days together that you wanted to put all of your energy into your work. That was Ruburt's objective.

He did not of course understand what the complete results would be. He felt that the physical could be safely dispensed with, and did so by degrees. Whenever physical mobility is demanded as an auxiliary to his work, then he produced physically—on your tour, at the high school engagement, and so forth.

(Seth might have added that these occasions were still subpar physically however, to others who were not impaired. Not to mention the emotional turmoil and worry about whether the affair could be carried through.)

He thought that he would have your approval, that you also would do anything necessary in order to put all of your energies into your work. He thought he was showing you he was (underlined) determined to take advantage of the opportunity you gave him.

In the past you often railed against Saturday chores while he was quite happily enjoying them. To show you that he could be like you he adopted your attitude, hid any enjoyment he used to feel from them, and took steps to cut these out of his life as far as possible; as he felt you would do had you the chance.

(Never in my wildest fancies would I ever consider adopting physical ailments in order to avoid doing such a thing as chores.)

You would have fallen into many problems yourself with the attitudes you had if the opportunity had come to you first. Do you follow me?

("Yes." But I still wouldn't adopt physical ailment, etc.)

You have also learned then through seeing your attitudes put into flesh. These were joint attitudes, now. I do not mean that Ruburt put your attitudes alone into flesh. He has a one-track mind in that regard, however.

When your communication system did fall down, the situation was at its worst for him. At an unconscious level he felt he was doing what was right, that you should approve of it, that despite the inconvenience and the physical soreness he was sticking to his guns.

As this began to take more and more of your time however, he became concerned, for he did not intend to have his work at the price of your difficulty with him. He felt guilty enough that you had to work outside. He could justify some small inconveniences on your part, but not your continued unease and worried concern.

Whenever he had a work problem he hastily then withdrew more physical energy in order to go inward with greater acceleration. The key is, he thought this was necessary. He took literally the idea of putting all of your energy into work.

The body's exuberance has been hidden and denied. It is given some exercise, when you go dancing; sudden exercise after inactivity. You have no daily structure for physical exertion or daily activity of any kind. The body's exuberance must be gently teased out, now, because it has been forcibly restrained.

Ruburt believed his place was in his room. Time spent in the preparation of meals, in your social activity, in travel, was wasted time, and his attitude was largely shared by you. He simply put it into greater practice.

The idea that being is its own justification is important here: The rights and privileges of the body cannot be long ignored, though Ruburt's body has withstood very much. You should be thankful under the circumstances that the condition was not worse, for the body's own resiliency fought back, and provided some balance out of its own sanity.

The body often would not allow sleep, since the muscles simply needed to be used. They would jump on their own simply for the exercise, regardless of suggestions that sleep come. You both minimized the importance of physical life to a large degree. Your nature and the circumstances prevented you from falling into a like but similar sort of situation.

When Ruburt felt, as I have told you, that you no longer loved him, then he had less use of the body. He feels his body's condition should tell you how devoted he has been to his work, instead of getting at it for not walking right or eating enough. He feels you should consider his condition as one of the means adopted in a goal in which you both believe. He was then afraid of giving up the condition for fear of using physical energy at the expense of mental energy, and hence at the expense of his work.

(I couldn't agree with these ideas less. It may be beating a dead horse, but let me say that I've told Jane time and again that I don't consider her physical condition an acceptable price to pay for any sort of creative achievement. This idea hasn't penetrated, though.)

You both always railed against overweight people. He did not think that would bother you then. *(But it does, terrifically.)* Again, he did not <u>foresee</u> the results. When they became obvious he decided there was nothing to do but put up with them if the end was justified.

(This statement struck me so forcibly that I simply had to stop writing for a bit in order to recover from my amazement. I asked Seth to wait.)

He felt you did not want him in bed anyway, so you would not complain there. He tried then to attain the goal in ways that would not upset you, as far as his understanding went at the time.

(I found all of this quite incredible, etc.)

When your communications were reestablished, he began to see that you suffered far more than he supposed from his course of action.

(I explained this to Jane last summer. But that was six months ago now, and

there has been no change.)

When he <u>began</u> it, as explained, your personal relationship was relatively at an unstable point. He did not feel he could depend upon you, and so went inward in the way given.

Now take your break. You may end the session if you prefer.

("No."

(10:32. During break Jane received a phone call from New York City; the caller, a girl, told of the death this evening of Francois Nesbitte. At age 46, of a heart attack, etc. Resume at 10:46.)

Nothing could sway him from that course while he believed it was the right one. When the two of you became more emotionally open, then he began to doubt it.

He wants you to leave Artistic and paint full time, to make up to you what you have suffered on his account, and also because he now believes that is the correct course to follow. I will go deeper into this in our next session.

<u>Part</u> of the reaction had to do with past conditioning, and was all interwoven. He was so often told "Do not fritter away your energy," "Do not go in so many directions at once," "Restrain yourself," and so he was making sure that he avoided these pitfalls.

The condition with the teeth simply resulted from keeping a tight upper lip, clamping down the jaw. He made his bed, he would lie in it. To relax meant to let down the guard, and distractions in. The physical strains altered the appearance of the teeth, then. Physically there were infections, enough to maintain the condition and no more. The condition had certain invisible boundaries that were carefully maintained. Only when the body objected and went over those boundaries did he become frightened, for he saw then that he lacked the control over the body he thought he held. He could not silence all of its objections.

He never planned on the condition becoming permanent, but only as a conditioning process to be dispensed with when no longer needed. He also wanted you so see how hard he was working, so that you would not resent his being at home. This also showed that he was paying for the privilege. He did not intend that you pay also.

In the beginning you encouraged him, and found such signs of withdrawal as indications of his maturity. Again, you both in the past found any endeavor disconnected from your work as a distraction. He saw to it that they were cut out and dispensed with in a large degree.

The dancing always did him good, and you also. There were sometimes physical repercussions following it, simply because the muscles were so <u>unused</u>

to the activity.

I will close with one note, however. Under the circumstances the vacation idea, with or without variations, is a good one, during which focus upon the physical aspects of life should be emphasized and encouraged. Do you have any questions?

("Is this vacation going to do any good? It seems to me there's got to be a strong change in his attitude, or the whole thing's going to be wasted.")

The rest, the changed focus, will be of benefit. The time given to simple bodily pleasures –

("But he's got to be willing to do these things..."

(I was quite skeptical. I was remembering a lot of other such statements by Seth about vacations, etc., none of which accomplished anything that I could remember. I was remembering now what Seth had said earlier in the session about Jane's attitude toward vacations, chores, etc., being a waste of time since these things took her away from her work.)

The stimulus of changed physical surroundings will be of benefit. The restaurant food will also be a stimulus to his appetite, and the changing physical sights alone refreshing. The change will also break old patterns of behavior, and will help therefore in changing his attitude.

(I didn't believe any of this, and still don't. I let Seth see my disbelief, but said no more. Nor have I yet seen a vacation break any patterns of behavior, or change any attitudes. After the session, I told Jane I would have to see it to believe it.)

Now you may end the session or take a break.

("We might as well end it, then.")

Your understanding will also help, for he thought that you agreed with the basic premise.

("He's known for at least a year that I didn't agree at all—and probably longer than that, Seth.")

He did not understand that you did not basically agree. Now I will end the session —and I hope that you are glad of the information.

("I am. Good night, Seth, and thank you very much."

(11:05. I think the session probably the most important that we've achieved, though this importance is built upon all those that have gone before, of course.

(I still intend to leave Artistic at the end of January, though some of my ideas have changed. Now I wonder if Jane will take my painting full time as a sign that her course of action was right all along, and simply intensify her withdrawal. Earlier today I told her I didn't have any more time to wait, because of my physical age, that I no longer wanted to wait, etc. Easy to say. I have no idea whether I can bring it off, but I feel I might as well try. I feel exhausted, and that every other avenue has

been explored.

(*There follows the translation of the Sumari quoted at the beginning of the session:*

The body knows its splendor.
Beware those who would deny it.
Like a stallion it will rear up and kick you
If you rein in its power.

(*Jane translated this Wednesday morning. It's very interesting to note that even though I wrote the original in Sumari, she is the one who makes it available in English. When I wrote it I had not the slightest idea of its meaning, etc. The same applies to the verses I wrote for her Christmas card.*)

DELETED SESSION
DECEMBER 29, 1971

(*This is the regularly scheduled session for December 29, 1971. It is deleted from the record.*

(*Jane experienced a bout of crying at the supper table this evening. Material came up to her consciousness after she arose from a nap at about 5:30 PM, and began preparing the meal. I encouraged her to talk about what was on her mind even though her supper got cold, etc., and was sure Seth would cover the subject this evening.*

(*At 8:52 I wrote the following in Sumari as we sat waiting for the session:*

Et u non regon du me nenorg agghor
Pe tu re sansori do du rantu gorheg.
To porney tu verg monet grusharky po
Ter kor ce tu cet ve can ka tonly du
Prevoort kliner per to andi to very yaz
Zu tu sa sen sor pruken ve do.

(*I didn't show Jane this, and ask for a translation, until after the session. Begin at 9:14.*)

Now. Good evening.

("*Good evening, Seth.*")

Ruburt, I understand, has given me free rein. (*Somewhat humorously.*)

There are some things I believe you understand about your lovely companion. One thing however is a great consistency that escapes you, beneath all the shifting guises of his behavior.

He has several important gifts of character, now, as separate from abilities. One is enduring persistence, massive inner intensity directed toward his goals. There is also an ability to endure unpleasantness, or even pain, if he believes it is for a great-enough principle.

Now all of these qualities are noteworthy and can be used to advantage. The built-in problem is that he will pursue a course with dogged stubbornness and determination once he has adopted it, until it results in the desired end or is <u>proven</u> disastrous.

Now this has been consistent in all of his behavior. For what he believes in he will try to jump any hurdle, and be willing to suffer almost any indignity. On the other hand he resents the slightest inconvenience that is not connected with his goals, and rises up vehemently against even the slightest restraint that he considers beside the board, or aside from your joint and individual purposes.

He railed, again, about the psychic work, but this, while important, was deeply recognized as a part of his nature, an extension of it long before he consciously accepted it. Do you follow me?

("Yes.")

Now. Intuitively he has always believed that you should leave Artistic. He was somewhat frightened over the circumstances some years ago, when you had no money behind you, but even then intuitively he felt you should do so.

("Can you wait a second, Seth, while I turn off the heat?"

(We were holding the session in Jane's workroom across the hall from the living room, in order to obtain more privacy. It was so hot that Jane had been peeling off articles of clothing ever since the session began.)

Yes—but the heat is on.

("I understand," I said as I turned the radiator knob.)

Open the kitchen window, also.

(After I resumed my seat:) The conflict was obvious, then, he had determined to write, to make his living in that manner. He refused to make a <u>pattern</u> of jobs. At my instigation he began the classes, which led him, though slowly, into other areas of financial development.

He has determined that he will not push you in any way. Because of your age difference he took it for granted that you knew more than he, and when he had pushed you to Florida it had not worked. He determined he would never push you again.

He was ready for you to leave Artistic and take your chances as soon as you had a thousand in the bank. You see his nature.

("Yes.")

As a woman he appreciated your concern for security, and part of him <u>was</u> frightened to think of your giving up the income then, but the greater intuitive part felt that you should do so. He would not support you with a job, but he <u>would</u> do so through his books and other endeavors.

You did lose communication for some time. He did not know if you were really satisfied with your work or not. If you were, then he did not see why you did not take the chance. If you were not then all the more reason why you should take it, to give yourself the additional time. He felt deeply disloyal to think that you should be doing something you had obviously decided not to do as yet.

He felt when or if he spoke of this you were deeply hurt, thinking he did not understand your sacrifice—the job, but he did not want your sacrifice. He wanted you free to do your painting. He thought that you would not be satisfied to quit unless he had a job, and this he could not do because of his own commitment to his work.

(I long ago gave up on any thought of Jane taking a regular job—perhaps several years ago, etc.)

He felt trapped, then. He withdrew physically, throwing all the more energy, he thought, into this course of trying to produce a book good enough to free you both. When the rewards financially began to pile up and you did not make a move, he began to think it was futile.

(This is the material Jane told me about, tearfully, at supper time, etc.)

It was you who always said you wanted to put all of your energy into your work. You, whom he followed with such enthusiasm. He would waste his body for you and his work, but you would not take that step. He could not understand why. Operating, again, on his part were those doubts: could he really make a go of it if you quit? But he was more than willing to try if given the chance.

In your discussions you came back to: "Yes, but I can't depend on you to take a job to help out." Of course you couldn't. He thought that was understood. He could help you his own way, and that was not his way. His commitment forbade it. He thought your commitment forbid you, too. He felt in the last years that he could sustain you both financially, with your psychic support, if the stimuli were there, and he knew you were doing what you wanted to.

He has no intentions of getting a job, but he considers this a tribute on his part and yours. He began to feel that the status quo would last. He wanted the impetus to come from you, yet realized that your concern for <u>him</u>, lately, made this relatively impossible. So he seemed caught.

Beyond this the daily and <u>yearly</u> steady living pattern was frightening to him in personal ways. He had always determined and said that he would not marry someone who stuck in a house on the corner of Main and such and such a street. This meant simply that the conventionally-accepted pattern was not acceptable to him.

He saw the two of you writing and painting together. Since you have no other close contacts this emotional bond was important. Because he concentrates with such intentness he needs changes of environment physically as counterpoint. He saw himself writing books, then taking a trip to break the routine, returning again and plunging into work.

He long ago relinquished the idea of freely dashing around the countryside. He needs a home base deeply, as you do, but your job here also restrained you both. He felt you did not understand this need, that it was not logical.

The money meant little if it did not bring you what you wanted or even provide an environment that was more desirable. He thought: another book, more money in the bank to pay taxes on, you still at your job, no trips, just another book for more money. He felt you were throwing his gift back in his face.

This is apart from the creative endeavor of the books. For these—to do his thing—he drained his body because he thought he had to, and for what reward?

He was also afraid of losing what you had, disrupting the pattern of current life, particularly if you did not feel ready. He became deeply worried for you, and looked to you for leadership. He felt you abandoned him as far as your joint concern with your work was concerned.

The psychic work took up more of your time. The obvious to him was to quit your job *(Jane, as Seth, almost laughed)*, paint, and have the time you needed. You seemed willing to make no adjustments of any kind. At the same time he felt you would begin to resent the time spent from your work, but you would cling to the job like a lifeline until it was too late.

As he saw your friends making adjustments to the best of their ability, he became more frightened. It seemed neither of you would make a move physically. He felt imprisoned in the second story of the house with his work, but he gritted his teeth and continued.

The few remarks he made never showed his deep emotional discontent. You would say "But you will not get a job," or "You are not able to," and that would make him think you did not understand at all. Of course he would not, and you should not.

He appreciated the time you gave him, but he did not want the sacrifice of yourself. It was to his way of thinking a perverted gift, for which he could give no adequate acknowledgment—a gift that denied what you wanted was no gift but an unendurable burden.

He felt you should know this. He would never bring it up. His fear was too great. You would think he would not understand, or that he did not appreciate what you were doing. With what he was putting himself through, <u>unnecessarily</u>—but he did not realize it—then he could not understand why you did not insist on doing what you said you wanted to do. Either that, or admit you did not want it.

Much of this had to do with the picture in his mind, quite unconscious, of what he expected life to be. It involved both of you working against any impediment <u>together</u>, taking trips together, and having a freedom in <u>that</u> regard, a mobility because of your life-style.

Symbolically the job meant to him a great psychic rift, <u>after</u>, now, he felt you had enough money in the bank to hold you awhile. This did not operate, obviously, when you did not have the means. He worked then to get them.

He felt you resented his being home. You used to say "You don't know what it is to punch a time clock," he thought resentfully. He took it as an accusation. He felt deeply that you had no one but yourself to blame if you did not quit. The money was there to be used, and you were blaming him when he did not deserve it to that degree.

These thoughts smacked of disloyalty. He would not admit them consciously. He was afraid of demanding that you quit for fear you would say "I will quit if you get a job," and this he could not do because of his own commitment.

When he moved into this apartment the idea was "If Rob will not use the money then at least I will have more space." He felt deeply misunderstood despite any ideas of logic or reason in conventional terms. He felt deeply that you should have left years ago, that your own intuition should have told you this. He was at a loss to understand why you did not, or why it <u>seemed</u> (underlined) you would insist upon a job on his part before you would leave.

With the dream book he felt, <u>beside</u> the material already given that it was useless. There would be more money in the bank and to him is was blood money, rotten or spoiled like fruit overripe and unused. He felt you were denying your own talent and abilities. You told him to trust himself constantly but you gave him no example, only words, for you did not trust yourself to that degree.

He knew quite well that you would be both casting yourselves adrift financially in conventional terms. He remembered in the past how he felt withdrawing money from the bank. He was quite aware of his own fears also, but he felt that the stimulus would offset these, and that you would not add your courage to his when he was faltering. Unless he did something, he felt, the status quo would continue.

The morning symptoms are clearly related to the fact that you work mornings. The exaggerated weekend symptoms are related to two factors: One, the chores that he feels you thoroughly resent, and two, the Sunday situation when your mother is home. He feels that all of you are not being kind to her, merely supporting her, to bolster up your own ideas of yourselves as sons. This also has to do with disruptions not connected with your work, for which he has no patience.

You may take your break.

(10:14. At break Jane experienced a real outburst, during which she said most forcefully that she wouldn't get a job, had no intention of doing so, etc. I thought this was material she had harbored for a long time. I hadn't asked her to get a job recently. Anything I said concerning Jane and jobs referred to past experiences, which hadn't worked out, etc.

(I didn't understand whether Jane considered the last five years wasted or not, however, including the books, the psychic work, the painting, etc. I said for my part that the end of January would mark a change in our way of life, and that I didn't think we'd ever return to the old—it obviously left too many things to be desired in spite of any accomplishments, etc. Resume at 10:40.)

Now. He considers the achievements highly important. It is for that reason that, misguidedly, he drained his physical energy and cut out all distractions.

He was also very deeply aware of your part in them, in the sessions, and in your support. To that extent they were their own reward. The secondary benefits, to him now, the financial rewards, lay latent. He felt they should be plowed back in—used for you and your work, and that you were not taking advantage of these secondary rewards, that they lay unused when they should furnish you, now, with the opportunity to do your painting.

He felt that it was inevitable, or should be, for you at one time to devote yourself to your painting, that you knew this, that is was always ahead of you, and that it was being unnecessarily put off.

He was afraid that you would grow more deeply to resent this, and that you would not rouse yourself in time to do what you must do. In the beginning he was afraid of taking the chance, but not taking the chance became finally unbearable. He was afraid you would not do it. He did not want to be the one to apply the stimulus. He wanted that to come from you.

Because of his love and loyalty he is deeply concerned about your work, and development. He was afraid of casting you into a situation before you were ready, and it seemed to him if you did not initiate the action you were not ready. He is afraid, naturally enough of the change, but the fear of not making it is far greater. He is determined that you have the chance despite any consequences, despite natural fears or anything else.

He is also intuitively sure that without the stimulus you will never develop your abilities fully. There will be other crutches to fall back on. He knows that this is something you must do, that it is more important even than financial insecurity, that a deep portion of your being will be forever unsatisfied if that course in not followed.

He feels that he is forcing the issue, but that he must force it now. He fears that there can be no more reasons legitimate enough to deter you, it is a challenge you know you must face, and that the best service he can be to you is to bring it to a head.

Automatically the living conditions will be far more to his liking. You will automatically have a freedom with time and space. He is banking on the stimuli to bring about greater book sales, greater productivity, further books and sales to help finance the establishment while you encounter your own abilities.

He feels you will be psychically more together, working more effectively as a unit, that your efforts will be directed more clearly toward what you want. It is the life-style he feels that is natural to you, and if you deviate from it for too long you become less unified and relatively listless. He feels then you will be working once again actively toward a common goal, with a life-style suited more <u>daily</u> to your natures.

(Leaning forward, somewhat humorously:) Now, I concur.

("Okay, So do I.")

The problems are being brought out into the open where at least you can deal with them in their <u>proper</u> dimension, in the way meant for you to handle them. This does not mean all will be roses. I am not making predictions this evening, but if you go ahead with courage and conviction you will <u>know</u> you are doing the right thing, and you will be creatively and financially rewarded.

There are other endeavors that can be tried, and <u>any</u> of them will pay off financially, <u>and</u> help you and others and free your minds; even though they may take some time from say, your work, they would be united concerns, reflected in your work, not energy directed completely outside of your concerns. I am speaking now of some of the ideas Ruburt listed.

You may take a break or end the session as you prefer.

("We'll take the break."

(11:04—11:17.)

Now. The fears and doubts connected with such a course have been buried and not faced, so do not be surprised if they become suddenly apparent to you. The consequences of not taking such a course should also be quite apparent to you. You would feel cheated and betrayed by both yourself and others, never knowing what you could have done had you given yourself the chance.

Your society is not going to offer it freely. On the other hand, only those with the determination to <u>seize</u> the chance will take benefit from it in the conditions at the present time.

The situation will automatically bring up problems and challenges that you have put aside, but also offer possibilities of development <u>because</u> of the altered focus, not otherwise possible. Do you follow me?

("Yes.")

For now then I will bid you a fond good evening, and I will do all I can to help you when you request it.

("Thank you. It's appreciated."

(Seth now made some comments, here not recorded, about my using our recorder for more information, but as usual I was hesitant because of the time involved later in transcription. This was the end of the session. Jane's trance had been deep all evening, the pace fast.

(At 11:25 PM I showed her the Sumari verse I had written before the session, and requested a translation. "That's your first chore tomorrow morning" I said. Jane then handed the page back to me and asked me to read the verse. She listened carefully, then said she "got something on the first line." I hadn't expected anything on the verse translation this evening, especially after a long session.)

(Then Jane translated the whole verse. I wrote the words down as she gave them:

Those who are given gifts by the gods must use them.
Polish your gifts in the morning,
Shine them with yearning,
Pluck them from the trembling trees of creation
Tenderly tuck them into the basket of your loving endeavor.
Use them or they will turn from fruits into stones that
Are heavy.

After a pause Jane said, "There's more. That's all you got, but there's more to it." This was another surprise. At 11:30 she went back into the Sumari trance and delivered the balance of the poem. It isn't included here since she has made her own copies for her Sumari notebook, of this one and the three poems that subsequently followed. My original notes contain a list of the times each poem took — only a few minutes — plus a few comments. The session ended at 12:15 AM.

(Jane was really bleary and sleepy by the time she was finished. I thought her performance remarkable, and the poems of high quality. "I just sit here and they come out," she said, but obviously there is much here for us to learn.)

DELETED SESSION
JANUARY 3, 1972

(This is the regularly scheduled session for January 3, 1972. It is deleted from the record.

(A note: this afternoon Jane began translating the long letter I wrote her in Sumari on December 31, 1971. It appears to be "The Sacred Script of Regulations." I had no idea of the letter's contents when I wrote it, on impulse. It is three pages of rather closely-spaced lettering, with some numbers incorporated in a few paragraphs, a couple of diagrams and a symmetrical symbol resembling a mandala. Jane tried several times to get something on it recently, without success, then abruptly this afternoon it began to open up to her.

(At supper time this evening I explained a few problems of a technical nature, connected with my painting, to Jane. I believe I have solved some of them, or at least am embarked on the right course after a very long period of trial and error. They involve mostly portrait work, and such mundane things as the handling of paint, both opaquely and thinly, and the symbolic meaning behind these things. I told Jane I wasn't asking that Seth go into these this evening; I preferred that he talk about Jane or the Sumari work. I made the extra effort to explain these concerns to Jane because I feel it's part of the resurgence I seem to be experiencing since we made the decision that I leave Artistic at the end of this month.)

Now. Good evening.

("Good evening, Seth.")

Give us a moment. Problems are often set as challenges, to be accepted and used for a greater purpose.

There are multitudinous themes interbound in any society at any given time, and they are all related. There is meaning in all of them. In the eras of the great artists, civilization was united by a series of revelations, ideas and also distortions. The artist was an important part of his society.

The distortions grew so great that the whole structure crumbled. Many artists relied upon the stereotyped constructions of their age, rather than looking within for their own revelations, so that art could have become the frozen art form—painting could have—that showed clearly the spiritual immobility of a people who finally grew dry.

The world from that initial creative center had to expand. It could not do so by imposing its culture, however admirable in many respects, upon others. The culture had to change, the foundations of art had to change, the old images had to be <u>in your terms</u> (underlined) demolished, for they had begun to freeze the birth of new insights and creative feeling.

The artist became at that point truly an initiator, no longer supported by the cultural society. While the majority were still immersed in the old, the artists were already experimenting with the new, and became to some extent outlaws to their own people.

Those minor artists who still continued to follow old patterns often did so because they were honestly not initiators or creators, merely facile. They belonged to the (in quotes) "mass mind" of the time, therefore they did not have to feel apart and were accepted.

You think you have harbored under great disadvantages, being born into a society that makes true creativity so difficult.

True creativity is far more apt to flourish, however, to the extent that you are not trapped by the "mass mind"(in quotes), and not tempted by the inducements. *(Long pause at 9:10.)* You chose the circumstances against which to pit yourself. The kind of art you will produce is not meant to be the art of youth. It is not what you intended. Your insights and intuitions were to be sifted through earthly years of knowledge and experience. Through these, childlike wisdom will indeed show itself, but a wisdom that has been tried, that is aware of its own integrity through the seasons.

An early acceptance would have tempted you to rely upon the facility before the inner spontaneity even began to grow to maturity. Your early comic book work should have told you that. You were quite facile and could have done well with it longer in other fields of activity—TV for example—had you chosen.

(I was very facile—so much so that a large part of my early work consisted of finishing off the work of others so that it would reproduce well. In the comic trade I was an "inker," and had more work available than I could handle. I also made a lot of money at an early age, in those days before high taxes. A comparable income now would amount to several hundred dollars a week.)

You did not chose that easy way for a reason. You knew you were preparing yourself, but the time of preparation was extended beyond what it need have been. *(9:20.)*

The psychic developments are also interbound in your own work, because you doubted yourself the preparation time was extended by you. The final period was and is to be one in which your energies are directed to your work without the outside job, for finally you began to feel that you were not doing what you should do; this itself inhibited your trust in yourself further, and therefore the development of your work.

Trust between you and Ruburt was also a prerequisite according to your own plans, set earlier. The impetus to help you is a built-in one, also meant as a further stimulus to Ruburt in his work and in our work. Already the energies of your natures are beginning to regroup. You have therefore a firm foundation from which to begin your endeavors as long as you understand and believe that you have.

If there have been built-in time bombs, as Ruburt once said, there have also been built-in points to lead you into new highly-productive areas.

Now. The yoga is good, a confrontation of Ruburt with his body, leading to a reconciliation. He must not strain, however. Already energy channels are <u>beginning</u> to clear. The willingness and recognition have occurred mentally of course, to make the exercises possible.

I suggest you take a break and we will continue.

(9:25—9:37.)

Now. The inhibition you were enforcing upon yourself by working outside was reflected in your work inevitably, as soon as you became aware that the course no longer served its purpose. You were not one with yourself or with your course of action. You were somewhat apart from yourself then.

In your sketches you allow complete freedom. The sketches sketch themselves through you, so let the paintings paint themselves through you in the same fashion, and miracles of technique will follow automatically. No problem of technique will exist, in other words.

Read again the material I have already given you, the suggestions on your paintings. You can use purple or violet with too heavy a hand, and the brown becomes lost then. Rise up the importance of yellows or colors signifying light. Let them shine through. Do not smother them with opaqueness.

Let your preliminary sketches be as spontaneous as your ink sketches. Then imagine the colors as appearing from within, not applied from without but shining through. Remember the incredible individuality and integrity and possibilities of each line. You can sometimes forget this in your painting sketches, while you are quite aware of it in your ink sketches.

Imagine the colors as waves of light, not as applied *(with gestures)* or added onto, but as growing out of, filling the preliminary sketch as blood fills the body.

(*This is excellent material, as I told Jane. I explained to her after the session that I wasn't sure about the reference to purple or violet, which I seldom use directly because they are hard to integrate into a painting—at least for me. By the next day, I may know why Seth made the reference. The reds I use, being cadmiums, can take on a decided violet cast when mixed with white. This must be kept under control. The painting I am working on now features a cadmium red shirt on the subject, and has given me some trouble because of its tendency to turn purplish if not watched; since Jane has seen me at work on this portrait often, she may have picked this up, although I haven't mentioned it to her. I did explain to her before the session my dislike of too brown a cast to features—this was one of the points we discussed, as mentioned earlier.*

(*The idea of letting the painting fill itself with color "as blood fills the body" is excellent.*

(9:43.) Now give us a moment.

Your Sumari statement. This is, in English, the memory of a covenant—and that should be the word in Ruburt's first line, instead of regulations.

It is indeed an ancient covenant. It is a translation of many manuscripts that have appeared and disappeared throughout the ages. In your terms the <u>initial</u> statement was a physical reminder of a covenant already made before spirit was made flesh.

You and Ruburt made it, in your terms now, together. You wanted to remind him of its importance. You have been Sumari together; you are now. Some of Ruburt's early poetry about the two of you was a reflection of that knowledge.

It was because of this that you decided beforehand on the development of the sessions. There are rites *(spelled)* that were used in various civilizations to stand as ceremonial reminders of this covenant. The Incas knew some of these. Christ knew them, but they were thrown away by his followers. The Hebrews knew but distorted the information. The Lumanians knew, but tried to override the body.

Now the covenants are appearing again. No man can be a fanatic who truly follows this covenant, for the soul nor the body is exploited for the seeming benefit of the others. The covenant is written in your genes.

(*"Can I ask a question?"*)

You may.

(*"How could I write this covenant in Sumari when I didn't know what I was writing? I've wondered about this before. It's so easy, yet I couldn't do it in English."*)

If you remember what I told you about the language, then you will see clearly.

(I couldn't remember offhand. "When I'm writing, I don't know what I'm writing.")

You don't consciously know. You need the connection yet, you see, the bridge of the language across which the meaning of the language can come. Do you follow me?

Now you may take a break.

(9:55. Jane's trance had been good, her pace mostly fast. I explained my second question to her now, to save time: Is what Jane gets a literal translation of what I write in Sumari, or does my Sumari act just as an impetus for her to get her version of it, etc.? Resume at 10:19.)

Now. I know you want an answer to your question—

("It can wait.")

—yet the question itself limits the answer I can give you. It does not have to be an either-or proposition, for example. There is no contradiction between the two alternatives you gave me. The covenant exists quite vitally within the depths of your being.

(Humorously:) Truth often appears hidden in the most exquisite of nonsense. It often disappears in the most weighty of tomes. It is not an imaginary covenant, yet with the aid of the imagination you can approach what it is.

Now some strong portions of Ruburt's energies are already working in your joint behalf. The exercises are important symbolically because they show he is willing to spend time with his body rather than ignoring it. The intent will add to the exercises' effectiveness. The body will be encouraged to free its rhythms and reestablish its natural ones. Energy will be released, but *(smiling)* three days is hardly enough for him to expect great results. The results will come from the changed attitudes. These themselves brought about the desire to exercise, and the desire flowed outward from your decisions. Areas of the body are being manipulated and literally washed, that have been relatively untouched and denied energy in the past. The exercises, and again because of the inner interests, will bring about a weight gain, normal bodily weight as the adjustments continue.

Quite literally he felt no deep need for exercises before. It did not serve his purposes. I am going to give you a shorter session this evening, and unless you have questions I will end it.

("I guess not.")

This is to compensate for your long session.

("That didn't bother me any.")

There are developments still occurring, or rather the developments begun are only begun; and with that enigmatic statement I will end the session. *(Louder:)* My heartiest regards to you, and a fond good evening.

("The same to you, Seth. Thank you very much. Good night."

(10:31.)

SESSION 602
JANUARY 5, 1972 9:15 PM WEDNESDAY

(The session was held in apartment 4, across the hall from our living room. Jane's pace was good, her eyes open most of the time, her voice quiet.)

Good evening.

("Good evening, Seth.")

Now. Any time you want to record a session and have it typed up, then I will deal with recordable material.

("Okay." Seth said this because I was tired tonight. We have been having some deleted sessions lately also.)

There are several issues and avenues of development in the Sumari experience. It will unfold, therefore. The statement is, comparatively speaking, a simple one, so that we can see what Ruburt can do with it.

(Here Seth refers to the three-page letter I wrote to Jane in Sumari on December 31, 1971. As I said in the notes for the deleted session of January 3, 1972, the script appears to be "The Sacred Script of Regulations." Seth changed the word regulations to covenant, however, in the January 3, 1972 session.)

(I had no idea of the script's contents when I wrote it out on impulse. It consists of three pages of rather closely spaced lettering with numbers incorporated in a few of the paragraphs, a couple of diagrams and a symmetrical symbol representing a mandala. Jane tried several times to get something on it, without success, then abruptly on January 3 it began to open up to her. As of this writing she is working on the last page. It is most interesting. A copy will be added to this session, hopefully, if I can remember to do so after having it duplicated.)

Corrections will be made if necessary when he is finished. In time the Sumari language will be replaced, you see, by symbols, hopefully fairly faithful representations of symbols used in some ancient manuscripts. The information obviously precedes *[the]* manuscripts.

The data was also given as I told you by speakers before the time of recognized written language. Some of the speakers were Sumari, and so we will often deal with speakers who were Sumari. Therefore the material will have a typical Sumari slant and interest, a characteristic focus upon certain areas.

Other speakers of different groups would "specialize" (in quotes) in the same way.

Sounds obviously existed before language. There is a pattern of sound beneath all languages, a bed of vocal communication that lies behind all language and alphabet. The vocal sounds of the Sumari language and characteristics as they are presently apparent to you will, hopefully, lead toward these clearly understood but logically unstructured sounds that are recognized by the organism and by the inner self, but ignored by the reasoning conscious mind that focuses upon the logical language.

The word in English is onomatopoeia—*(My phonetic interpretation*

("*Do you want to spell that out?*"

(Leaning forward humorously, eyes wide:) I cannot spell it. There are some (in quotes) "defects" of Ruburt's that are even hard for me to surmount, and in this particular case for a special reason. Just add the note, as I do not want to get off the subject. The word, onomatopoeia *(there is a chance the first letter should be A instead of O)* comes closest to explaining the inner nature of such sounds.

In your language there are words that <u>sound</u> like the reality they try to represent. These are called onomatopoeia. Hush is an example, the word hush. It is understood as a quieting agent. When you say it correctly the breath is slowed and leaves your body: hush-sh-sh-sh the sounds finally seem to disappear.

The body's feeling, the sound of the words, convey(s) the message. So independently of any language there are sounds that in themselves convey such messages, that act upon the physical system. Their utterance demands certain characteristic uses of breath. What is felt by the organism approximates the meaning of the sounds, and to some extent <u>is</u> the meaning of the sounds.

Such feeling-tone "words" (in quotes), with pantomime or the expressive body, can therefore come closer often than structured language to convey various levels of emotion, to explain levels of subjective feeling that are often distorted in recognizable words.

More than this, they act directly on the body. Physically speaking it is one of the earliest forms of communication. This may lead to the suspicion that I expect you to return to the grunts and groans connected in conventional thought with the cavemen; such is far from the case.

This is a vital basic method of communication, <u>upon</u> whose inner intuitive and organic structure all other languages are formed and based.

(9:35.) As a method of freeing you from stereotypes then, this is important. More than this, intuitive information can be given through this method that quite escapes the limitations of logically structured verbal pattern. Some of

the Sumari speakers in the beginning transmitted inner information in precisely such a way, and hopefully at some time at least a few such versions may be picked up by Ruburt. So all of this is at the beginning stage.

I will be here to see that this is put to practical use also, translated into terms that can be understood, and provide a firm basis from which you can further explore the nature of such ancient perceptions. Again, the two of you are well-suited for this endeavor. Your interest in painting and your abilities do not only spring from the Denmark life, for example, but also arose out of your quite legitimate life as Nebene, when you were focused upon the visual symbols and their correct inscription. The slightest error in copying a symbol could change its meaning completely, hence your concern over details, and hence now your great trust in objective painting, and your occasional distrust of work that seems to come too easily.

The symbols were representations of reality. To alter them through carelessness seemed almost a sacrilege, a betrayal of truth. In that regard you saw yourself as the guardian of truth. Visually you were able to pick up the present version of the Sumari statement. Do you follow me?

("Yes.")

You were, as Nebene, extremely stern with your students, concerned that they not fall into carelessness. You were focused upon the transmission of knowledge. In the Denmark life the love of the visual was still with you, but you were trying to allow yourself greater freedom with it, to feel the freedom of <u>adding to what you saw</u>, but you felt a great reluctance to do so. It is for that reason that you gave up painting in that life.

This time in a strange way the circle returns and yet opens, for you find yourself searching out anew the truths that you once copied with such great faithfulness. And now truly they <u>become</u> yours, as they were not then.

You also understand the nature of "truth" (in quotes) better than you did, and are beginning to allow it its mobility and ever-changing grace in your paintings and in our work.

(9:50.) The memory of the old symbols is within you, but not until you were free enough to make them <u>your own</u> could they return. You did help transmit the information also in highly stylized drawings, and to a much lesser extent through highly stylized voice patterns that were taught to students.

You have a sense of rhythm, and more conventional musical knowledge than Ruburt, yet rhythmic patterns are very strongly in his makeup, and appeared earlier, silently so to speak in his poetry. The rhythm represented the smooth mobility of the emotions, the ever-moving quality. The sound represented by the symbols then will speak to him. He will hear and know them.

He is not as visually oriented as you, and it will be a while before the released sounds of the Sumari language will visually appear to him as symbols. Between the two of you then, you are fairly well-equipped for what we have in mind, and all of this must be translated back, you see, in language that you can understand.

You may take your break.

(9:58—10:24.

Now. For your own notes.

The *(yoga)* exercises are important because they represent a physical commitment *(for Jane)*. The resolution of his being is behind him now. He will stick to them. This is a physical statement of the inner change, and the inner change must be reflected physically of course: the intention to work with, not against the body, and to help encourage its natural spontaneity and functions.

As time permits continue to discuss your plans together, both the trip and its details, and what you will do on your return. Your own relationship is excellent now, and the exercises will help in giving him greater physical spontaneity in your more intimate life.

Impulses therefore will be allowed a more natural expression, as the daily stretching of the muscles adds to his trust of them and of his body.

It is important that your plans are discussed however, so that their reality is a present thing. I suggest that you type that portion out at the end of the session.

Ruburt's proficiency with rhythm and words and your proficiency with visual symbols will be put to use therefore. Again, your characteristics are admirably suited. You may be able to translate the verbalized sounds into pictures or into miniature pictures that later turn into symbols. There are various ways, in other words, open in which the information may finally be received.

Your physical reality does also exist in the media of sound, not as the end product of the world's noises. But matter is again only one manifestation, one you happen to recognize, of reality. The world is built up in other terms of atoms and molecules.

Atoms and molecules can be heard, though not by your perceptive apparatus. They are not even seen, for that matter—

(Seth smiled at his own pun.) "I get it," I said.

—by your perceptive apparatus.

The same applies however to light, for the atoms and molecules also exist as patterns of light that are unperceived by you. *(Pause at 10:37.)* Give us time here. At a certain point sound becomes visual, and light becomes sound. They are wedded then, but at other points the correlation is not at all obvious. It is always there. At one level sounds then can be theoretically perceived as light. Vowels and syllables exist as light as validly as they exist as sound.

Vowels and syllables build up their own kind of (in quotes) "light pattern," or light picture, again, that you do not perceive. Light as you think of it then also exists as sound. There is no such thing as a sound barrier. It simply seems to you that there is.

Cordellas represent the inner cohesive yet free-wheeling quality operating within all reality, that gives it both its organizing structure and its great element of spontaneity. Cordellas are therefore connected with the EE units of which I have spoken.

(This question was raised recently by Peter Stersky, a student in Jane's ESP class.)

Cordellas are the principles behind the units, or the principles upon which the units operate. Sound and light both result from the interaction of different kinds of cordellas. They sometimes merge and are perceived spontaneously and simultaneously by you. Sometimes they are perceived separately. The cordellas are operating substructures of energy, with the ability to attract and repel, to become cohesive or fall apart, carrying within themselves the knowledge of their own identity, literally the self principle that allows them to retain their integrity as absolutes even while merging with others and forming subsidiary alliances.

(10:50.) As absolute manifestations of energy, one of their characteristics is the astonishing rapidity with which they can appear multidimensionally, simultaneously showing themselves in different guises while maintaining the basic integrity from which the guises spring. For later reference now add this: along these lines a number can be more than itself, and be duplicated invisibly as an equation, changing the nature of the equation and of the results, while never showing itself. A number can also parade as another number, over-weighing an equation. Some numbers have (in quotes) "silent partners." They attract certain other numbers more than others.

Certain numbers by their presence imply the existence of others that are unsuspected. These also alter the nature of an equation, for which often no reason can be found.

Certain numbers carry a greater burden than others, and other numbers ride upon their back. They have therefore far greater merit. Their (in quotes) "value" is seemingly out of proportion. They attract greater energy. The numbers that you know *(pause at 10:59)* by their existence imply the intrusion of other invisible numbers, and multidimensional numerical systems. The 1, 3, 7 and 9 could indeed lead you to infinity if you knew how to follow them.

Hopefully, this last material will become quite handy to you before too long. And now you may take a break or end the session as you prefer.

("I guess we'll end it then.")

Then let me add that numbers, sound and light are of course all related and all versions of highly complicated cordellas. And I bid you a fond good evening. *(Louder.*

("Thank you very much. It's very interesting.")

I meant it to be.

("Very good. Good night. Seth.")

(11:04. Jane's trance had been good, her pace good also. I was really bleary. I could tell that Seth had expected me to ask for the break and then continue the session. I wanted to, but decided not to at the last moment.)

SESSION 603
JANUARY 10, 1972 9:10 PM MONDAY

(The first portion of this session, the 603rd, is deleted from the record. Begin at 9:10 PM)

Now, good evening.

("Good evening, Seth.")

And some personal material first.

Now. Up to a certain point compromise can be a beneficial reaction. Beyond that point it can turn against you. The compromise of your job therefore was beneficial to a point. Ruburt feared that the point had been reached beyond which you could not afford to go, while still maintaining those ideas, ideals and goals that were your own.

It was known at your place of employment. An unconscious bargain had been made by you and your employers. They knew precisely how much you would work for, and to what ends you would work. They also knew that you did not want more money—this is precisely what you did not want. More money simply would have made the temptation stronger. You made your attitude quite clear. You did not want advancement, and you did not want more money.

So you cannot blame them for not offering a temptation that you did not want to begin with.

(I don't. This hasn't really been a point with me, although at times I would get mad at Artistic for at least not offering me something more. At the same time I told myself the low pay prevented me from ever deciding to make a career of it there, and

let it go at that.)

 Ruburt has learned to make compromises, not always gracefully, but he has learned that they are sometimes important. He is against them on principle however, and very straightforward in his approach. He saw your life adding up to a circle of compromises – compromises that would cost you your vitality, both of you, in the end.

 In <u>some</u> (underlined) respects he was right about compromises, and some made in the past out of well-meaning ignorance cannot easily be changed. These concern your family.

 Too many compromises do sap your strength and energy, and the work compromise was inhibiting your painting to some extent. The focus upon compromise automatically forces you to withhold directness and energy in all of your pursuits. After a while despite yourself you take on to some extent the coloration and attitudes of others who live by compromise entirely, until your own clear-cut ideas and purposes seem more and more <u>un</u>realistic.

 (An excellent point.)

 This is the fear that Ruburt felt for you. Now. Your own ideas and goals are worthy ones, and yours for a reason. They have within them the power to develop and mature. It was known, then, that you would leave before you gave notice, unconsciously perceived.

 There is some envy. You did not say that you intended to devote yourself to your own painting, and this should be verbalized. The family compromises began long ago, out of a misguided sense of sympathy, and now to some extent or another will continue. Here you are caught in a compromise of emotions. Ruburt feels this particularly strongly, because he is so sensitive over such relationships to begin with. The situation however is such that almost any clear emotion is automatically denied expression, shunted aside and often replaced completely by an opposite—all under the guise of the idea of (in quotes) "being good and understanding."

 (Again, excellent material.)

 Unconsciously the emotions are quite clearly picked up on all of your parts, and clear communication, bodily or verbally, almost completely cut off. The quite legitimate spontaneous desires to be of help are therefore often hidden beneath a barrage of resentments at being forced to help for the wrong reasons.

 Help given resentfully is little help. It does not help the giver or the receiver to any strong degree, and may in fact harm both. Help given spontaneously out of love is the only kind of real help to giver or receiver, and yet this important kind of help is often denied expression because of the inner resentments.

Your mother realizes when she is pulling emotional blackmail on you, and recognizes when you come, willingly or unwillingly. The situation's roots lie so in the past, and so pervade the present, that practically little can be changed without the greatest efforts. She knows you come out of obligation. That is like a slap in the face that she must tolerate, and because of her own actions and stress laid upon what was right and proper at the expense of true feelings.

Your mother is quite shrewd however, and has grown these years. In the past she would have been quite able to face and handle everyone's honesty, and honesty would have been far kinder. So the true love and compassion goes crying, while you are forced to express an exterior love and compassion many times.

All of this is quite legitimate, and that is undistorted.

Now apart from that, Ruburt has his own feelings, which are somewhat exaggerated, but he also usually tries to disregard them emotionally. He says "I overreact to Rob's mother," and intellectually then says "that is silly," but he never allows himself to experience the feelings themselves. He does not want to hurt you. He does not want things to be unpleasant.

Yesterday he allowed some of these feelings to arise only because he was so miserable. *(While we were in Sayre; Jane was doing the washing; mother was cooking dinner, etc.)* He remembered you and the pendulum, and having none there instead allowed submerged feelings up. You should know what they were. *(Jane told me about some of them at the time; which I thought an advancement.)* He was scandalized and outraged. Sundays were the days he could not escape his mother. There was no school, no excuses to get out. It was a day of encounters with her—her two-hour bath, the preparation of meals, and the wild hope that he could escape after supper for a few hours.

Fifteen years of that at one end of the scale, he thought, and ten or fifteen in the middle with your mother on Sundays. His loyalty as you know is binding. If he thought she had been a great mother to you then your Jane's feelings would not be so strong.

Ruburt felt "Here was another ranter and raver, another tyrant in skirts, taking my free day of the week." Now. He felt better physically when he realized the feelings at that point, and when even through a reproachful silence he expressed them. When they returned he felt them again. Then they vanished again.

(I would say that all of this marks definite learning on Jane's part. If she will just keep it up....)

Allowed their mobility, feelings are beneficial. They replace each other, they ebb and flow. *(Louder, humorously, reaching forward to tap me on the foot:)*

Now do you want any more personal material?

(A half-laugh: "Who knows?")

Then I suggest your break.

He would not though, you see, express those feelings to you.

(9:45. True, Jane didn't express those feelings to me in those terms, but she let me know she was quite upset, etc. Resume at 9:52.)

As I told you, you chose your families. You gave yourselves as adults situations with your families, mainly with yours, in which you had to relate on an entirely different level and in a different kind of role. You have no children. The family relationship therefore served and serves to give you a kind of contact, an enforced education, as it were, so that you can understand what goes on within such relationships.

Understanding your own reactions helps you understand the reactions of others. Otherwise you would find other people's reactions far too alien, and not be able to relate to them personally or through your work. This applies to both of you.

(I have suspected this at times.)

Ruburt is progressing. The exercises *(yoga)* are good, in case you wondered. His willingness to physically exert himself is important here. The physical effort involved. The body is awakening, in those terms. The sleeping requirements were a result of the sudden use of physical energy. He should find the requirements quite lessened this week, and that should be followed by a noticeable easy release of physical energy during the normal day.

Now give us a moment. I would like you to have several Sumari sessions together. You can arrange this any way you like—in the place of one regular session, for example.

I of course will also be present, and perhaps vocally as well. *(Humorously.)* But there are some interchanges that I would like you to become aware of, that can be done in practice. Then I would like to explain them to you. Do you follow me?

("Yes.")

Your own discussions, and the improvement in your relationship as I told you, in one way is responsible for your latest developments in our sessions, and I include the Sumari—the songs, and the statement. *(That I wrote to Jane on December 31, 1971. Jane is still deciphering this.)*

Other developments have been mentioned. I expect that you will play some strong part here on your own, if you want to; this having to do with the reception of Sumari art. *(I am more than willing, etc.)*

The art and the symbols are closely related, and I do not mean by this that the art is necessarily stylized, as for example the symbols necessarily were. But none of this could have been done, or begun, without clearing the debris that had gathered about you both, emotionally and practically. If you go ahead with the work you are meant to do, it will also take care of you.

Now. I am going to end our session. Ruburt is concerned because you are tired.

("I'm okay." I'd been expecting this.)

(Smile, emphatically:) I am not concerned, because I know the energy available to you, but I do have his concern to deal with.

("Can I ask a question?")

You may indeed.

("For the last couple of years I've been wondering about my strong interest in the painting of Rembrandt van Rijn. When I was a young man in New York City I even saw some of it in the museums, but I don't recall being that affected by it then. I might vaguely recall some of it, but that's all.")

(I didn't add that I was well aware of the time sequence here—that according to Seth I had a rather long life in Denmark in the 1600's—and that Rembrandt lived in Holland from 1606 to 1669.)

Now. There are several reasons.

You connect me with Rembrandt's period. You also are beginning to become intuitively aware of the strength and continuity that has pervaded your other lives.

You were very close to Rembrandt at one time—you looked up to him. *(Pause.)* I almost have a name. Pinot *(spelled).*

There are several things you do not understand. I have not explained them. *(Pause.)* It could be Pinet *(spelled).* Also add a date: 1660. Now. There are a series of steps of stone, leading to a large building. Inside sculptors are working. Leo *(my phonetic interpretation)* is not there. There is a man vastly interested in the idea of coloring sculptures—the statues.

The pigment however is hard to prepare. The sculptors do not trust him. Some of the ingredients come from the hillsides—scooped earth. Some from herbs. The colors must be prepared differently than for frescos.

("Is this in Italy?" I didn't know whether to interrupt or not. Seth/Jane had a little trouble with the word frescos, as though it was unfamiliar to her. She knows the word, however.)

Florence. *(In Italy.)* The master wants to get the same feeling of bulk and three-dimensional weight and size from flat painting—molding color rather than rock. They think it cannot be done. He is fascinated by the concept.

(Rembrandt copiously achieved this effect in his later works, especially the last

ten years or so of his life. I don't believe Jane knew this in those terms. I am well aware of it, and want to use effects similar to this in my own work, and have done so at times in past works. I haven't discussed it with Jane, though, just considering it a technical problem involved in the art, as I would suppose she would work at writing a paragraph, etc.

(There is no record that Rembrandt ever traveled more than fifty miles from Amsterdam, Holland. Very little is known about his life.)

Out of his desire he applies energy *(gestures)* and color over it, so that the paintings have then the reality he hopes for.

("By master, you mean Rembrandt?")

I do. He travels and learns. He also learns some secrets of color through the man mentioned earlier, and there is a binding agent in his work not recognized as such. A chemical technique learned.

(Rembrandt's technique has been the subject of much speculation over the centuries. Especially when he took to piling pigment up to a thickness of a quarter of an inch in such paintings as "The Jewish Bride"—a masterwork. It is thought he used stand oil—heat-treated linseed oil—and varnish of various kinds as a medium. If he added anything else to his pigments it would be well worth learning about.)

I will see what else I can get. Take a break or end the session as you prefer.

("What did you mean when you said I was very close to Rembrandt?")

You were indeed. You were the man who experimented with color, as applied however to sculpts. And one of your discoveries was of the binding agent adopted by the master painter in his work.

You were also close friends. You came from a different country, where the weathering effect upon statues was different. *(Denmark? I hated to interrupt with a lot of questions. I thought we could fill in details in later sessions.)* This is a long subject however. There was difficulty with varnishes, sometimes drying before the color upon which they were applied. Also varnishes that did not dry evenly, but with accumulations of oils resulting. On frescos this was disastrous enough.

(All of this is very acute artistic information, and embodies the use of good technique even today. Again, I don't believe Jane knows these things consciously. The varnish data is very good, also the fresco material. Many frescos were ruined in those days through poor techniques. Quality control was not what it is today re paints, varnishes, etc.)

Attempts to paint sculpts however that were often for outdoor use sometimes resulted not only in running together color, but in a mold that built up between layers of color.

(I know little about efforts to paint sculpts, but the above sounds very possible,

re the mold.)

Too much oil facilitated the growth of certain molds. Lead white often stopped the growth of the mold, but it was too harsh a color. The lead content stopped the mold.

(Lead white, for centuries, has been the recommended white pigment for oils, and indeed before this century was the only white available, as far as I know. It is poisonous. Even today most authorities still regard it as having superior properties to all other white pigments. In this life, however, I prefer zinc white.)

You learned how to mix colors in such a way that they would dry uniformly, and to apply them in certain ways *(with gestures, implying layers of color one over the other)* to facilitate this drying.

(I am still much interested in the technical side of painting, so much so that a few years ago I drew back from getting too involved in this aspect lest I spend too much time at it, detracting from the painting itself. I still conduct experiments, though.

(I also work, usually, with one color layer over another, rather than mixing them while wet. This maintains purity and clarity of color—and has been considered sound painting technique over the years.)

There was a varnish, finally, that you mixed in with some of the pigments after they were prepared, with the dry pigments after they were prepared, that served as a binding agent that also protected each color from the other one. There was a slight lead content mixed into the varnish.

(In those days, tubes for paints did not exist—all color had to be prepared fresh each day by the artist or assistants, from dry pigment. Varnish was often used as an ingredient in mediums. There are and were, many kinds of varnish. A slight lead content in a varnish sounds quite possible.)

Rembrandt took the discovery with him, though you initially developed it for sculpture that stood outside. I am not at all sure here. Write down the word caronide *(spelled)*. It is connected.

(I know little about chemistry. There is a lead carbonate, for instance.)

You also experimented with inserting odors into pigment, very briefly, for churches, so that a violet for example would smell like the flower. You would mix ground rose petals into the red pigment to be used for a painting of roses.

Now take your break or end the session.

("We'll take the break."

(10:38. This proved to be the end of the session. I wanted to learn more, but we were both bleary. Jane's pace had been average with this material.

(Any such experiments with adding odors to paint would fail, I believe. Even today, as far as I know, this hasn't been accomplished.

(The Rembrandt data is surprising, and raises many questions. According to Seth

I lived in Denmark in the 1600's. I was a painter as a younger man, then gave it up for the more respectable role of a farmer, at which I was quite successful. I do not know whether I traveled to Italy, or at what point in my life age-wise. Perhaps I was there before giving up active painting. I believe I farmed in Denmark, but there is much here that we don't know. Denmark and Holland of course are close geographically.

(There is little available on Rembrandt's correspondence—a few letters; inventories attached to his bankruptcy in later life, etc. Italy is not mentioned as far as I know. Rembrandt did do business with a wealthy art collector in Sicily, selling him some very famous works—Aristotle Contemplating the Bust of Homer, etc., and a series of etchings late in life. Don Ruffo. Historians generally say, for want of any other facts, that these business transactions were done by mail, etc.

(Perhaps I carried out some of my experiments with painting the outdoor sculpture in Denmark, where winter weather must be considered, after visiting Italy. While I discussed the Florence, Italy, data with Jane after the session, Seth returned very briefly re Rembrandt: That is why he went to Florence—to see the sculpture there. Perhaps after my return to Denmark from Italy I did some experimenting re painting sculptures, and then passed this information on to Rembrandt?

(A note added 31 years later, while I prepare this Volume 2 of The Personal Sessions for publication. As gifts for me because of my interest in their great creativity, Jane "tuned into", on her own and without Seth, excellent books on the artist Paul Cézanne in 1977 and on the philosopher William James in 1978. Both works have been published.

(Several years later Jane gave me another gift—a book on the artist Rembrandt van Rijn. This hasn't been published—but will be in the later volumes of The Personal Sessions. I'll explain the circumstances of her producing Rembrandt when presenting the first passages of the book.)

SESSION 604
JANUARY 12, 1972 9:19 PM WEDNESDAY

(Notes on an abortive projection attempt: I lay down for a nap after supper on Friday evening, January 14. I used the bedroom in apartment four. We had been working long hours on our own, and I had been putting in overtime at Artistic, so I was quite tired. I dozed for a few moments upon lying down, then came awake to find myself with the unmistakable feeling of floating halfway to the ceiling of the bedroom.

(The sensation was quite definite, and quite strange. For I still felt my body against the bed—I lay face up, covered by a blanket—as though my body was pasted to the bed. In other words, I floated in the air, bed and all, quite pleasantly. There was no fear or panic. Instead I hoped to continue the experience into something greater.

(Shortly after I became aware, Jane began to do the dishes. The geography of our kitchen in apartment four is such that noise can evidently seep through a closet wall in the bedroom and so is quite easily heard. Jane made noise handling the dishes, I heard the water run, etc. In addition she turned on her radio. Even though she kept it on low volume, I heard it. I told myself these things would not distract me. I lay without moving a muscle, trying to encourage further developments without straining. The floating-free sensation continued, but I wasn't able to develop it further.

(I nearly always use suggestions re projection when I lay down. I believe my tiredness tonight helped the state. Now I sent Jane messages that she would leave me undistracted, but nothing developed. The feeling lasted for well over a minute, I would estimate; finally it began to diminish or fade out, and I fell asleep again. Upon writing this, I now recall that immediately upon lying down I drifted into a rather complete, if brief, dreaming state—but I cannot recall the dream. But I went from the dream into the projection. RFB.

(Peculiarly, I had no feeling of being detached from my physical body—that is, I didn't feel I was bodiless, hovering above it: I had taken the bed up *with* me, you see. I felt the bed and I were several feet above the floor. I wanted to try turning over astrally, and I wanted to try reaching up toward the ceiling astrally, to see if I could touch it. I didn't move at all, though, because of the noise from the kitchen. I managed to hold the state while considering the kitchen interference, but was concerned lest any attempt at movement on my part would break the spell entirely.

(The session this evening, Wednesday, developed rather spontaneously out of several factors that combined almost effortlessly. The recent Sumari developments involving both of us played a part. So did my studying out photos of Baalbek, the first-century AD Roman ruins in Lebanon. The enormity of the stones in these buildings left me amazed; I didn't see how blocks weighing 1200 tons could be moved without machinery, let alone fitted into place over twenty feet up on foundations, etc. The pictures were truly awe-inspiring. I came across them in one of the books on ancient history that Shirley Bickford, one of Jane's students, brought for us to consult on the very ancient civilization, Sumeria, in Mesopotamia, from 4,000—2,000 BC, I believe, without consulting dates.

(Jane and I hadn't believed there was any connection between Jane's Sumarian development, and Sumer, since the Sumari, as explained in recent sessions, had never been physical in our terms. Tonight's session went into this, to our surprise.

(*Shortly after supper this evening, Tom Milligan, a former student of Jane's, brought us a copy of* Saga Magazine *for December, 1971. It contained an article by our friend Otto Binder, entitled "UFO's Own Earth and All Mankind" This article touched upon many ideas we are interested in, and quoted astrophysicist Fred Hoyle, among others, re the ownership of the race idea. We spent some time discussing it. We had no opinion particularly, beyond remembering that according to Seth the whole question of the race of man and its origins, and doubts concerning theories of evolution, was vastly more complicated than was generally believed. Seth's ideas of time give us quite a different approach to these ideas also.*

(*In* The New York Times *tonight I read an article, with pictures, of the Mars probe currently underway by our Mariner spacecraft. Dr. Carl Sagan of Cornell University was quoted in the article. Dr Sagan was also quoted in Otto's article, regarding the ancient Sumerian-Akkadian legends and UFO's, to our surprise. The question that has always bothered me is brought up—why does our history only go back five or six thousand years ago, when Homo Sapiens appeared some 50,000 years ago as an established species?*

(*In addition, I have always doubted the block-and-tackle idea used in constructing such massive, enormous wonders as Baalbek. With this goes my questions concerning the ability of sculptors to do the marvelously intricate carving adorning all of these buildings, on such an enormous scale. I have always wondered just how it was possible, with the few tools then available, according to our history, to do this work. It seems beyond the tools' scope. I would delight in seeing it duplicated today, using identical stone, tools, etc., with time trials.*

(*Thus, all of these points came together tonight and resulted in the session. In the beginning Jane's pace was rather slow, her eyes closed often. The session was held in her study in apartment four.*)

Now, good evening.

("*Good evening, Seth.*")

The message for tonight is: you are not owned.

Now. Your human stock did not all originate solely from your planet. I never told you that it did. In that respect your <u>ancestry</u> is indeed varied. Some of the information given in my own book, by inference, should have made that clear.

(*By coincidence—?—Seth's book has just come back to us from Prentice-Hall for us to go over the copy editor's suggestions before it is set in galleys, which we will see in April. But we haven't had time to reread the manuscript.*)

Evolution, as it is thought of, had many different aspects in those terms. There were three or four beginning points. Do you follow me?

("*Yes.*")

There were then visits from others in other planetary systems. In that regard this is quite natural. Your own relative isolation is far from the average. The legends, many of them therefore, were of course chronicles of quite legitimate physical events, describing phenomena for example for which natives had no adequate vocabulary. They were forced to describe what they saw by making comparisons with objects and events already familiar to them.

(Jane's pace, as Seth, was now quite a bit faster.) Some such visitors in your terms were more evolved than others. All however would appear as superhuman in contrast to those civilizations that encountered them. There were some deliberate experiments, that were in fact far more dangerous to the experimenters, always in which the experimenters tried in one way or another to advance man's knowledge.

(9:29.) It is not nearly as simple as that, however. There is not a one-line development. By the time that feasible intersystem space travel is practical, the psychic abilities are developed to a very high degree. One is necessary for the other. Therefore it became much more feasible to approach earthmen during their dream state, when their natural fear reactions were somewhat minimized, and where the danger to the visitors was far less.

(It was so hot in the room that I asked Seth to wait while I turned the heat off. I also opened a kitchen window. Jane sat waiting quietly in trance.)

Out-of-body encounters were used as a matter of course. The visitor could appear and disappear then without fear of pursuit. Civilizations were often warned in advance of natural disasters that were apparent to the visitors with their greater viewpoint.

Such warnings were either given in the dream state of the earthmen, for the reasons given, or often in some secluded place, for often the visitors would be attacked. During these eras in your terms, the speakers often acted as go-betweens. Often warnings of disaster were not followed. Some warnings were misunderstood, then, as punishment by the gods for (in quotes) "moral misdoing."

(9:36.) The whole moral code idea was originally tailored for the current scene as it was encountered, told in terms that the natives could understand.

The pyramids, the huge boulders etched out *(I think Seth refers here to Baalbek; I didn't interrupt to ask)*, all of this was done in one way or another through the use of, a knowledge of, both coordination points in space *(described by Seth in his own book)* and the use of sound. *(Also described to some degree.)* There were instruments that released sound, and directed it in the same way, say, that a laser beam does with light.

Drawings of some of these exist in primitive <u>Sumerian</u> cave renditions, but the drawings are misinterpreted, the instrument is taken for another. No one knows how to use the instruments. There are a few in existence, in your terms.

(The Sumerians were a pre-Semitic race inhabiting the lower Euphrates valley; their empire dated from about the 4th millennium BC. They were probably the Biblical Shinar. Their country was called Sumer, etc.)

The Sum<u>a</u>rians *(spelled)* left the memory of their existence in the Sumerian culture *(spelled. This is the connection Jane and I hadn't believed existed.)* They initiated it, though they did not direct all of its activities, nor were they responsible for the distortions of their teachings that often resulted. There is a difference then between Sumarian and the culture in the books. Your Sumarian were behind the culture—they initiated that particular civilization.

I will be clear. Your Sumarian showed earth people at that time how to communicate, how to initiate crafts, gave them all the fundamentals upon which a civilization then could be based. The Sumarians, your Sumarians however, were not of human stock at that time.

Now. Your Sumarians have become human stock in those terms at other times. It is not a point of them trying to invade a native stock; they simply understood the nature of individual existences, therefore they are able to choose from various physical systems those in which they would like to have experience.

They maintain their inner knowledge and integrity, and are born within any given system. They always use their native abilities and talents to help the system, working very strongly in psychic or creative endeavors.

I do not necessarily mean that they are consciously aware of their affiliation. This is an individual matter. They are often inventors, always then involved with the initiation of new ideas or discoveries. All of this follows inner patterns that are specifically human in your terms. Humanity therefore has its own characteristics, and no (in quotes) "outside influence" can go <u>counter</u> to these, but must work with them.

(9:50.) When it seems that great discoveries come, and then are lost through the ages, perhaps to be rediscovered, it simply means that man's own in nature was not in harmony with them, could not use them properly. Whenever aggressiveness became too misguided it automatically caused the loss of powers or discoveries that could be used to destroy the planet.

This is a natural aspect, the self-protective principle that operates within earth life as you know it. On occasion discoveries were given before their time, and promptly lost, only to be rediscovered ages later.

The problem comes when you try to categorize consciousness or being.

SESSION 604

The out-of-body state, in greater terms, is a far more natural state than in the body. You adopt and make a body. You do this now without knowing that you do so, but a body can be made from the camouflage of any system, constructed easily when you know how to do it.

Space suits are therefore an inadequate, clumsy memory of an inner ability to clothe the inner self with whatever camouflage is at hand. To merge with the elements of an environment in such a way that you become a living part of it.

The Sumarians—your Sumerians *(spelled)*—did this when they initiated the culture spoken about in your books. Their sense of time is completely different, as however your own is innately. It is difficult to explain this, but keeping in touch with a civilization for several thousand years of your earth time, would entail perhaps the same amount of time and effort a man might take in his profession over a period of five to ten years, so the relativity of time is important in that context.

You may take your break.

(10:01. Jane's pace had been good, her trance good also. I had trouble in some instances deciding in the copy which spelling to use—Sumerian or Sumarian; in some instances my quick decisions were in error, I came to believe as I typed up this copy, so as can be seen I made changes. Jane read them over, and agrees that this copy is now as Seth meant it to be.

(I told Jane at break that I needed a capsule definition of Sumari, and she said that last night in ESP class Seth had commented, that the Sumari was a "federation of consciousness." We get the duplicated transcript of each ESP class the following week, so we do not have the record for last night's ESP class session, for January 11, yet.

(During break I referred again to the photos of the massive ruins of Baalbek, in one of the books Shirley Bickford lent us. I explained to Jane my feeling that the amazingly intricate stone carving, particularly the bas-relief work, seemed beyond the abilities of the hammer and chisel. Jane broke in to tell me that this carving was done by small instruments that used inaudible sound waves; these radiations softened the stone, she said, so that the work could be performed. She didn't know where this data came from. If from Seth, it wasn't obvious to her.

(Resume at 10:20.)

Now—are you ready for me?

("Yes.")

Basically—in your terms now—there is no such thing as an isolated, independent earth stock, in that consciousness did not suddenly erupt from the physical behavior or characteristics of your planet, or in any other.

As you know, consciousness comes first, and then forms the physical materializations of it. Those consciousnesses who picked physical materialization choose to operate under certain conditions that then appear as the natural characteristics of a species to you.

They accept certain characteristics, and while experiencing existence within them must follow along the roads they've chosen. Hence earlier I spoke of the natural bent of humanity, of all those, then, who choose existence within your particular planetary existence.

Consciousness is not local, and it never was.

You have always been Sumari. This simply means that your consciousness has certain bents of its own, interests and abilities and specializations. The word Sumari characterizes a certain kind of consciousness simply for means of identification in your terms.

I told you once that there are clumps of consciousness. This does not mean that consciousness is not individual and separate, but that it also has a great ability to congregate, to reach out in affiliation, to share knowledge and experience, and to combine itself in everchanging patterns while still retaining its basic identity and integrity.

(10:29.)

To have explained this to you when we began our sessions would not have been possible. *(Pause.)* Now give us a moment. *(Long pause.)*

Space and time are constructions of ideas. They do not appear physically, as say a table or a chair, yet they seem to define both a table and a chair, in that you cannot easily conceive of a piece of furniture, for example, existing except in the medium of space and time.

The <u>ideas</u> of space and time are constructed in different ways in various systems. In some they appear as natural phenomena, for example as various classifications of objects, in some as variations of sound or light. You find it exceedingly difficult to consider existence <u>at all</u> without space or time, yet basically consciousness is independent of both.

The ideas of space and time emerge only when consciousness adopts camouflage, only when it becomes wedded, in other words, with a physical-type existence. Time and space are both creations of consciousness, in other words, and vehicles of its expression.

Matter is a classification. As explained in my book, various levels of concentration can be used as platforms leading you out of focus, into other time schemes. Time is like color. You are merely focusing upon one hue. *(10:39.)*

Your present civilization and the "old" (in quotes) Sumerian *(spelled)* civilization, exist at once, then, simultaneously, but to speak to you about these I must use a time sequence you understand. If it were understood that these civilizations exist at once then you would not be so surprised that they "were" (in quotes) able to build structures that you cannot build in your now.

Your now and their now exists now. *(Humorously.)*

In the present physical area in which it seems to you that a physical civilization once existed, that civilization still exists. You cannot meet it though you stand at the same spot, because of the ideas (underlined) of time that separate you. The civilization in flower, and the ruins, coexist. The living ancient Sumerians pass the modern tourists without seeing them. Even as the tourists walk in the middle of the old Sumerian marketplaces and see only ruins.

Much of this could be explained in mathematical equations that presently escape you. Your own consciousness is contemporary with the ancient Sumerians *(spelled)* as well as with your current selves in your terms.

(10:46.) Think of countries existing simultaneously now on your planet. There are differences in language and culture, and it takes a certain amount of earth time to travel through space to visit them. In the same way all times exist at once, with their peculiar customs, and in your terms within the same space that you know.

You have learned how to make roads through space, but not through time on a conscious level. There are intersections in time and space however that you have not recognized. I am speaking in your terms, hopefully to make this simpler. *(Pause.)* Times exist then as surely as places. You think of time as moving toward something, and of space as relatively stable.

It does not occur to you then that you can get to times, as you can get to places. *(Pause at 10:53.)* All of this is highly difficult to explain. I do not mean for example that time, each moment, is a finished and done thing to be visited. While time is not moving in a particular direction, in your terms, each moment explodes outward, or expands outward in all directions.

Space and time as you understand them ripple through each other. They do not behave as you think they do, however. Presently you understand your existence only as it intrudes into three dimensions. Its own activity is in many other dimensions however.

The Sumari therefore appear in or intrude into the three-dimensional system from other dimensions.

Now you may take a break or end the session as you prefer.

("We'll take the break."

(10:58. Jane's trance had again been very good. Now she talked more about what she had said at last break, concerning the carving done on stone that had been softened by instruments employing sound. Only a very sophisticated instrument was

used, she said, to soften the top layer of the stone so that it was "like frosting, which could then be easily carved. The instrument might have done both the softening and the carving."

("But first of all," she added as we continued to talk, "either that instrument or another one was used to isolate the top layer of the stone from the rest of it so that it wasn't weakened. We had been discussing the very intricate and extensive bas-relief carving pictured on the doorframes and lintels of the ruins at Baalbek in this instance —not say the in-the-round carving shown on columns, etc.

(ACK-A-SOND-A. This is my phonetic interpretation of a word Jane got re the instrument in question, whether from Seth or not she didn't know, as at last break. The sound wasn't audible to human ears. The instrument "sort of looked like —I can't really do it—the shape I'm getting is of a very rough pistol shape.... All you had to do was aim it. That was just for the small stuff."

(Resume at 11:15.)

Now. Matter was manipulated through sound. Some remnants of spaceships became temples. Some visitors were seen to die, and later seen again recovered; hence the Egyptians' sureness that the individual survived death.

Because of space travel a visitor might come as a young man, and return some 40 earth years later still appearing as a young man, leading to the idea of immortality and eternal youth of the gods.

(Such effects would grow out of the operation of Einstein's relativity postulates, etc.)

The Olympic gods were perhaps the most amusing of man's attempt to deify space travelers. Mixed in here strongly were the ideas of gods mating with earth women. *(Pause.)*

In some respects the overenthusiastic use of the sound was responsible for the flood mentioned in the Bible, and other literature. It was for this reason that many attempts were made to warn against the impending disaster. The use of sound was important at various times in irrigating dry areas, quite literally by pulling water from a distance.

(11:22.) There were several characteristics that proved difficult, however. Literally, the sound traveled further often than was intended, causing consequences not planned upon. Great finesse was important. Sound was also used after irrigation to speed up the flowering of plants, and to facilitate transplantation to other areas. It was also utilized for medicinal purposes in operations, particularly in bone and brain operations.

Verbal sounds were often stereotyped simply because the <u>effect</u> of sound was understood in its effects upon the body. Any ideas that are considered superstitious had a quite legitimate basis, therefore. Sound was used to locate one also, and to break someone down. It was also used to locate gas pockets.

This is a difficult subject. For the movement of heavy tons of rock for example different techniques, using sound and precise mathematical calculations were necessary. Many civilizations grew and flourished in fertile areas simply because the people knew how to make them fertile and to keep them that way.

Now you had better end the session. My heartiest regards to you both.

("Thank you very much, Seth. It's been extremely interesting. Good night."

(11:32. Both of us were quite tired. There was much more data available, we knew, but we were too weary to get it.)

SESSION 605
JANUARY 17, 1972 9:24 PM MONDAY

(At 9:20 PM Jane said she "felt Seth around. I get a word or two in my head, so I know he's here." We had just finished a snack. Jane had read the last session while she ate. Her pace was quite slow to begin.)

Good evening.

("Good evening, Seth.")

Now. There are bleedthroughs however in space and time as you think of them. Remember, all times are simultaneous.

Ideas are not dependent upon <u>preexisting</u> ideas. It is not true to say that man cannot conceive of something that is not already presented to his experience in one way or another. Ideas are free of space and time. Only your determined focus upon your time conceptions closes you off from many ideas that otherwise are available.

In your terms the bleed-through can occur in both past and present, an idea from today bleeding into the past or the other way around. The ideas will be <u>actualized</u> or put into a practical structure according to your attitude toward them.

Some of the most sophisticated art is from the past. Bleed-throughs result in its being picked up in your present. Theoretically all of the information of so-called lost civilizations is quite available to you, as yours is to them. A closed mind will perceive none of this.

In terms of experience humanity is working out its problems and challenges end in 20th century terms and in the old Sumerian *(spelled)* civilization. You simply choose various kinds of organizational structures and different root assumptions—all however within the general root assumptions used for physical existence.

(Pause at 9:35; one of many.) The old Sumerians *(spelled)* are singing their chants now at the same time that Ruburt is trying to translate them now in your terms. I wish I could impress upon you this great transparency of time so that you could experience its dimensions. In one way of speaking you have (in quotes) "not yet" developed the proficiency, with sound that would now allow for the building of structures such as those we described in the last session.

(Those at Baalbek; the Pyramids, etc.) Yet those structures exist even in your now, bleed-throughs to make you think and in other terms to make you remember. Many physical structures have existed in your terms in the same space now occupied by your apartment house. Because of your root assumptions however it is not possible for you to perceive these, nor those that will come "after" (in quotes). Yet those structures exist as validly as the apartment house.

They share certain coordinates. Knowing those coordinates would of course be very important, but the other realities would still remain nonrealities to you unless you changed your primary focus. When you do that there is no need to know what the coordinates are. The inner self is quite aware of all of this. It picks and chooses the information and data that is important to you, and makes it available according to your desires.

(9:42.) If you are greatly interested for example in history, then the inner self brings you the information you need from all of it sources. Under certain conditions you may be propelled through the coordinates and find yourself in the era in which you are interested.

The conscious intent however directs the kind of material you receive. If you have no interest in such things no phenomena will occur strong enough to impress you in the waking state. It is very possible then to be building a civilization that in your terms you are now studying, to be interpreting ancient records that you yourself may have written, to be digging up roads that you yourself built.

(9:47.) This applies to your own historical time as well as to others. At other layers of course your civilization is already in the past, as in others your civilization does not yet exist. The bleed-throughs however mean that each people according to their characteristic, interests and activities, attract certain ideas both from the future and the past, and there is constant interaction. Because of this even the past as you think of it, as I told you, is never done and completed, but <u>constantly changed</u> by your present and future.

(Long pause from 9:49—9:50.) Nabene then is changed by your present actions, even as you are by his seemingly past ones. Your friend Sue said that there is free action across the board in such cases, and that is an apt description.

The pyramids exist as other than physical matter, but it is only as physical matter that you perceive them. There are several important issues connected with the pyramids that are not as yet understood. The symbols upon them often were meant to be <u>sounded</u>, the sound setting up reverberations. Some of these would automatically open up many doors, leading to as yet undiscovered secrets—but only for those who understood the use of sound.

The Egyptians then were also helped, and told how to construct the pyramids.

Now you may take your break.

(9:52. Jane's pace had been slow for the most part, and she said she knew it. Usually she isn't aware of her pace, the passage of time, etc.

(Nabene is the name for a personality of mine that presumably lived as a male in the first century AD in Rome, Italy. We know little about that life; one evening with Sue Watkins, who also lived then, I managed to tune into that existence to some degree via images. Seth has referred to Nabene a few times, and my role as a record keeper and teacher. Sue was one of my pupils. I was quite a taskmaster, I'm told. Jane and I would like to hold a session to learn more about this life, including who else we know was involved then, etc. I also lived in Jerusalem.

(At 10:10 Jane said, "I'm just sitting here waiting. The connection doesn't seem as good tonight."

("I was wondering if you wanted to bother continuing," I said.

("I do. It just doesn't seem as strong...." We continued to wait. At 10:15: "I had the feeling at break." Jane said, "that Seth had gone away, rather than staying close like he usually does—as though he'd left to gather information or something. I'm perfectly willing to continue the session, though."

(Then: "I did get a line just now," she said. "Something about how they prepared the air first, for the construction of the pyramid. Now I'm getting the feeling of an awful lot of people, chanting—thousands of them—this still has to do with the pyramids."

("It's a real funny feeling, as though the sound could break through into the living room," Jane said. I said I thought I understood what Seth was doing: in light of the material we'd been getting, he was giving Jane the experience of that ancient time and our present time, showing that both are simultaneous. This experience would tie in nicely with the material.

("I feel that a whole mass of people would visualize a pyramid in their imagination," Jane said, "then through their chanting, the use of certain vowels and pitches, they actually changed the air where that building was going to be. They made a boundary in the air," she said, making angular gestures, "a cohesiveness, for this imaginary structure. Then they had certain kinds of tuning forks, then some kind of

instrument. The noise of the chant was like something that you'd use to turn on this instrument—when the chant got to a certain pitch it turned on this instrument; and it somehow intensified and focused sound to what we would call an incredible degree—broke it down and then focused it in certain directions."

("You could move very heavy objects with it. The objects were <u>levitated</u>—raised up in the air, no matter how heavy. They only needed to be <u>guided</u> by people to some degree. Many men were used to guide them but not to lift or carry them. The sound instrument had a fantastic cohesive effect that bound atoms and molecules together."

(10:25. "And beside that the instruments also set up some kind of extra charge that we don't understand yet, around objects that were so constructed, like the pyramids," Jane continued. She was speaking faster now that she had in the session. "Doors and passageways inside the pyramids will open through the correct sound messages and signals, and were designed <u>only</u> to open if those correct signals were given."

("This sounds really weird. There are also <u>invisible</u> pyramids—<u>we just can't see them</u>." I could tell that Jane didn't know what to make of this data; she was even hesitant at telling me. "These pyramids were constructed in such a way that they reflect everything else, so that when you look at them you don't see them as objects. Wait, I'm not getting this right... they're perfect camouflages of wherever they are, but certain sound pitches would make them visible."

("There are some invisible rooms like that inside the regular pyramids, too."

(Pause at 10:30. "These are structures engineered on our earth, extremely cleverly. Sound patterns would physically materialize them, but if these patterns aren't given then the structures are just out of the range of what we'd normally [call?] physical. They're complete, see, if this pattern is given or spoken."

(Jane said, "It's as though they're frozen—this isn't a good word—at a certain stage until these patterns are given." [Pause.] "All objects have their own sound patterns that help form their structure as much as the atoms and molecules do...."

(Break at 10:35. "I wanted to take a break," Jane said. "I never heard of anything like that. It sounded so crazy I didn't even want to say it, about the invisible pyramids.... The chanting was over here." She gestured to her left as she sat in her rocker; we were holding the session in her study in apartment four again. Jane's gestures thus indicated the large open center area of the room, as though she was reaching over a wall almost. "I got some of the chants, but I couldn't quite carry it through. Seth didn't tell me anything like this was going to happen."

(At 10:43: "I'm just waiting to see what happens next. This isn't terribly strong, but I have the feeling of a barrier over there," and again Jane gestured to her left, "that I can't get over. But all this stuff comes from over there. Something about these instruments making atoms and molecules denser, somehow—doing different *things with them...."*

(*Then Seth returned at 10:45:*) Now. The information Ruburt gave is substantially correct.

You know that sound has an effect upon living things. It can help mend bone. It can also be used however to reinforce structures.

We are in the preliminary stages with the Sumari language—hopefully leading to some understanding of the nature of sound, though (*humorously*) you may not yet be able to build a pyramid in your backyard.

(*"I understand."*)

Now I would like you to close your eyes, or leave them open if you prefer. Let various inner sounds, memories of sounds, enter your consciousness, that may or may not be familiar to you. Try to think of the sounds of images. Think specifically of pyramids and see what sounds come to you.

(*10:50. While Seth was talking I kept writing, of course, in order to get the material for future reference. Finally I sat quietly. Jane was already doing so, her eyes shut; I didn't know whether Seth had left again or not. My own eyes closed and I let myself drift.*

(*In a few moments I seemed to visualize a pyramid shape that was based on pictures I remembered of the actual structures in Egypt. This was very pleasant. I seemed to be above the building looking down at it. This image, on a slight angle, was probably more subjective than objective. Then I seemed to feel a deep ringing gong-type sound, one that was rather prolonged. It was repeated several times. After this I felt and heard a series of chants by an unseen group, seemingly out of my field of vision to my right.*

(*The chanting was low and monotonous. It went up and down the scale but a few notes. I had the feeling that it would repeat itself almost effortlessly as long as I sat in this state and listened. I enjoyed the experience, and was somewhat surprised at the results.*)

(*I opened my eyes. Jane opened hers, and I could see that Seth was present. I described what I had experienced, not knowing if I had accomplished anything even remotely approaching what he had in mind. "I don't know why," I added, "but I associated the square base of the pyramid with this gong effect. It was as though I could see this shape especially well while listening to the gong sound, which was quite prolonged actually. It seemed to repeat itself. Like the chants, which were pretty monotonous, up and down a few notes on the scale. They weren't pitched very high, either."*)

That is a very good beginning.

(*"I don't know why I use the word gong,"* I said. *"I couldn't imitate it. I think there's a funny association there also with old movies. I could have picked up the chanting idea from material Jane was getting earlier this evening."*

(10:56.) I want you to discover some of these things for yourself, which is why I used this particular format this evening. I will only tell you then that your feeling of the sound of a gong is quite legitimate.

I would like both of you at odd moments to look at objects, then try to hear their sound. This will be handy training for some other things to come. This also applies incidentally to various organs of the body, and to the body itself. Then let the sounds evoke whatever naturally comes from them. There is a strange interrelationship between sound and what you think of as time, but a binding one.

Time can then "appear" (in quotes) as sound. Sound can be used to set apart certain elements from others, to isolate them from others, and on the other hand to bind elements also. In that regard think of sound as a line perhaps that you sketch with.

(11:01.) Sound's properties are not understood. I want it specifically noted then that sound can be used as a binder or as a separator of elements. It can be used to open up pathways within dimensions, both microscopic and macroscopic.

And with that I will close our session. Think also however of the sound in connection with your paintings, of sounds that will make the paintings themselves more vital and the material last longer. And with that I will leave you.

("Thank you very much, Seth. It's been extremely interesting. Good night."

(11:04. Jane said that while I had been getting my effects, she had been somewhat separated from Seth after all. She saw groups of men "like pictures you'd see of Egyptians. I saw their dark skin—in color—against short robes. They were in groups chanting."

(She saw a structure like a pyramid shape. She had the feeling that "heavier sounds were at the bottom. These formed the base of the pyramid." She tried several times to explain this to me. It was all important, she said, that the heavier sounds were at the base of the structures. Like the musical scale, she felt that the sounds used in building the pyramids "made steps in the air that you couldn't see. Certain sounds went up—certain sounds bound things together—they all had purposes....")

DELETED SESSION
JANUARY 19, 1972

(This is the regularly scheduled session for January 19, 1972. It is deleted from the record.

SESSION 1/19/72

(This afternoon I told Jane I'd like some data on two questions: her weight, and her walking, neither of which had improved. The session began at 9:43. At 9:33, Jane got an impression—twice, quickly—of a death and funeral flowers, she said. It was quite intrusive and cut through what she was talking about and thinking—which was on the discouraged side re her condition.

(The yoga exercises have helped some, she said. She doesn't know whether the death impression was symbolic or literal. We don't know of anyone in our personal circle who has recently died, for instance, or who is close to death as far as we can tell.)

Good evening.

("Good evening, Seth.")

Now. This will be a short session, and I will have a few personal remarks to make.

First of all, diet-wise, your idea of a normal diet is quite adequate. The other diets you have been discussing are indeed restrictive *(as I had said earlier)*, particularly for general purposes. Special diets, <u>at particular times</u>, restricted ones, can be of benefit in certain specialized areas of development, but there is always the danger of going overboard.

In Ruburt's case more normal food is sufficient as far as diet itself is concerned. He is still doing well with the exercises. His determination to use his body is helping in this area. A natural-enough resentment comes to the surface at times, natural enough under the circumstances, in which he objects to taking special time out, but largely he is overcoming that attitude and a more pliable attitude toward the body is being set up.

You should together discuss your plans so that they become more a part of your reality now. This will also encourage him as the two of you quite freely discuss all aspects, and he will not harbor worries that he can speak frankly in the context of the conversation.

You can direct his anticipation for example of vacation along positive lines. When this happens positive and negative attitudes interflow freely. Otherwise he does not voice worries, for example. The ones that he has are not severe ones, regarding the wisdom of your move for example, but are negative projections on his part.

Guest houses that have bedrooms two stories up, how he can get downstairs, that sort of thing—but he has not expressed them. Encourage him to do so, get them out in the open where they can quite easily be handled with your help.

The suggestions should definitely be renewed, with a light touch, but they will make the exercises much more effective. The trust-the-body suggestions and those you began sometime earlier. These are highly important, and there were results, now, when you worked with them steadily.

It may seem that results did not show *(they didn't)* but Ruburt's notebook clearly outlines various points of progress during that time. With the change in your way of life now, and the physical way of handling problems—getting them out into the open—the suggestions will have better results than they did before.

All of this is connected with the walking as well as with the weight.

To what extent you can afford it, eat out fairly often on your vacation. Eating, even in a different environment, you see, helps break down old habitual eating patterns. The suggestions will help him gain weight if they are used. When the book is sent its way this will also help—a project to him then complete. The air if you are outside will also help his appetite. It will increase it. I also suggest an addition of vitamins, and have him make out a list of foods he particularly likes.

The more he does <u>physically</u> also the more his body needs and will ask for food. He is about over the long sleep cycle that followed directly on beginning the exercises. You have tried to watch your comments concerning food to some degree. This has resulted to his adding more to your evening meals. He has had gravy for example, and potatoes more frequently, where before he would not.

The menstruational cycle is beginning to come around, and more intimacy on your parts would facilitate this.

This is all I am suggesting this evening. Instead I want you to talk about your trip, and have Ruburt get rid of some of the worries connected with it, so that the positive elements can have greater sway. Also discuss your other plans if you wish, but use the time to communicate in that manner.

I will listen.

("Okay.")

(10:06.)

DELETED SESSION
FEBRUARY 16, 1972 WEDNESDAY 8:20 PM

(Deleted February 16, 1972. Marathon, Florida. 8:20 PM, Wednesday.

(Just as we had talked at the end of the session on January 19, we talked for hours before tonight's session. First we took answers from my pendulum. I had always thought that method very reliable—and so it was once more. Amazing, the beliefs that seemed so obvious, yet so persistent!

SESSION 2/16/72

(Jane became so excercised by those answers that she scribbled her own notes and doodles [some of which are presented here], then pounded out on her typewriter, misspellings and all, her further reactions before tonight's session.)

2/16/72

① JANE feels GUILTY NOT WRITING — INCREASED SYMPS — ON VACATION!
     "   "   "   doing anything — "   "   " CAUSE OF

② UPSET BCSE I WASN'T DOING ANYTG ON VACATION? } BOTH CAUSED SYMP'S.
    FELT SHE SHLD BE WRITING, ON VACATION

③ SPECIFIC PART OF JANE'S SELF CAUSE PSCL SYMPS — CAN BE REACHED WITH PEND.
THIS PART OF SELF TRYING TO PUNISH JANE.
BUT NOT FOR HAVING CR. ABILITIES. OR FOR USING THEM.
THIS PART OF SF AFRAID OF OTHER PEOPLE — TRIES TO FIND SECURITY BY HIDING. FEELS SAFE WHILE INSIDE — AFRAID OF BEING LAUGHED AT. (PEND. AGREES WITH JANE'S DESCRTN OF BEING RIDICULED AS A CHILD, etc.)

④ PART CAUSING SYMP'S ENOUGH AFRAID OF PEOPLE TO TRY TO ISOLATE JANE FROM THEM. KNOWS REASON FOR FEAR — STRONGLY CTD WITH SYMP'S.

⑤ — OUR TALK — JANE GOT INSIGHTS INTO EARLY LIFE SITUATION. etc.

⑥ — THEN JANE WRITES PAGE ① A ON TYPEWRITER.
— HER PENDULUM TELLS US HER INCREASED SYMP'S DUE TO HER NOT WORKING WHILE WE ARE AWAY. <u>STRONG EMOTIONAL REACTION.</u>

    CHARGED — TO BOTH US — HOW COME THE TROUBLE — WE WERE SUPPOSED TO WRITE + PAINT — TO HELL WITH EVERYTG ELSE — SHOULDN'T BE LIKE OTHERS. WE DID WE'RE NOT SUPPOSED TO BE LIKE OTHERS. WHEN I STOPPED POLICING US, JANE TOOK OVER — SYMP'S WAY OF STOPPING US FROM GETTING INVOLVED IN WAY OF LIFE LIKE OTHERS — MY JOBS, RATIONALIZATIONS — HERS TOO — SAT ON THE

FENCE, WHEREAS WE SHOULD HAVE FACED OUR
COMMITTMENTS — TOLD OURSELVES FALSEHOODS — NO REAL
MYSTERY FOR SYMPS — WE BLAMED THE EXCUSES.

⑨ — ~~JANE~~ THERE WAS MORE, QUITE EMOTIONAL — JANE SAID
SHE WANTED TO SHOUT & YELL, BUT INSTEAD SPOKE THE
ABOVE RAPIDLY & IN A NORMAL VOICE.
   THEN CAME ⒜ IN AUTOMATIC WRITING, MORE OR LESS.
   PAGE
                                                                    ②

⑧ —   JANE'S OTHER SELF THEN SPOKE ABOUT ME GETTING
SICK, GOING BACK AFTER, ETC, WHEN ALL THE TIME I KNEW
WE SHOULD JUST WRITE & PAINT, REGARDLESS OF PARENTS,
SOCIAL PRESSURE, ETC — ANYTHING.
   WHEN I QUIT POLICING US, THIS OTHER PART OF
JANE TOOK OVER. MUCH MORE, TOO FAST TO WRITE DOWN.

Both go to work.
Excellent chances if
both apply selves
to joint work, as
you should have been
doing all along. Plan
together concentrate
AM on work — the
con can not being kept
into work goes into
symptoms

SESSION 2/16/72   71

JANE WRITES:

the body in youth served its purpose; it can grind the soul to a pulp if left free to follow its natural desires become gross and fat and flabby and gluttenous; betray the self into death by giving birth; destroy the fine tuning of the mind, that becom sunken in mires of flesh - and hence decay. So let the self discipline and deny the body, hamper its desires and its freedom , force it into subjugation in exact proprotion to its needs and strength let it suffe; this body left alone is particularly gluttenous of life- its idea o f it, overly sensuous, therefore the means to sensuous living are deni give the body an inch and it takes a mile.....

the mothers body was also gluttenous.....the bodys desires are dangerous, not moral..... bad heritage from mother and father too sexy....its activities devour minds activities; given freedom might be unfaithful like mother and father, gluttenous sexually; and or have child, either course disasterous. up to recently, in ver beginning rob an unwitting allie, felt same way, only got appalled quicker but still what he wanted too. he was always my moral allie everything devoted to his work then he changed...... i was always wi willing to sacrifice everything to tit, once he was now he isnt. says the sacrifice is too much. I', not convinced you can police yourself consciously enough, that you wont give in to the glesh, be fleshy at the expence of work.......i cut down the range of temptation.

Now—let me proceed at my own rate, and in my own manner. Your questions will be answered, but let me go about it in my own way, and not start out necessarily with question A.

Some of this, then, will be in the nature of necessary review. Apropos of your own discussion earlier this evening, I have a few remarks.

First of all, Ruburt idealized you, as you know, in the early days of your marriage and courtship. The poetry to you clearly shows that he did not regard you in the same light as ordinary men. He did feel to some extent after your move to Elmira that you withheld leadership. This was twice the crushing blow because he overidealized you to such a degree to begin with.

I told you some of this was review, but pertinent. He felt that when <u>he</u> had initiated action in the past that it had not worked, and he was then afraid of initiating new action, so he kept waiting for you to do so. This mainly involved the idea of leaving your job, particularly as money accumulated in the bank.

None of this was spoken, and he felt it disloyal. He felt that you would interpret any such feelings on his part as aspersions against your manhood. He was finally driven to voice some of these attitudes as the years passed; particularly after your 50th birthday and his 40th, he became literally panic-stricken, yet you did nothing, to his way of thinking.

(*I explained to Jane that I've never felt any aspersions against my manhood; that has never been a problem with me. As far as the idea of doing nothing, I explained to her that I thought saving money would enable us to get our own living quarters eventually, and thus solve some long-range problems. As soon as I realized that she was rebelling against a way of life that we had fallen into, probably mainly at my unwitting behest, I tried to make amends by leaving the job, etc. I would say the realization became conscious late last year; I kept the job until we finished checking the script for* Seth Speaks, *by the end of January.*)

Success to him now would automatically put you in a poor light in his eyes. There was the struggle to succeed and not to succeed. He felt you were not putting yourself to the test, that you were holding back while he was putting himself to the test, and often not doing too well.

(*Again, I don't consider that any success of Jane's would put me in a poor light. I have been for her success, especially since I began to understand my poor reactions to the publication of her first book—jealousy, etc.*

(*A quick recheck with the pendulum as I write these notes reaffirms that I want Jane to be a success, that I am not jealous, that I am happy to have left the job, and that I want to be a painter.*)

The fact that you would say "I am giving you the opportunity to do this by my job" entrapped him further, for he felt basically that underneath this was another reason: that if you wanted badly enough to paint all the time that you would do so, that you should have done so, that you should do so, that you would and could have managed without jobs, particularly in the later years, and that you were betraying yourself and therefore him. He did not feel this was his responsibility. It was a reversal of the leadership for him to tell you what to do.

(*I agree with all of the above, except that perhaps leadership should be a mutual thing in our case, one's strengths bolstering the others' weaker points, etc.*)

He did not want to admit these feelings to you or himself. He felt also, in the past, that if he told you to leave the job, and it did not work out as you wanted, that you would blame him, as he thought (underlined) you blamed him for the move from Sayre.

As his own early youth vanished and nothing was done, he grew more frightened. He saw your lives blurring into those lived by others, the fine lines of purpose finally becoming dulled.

The psychic work was quite all right as long as it added to or blended with your own creative endeavors.

Now besides all this, as you know, because of his background he has a great need for emotional give-and-take and reassurance. This must come largely from you. It is and has been a sore point. As he became afraid that youth left him and that your drives to paint and write were not as secure and overriding, then he became even more in need of reassurance.

Because of the situation, of course, it was even more difficult than usual for you to give it. This in itself aggravated those old fears concerning sex and the body—that it would lead him astray. If you did not—I am using his terms now—flirt with him and play with him in those terms, he was afraid he would look for that assurance in other men's eyes.

All of this contributed to the hampering of body motion. For whatever reasons, he never planned to marry a man who would go away to work each day, but saw you both involved in a jointly-shared comradeship of work and love. You, it seemed later, grabbed hold of a job with great tenacity and would not let it go, and he grew more and more afraid of suggesting that you do so.

Since you did not do so on your own, he was afraid that this meant that you did not want to. He would be forcing you into a position that you were avoiding with all your might, regardless of what you said. He felt forced into a corner, with life slipping away.

He wanted to shout your decision *(to leave Artistic)* to the skies of course, and thought he was quite reasonable by saying nothing for a while, at your request; yet secretly he thought that your attitude of silence meant that you were not proud of the decision, did not want it known, that you were acting ashamed of it and wanted it kept quiet, rather than as a triumph.

Now. The feelings of pessimism belong to you both, and help in keeping the symptoms in a stirred-up condition. They are a strong part of your problem, and there is a negative feedback that operates in that regard.

You still do not encourage, now, lovingly (underlined) Ruburt to discuss his fears. The two of you do not consistently bring them out into the open. Some could be easily dismissed if you lovingly said "These are harmless. Don't you understand how silly they are," but without accusation.

The daily habit would reap great results. I have told you both often—Do you want a rest?

("Yes."

(8:47. My hand was tired. At break I did some ranting and raving to some degree. Jane said she didn't want to continue the session if it made me feel that way, but I answered that I did want the session continued, etc. Resume at 9:00.)

Now. It is precisely because Ruburt places such high value on your work and ability that he was so concerned. Had you stopped painting, you see, the dilemma in a way would not have existed. He felt you were denying yourself the one thing you wanted out of life above all others.

(This material, on up to break, is largely in answer to things I said, and questions brought up, at last break. It's very well done.)

The more he valued your work the more concerned he became. He often in the beginning resented the psychic work precisely because it took time from your painting for transcripts. Therefore behind all of this is his high estimation of your abilities and work, and his refusal to see you trapped so that you do not have full time to use them.

He was angry at your mother for whatever ideas she gave you that prevented the full use of your abilities. One of the things Ruburt resents most about your mother is her lack of understanding of the nature of your artistic abilities. Ruburt considered your mother an enemy in that regard.

So it is not that in Ruburt's eyes that what you have done is not important. Its importance however in his eyes brings about the responsibility to go further. The steady, unvarying devotion that you have for him is always appreciated, never taken for granted, but he feels he would be denying that devotion of yours if he did not see to it that you had your chance to work.

Now give us a moment. *(Pause.)* The value of your lives together and separately does not appear to you. Your effect upon others, even before the psychic work, has been literally invaluable to many people. You have been beacons to them. You go quite literally into areas into which many cannot follow. You go for them and for yourselves, this being the nature of creativity.

Your relationship alone, as unsatisfactory as it may seem to you at times, has served, and will, as a beacon for many who have not dared to <u>try</u> for so much, who have not dared to accept the challenges that you have accepted.

All of this should be kept in mind, and I tell you so that you do not concentrate upon the difficulties, and find no merit in your lives. You are both responsible for the psychic development, and without your steady devotion so many, Joseph, would not have been helped. You do not know these people, that have read the books and benefitted.

Now we will take a break. Do not blame the good people.

("Okay."

(9:10. Seth spoke thus because of a lot of noise next door. Newcomers were moving into the unit beside us; I heard a child's voice also, which at once made me angry. Our landlord had told us earlier that people from Canada were coming to stay a week or ten days—in other words, as long as we would probably be here—but he hadn't mentioned children. I frowned, then Seth spoke. One more problem, I thought, even if only temporary. Jane and I had a good discussion, though. I thought the material excellent. Resume at 9:22.)

Now. With each book that Ruburt produced, he felt guiltier that you were still at the job. He was afraid that both of you would become too timid as time went on to make the move that he felt you must make, and that the necessary opportunity would slip through you fingers.

Regardless of the earlier overidealization he still thinks, you see, that you are unique among men, for true love allows one to perceive the sublime uniqueness of the beloved. Beside your own drive to paint, he saw you through the eyes of his own drive to create.

He feels you also have a role to play in the psychic work that you could not play with a job.

Now. A separate point, returning now to a discussion of fears. Before you left for your trip I told you of some of Ruburt's negative projections, and advised you both to discuss them. I remember the night well. You had a snack and went to bed, and that was that. And I spoke in stern terms.

(Jane remembers this session better than I do. It took place in January. Anyhow, we didn't have any such discussion as recommended, etc.)

Because you made the decision to leave does not mean that automatically the negative thought patterns are relieved. When Ruburt had fears about his physical abilities during the trip before the trip, they were not thoroughly discussed, barely mentioned. Together you should have seen that under the circumstances they were "natural extensions" (in quotes) of past habit. Some of them ordinary-enough concerns that anyone would have embarking upon a trip, about money, etc. hardly dire, and easily dealt with if aired; but he was ashamed of them. They were negative and to be hidden.

Loving encouragement in getting rid of those would have taken care of the trip difficulties. Instead he tried to smile and shove the trip fears under, and you let him.

You both still lacked the communication of your desires and fears. Simple feelings go unexpressed.

Now there are reasons for all this. I will see that you get them, but in the meantime you both can make an effort to express feelings. *(We have already begun, with good results, as I type this the next day.)* It will become easier as you go on. *(Humorously.)* The nonexpression leaves the door open for all kinds of misinterpretations. Some of the difficulty here had to do with the fact that Ruburt uncovered his body in front of others, which to him made him feel vulnerable, pointed up the contrast *(with others)*; he would not let the normal feelings have release. He should have cried quite honestly in front of you, and you should have then tried to reassure him of those positive elements of his appearance.

Earlier however he would not have so bared himself under any circumstances. He purposely put himself in a position where the physical was stressed. This was an advance. It also meant however that you should have both honestly faced the feelings aroused. Instead he tried to hide them.

(I had noticed of course when Jane began to wear brief garments here, but I assumed she had simply decided to do so, and so I considered it a distinct advance. It completely escaped me that she was hiding feelings about revealing herself. Questioning her before writing these notes, I learned that she had indeed covered up feelings of inadequacy, crying, etc., regarding her appearance as compared with others.)

There are points in the session that I want to elaborate upon, and several other comments I want to make for now.

Again, your loving encouragement that he can, for example, go down a step is highly important and supportive. Because of the reasons given earlier in this session, he retreats and hypnotizes his muscles into believing they cannot act such and such a way. He tries quite honestly to perform an act while believing he cannot, so that the muscles do fight themselves, and hurt quite painfully.

Your loving encouragement therefore helps ease the transition into action, again, quite practically, regardless of the reasons for the self-hypnosis—

("But we're not really going to get anywhere until he gets over that self-hypnosis.")

—and until you encourage the free flow of feeling; and you can. The situation is not nearly as hopeless as it appears, and I tell you, Joseph, that your joint feelings of hopelessness are as hypnotizing as what I just explained to you of Ruburt's actions.

I cannot put it to you more simply than this: as long as you persist in considering the situation hopeless, then it is and you make it so. The moment you break out of that circle, the moment improvement begins and continues.

("Then he hasn't been out of that circle since this business began." By this, I meant for at least the last five years. I should have said so, but Seth picked up my meaning.)

He has not indeed, except for two periods, and neither have you. The fact, however, that you have left your job gives you a strong advantage and starting point, but you must use it. This means that you must first of all honestly admit your feelings about leaving your job; both of you, both your fears and hopes. Then it means that you do not waste time and energy in apathy, or in crying over the past, but that you see yourself at last beginning upon a course of action that is highly important. And a course, incidentally, that many people are not <u>graced</u> to follow. Your abilities give you added dimensions of mental and spiritual natures that you take for granted.

They are so a part of you that you do not recognize their relative uniqueness, and it is important that you do. Others recognize these qualities quite well in you, and their lack of them. It is highly important then that you try to sense this, be thankful for it, and not concentrate upon what seems to you to be the tragedy that you did not use them fully earlier.

<u>Quite frankly, they are of such a nature that youth could not bring them to fruition. This you and Ruburt should underline and remember. You could not use them as a youth, fully, anymore than Ruburt could have used his psychic abilities without gross distortion</u>. Underline the last several sentences, and take my word for it.

Now for tonight I will let you rest, but there will be other sessions; and I suggest that you follow the plans that you began today.

("Okay.")

I bid you a fond good evening.

("Thank you, Seth. Good night.")

(9:52.)

DELETED SESSION
FEBRUARY 19, 1972 SATURDAY 9:05 PM

(Deleted. February 19, 1972, Marathon, Florida. 9:05 PM, Saturday.

(Today Jane and I visited Key West, some 50 miles from here. We asked about rates at several motels, etc. After the excellent session on Wednesday, February 16, we hoped for good improvements in Jane. Yesterday there were some. Today on the trip she was noticeably slower, had trouble going down a step. We took a nap upon return-

ing. I arose with several questions that I wanted answered in a session tonight; the trouble with steps, why she took a turn for the worse after the tour for The Seth Material, *etc.?*

(*We talked briefly after a late supper. While washing up, Jane told me after she was finished, she "got" that she was worse in Key West because she should have stayed here and worked today. We went to Key West with the idea of possibly spending our last week there, but found prices too high for us, at least on such short notice. After the nap, I suggested we might stay here the next week, to work, have a couple of sessions, etc., and Jane agreed.*

(*When Jane came out of the bathroom after washing, she said several times that she was getting this information, that it had a strong charge behind it, and that she "didn't know what to do." She repeated this phrase several times. The feelings wanted to explode, she said. She had experienced similar feelings some other times here in the past week, particularly after the last session, and made an effort to discharge them reasonably by talking. I thought that probably the feelings should be allowed to come out violently, but we were inhibited by our surroundings, and probably fear, etc. At any rate it seemed a great help that we had even reached the feelings. I asked Jane, rather impatiently at last if she could discharge the feelings in a session, as we had planned.*

(*She said she thought Seth was trying an experiment, that it was better to do it this way. She could feel Seth about, but he was letting her go ahead on her own.*)

(*It was a colder, very windy night here. The wind had been blowing strongly—to 30 miles an hour, and even more—for over 24 hours. We had the heater on in the efficiency. We sat in the kitchen. Jane's voice was average, so this meant that often I had to ask her to repeat a phrase because the various noises almost drowned it out. She said later that she was in an altered state of consciousness. She knew what she was saying and remembered some of it. Her eyes were open most of the time. Her pace didn't exceed my writing speed, but often it was close to the limits. A mild anger showed itself at times.*

(*Therefore, at Jane's suggestion I began to write down what she said. It must be remembered that at the start of this experiment neither of us knew what would develop.*)

All right *(Jane said)*, call me the creator, this part of me that's talking. We're using it to designate what I am. I'm composed of your strong drives for creativity. My purpose is to protect and direct your energies specifically in the areas of writing and painting. I'll state what I think simply. I want this dialogue because my purposes were not being met. My efforts have obviously worked against themselves.

Strong moral ideas welded what I am together—welded the creative drives like glue. Part of me was born in Ruburt's childhood. This part was strengthened by your own ideas of work and creativity. You became the policeman. I relied on you to see that Ruburt's creativity was channeled and used, protected, but most of all not frittered away.

Many aspects of your joint ideas gravitated toward me. Other areas of living were all molded together so that unity would result. You would have, for example, no desires that would be basically in opposition to the creative one.

Your creative drives became a part of what I am, so that what I am includes the strength of both of your creative drives. I believe that you both must write and paint a reasonable amount of time daily. *(Pause.)* I was always against any jobs that would divert you as long as you were not in dire need, in which case I was willing to suspend my judgment.

You began to change your ideas. I expected them to be unswerving. When it seemed you would not police the two of you with the <u>intense fervor</u> necessary, I began to do so, and took upon myself all those attitudes that had been yours. It was easy. Ruburt is literal-minded in many ways. He looked up to you. The constant suggestions took root, and I used this for my purposes.

I am literal-minded, in that I believe you are meant to be creators, and I have done all in my power to see that you did not swerve. I considered your position dangerous, more so as time passed. My methods however obviously are not working now, so it becomes necessary that I communicate with you.

(Long pause at 9:31, eyes open. I didn't ask any questions.)

There was difficulty with the books. My drive was being met, and yet the money was being used to support a status quo that I could condone only for the first several years in Elmira.

I do not want you to go hungry, or to be unhappy. I do not want you to be in want, but outside of that nothing else concerns me but your work.

You two more or less made me a promise that Ruburt would begin working sensibly on his book again *(after last session)*, and instead you took a trip. I consider this a betrayal—a small one, but quite indicative of your behaviors.

My methods have not brought about what I wanted, however. Now you spend half of your time trying to figure them out, and what is wrong with Ruburt—time that you should be working. I do not care if both of you die poor, but I do demand that you live using your abilities.

That purpose unites you, and when you are not tuned to it completely you are unhappy or sick, one or the other. I am protective because I know that this is so. It is the purpose that gives everything else in your lives meaning. Because I am attached to Ruburt now, his ideas of course color many of mine, so his fear of the passing years developed upon your fear of them ten years ago, projected now into <u>your</u> future, as ten years older than he. So to me you have no right to have a job.

I understand you have left, but I expected a full concentration on your work and plans. Unfortunately there were side effects from my methods, that make Ruburt's condition an impediment to the very plans I want.

(Pause at 9:40.) These themselves led you to concentrate on his condition here. On his own, in other words, he picked up negative habits, apparently as a side effect of my methods.

I considered the trip a scandal today. The vacation itself an excellent idea if half of it were devoted to work. I go along with the psychic development, as long as it adds to your work and influences it. I am suspicious of it if it prevents you from painting, because of notes, but this does not bother me when you are painting also.

My demands, to me, are simple and reasonable. More than that, I see no others worthwhile. All you have to do to please me is work a reasonable amount of hours daily; then I do not care what you do, but I expect that purpose to govern and direct your lives to be the focus about which all other events happen, not a sideline.

I abhor hobbyists. All of what I am has been, and is, to keep you from falling off the fine line of concentrated, intensely concentrated, creative endeavor *(pause)*, that is the purpose that drives you both.

I accept no substitutes, and in that respect I am like a jealous God. I am also somewhat like a computer gone amuck, however, if my methods do not meet my ends. I want the main energizing portion of you directed into your work, both of you. Now they have been directed toward Ruburt's condition. The condition will vanish automatically if these ends are met. They are side effects.

You said once that you would like to live on a mountaintop, and never go out, and just work and have no distractions. Ruburt was carrying this out in his own way.

If you work on your own, both of you, then I do not need to police you. You are free to play and wander when your work is done. I tried to have him sit and write books, chained to his chair, don't you see. The purpose twofold: to see that he worked creatively himself, <u>and could not have a job</u>, and to have money so that you could paint full time.

The more the books were written, the less willing it seemed you were to do what I wanted. The struggle made it difficult even to create for a time. I was caught between using my energies to help Ruburt create, and trying to get money through the creativity for you to quit. This itself hampered the creative drive, hence the dream book difficulty.

You would not quit anyway, so I created a book that would not sell. This did not seem to help. Ruburt became anxious. I released the creativity full force then in the beginning of *Adventures* and the new *(Sumari)* development.

You finally began to realize that I wanted you to leave the job *(long pause at 9:55),* but the negative attitudes that had built up attached themselves to the new projects—something I did not foresee. My power is the strength of both of your drives. *(Pause for a cigarette.)* I am a part of you, then, the part that always hated your job, and can scarce[ly] forgive you for keeping it so long. I understand it was necessary for a time, but all thoughts of security beyond the daily necessities mean little to me. I want you secure enough to work in peace. Outside of that I have no interest.

(10:00.) I see the spontaneity of your sketches, so good, many of them done at the job, kicking your heels up at the job—the spontaneity in direct opposition to the work demanded of you there.

To me, my demands are simple. I rage when neither of you work as you should. Show me you do not need a policeman, that if I let go you will not slide away from your goals. I <u>am</u> a taskmaster. That is my role. I am reasonable, however. I am willing now to negotiate. In negotiating with me you negotiate with yourselves. I do not accept compromises. I do accept solid work and firm intent.

I have not compromised. You have. Now I state my purposes and conditions plainly. Seth thought you would find this direct statement even more informative than his indirect description of it.

I need your cooperation now, since the methods that I chose have fallen so poorly. Apparently I must allow you more freedom,<u> but you must use the freedom to do what I want you to do.</u>

("Well, we're perfectly willing to do that."

(The portion of Jane that was speaking gave no sign that my voice had been heard.)

I am tired. I have done my best. I do need your understanding and cooperation now. I have worked long and hard for you; though it <u>seems </u>that I have been a tyrant, I have always tried to be the servant of your own abilities.

("I understand.")

I am dismayed. I did not think Ruburt would work unless he was chained to his chair, so I chained him, both to do his own work and force you to do yours. Then you both fought <u>me</u>. He did not like working chained, and I tried to make the chains appear as natural as I could. He is not physically harmed to any great degree *(one of the questions I wanted discussed tonight, although I never mentioned it to Jane)*, or maimed. I can say however that for some time I did not care if he was, if these purposes were met. I see now that they would not be, that instead all your time would be spent concentrating upon the condition that was meant as a protection, until no work was done—hence my dismay. I was not appreciated, though I did my best for you.

("I think we appreciate the intent. It's our nature to be creators, but finally we had great difficulty creating under the conditions mentioned. The situation became self-defeating."

(At 10:14 Jane sat with eyes closed, giving no sign that I had been heard.

I suppose you will have to be on your own now. I have done all I can *(crying)* and have....

(Jane broke down in tears now. I held her up in her chair as she cried. I felt like crying too. The portion of her personality that had been speaking sounded hurt and defeated, and in the process of retreat. I am not trying here, now, to judge this portion—herein after called "it" for convenience—or to say that it is going to vanish forever, or release its hold overnight. We will see.

(Jane tried to say more. I talked to it, offering reassurances, saying we didn't require it to leave us, but merely to understand our need for freedom. The physical freedom symbolized creative freedom, I said. To us freedom of motion meant creative freedom. It agreed, as Jane cried. She became very relaxed in her chair, so that I had to hold her upright.

(By 10:25 the tears seemed to be over. Jane felt so limp and relaxed, I told her, that it seemed she had shed two tons of weight. The crippled black cat we've made friends with here cried outside our door, so I let him in and fed him. We split a beer. I held the cup to Jane's lips because she said she was too relaxed to hold it. As I wrote these notes she half lay on her own chair with her head in my lap—a position she hadn't taken for years. She yawned again and again. She didn't want to lay on the bed.

(I hoped the portion of her consciousness that had contacted us would now let her have her freedom. Certainly her state at the moment was a good sign. Many yawns at 10:40.

(Jane said she was in an altered state of consciousness as she delivered the material, yet was aware of what she said as she said it. "I felt this real sad 'Okay, I'm going,' at the end," she said. It had wound up confused over what to do, but I thought we could help it understand as the days passed. I thought she was achieving, or trying for, an integration of drives that might be very important. I hoped that the motivations behind it would rise to join her ordinary consciousness.

(As we talked at 10:45 it almost returned. Jane said she got, several times, "and all that for nothing," so I repeated our ideas. I made it a point to reiterate my statements about freedom being absolutely necessary to us in order to create, and that we

requested its help and assistance with these limits or goals in mind. "But I'll be just as happy," Jane said, "if it goes away altogether." The only concern I had in this respect was that it represented creative drives, if in a distorted form. I wanted the drives to remain with us for our use without limitations, so I wasn't sure if it should be dispensed with completely.

("There must have been a fantastic charge behind it," Jane said between yawns. "For a while there I was as light as air. Already I'm wondering now as I come out of it: am I okay now, am I free? How are my knees going to be when I try to get up?" etc.

(10:55. "I'm not sure I should even think about it," she said, still yawning, but I think the relaxations reached to about here," and she touched her legs just above her knees. Previous relaxations, including one yesterday, stopped at her waist. "I can't understand it," she said. "I seem to be getting another one after coming out of the first trance... Going back in...." She didn't, though. I helped her to the john. Afterward she told me her knees felt better than they had in some time.

(Later the next day, as I write these notes, she told me her knees are "working, bending somewhat," as they haven't been doing. She has been walking stiff-legged.)

DELETED SESSION
FEBRUARY 21, 1972 MONDAY 9:43 PM

(Deleted. February 21, 1972, Marathon, Florida. 9:43 PM Monday.
(This session is a continuation of those for February 16 and February 19. Jane's voice was very quiet.)

Now—you see how softly I can speak.

("Yes.")

Again, let me start off in my own fashion.

You, personally, have been gravely perturbed because of your job for some time. You tried to shove the discontent aside, hoping that you could continue it to practical beneficial ends. You were to some extent outraging a portion of your being, for whatever reasons.

The basic discontent colored your other attitudes, both toward your environment, your own work, and other people. (Very good.)

It became—relatively now—a displaced discontent. You felt that there was nothing you could do about the situation, that there was no reason to worry about it, but the anxiety was displaced then, draining your energies.

Now, we are speaking comparatively here now, you understand.

("Yes.")

When you begin devoting your time to your painting you will be satisfying then a deep need of your being, and therefore energized. You will feel personally that <u>you</u> are solving problems that <u>you</u> are meant to solve, problems that are nevertheless created challenges having to do with the nature of painting, problems then and challenges that you consider quite worthwhile.

This will give you a much more optimistic attitude in general. Personalities are as diverse and unique as flowers or fish. There is no need to compare one type of personality with another than there is to compare a toad to a bird, or an ant to an elephant.

It does help however if you understand that birds must fly if you are a bird. It does help for example if elephants do not try to build anthills. So there is no need to compare personalities in a judging way, merely to know your own.

Ruburt's energies will be released in the same way. I am sure that you appreciated the encounter that took place the other evening, under my auspices. *(On February 19.)* What was said should show you that Ruburt's condition also became the focus of your combined discontents, the physical picture of it. The energy to maintain it, <u>almost</u> (underlined) in direct proportion to your combined discontents, was composed of the displaced energy not put into your prime purposes. This is difficult to verbalize precisely—

("I understand." I thought Seth was doing very well.)

—built up by unsolved problems. A concentration upon your individual and combined work, your practical plans in that direction, will promote an enthusiasm that you have not felt jointly or individually in years. You will <u>know that you are on the right track</u>.

(Quite humorously, Seth's voice burst out loud and strong, to rise above the roar and screech of a nearby car taking off at high rpm from a standing start. The voice then quieted at once as the car roared away.)

The symptoms therefore will be released as that energy or concentration is placed back where it belongs, into creative and practical action. You felt as if you could not move also, and before Ruburt's symptoms began. You felt this psychologically; do you follow me?

("Yes.")

Your discussion this evening was beneficial and showed a point in progress on both of your parts. Earlier Ruburt would have become alarmed and frightened, felt you were being negative, and discouraged at any verbal and emotional encounter with the feelings that you expressed, precisely because they brought into the open feelings of his. This time however he recognized that earlier he would have brooded and gone to bed, leaving you to brood alone at <u>his</u> ways.

The ordinary fears connected with any such discussion should be discussed. Only in this way are they faced, encountered <u>and</u> cast aside. They do not grow then in secrecy, and gather charges.

Do you want a rest?

(10:04. "No, I'm okay for the moment.")

The change of environment has been and is good for both of you in ways you may not presently comprehend. A few you glimpse. It is obviously good for you to look at the world simply from a different viewpoint. It is particularly good that you see the situation here in Florida, on the spot, so that you feel free in making choices—a real Florida, not a fantasized one.

Your journey will also allow you to perceive your Elmira *(New York)* environment when you return in a fresher light, and your circumstances there.

A point, if you do not want a break now: <u>Concentration must not be on Ruburt's symptoms</u>. Underline many times.

A point now that I want you to heed in advance: In the past, because of joint negative attitudes, I have given the reasons for some of these. Improvements in Ruburt's condition were <u>ignored</u> (underlined) largely by both of you, and instead concentration was upon the symptoms that still remained.

After the first bad bouts for example, when he improved enough to go up and down stairs without even limping, when he was agile enough at least to climb some rocks at the Glen *(Enfield, near Ithaca, NY)*, to swim after being largely incapacitated, you both acted as if the improvements meant nothing, discounted them largely, and concentrated upon those symptoms that did indeed still remain.

I am not saying that he was completely better then, but the improvements far outweighed the symptoms at that time. Do not let that happen again. That was the result of discounting improvements as they <u>did</u> show themselves, and this applies to both of you.

Now I will give you a break, and continue.

(10:13—10:15.)

Now—tell him what I said later.

("Okay.")

You chose to do what you did, individually and jointly. In <u>narrow</u> terms you can say that you both made a mistake. In larger terms no error was made. You simply happen to be dealing with the area of activity in which terms like "mistake" appears valid. Do you follow me?

("Yes.")

Practically speaking, while you had any kind of a job you were ill at ease and off balance. You compared your lot with that of others who had jobs also. There was only a difference in degree.

Your own attitude was partially set by your father's innate and quite strong sense of independence. He hated to work for anyone else. The same applies to Ruburt's background, mainly with his grandfather. You would have felt freer had you tried to freelance; for freelancing, while it would have produced long range its own problems would have allowed you a greater sense of freedom.

Here you were influenced, where Ruburt was not, toward a job because of ideas of security that came from your mother, and, despite your conscious evaluations, from the activities of your brothers. Your having a job made sense to you therefore for these reasons, more so than it did to Ruburt, who had no such countering influences. Now give me a moment. *(Pause at 10:27.)*

The entire environment concerning your brothers' homes, and the implications, always upset Ruburt, for he sensed that influence.

I want you to anticipate then that uprush of energy you will most certainly feel. The problems that beset you were so aggravating precisely because in a sense they were not your natural set of problems. You always have the energy and the means to meet the deepest needs of your own personality, but not to meet the needs of other kinds of personalities.

(Very good.)

Now. I will tell you something else. You felt that you owed it to your mother to try a secure type of financial arrangement, as far as you were personally able to do so. You realized that a full-time job was out of the question. Remember at least that you did not fall into that trap, and that you both had enough sense to avoid it.

The type (underlined) of commercial art you did as a young man was not the answer, but served many purposes. It gave you prestige and money. It gave you practice, but beyond the point that you pursued it, it could have frozen your abilities. The prestige and money, tied to your mother's hopes, could have led you into other channels of commercial art that would have led you completely astray as far as fine art is concerned.

To you a part-time job helped compensate. You feared losing status in your family's eyes by casting yourself completely aside into areas alien to them. You also felt that this would equate you in your mother's eyes with your father. She, your mother, went with the main stream. Your father did not. You did not want to hurt her feelings particularly in the beginning. Your mother did think of Ruburt as a threat, for she recognized at once that Ruburt would not encourage the tendencies that she herself respected.

All of this I tell you because it should help clear up some of the reasons for your actions. Beside Ruburt's "natural leaning" (in quotes) characteristic dislike of families then, there was the "outsiders" argument, and you were often put in the middle.

Your family to Ruburt was one of society trying to make you toe the mark, hence his often exaggerated reactions. As you know, spontaneously Ruburt would state your position to your family as a symbolic statement to the world at large for those reasons.

What you do in that regard is not nearly as important as an understanding of your attitudes. The basic "problem" (in quotes) again therefore has festered, gone underground, in the past. It was obviously one born from your basic creative natures—a challenge rather than a problem, but one that was interwoven with all kinds of social and economic and family connotations.

Finally your way of life became not a symbol of what you were, as it <u>was</u> for a while, but more largely a symbol of what you did not want to be, jointly and together.

Ruburt did not have, again, those influences working on him that worked on you to prolong the situation. Danger signals only too apparently showed with you as soon as you accepted full-time work. They became unbearable, and you quite the course quickly. The part-time course filled some of those other mentioned subsidiary needs however, so this you found more bearable.

Ruburt also of course knew this, as he knew about your curly-headed friend the other night *(at the Hurricane bar, amused)*, and he reacted vehemently, particularly against your parents. To help support your mother, particularly in the beginning under the situation as he sensed it, and with all of his other anti-mother sentiments, was the greatest of outrages. This is another reason for his actions on the Sunday visits. Hopefully, this will help you both understand.

You can have a break or I will continue.

("We'll take the break."

(10:51. Jane's trance had been deep, her pace fast. 11:01.)

Now we will shortly close. I want to remind you however that I went to considerable pains to give you some of the important reasons why you both had a tendency, a strong one, toward repression. Why Ruburt began by repressing unpleasant ideas, and why you initially began by repressing hopeful ones.

("Yes. I know it." This material is at home, and will be reviewed when we get there.)

Now. If you understand the reasons, and do as I have suggested then you will be involved with the real issues, not <u>basically</u> (underlined) superficial ones—like why does Ruburt have trouble going down the step.

("Yes." This had been a question I had mentioned for tonight.)

<u>That</u> becomes merely another symbol for the inner difficulty. Do not concentrate upon that.

("I don't think we are, now.")

Part of the difficulty is that it has become a symbol of Ruburt's disabilities at this point. At home the stairs are the symbols. After working one day, Ruburt expects instant results. Now there have <u>been</u> results. As you begin to make your own work plans, and work, this will also generate results. Remember the encounter *(of February 19)*—it was with a part of both of your personalities, not only Ruburt's.

I suggest that you do some sketching. Now. As you progress our sessions can also be freed for other endeavors. As the natural flow of your energies returns to your work, so will greater energy be released in the sessions as well. The part of the sessions in your lives as applied to your Elmira existence so far will be covered at another time. Obviously there is a connection, you see. And <u>now</u>—I bid you a fond good evening.

("Good evening, Seth. Thank you very much. Good night.")

I could come through far stronger, but I do not want to frighten the natives.

("I understand. It's appreciated.")

(11:13. Again Jane's trance had been deep. She didn't remember any of the material. We had just begun discussing it when Seth returned briefly.)

Remind me at our next session to say something about spontaneity and scheduling, as applied to your daily lives. Ruburt does not like scheduling from <u>without</u>, applied from the outside, in other words. And neither do you.

("All right.")

(11:14.)

DELETED SESSION
FEBRUARY 24, 1972 THURSDAY 8:50 PM

(Deleted. February 24, 1972, Marathon, Florida. 8:50 PM Thursday.

(This afternoon I wrote Jane a three-page statement. It was based on the three previous sessions held here, and my thoughts growing out of them. I included a few lines of Sumari at the end of it; Jane hasn't translated these yet.

(At 8:45 PM I used the pendulum to clear up an ache in a tooth. I learned the trouble was based on my fear that Jane wouldn't accept, or believe in, the statement. My action led Jane to tell me about her teeth and sinus bothering her before and during our trip down here, for about three weeks. I told her I was floored to learn that she'd let something like that go for so long before trying to learn anything about it's causes, etc. This of course was a tie-in with the repressions on her part that I'd written about in the statement today.

(This evening we sat waiting for a session, or whatever else might develop. Jane heard her mother's deprecating, scathing voice, quoted it to me, and said she

felt quite uneasy. She felt as though "different parts of me are casting about for the best way to give the material tonight—Seth, or some other part of me, whatever we decided. I even got the idea: Now here we have the body 'kind of thing,'" she said.

(My face began to feel better, although I still had an occasional twinge. I thought this not surprising under the circumstance. At 8:45 Jane said she felt herself dissociating. She said we could have a regular session probably, but she waited to see what the best way to proceed would be. Then she began to speak at 8:50, in a very quiet voice. Eyes open often, etc.)

The other night you were talking to a portion of the personality who called itself the creator. It was actually a composite of the creative self and the conscientious self.

I am the creative self. You see me in the poetry, the psychic developments, and Sumari, but I have been forced to follow certain lines, as you suspected, despite my nature. Far more than Ruburt suspects from the beginning, his natural creative drives were also used to their ends, both religious, social, and as a way of gaining approval.

He always needed approval, desperately. I was often forced to structure my work along lines that would bring approval. *(Pause.)* He feared the psychic developments, though they were one of my most creative endeavors, because he was afraid they would bring scorn instead.

Sometimes his intellect has worked with me, sometimes not. I am far more resilient, pliable, flexible and daring then other elements of his personality, which are fear-ridden. Some of his attitudes have to do with his parents, in that he fears he could become like his father—undisciplined and <u>slack</u>, loose and amoral.

His mother's scorn told him this was a part of a bad blood heritage, an inevitable part of his condition. Ruburt felt that his <u>mother</u> only liked him because of his writing. In the early novels his repressed feelings could be expressed. They were creative, but also safety valves. I made art out of them.

I need freedom and agility of thought, where he tends to repress me unless I conform to definite ideas of good and wrong. I found the conscientious self then an uneasy partner, and a growing hindrance.

The repression in one way I used in the novels, but when the habit becomes too ingrained I find it difficult to retain, to transform into art. Some of my material comes from Ruburt's repressions, but when the habit allows for too strong a charge, constantly rebuilt, this is a hindrance.

I often help, and have, by recharging him, as I did in all the creative developments to date. But then he must think "Is this good or is this bad? Am I being too free?" I can handle the early repressions. The <u>habit</u> of repression dropped its hold to a great degree when he met you. The situation of your illness brought it back, and from there it gained hold again.

You know that panic is behind such repression, and a misguided idea of self protection. Inhibiting thoughts inevitably inhibit body motion. For his own benefit and mine, two or three times a week he should sit down and write out his feelings, as he began to do last summer. All kinds of repressions will come to the surface.

You must understand that for nearly 20 years he lived in an environment in which expression of dissent brought instant retaliation of the most frightening kind. Outright punishment—hair-pulling or cursing. Verbal humiliation was easiest to bear, but his mother would immediately show all kinds of extremely serious symptoms, for which Ruburt would be adamantly blamed.

His mother would pretend suicide just to punish him. He felt therefore that he caused your illness, that in a way you were punishing him for the frivolousness that made him suggest you leave a conventional background and your parents, and go with his father in Florida.

(And of course, this makes me think that our staying her at the Overseas Motel, in Marathon, is probably the poorest choice we—I—could have made. Our cottage here is within a hundred yards of the spot where we camped with Jane's father in the late 1950's. I would say now, without checking with Seth, that any thought of nostalgia we might have derived from returning here would have been better ignored. We will not come here again. Our stay hasn't been too pleasant for a variety of reasons, including noisy neighbors, etc. We made one half-hearted attempt to get out a week ago, on our trip to Key West.)

When you became sick he thought "Aha, mother was right, I do destroy everyone I touch, and now I have made my husband sick." There is a great division of energy, as there is in all creators, but in his case between the need for spontaneity and discipline, safety and freedom, and these are clearly seen in the body's condition right now.

(Additional thought re the notes just above: I suppose that if we enjoyed clear channels of communication between all parts of ourselves, we wouldn't have returned to this spot—or if we had, no charges would be involved. I pulled in here after we had passed it; it was at the end of a day of driving, I was tired, and thought of the place. We hadn't decided to come here while in Elmira, or on the way down. And if Jane had been aware of any negative influences here, if they exist, she would have prohibited our returning.... Perhaps our stay here did lead to this very important series of sessions, though; we are learning much from them.)

Quite unwittingly because of your own nature, you tilted the balance for a while. He picked up your ideas of discipline in the beginning, then latched upon them in his own way. He felt you did not trust his judgment, remembering what he thought of as key points in your life, when his judgment seemed wrong or when it was criticized.

These seemingly small episodes were nevertheless important. Because in the beginning you emphasized discipline, he felt you did not think him capable of exerting it on his own; that while you were attracted to his spontaneity you feared it and his energy. He felt that you believed that, given a free hand, his habits would be too exuberant. He would have, or would keep, odd hours, no schedule, be messy.

(9:15.) He felt for some time that you were intrigued by the spontaneous parts of his personality, as long as they could be controlled, kept proper and in their place. This had to do with the love-making also. He tried then, because of his loyalty to you, to temper the <u>percentages</u>—to be more one way than the other. You had this effect because he did idealize you to such a degree. It was not a fault of yours.

When you became ill then the repressive state reasserted itself. You follow me there: because of the mother situation it was not safe to speak of illness at all. He could not bear to be responsible for your condition.

After that he feared deeply that all adverse comment of his, or negative remarks, would make you worse. Your illness frightened him more than anything else since his life with his mother, because he could not allow you of all people to be ill because of him, as explained.

From that point on he kept any negative thoughts or criticisms to himself, and during that time he feared that you almost disliked him completely. The habits of repression took great root. Rather than hurt you he would put himself into harness. Once <u>begun</u>, these feelings attracted to them <u>others</u> from the past, so that <u>I</u> was appalled and finally had great difficulty.

He felt his success put you in a poor light in your mother's eyes, and the eyes of society. An impoverished artist as a husband he could take with great pride. Once the part-time job continued and kept continuing however, once you had a job steadily, then he felt that others compared you, not with other artists but with other ordinary men who had jobs. And there, under those conditions, you made poor showing.

He felt these feelings extremely disloyal. He felt your mother was silently accusing him of putting you in a poor light whenever he succeeded. He wanted you to state your position, and say "I am an artist" to her and to the world, but he deeply feared that you considered that attitude irresponsible, frivolous, not practical; and worse, that you felt it negated the sacrifice you made by keeping the job for so long. *(Not so, etc.)*

For all of these reasons the habits of repression continued, for any critical comment could bring up the whole barrage. The slightest remark that you made that he did not agree with was the symbol for these inner deeper feelings. He dared not criticize you for anything, or even disagree in normal conversation, the charge was so great.

You did not communicate yourself too well. Because of his abilities he picked up your feelings all too clearly, but because of his <u>fears</u> he picked up your negative feelings. He was afraid you were not an artist after all. He knew you were not a Sunday painter, but he felt you were greatly repressed in your work, and that any breakthrough could only come when you focused upon it, your work, regardless of other consequences.

He interpreted what you said at times to mean "You are ungrateful for my sacrifice," but he did not think the sacrifice in those terms was necessary after the first years, and that such sacrifice could destroy your ability, your fine purpose.

He therefore did not discuss any issues with you concerning his own discouragements or fears as they happened. He felt guilty enough because you were working. He did not want to lay extra burdens on you, but he came to resent everything that was provided by a job.

Though you have left the job, the <u>habit</u> of repression is still strong. I know this is a burden on you, but it is important that both of you understand the repression. In some ways he has made poor judgments—for example in dealing with editors. Part of this was caused <u>by</u> this need for approval.

He also interpreted your comments however as indications that, left alone, he would not behave with competence, that he was <u>not</u> able to cope, that he would not be able to learn through experience how to deal with editors, for example.

For many years, at least seven, he has been deeply concerned about your work, a repressive element in it, and the psychic freedom he felt you needed to release it. Because of the age difference he became very worried. Your best energies were going into your work, he felt, at the job, not into painting, and the very focus divided you. He felt it disloyal to recognize the repressive element in your work, and tried to pretend he did not see it.

(Jane and I are going to discuss this element in my work. I'm curious to know what she knows about it. I need all the help I can get, etc.

(9:37.) One of the best influences on him are the few pages in a book by a psychologist about the creative personality. He knows what they are. *(The Essence Of Being, by Abraham Maslow.)* They release him to a strong degree, but

in the past there has been a bearing down afterward, a renewal of repressions, if he became frightened if the spontaneity has worked.

With your help he can avoid the second reaction. You know what I mean. *("Yes, but I'll have to know when it's happening." Meaning that Jane will have to tell me.)*

The passages allow him to give me freedom, and also release the physical mechanism to some notable degree. If he does not repress any fears following the release, then improvements will continue. He did not realize this, so the information above will be of great help.

I am an ally because I can help express those repressions. I have the energy to do it creatively if I am not hampered. Read this together with the other statement. You are on the right track. Once repression is really faced as a problem it can be overcome, because all portions of Ruburt's personality now realize the danger involved, and know that the pattern must be broken.

There may well be emotional charges expressed. Do not be afraid of them. They will clear the air.

(9:45. Jane slowly began to come out of it. Her eyes were heavy, closing often. Her pace had usually been fast, and she had taken now breaks. "I feel real funny," she said at last. "Intellectually part of me is appalled but I feel triumphant also because I've got a clear channel up through here—"she indicated her stomach, chest and throat—"and got the material out. But I really feel strange. Part of me feels like getting sick and the other part like laying down."

(Jane got two more bits as we talked: The creative self had to disentangle itself from the conscientious self to get this material out; and she had ambiguous feelings about her books because she felt they put me in a poor light. Then the creative self returned at 9:50:)

Part of that was because Ruburt was sensitive to your own negative feelings or fears, and picked these up. Basically he trusted both you and your work, as I have. The physical condition was also meant as a signal, saying "Look what is happening." The body trying to speak out, where he would not.

It served that purpose, and as mentioned elsewhere it served as a symbolic statement as he put himself <u>behind</u> you. You used to say in a critical manner that he would not wait for you to open doors, and run ahead of you on the street. He took this to be a statement that he was running ahead of you, and to slow up.

The very fact that all of this now comes into the open is most advantageous; though it has been mentioned before, the peculiar <u>tie-ups</u> have not been described this well or this adequately. Please read this carefully. You need not fear that you must watch every word, and so forth, as long as communication both ways is maintained. Your own habit of repression in the past helped reinforce

Ruburt's, so greater communication helps you both.

Nothing you can say, vocally, can be as severe as Ruburt sometimes imagines your reaction to him, so do not feel that you must remain silent on any issues. That only compounds the issue.

(*10:03. Jane was out quicker this time, etc.*

(*While I was typing up this material on February 25, Jane got the translation of the Sumari I wrote her at the end of the statement of February 24. Both the statement & the translation, which I think is excellent, are included with this session.*

(*I would suppose the statement played a part in bringing this session about, since it posed questions dealt with in the session. I think though that this part of Jane's personality would have spoken also, since the conscientious self had its say on February 17. Now that the conscientious and creative selves have spoken, probably Seth will speak next.*

(*Jane's suggestion that she can consciously know whatever she needs to know is a good one. She has been using it before sleep for two nights. Last night after the suggestion, she received a good insight, and was able to examine it instead of repressing it. And again this morning.*

(*Now for my statement, Sumari, etc. :*

(*February 24, 1972. Thoughts—after the 3 sessions here in Marathon, of February 16, 19, and 21, it finally dawns on me—I finally put the material in the sessions together—and realize that a more basic quality behind Jane's symptoms is repression. The task then is to learn what causes this. A good question would be: "What am I so afraid of?" This is much simplified, of course.*

(*This morning Jane got quite angry at her conscientious and creative self. After the revealing session of February 19, she expects more dramatic improvements. This morning she found herself rebelling against what she considered to be the conscientious self's domineering tactics—work before anything else—etc.*

(*I got the insight at noon that the conscientious self, or "it", was so tyrannical because it is being constantly fed charged material, fears, that are steadily repressed. These come from her childhood, her religious upbringing, her own strong moralistic and literal nature, plus probably reincarnational data about which we know very little. Plus overidealizations about me and my work, etc.*

(*The tyranny results from "it" not being allowed to express itself in usual ways, I thought. Jane is perfectly able to work a daily quota of time without overseeing, just like anybody else, and to do all the other normal things people do, like take vacations, etc. If all parts of her being are allowed expression, I said, there would be no extreme reactions, as in the symptoms. Therefore we must learn what is being held back, what is seemingly so terrifying, that it dare not be faced.*

(*A small incident to illustrate: Yesterday morning at 8 AM, the tenant in the efficiency next door played the radio very loud outside our window for over an hour. We both were mad, and felt like yelling, etc. Later that morning I asked the man and his wife to not do that. They agreed. [This morning we slept undisturbed.] But when I came inside after speaking to them, Jane said, "I wouldn't dare do that." At the same time she was smiling, and very pleased that I'd spoken up. [I had decided to speak up regardless of the consequences, though.]*

(I took her reaction to speak of her faith in my leadership in this instance. In other instances, I told her this noon, I believe she lost faith in my leadership, as detailed so well in the three sessions held here. This would arouse all kinds of panic feelings, since she wouldn't dare speak out—and so she, and "it", would feel that she had to furnish strong guidelines for her own protection—keep her writing rather than take jobs, etc. The symptoms resulted. All of this, until just recently, on unconscious levels.

(Last night we went for a walk: Jane said she was disappointed in my reaction to her ability to walk a little better, and so was worse when she went to bed. I replied that I would rather she wouldn't tie up her state of physical being with my reaction.

(The two instances cited here actually represent good improvements on Jane's part, in that she allowed me to learn what was involved. I think the continual repressions over the years have let the conscientious self grow out of proportion. I think also that the conscientious-self or "it" made a creative advance on February 19 when it stated its tactics were bringing about the very thing it did not want—Jane's inability to work in freedom. My thought at the moment is that more expression on Jane's part will free the conscientious-self to perform its own balanced role, and to actually retreat in doing so.

(I told Jane I think that if it is not fed a steady diet of repressed material—which it may not even want—the conscientious or creative self is perfectly capable of doing its job without excesses. There will be no fears of unrestrained sexuality, or not working creatively, of overidealization of me, or my work, etc. All of these ideas, I feel, evidently grow out of repressed, unexpressed fears that have built up over the years, and have been taken over, or dumped upon, the conscientious and/or creative self.

(I told Jane today that when a fear is expressed, it takes its natural place in the scheme of things and no longer grows unseen. Jane at first said during our talk that she must hate many things—but it seems that hate would only be a mask for fear—hence the suggestion that instead of asking herself what she hates, a more basic question is "What do I fear?"

(Jane today revived what is evidently an excellent suggestion—to the effect that "Whatever I need to know will rise to my consciousness." She used this suggestion as she lay down for a nap. She is sleeping as I write these notes at 2:20 PM.

(This morning when she expressed resentment at her conscientious or creative self, Jane said it took her a long time to get mad—several days in this case—after the session of February 19, when the creative self spoke. This delayed reaction may be, partly, her very cautious way of allowing an adverse reaction to surface, and it may also simply reflect her nature.

(My thinking at this time is that when we allow ourselves expression freely—painful as it may be at times—and live in ways that are in keeping with our natures and abilities, we will achieve that necessary and vital balance that automatically results in creative work, health, whatever material success we require, etc.

*   *   *   *   *

(To me, Jane's creative ability to translate my Sumari into English, as she did on Friday morning, February 25, 1972, was magical indeed.

I epa togen re peta upialingor
qua so ne togenir raw personigenter
so ne a peco geni literop
to be so qer nat rupor portille
per zuggerli graw upi shaperto

- Rob

We are two swallows
Above the land masses
Yet the earth and the water
Propel our wings.
Our thoughts and our feeling
Flow through and fill us.
We ride them
Sustained by their thrust.
Who doubts this power
Doubts wings, land and water
And cannot fly or rest.

- Jane

(Then she wrote: Feeling I've been so afraid of my personal thoughts and feelings—thought they were so bad that I don't know myself. Invite self now to be aware of them—all of them normally, be astonished at their power, beauty and variety.

They aren't all negative. And even those have a power that is good when released. Can be a new kind of creative joy—a discovery that will really release me creatively, psychologically and physically. Been afraid to know myself; distrusted so never allowed self to see how good I am.)

DELETED SESSION
FEBRUARY 26, 1972 SATURDAY 9:59 PM

(Deleted. February 26, 1972, Marathon, Florida. 9:59 PM Saturday.

(We were due to leave here tomorrow morning; we were all packed, etc. Our landlord, Rich Elgersma, visited us this evening and told Jane and me about a trailer and lot that he could have acquired not long ago for $1300.00. The news made us regretful in some way; it seemed to suggest answers to some of our own problems re living costs, locations, etc. Both of us liked it here. The weather has been very charming indeed.

(Today in our talks Jane and I said a lot of things about our goals, purposes, distractions. Jane talked to several people here today who reminded her that there was always a need to be filled regardless of location, about such things as reincarnation, dreams, etc; this also made us feel that we could work out here, in living arrangements and income, as well as anywhere else. In addition, my pendulum told me today that my hand symptoms stemmed from my fear of failure as a fine artist—nothing else.

(Jane suggested this session abruptly, after 9:40 or so; I thought it would deal with what we had talked about today.)

Now: give us a moment, and again let me begin in my own way.

Unconsciously you feel that because you are the oldest son you should be the money-maker, in your mother's eyes; but she never considered painting as such as financially rewarding. You still do not want to hurt her feelings. You are still trying to be yourself and the self you think she wants you to be, as far as you are able. Certain concessions for example you would never make, but you are still unconsciously bothered here, whether you know it or not.

Some of your own energy has been held back then from your work for that reason. You often tie yourself in knots, considering alternatives, none of which are ever taken. Hence a continuing sense of upset results. This is also the result of so double-checking impulses that few of them are followed through. As a result <u>no</u> clear-cut decisions are made, and the feeling of being off balance ensues.

When this continues you project negatively on <u>all</u> alternatives so that change always seems disruptive and negative. The possibilities of its creativity are often forgotten. You have both done well communicating your feelings lately. Ruburt's idea of actively searching out his usually repressed feelings is excellent.

He also often voices some of your own fears. Together this helps both of you. These feelings may be charged because they have been so repressed. He is learning, just lately now, how to release them, and the body <u>is</u> beginning to let go. But do not let these repressed feelings blind you to the beneficial qualities of your situation right now, or its creative possibilities.

You both do have an inclination to overstate your problems, and concentrate on them in an effort to solve them, and as you know that is not the answer. Ruburt should write in a personal diary if he prefers, but write his feelings several times a week. A half-hour at a time is fine, plus the effort to express any normally negative feelings at once.

Releasing the habit of repression will itself allow the body to relax, and be released. A moment-to-moment check on his condition is not necessary.

Now, because it seemed to you for so long that <u>you</u> could not move freely in your own life, that you did not paint full time, you got in the habit of automatically viewing all change as negative. You could not do it anyway. To realize its possibilities therefore would have been a torment. So recognize that element and its reasons now.

The effort made in any creative change would be nothing compared to the constant feeling of unease that could result simply from a fear of change. In a fear of change there is only tumult, and no peace. As you know, it does no good to worry about the time you may sometimes feel was "wasted" (in quotes) in the past. Great damage can result however by projecting such feelings of time waste into the future.

Do not compare your *[joint]* position with anyone. It is unique. Because it is, the possibilities are endless. If you magnify your limitations you create your own prisons. If you enjoy those freedoms that <u>are</u> yours now, you automatically increase them. You are in a clear position at this moment. You cannot expect a blissful time innocent of problems. That is not the nature of life or of existence.

Your set of problems are of the most creative kind. They are problems from which great potentials can emerge. Your full energy for work and your creative drive is released, and will be, as you creatively use and understand your problems, but not concentrate upon them, not let them close your eyes to the joys and freedoms that you have. <u>You get what you concentrate upon. There is</u>

no other main rule.

You have a relationship not only unique, the two of you, but one that also serves as a springboard for creativity. You have talents and abilities that carry with them satisfactions that you both often blithely take for granted. They are so a part of your existence that often you are not even aware of them, yet their absence would show you the relative darkness in which the majority of people live.

You are not financially in any desperate need. By many standards even Ruburt's health would be considered excellent. A concentration upon the healthy parts of his body will help increase his health. That is the point I am trying to make here. Be thankful for what you do have, and it will be increased.

Releasing the repressed feelings will also clear the way for freer expression of joy and exuberance, so while repressed feelings are being freed, do not forget to concentrate upon the positive aspects also. You do both, when you are together—often now, but not always—still concentrate upon Ruburt's symptoms, so that they seem to block out all else. When either of you forget yourselves in work, conversation, other people, then the symptoms automatically decrease to some considerable degree. Now take your break.

(10:31—10:40.)

Now. Several portions of the personality have already helped in the release of repressed feelings; the conscientious self particularly, which was the greatest repressor. In any cases of great repressive nature, one part of the personality may act alone in the beginning but later it must get the cooperation of other portions.

(This was a question we had discussed at break.)

Any release therefore involves all of these cooperating parts. They follow the leader, so to speak, each part repressing various areas. In what has happened in the last few days, the conscientious self gave its consent to the release of various groups of thought and feeling it previously kept hidden.

Other portions followed, beginning to release those feelings generally under their sway. The sexual implications last evening, generally under several various areas of personality, could not have come into consciousness, for example, without the consent of the conscientious self, which says often "No work, no sex." And often says "No sex anyway. It must go into 'good' creative work."

On your return I expect you to concentrate your energies in both of your works, then in maintaining communication. Now the sexual area can serve as a great aid, and will be quite illuminating. Ruburt's ambiguous feelings and the various stages of repression are clearly seen there. There are points where he wants to cry, and if he lets himself feel these stages you will be able to recognize them and go beyond them. They are symbols of course for release of various kinds, and the blockages or points of conflict will clearly show.

Motion will be cleared through. The combination of emotional and physical release will be invaluable. Symbolically it also represents of course your relationship. Motor responses can be cleared in that fashion. Inhibiting points, again, under such conditions, will be easily recognized. Any emotion at that point should be released. It will clear the motor capacity at that level.

Emphasis should not be on performance but on expression, and Ruburt particularly encouraged to express all feelings, no matter how ambiguous. There are natural results, activations of hormones, quite necessary, that are released at such times that greatly benefit the system. The ambiguous feelings must be expressed. The drive, when it shows itself as last evening, is often irritating because the muscles and nerves connected have been so held back, instead of a clear flow of sexual energy then.

Ruburt experienced a jerky irritation of muscles and a jangling of nerves. The repressed nature however came through, which is a definite advance. The sexual area is charged for him for those reasons. Here most of all he is afraid of letting go, and yet the pressure of course builds.

At one time when communication was poor, he tried to use your moments of tenderness as opportunities to tell you his worries. It seemed to him then (underlined) the only time. This turned you off romantically. The less open communication you had, the more he seized that opportunity to speak.

With all of his repressions, love-making became the most loaded time, for in a moment of weakness he feared he might spill out his feelings about your job and all the other material that has come to light.

Now you can take a break, end the session, or continue at our next one. *(We'll take the break and let him decide."*

(11:00. Jane remembered some of the data, and knew it was charged—she could feel it. Both of us were getting tired so we ended the session.)

SESSION 606
MARCH 3, 1972 10:25 PM FRIDAY

(This unexpected little session was Jane's first upon our returning to Elmira, NY from Marathon, FL. We arrived home March 2, bleary from five days of dri-

ving. We were still tired today, but were in the midst of cleaning up both apartments before settling down to work again.

(*The page proofs for* Seth Speaks *were waiting for us upon our return. We were delighted with them, and had already begun to read them. As we sat at Jane's worktable looking them over, I remarked that the notes were well written—this was my particular work. Jane said she felt Seth around, tired as she was. I asked if he could say a few words; she told me to get paper and pencil.*)

Now, good evening.

(*"Good evening, Seth."*)

I am not going to keep you—

(*"Okay."*)

You do not need to take all this down, just the good points if you prefer....

(*I left out a few sentences, then.*)

It must have occurred to you that you have writing abilities, and no time, it seemed, in the past to exercise, develop, or use them. So see how nicely and easily you were led along those lines.

(*Through writing the notes for* Seth Speaks, *etc.*

(*"I believe I've thought of that."*)

Now. The joint endeavor is of course important—and there will be other joint endeavors of various kinds. They will be highly creative, and quite rewarding financially also.

I was simply dropping in on you briefly upon your return. You noticed of course Ruburt's energy suddenly materializing upon his return.

(*"Yes." When we reached Troy, Pennsylvania, yesterday afternoon, some twenty-four miles south of Elmira, Jane told me she felt revitalized suddenly.*)

Your trip served among other things as necessary counterpoint. Being away from the life to which he was accustomed, he could on his return see it more clearly, and appreciate it for what it is. I will have more to say as I continue at our next session, with personal material already begun. And with that I will close.

(*"Thank you. Nice to hear from you."*)

You will be hearing from me for some time.

(*"Good. We'll look forward to it. Good night, Seth."*

(*10:30.*)

DELETED SESSION
MARCH 6, 1972 MONDAY 9:15 PM

(Jane went for a walk by herself after supper tonight, and got mad at herself because she was so slow. When she returned home she used the pendulum to learn that she had been repressing reactions to a statement of mine of the other day, to the effect that I didn't think she'd be able to get around well enough to go on tour for Seth Speaks, *if Prentice-Hall asked us to. Hence her slowness tonight, etc.*

(I remembered making the remarks, but hadn't realized her reactions to them, although I had noticed her increased impairment walking. Jane said the pendulum session helped. She took a nap after it. We had a talk before the session tonight. I reminded her of what Seth had said in the deleted session for February 26, 1972, in Marathon: "You get what you concentrate upon. There is no other main rule." I think this excellent, and plan to make signs for each of us to display in prominent places in our respective working areas.

(As we talked about Seth's statement, and decided we should concentrate upon beneficial things, Jane then wanted to know how this idea fits in with the importance of not repressing negative thoughts. As I started to answer Seth broke in:)

Now—let me answer that one, and give a living example, a recent one.

When you made the remark about tour, Ruburt repressed the fear invoked, wanting to show you that he no longer was so sensitive. Do you follow me?

("Yes." I was also somewhat dismayed.)

He feels that he unjustly puts you on the spot, now. Quite rightly, he does not want you to have to double-think before you speak. He repressed the <u>emotions</u> (underlined) in an effort to show improvement.

These repressed feelings grew just beyond the reach of consciousness, and just below the reach of consciousness, but <u>almost</u> consciously he began to wonder, to judge his condition now with what it must be. *(To go on tour.)* The feeling-tone colored his other activities.

Had the emotion been honestly faced and brought to the surface it would not have <u>been</u> hidden. The body would not have to express it for him, and it would have cleared the way for other compensating feelings as you encouraged him and pointed out the proper direction for concentration.

Crying is a cleansing and usually quite beneficial activity, releasing psychic as well as physical pressures. He has little use for it, or for people who cry, because of his mother's crying spells. Crying clears the air and guarantees that the emotion will not be repressed. It is a healthy sign. He shies away from this, fearing that it is negative, or that it will upset you and make him feel worse.

Fearing you see the noise, the undisciplined—to him—release.

Explain to him your feelings. It is quite natural for him at times to become discouraged. It is for <u>anyone</u>. When he feels that way it would be of great help if he simply cried alone, or went to you for comfort. He thinks of it as an admission of weakness. There is a connection here sexually with the giving-into emotion, period, in a bodily fashion.

I have several suggestions; the remarks you made before the session are most pertinent, and must be kept in mind. Also, the suggestions as you are doing them *(at night before bed)* should be also given in the morning, at least before work. To these should be added "I will react only to positive suggestions."

Before the day begins with work Ruburt should take a few moments, as he <u>has</u> done in periods of improvement, to dedicate himself to a creative and expressive day. The emphasis on <u>expression</u>.

There was a recording he made with *In a Gadda Da Vida* in which suggestions were given. This was of help, and I suggest he use it. When he feels he is in a bind, he should admit it and tell you. Such periods will then diminish. The effort to hide them is of no help.

Laughter is an excellent aide, and gentle humor. The gods are not as serious as Ruburt tries to be about himself. Again, your comments were most important, and contain the most helpful advice possible. Playfully now, for the relaxation and joy of doing it, let yourselves imagine the things you want to do, as a creative game, because of the intrinsic pleasure involved but without Ruburt expecting, or rather demanding, instantaneous results.

The results will come, but not if he checks constantly for them. This implies the fear that they will <u>not</u> appear, not the faith that they will. The sharing of any emotion with you will quicken the sexual activities, and it is in the area of discouragement in particular that Ruburt represses.

It involves the fear of criticism, that he will be criticized for being discouraged. Discouragement is natural, and is no problem once it is acknowledged and expressed. In fact it is a stage clearing the way for new action, and to a certain extent the handmaiden of encouragement and joy.

I expect that you will see to it that Ruburt follows the suggestions given this evening. I suggest that the session be placed in front of his old journal notebook, and that the list of material written by you also be read by him every day before work. Now you may take your break.

(9:20—9:40.)

What is involved here is the necessity to recognize and express emotion, period.

In helping Ruburt do so you will also find your own emotional nature released and enriched. Ruburt feels emotions deeply, hence the repression of them causes such difficulties. It is the conscientious self, incidentally, who attaches the idea of good and bad to emotions. I suggest that in a joint pendulum session you address Ruburt's conscientious self with this in mind.

Ruburt in past years tried to be like you, to emulate what he <u>thought</u> you were like, this fitting in with the overidealization. He would do anything then to avoid an emotional scene. Emotions belonged to parents, who were unreasonable.

He felt emotional displays on his part would make you cast him in the same light as your mother. Her tears put you on the defensive, he felt. He even felt you considered tears contemptible.

It was his emotional nature however and spontaneity that opened your eyes to the necessity for emotional expression. Because he idealized you so, he projected the same kind of feelings from you to him, thinking then that you wanted an ideal mate, not a quite human one. Letting him know that you are not afraid of emotional expression on his part is most important.

He has made gains however in understanding the extent of his repressions. Earlier he did not at all. The last session I gave, in Florida, is very important, taken with this one. The suggestions given tonight are given for his present period, geared to the present state of affairs, and will bring results, and excellent ones.

The concentration upon other areas is most important. I have some excellent material along other lines that I hope to be giving you shortly. Your financial situation is quite taken care of. It is taking care of itself, and your joint energies have already made their imprint. This is an accomplishment being made now, even though the physical effects have not caught up with you.

(To me:) There are several intuitive developments regarding your work that are already in the making, and will bring you great pleasure and a sense of accomplishment. *(Long pause.)*

Ruburt's condition will improve because of other developments, success in his work and other areas that will automatically bring about a concentration away from symptoms. This has already begun, though again the physical results have not yet occurred.

The necessity for <u>understanding</u> what is behind the difficulty is still necessary, however, and the steps I outlined must be followed.

Now because I am so far ahead of you in regard to typing, I will close the session. You are embarked however upon a road leading to some fascinating events, and accomplishments that would not have been possible earlier. And have a more playful attitude, both of you. It is the best medicine. There is nothing for either of you to feel hopeless about. I bid you a fond good evening

("Thank you, Seth. Good night.")

And whenever you want to give the notes the boot and use the recorder, I am ready.... I expect a new state of affairs, with these suggestions started immediately.

("Okay. Thank you. Good night."

(10:10. Jane said she felt better already. Then Seth returned.)

One more remark. Your idea of getting up at five is (underlined) an excellent one. It will increase your sense of privacy, hence minimizing feelings of resentment toward this place. But it will also make you feel that you are starting out the day with the sunrise and your work—a symbolic statement concerning your values. There.

You will also recall your dreams easier, and again those benefits mentioned in my book, you proofreader, you.

("Not yet, I'm not."

(Meaning that my turn at proofreading Seth Speaks *hasn't come yet. Jane is still doing her stint at it. Now at the end of the session, she repeated that she felt much better.)*

DELETED SESSION
MARCH 22, 1972

Now, Good evening, and good evening to our friends. I will be addressing ____. Now before we begin, let me say a few things to you. First of all, as you well know, you cannot force spontaneity. You have it in your mind that you must be spontaneous, that you must let yourself go, and as you also know, spontaneity is not achieved in that manner. You want to feel free to give of your own nature, not when it is demanded by contract. You do not want to give upon demand—after your marriage you felt as if this was the case. You felt quite free to have an orgasm when you did not consider it something required of you—when you gave out of your own giving. You have always given of yourself—in many areas you have always been spontaneous. You do not want to give when you feel you must give. You do not want to give on demand. You can live with the idea of being a mistress, not wife—the two roles clash in your own psyche. There is a connection here between you when you know so much about hypnosis *("and yet not successful in going into it yourself"—I lost these words—and am paraphrasing Seth here).*

You judge yourself far too harshly however. You have a gift for bringing out the spontaneity from others, for calling from them qualities of giving and letting go, and in so doing you ride the spontaneity of others also—you can go along with it. It is only when you feel you yourself must give up yourself on demand—you are not able to let yourself go. This is from distorted attitudes of your own. The fear under those circumstances of letting go, and yet the fear has to do with the deeper fear involving the nature of your own inner faith—thoughts, of course, of being annihilated, not however by the emotions of another, but by your own.

You set up strong barriers in those directions—these have been added to by concentration upon the problem, so you become involved in this vicious circle. You try harder to give up when you cannot try to give up. The overconcentration prevents you from doing what you say and feel you want to do.

Your husband's attitude, certainly on the surface, has been understanding. Yet despite the surface attitude you feel, this is a duty, and you have set in your mind a bogeyman, called Orgasm. You have glorified what orgasm is—the unattainable, and therefore, the symbol of all the other qualities you want to achieve or think you should achieve, but do not have. The term, itself, sets up a barrier. In the spontaneous, normal natural feelings you have, you always question: How far am I going, how much am I giving? Always beginning with the idea that the orgasm for you is impossible to achieve. Your body has a set of contradictory doctrines—it cannot behave on its own. The negative taboos over the years have built up. Some of this can be immediately negated if you do one thing.

Forget the word orgasm. Forget what you think intellectually it means. When making love, simply become aware of what your body feels. Do not try to force your body onward. Use a balanced alertness and passivity. Simply be yourself as you are.

I know you have tried concentrating on pleasing your husband first of all. However, I suggest that you simply realize that your body is an important part of you that you have allowed to go begging—that its response can be perfectly adequate that you must release it from your own preconceptions—particularly from your idea of what an orgasm should be...that you allow yourself to feel freely.

Be aware of what your body feels without questioning—without wondering whether or not your body should feel more—allow yourself to feel your husband's caresses in the same way a flower might feel the sun.

Do not try to let go—forget the idea of letting go. Simply become aware of your sensations. Concentrate upon what your body feels. Imagine, the interrelationship, for example, between his hand and the particular portion of your body that it is touching. Realize that the simple atoms and molecules that compose your bodies are aware, and are vital and participating. Left to themselves they know their own joy and are aware of such intimate relationships.

If you will not try to have an orgasm—if you will simply allow your body to become aware of the sensations that it feels, then you will be at a beginning.

(Break.)

I want you to take it for granted that your body feels—but that you have often inhibited the feeling. Therefore, I want you in your lovemaking to imagine that your body is like a field—be aware as stimuli come to this field—feel it waken. I want you to concentrate upon feeling actively. I want you to be alert to the movement of muscles—the message of nerves. The body is affected by touch in the same way as a field by the wind, the sun and the rain. I simply suggest, therefore, that you become aware in the same manner—that you listen for what your body feels. It is you who have been blocking sensations that are there and do exist.

Forget the word orgasm. Become aware of what you do feel without questioning. Cease to strive for an orgasm. You are trying too hard in that direction, as with meditation. You are too earnest in that regard. In its own way hypnosis involves a psychic kind of play—meditation involves a psychic kind of play and lovemaking involves a psychic kind of play. You are too serious in your lovemaking, as in other fields.

Allow yourself feelings when you make love. Forget the great burden that you must have an orgasm.

Allow your body its simple pleasure. Do not begin by insisting it have a certain kind of peak—let it go to be itself. The same thing in meditation—let your inner self play in your meditation and let your body play in your lovemaking.

Make up certain games in your lovemaking. Involve your husband in them. Let him surprise you. Have the stress be upon, first of all, gentle touches. You know many of these sensitivity techniques. Use these. Let yourself be lost in the wonder of his hand upon your thigh, of the heat between the hand and the thigh, and forget the word or thought of sexual orgasm. You are laboring too much.

He is quite able to follow in these games, even to initiate them. You are quite capable in the terms of which you speak of having orgasm if you allow it.

When his lips touch your hand—if you do it in the sense of play and allow your native awareness to function.

In your particular case I would even suggest that you stay away from the normally accepted sexual areas for awhile, and enjoy instead of the content (?);

i.e. when he kisses your hand, and you are aware of the sensation of lip against palm and vice versa—be aware of feeling also in your hand on his skin. Lose yourself in that sensation. This involves active concentration on your part.

It may seem in your terms that orgasm demands a letting go—a <u>lack</u> of concentration. Yet instead, a high amount of concentration is involved, as other stimuli are shut out and consciousness is instead focused on visible sensation. This involves action on your part and the focusing of attention—then this will help clear away some of your difficulty.

I am trying to give you some practical advice. Expect another tape at a later time, and we will cover more regarding will. But I want you to follow instructions given this evening now.

(Jane [Ruburt] said something to me on the tape about having a strong feeling of resistance on my part—as though in spite of all I said about wanting to have orgasm, I really didn't want to—that it was a strong protective measure, as though my survival in one way depends on it.

(At which point, Seth started:)

Now—I would like to make a few comments regarding what Ruburt just said. First of all, if you will forgive me, you would have no difficulty at all having orgasm with a man to whom you were deeply attracted if he were not your husband, and if you could get over the moral barriers that might prevent it—if you could convince yourself that it was all right.

It is the fact that you are expected to have an orgasm, that causes the difficulty.

You feel that you are a warm, spontaneous person. You do not like to take orders—you do not like barriers—you do not like enforcements. You are the kind of person that likes to do things for other people, but not if someone demands that you do.

As a child, you would surprise your elders by performing chores when they were unexpected of you, when they were not demanded. When demands were made, however, you became either innerly resentful or rebellious.

The orgasm to you, then, stands for enforcements. The idea of performing in such a manner, giving in such a manner or on demand, as if it's expected of you—this is the difficulty.

You have created the problem in your own mind, of course, and reinforce it. The more you build up the necessity of having an orgasm, the more impossible it becomes.

You would be better off if you told yourself you didn't care if you ever had an orgasm in your life. And if you could tell yourself that, and honestly, you would have no trouble in having an orgasm.

But again the term betrays (?). What point, if you will forgive me, is reached when you can say: "Yes, now I'm having an orgasm, and now I am not, and the sensation begins and ends." A complex variety of feelings and emotions are involved—they rise and fall, but they do not begin and end in that particular regard.

In refusing to have an orgasm you are showing your rebellion against authority. A certain part of you insists it is being spontaneous by withholding the orgasm—simply because it is demanded or expected.

The same applies to hypnosis. When the condition is set up or the situation in which giving in, in your terms, is expected of you, and when the hypnotist is set up as an authority—you instantly rebel, and in your own way, you reinforce your ideas of spontaneity by refusing to go along with the authority. Going along with the authority is not being spontaneous to your way of thinking—it is conforming.

There is something in here also having to do with your feelings about yourself as a rebel—as one who does not conform, who stands apart. In not having an orgasm, to certain layers of your personality, now, you are maintaining your individuality—you are reinforcing the idea that you are a rebel, and free, but not conforming as is expected of you. The same applies to hypnosis.

There is also, within, that you do not want to be one of the masses of men and women who experience the same phenomena, in other words, the orgasm—that you want to be apart, and different, and indeed spontaneous and a rebel and walk along in your own way. There is behind it all also, a great embarrassment that you must share such a sensation with others, if you experienced it within marriage—it is expected within marriage—people looking at you, in other words, if you are married can say that you do it.

Before marriage, in the context of your relationship, however, this did not apply. Then having orgasm meant rebellion, meant being different, meant being spontaneous, and meant being apart from others. After the ceremony, it meant conforming to what was expected, being one of the masses, giving up your individuality.

I want you to think hard on what I've said to you involving circumstances and conditions.

You will realize by the time we are through that it is simply a difference of interpretation.

Certain parts of you are trying their best to help you, and they... (?). I will have some other recommendations but I want you to become aware of the symbolism behind...(?).

Before your marriage, you and he, _____, stood against the world in a relationship that you considered intimate and isolated, one of its kind. After your marriage, because of your interpretation and attitude, it seemed you became one of others, or two amongst many.

The act of love did not seem as unique—it did not seem to belong to the two of you alone any more, but you must share it with others, and you resented it. Certain portions of your personality were even embarrassed. The children were born because others would by implication share in the knowledge of relationship involved. You did not want to share this.

(Break.)

Now, from your early years, you did not want to feel forced to do anything, but wanted to use your abilities freely.

You are a great help to your patients because then you allow your spontaneity full play. You use telepathy very well in discovering their feelings—you use your inner senses in perceiving their difficulties and intuitively you are aware of the problems and able to help them rise above them.

You do not feel forced to do this, however. You feel to one extent, flattered, they are asking for assistance—they need your help. You are the authority.

Even in psychological circles you are to some extent considered a joyful rebel. Your methods are sometimes thought of as avant garde in comparison to many others. You think of yourself then as someone different, as a rebel, as able to help other people and as spontaneous and warm.

But when these qualities are demanded of you, in your mind, or when you believe you must perform them, you become frozen. This has also applied to one small area of your profession life also.

I am working from the present backward—so you will have to bear with me.

Again I want to give what practical advice I can to begin with and then we shall slowly get into deeper reasons and past implications.

I suggest, for example that you not make love in the bedroom, that you change your location whenever it is possible.

You must, above all things, stop telling yourself again that you must have an orgasm. You must stop thinking in terms of performance. You must begin thinking in terms of feeling.

When you honestly let yourself become aware of the slightest touch between your husband and yourself and honestly admit it and enjoy it, you are a step ahead.

There is no reason why you cannot progress in your meditations either—the two are so intimately connected and you have equated them in a strange manner in your own mind. This again is the problem of trying too hard.

You should use your own mantra—you resent using the mantras of others—the very fact that certain mantras are expected to bring you to a certain state of consciousness is precisely enough to make you decide that you will not go in that direction.

There is a study, I believe, in your home—try making love there.

Some of this has to do with feelings toward your father in this life. I told you we are working from the present backward. There seems to be the name J (?) in the background here somewhere and it's Dumold (?).

There is also some confusion having to do with your own idea of what male and female is and what is required of each. In your rebellion you see yourself as the male. Spontaneity and freedom also suggest itself to you as male rather than female. On the other hand, you feel yourself womanly. The male image of a rebeller, however, comes to a halt in your lovemaking encounters.

I am not saying that you identify as a male. I am not saying that you have problems in that regard. I am saying that the rebellious streak in your nature seems male to you.

I have another suggestion to make in the area of lovemaking—that you imagine yourself on occasion as your husband, and imagine what he must feel as he touches your body.

Have the lights on in your lovemaking encounters.

I suggest once more that you concentrate upon relatively few areas of the body: the hands, the face, the arms, the thighs. Become aware of your own sensations in those areas as he touches you there.

The field analogy mentioned earlier should help you.

Concentrate upon the idea of your body being a field awakened by the wind and the rain—awakened into sensation—not necessarily passive, then, but in a strange condition between alertness and passivity.

Do not resent the fact that your husband can have orgasm so easily, in your terms. You are jealous in that regard of what you consider his spontaneity. You envy him his pleasure while feeling you should not feel envious. In your present condition, however, a certain portion of you is still pleased that you have held out—that you are the rebel to the last, and that you have not given in.

The marriage contract itself has had therefore a strong fate, for what you did spontaneously is now demanded and once it is demanded, you rebel. I want to make sure you understand this.

You always seek in your profession, you see, to go above the others to seek new methods to be avante garde. To show that although there are many psychologists with degrees seemingly in the same category as you are, that you are, nevertheless, beyond them. Now do not take any of this in terms of guilt—there is nothing for you to feel guilty about. You have simply to understand why you feel as you feel, and not to inhibit your own feelings.

As I told you, we will go into deeper reasons, but for now, I want you to pay attention to what I have said, and to try these methods for they will work and they will show results if you apply them.

Use your own initiative for variations—think in terms of play—of a playful encounter, rather than serious encounter. Remember that the body, left alone, will find its own joy and pleasure. So concentrate upon what the body feels.

This means using your mind and applying the mind to the body—not blocking out the mind. Any love encounter is truly unique and different from any other and this you must understand. A love encounter is a way of expressing your individuality. In expressing it, you do not lose it—you are not less a rebel. In expressing it you become more what you are—you jump the bridge of communication beyond words, and this can be a simple thing involving merely the touch of hand on hand or thigh on thigh.

So do not label the experience you think you should have. Let your body and your mind become aware of what your body feels in these encounters.

Now there will be another tape within 3 months time if we do not see you earlier.

There are some remarks in your letter that I will comment upon and also go into background material. But all information given tonight should be helpful too and if you follow the advice given, you should become aware of a sense of sexual freedom and joy that is novel.

I bid you, therefore, a fond good evening, and my best regards to you both.

And that is the end of this evening's session.

SESSION 607
APRIL 3, 1972 9:35 PM MONDAY

(The first part of the session was held for Al and Gertrude Laux of Columbia Crossroads, Pennsylvania. Since they recorded it, I did not take notes.)

(The second half of the session was held for Alma Priestley, of Clearwater, Florida. She wrote Jane in March, 1972, about her son. Before the session Jane reread an earlier letter from Alma Priestley, and the carbon of her answering letter in June, 1971.)

(Seth resumed after a break at 10:00.)

Give us a few moments, please. *(For Alma Priestley.)*

Her own attitude is highly negative. The boy picks up from her now that he cannot be expected to do well.

Earlier she had a greater determination, a stronger faith that helped bring him through. With the years however she has become discouraged, and telepathically he knows this.

She is <u>too sorry</u> for him. She is also projecting the negative picture into the future. She feels beaten by the situation. A circle of reaction has formed about the family therefore, that so far is self-perpetuating. This is not her "fault." It is simply that the family has become weary, but the circle of reaction must be broken.

She must in her mind begin to change the circumstances. She should do this mentally. The two books that Ruburt *(Jane)* usually suggests should be read and used by her. The boy should be encouraged to continue painting, regardless of the fact that she knows nothing about it. Particularly he should be urged to use color.

The mother must change her own feeling of hopelessness, for this in itself becomes an added burden to the situation.

In Greece the young man was a senator, extremely brilliant, and emotionally immature and cold. He was very quick and impatient, particularly with the mental incapacity of others, yet he played upon their weakness in that regard. This was in Athens, and there was also a connection with Cato *(pause)*, and a Hebrew background.

(In all the sessions Jane has given, this is but the third time that Seth has referred to past-life connections involving historical figures. In each case the connections were rather tenuous.

(The dictionary tells us that the Stoic philosopher and statesman, Cato, was a Roman, and lived from 95—46 BC. He was called Marcus Porcius the Younger; his great grandfather, Marcus Porcius the Elder, was a Roman statesman who lived from 234—149 BC.

(Since Greece and Italy are close to each other geographically in the eastern Mediterranean, it was an easy matter for the citizens of both countries to meet, even in those ancient days.)

In this life, or rather before incarnating in it, the personality then chose to purposely minimize the intellectual area; not, now, to punish himself, but to understand in and through an exaggerated form, the experience of those far less mentally gifted than himself.

He is able to give his emotional abilities far greater freedom. In all of his existences he has been of an extravagant nature, impetuous, choosing extravagantly-opposite experiences. He did not choose to probe lightly or delicately, for example, various areas of experience, but chose instead to intensify each life.

The two books that Ruburt usually suggests are definitely recommended, and should be seriously followed as far as the family is concerned. There is still a great concentration upon the young man's weaknesses. This leads to further weakness and nonachievement.

The expectations must rise on the mother's part; the inner expectations. The exercises suggested in both of those books will help her. She must cease mourning over his disabilities.

There were connections in past lives that united mother and son, of which they are both unconsciously aware. She has been valiant. At certain tides she rose to peaks of high encouragement that helped him. But she must avoid the mire of negative expectation.

He is not unhappy, particularly if no one reminds him of what they think he is missing. She must have faith that the life was chosen for a reason, and then the reasons will become at least understandable to her.

I do not mean to scold her, but in her well-meaning sympathy she can hold down the native joy that he feels, when left to his own standards of achievement.

And now I bid you all a fond good evening.
("Thank you, Seth. Good night.")
(End at 10:23 PM.)

SESSION 608
DELETED. SETH'S PREFACE:
"THE MANUFACTURE OF PERSONAL REALITY"
APRIL 5, 1972 9:29 PM WEDNESDAY

(Before the session tonight Jane told me she thought Seth was getting ready to start another book of his own soon. Not tonight, she said, but before long. She had mentioned the same thing on Wednesday, March 29, when we sat for a session. No session developed at that sitting, however—in itself this is quite an unusual occurrence. She has no idea of subject matter, title, etc., for any projected book by Seth. It can be said that such an undertaking wasn't expected by us at this time, seeing as how we have just finished proofreading the galleys for Seth's first book last month.

(Jane's pace this evening was rather fast, but quiet.)
Good evening.
("Good evening, Seth.")

Now: Ruburt is quite correct. We are preparing for another one, and giving you a rest in between.

The volumes automatically unite the material, present it within certain frameworks of discipline. This does not mean that other in-between sessions cannot deal with helping others, or with personal material. As you now know, some considerable time is taken with your preparation of notes, and so I have been waiting a while.

Ruburt sensed this quite clearly, and as usual feels twinges, wondering what I am going to write about, and what kind of a book it will be. Such a book can be given quite normally and quietly along with your regular routine of sessions, adding to your own knowledge, and ultimately helping others also. I suggest the simplest of formats. Always the least complicated as far as any mechanics are concerned. Do you follow me?

("Yes.")

Most probably this time we will work in concentrated periods that can be broken by rests when you prefer it, or circumstances seem to call for it. Now in the meantime there are a few points I would like to make that have not been given in this particular manner; connections that are important, between the nature of matter, your perception of it, and reincarnational existence.

As you know, the mind forms matter. The physical brain only perceives the appearance of matter in one of its many manifestations. There are many gradations of matter, therefore, as I have told you.

Now: the inner self is the primary personal creator and perceiver, the seat of identity, a consciousness then with many faces. Each portion of the inner self creates its own reality, and perceives the structure of matter to which it is attuned.

It creates then the times, the events, and the places. These exist all at once, but the perceiving mechanisms are tuned in to one characteristic channel, so to speak. While you are creating the physical reality and time that you know, other portions of the self are therefore creating their own times and places. All of this must be understood along with the nature of physical matter to begin with. Otherwise it is impossible to understand how for example, an 18th-century town, a 20th-century town, and an ancient village can all exist not merely at once, but also on occasion in the same (in quotes) "location."

The subject of matter then becomes one of correlating inner data with outward experience and appearance. The inner core of the self has no difficulty in uniting and correlating the outward experience of its many personalities, but the subject of reincarnation cannot be understood without a knowledge of the nature of matter.

(9:45.) Often in the dream state and occasionally in the waking state, a personality will glimpse what seems to be a past personal event . When this occurs the perceptions have already altered it, so that it is very difficult to perceive at the same time the present physical location and the past one. Usually the perceptions glide to one or the other: that one becomes shadowy or indistinct as the other becomes stronger and appears three-dimensionally.

It would be impossible to proceed physically if the other simultaneous events had to be handled by one ego. These (in quotes) "divisions" of the self simply enable it to multiply its experience. Think of the subconscious now merely as an academic psychologist might; as that inner portion of the self who is concerned with physical survival. Bodily mechanisms, who holds memories too numerous for the conscious mind to follow.

(9:50.) Now. If all of those functions must be beneath present consciousness, you can see that no single ego-consciousness could easily grapple with several environments, times, or life experiences. Instead this is carried on by the core *(spelled)* inner self.

As the personal subconscious that you know maintains your familiar physical image, so does the core inner self beneath give this personal subconscious the power and ability. It does the same with other portions of the self that look out toward other times and places.

If you identify yourself with this inner core identity, then you realize that you (underlined) form other physical images of yourself beside tile image that you know.

Reincarnation, so-called, cannot adequately be considered then as a phenomenon apart from the nature of personality either, for it is a direct result of the inner self's attempt to project its personality characteristics outward into a world of physical actuality.

The idea of a time sequence *(pause)*, is a psychological method of separating such experience for practical purposes at a given level of development. The idea of time sequence is intimately connected, again, with the structure of physical matter as you perceive it, a way of separating and correlating experience so that it can be physically processed and correlated.

(Pause at 10:00.) The brain, as opposed to the mind, needs this correlation. In the framework of three-dimensional reality in which reincarnation exists, the structure of the body itself requires (in quotes) "time" lapses. Messages do not leap instantaneously through the nervous system. The mind exists independently of the brain, but with connections to it. It can perceive without time lapses. The physical body exists within an electromagnetic order.

There are points of correlation between the two of which the conscious brain is not aware, and perceptions that do not consciously register. In the same way that all individual <u>can</u> (underlined) know what is happening in another place without any physical communication, so he can know about his other reincarnational existences.

Now take your break.

(10:05. Jane's pace had been quite steady. She or Seth, hadn't been bothered by an eruption of noise from the apartment over us; several people entered there after the session started; there was much walking about, banging of furniture, etc, that I found quite irritating. At break now some of the people left the upstairs location, so it was quieter. Resume at 10:20.)

Now: I want to maintain the framework of our sessions even while I give you a mini-vacation before our next main project. Therefore, I will not keep you long. Ruburt is psychically working out some of his concerns over reincarnation in his novel, coming to grips with the subject creatively, and in ways that have deep meaning, not only for himself but for others.

Oversoul Seven and Cyprus do exist, though in different terms than he may imagine them, and the whole episode allows him to work creatively with fiction, and creatively with his psychic abilities.

The book is a way of teaching through parable. He teaches himself as he teaches others, and of course in the writing of the book he is also being taught.

I am not going to say more about our next project this evening, simply that it is in preparation. Do you have any questions, Joseph *(as Seth calls me)*?

("No. I guess not.")

Then I bid you a fond good evening. You Sumari, you.

("The same to you, Seth.")

Try sketching sometime with your left hand also. The results might be surprising.

("I thought I would, yes. Good night, Seth, and thank you.")

(10:25 PM.

(Jane started Oversoul Seven *in late March, 1972. She finished* Oversoul Seven *in late July, 1972.)*

DELETED SESSION (FOR MARY SMITH)
MAY 3, 1972

Stop shaking!

([Mary:] "Okay.")

Can you hear me?

([Mary:] "Yes.)

Then listen well. I will start out with a compliment. That is to set you at ease. You are warm-hearted. You try to help other people. You mean well, and you have many abilities. You also have all the energy that you need, when you learn how to release it. Now, give us a moment, and listen. *(Pause.)*

I will not answer your questions in the way that you asked them. First of all, let us deal with some causes.

You expected too much when you moved here. You expected many things —a complete renewal, a reversal of certain circumstances in your life—a new relationship with your husband. You overidealized the situation ahead of time. You thought there was going to be a second honeymoon. You also thought that you would enjoy having your husband around all of the time. Because of previous conflicts, that can be resolved, you did not enjoy having him around all of the time as you supposed that you did. There were also conflicts of direction, as to who would "rule the roost", and you resented his "taking over", or what it seemed to you to be. You were used to managing the home alone. You thought that you would welcome his cooperation and aid, and because, now, of other conflicts with him, in the east, in this life, instead, you resented his help. You wanted to rule as you had in the past. You wanted the home to yourself.

Now. There are two strong aspects in your personality. One having to do with the reason why you entered the service; a desire for order; a desire for excitement, but excitement within an ordered sequence. There is also, in this same respect, an organizational aspect to your personality that is not now being used to advantage, and therefore can have negative consequences. You like to organize things and people. It is in this regard that you found the presence of your husband distracting when the two of you moved. Do you follow me?

([Mary:] "Yeah. I thought that he would be home and we could...uh... he'd have more time to farm, and we could work something out, but I was really relieved when he went to, had to go to work at night and I could read and study by myself.

Now. You were disappointed, then, shortly after you made your move, and you began to retreat. Whether or not you are consciously aware of this, in your earlier life, when you became extremely nervous or upset or had a bad problem, you began to "shut down" stimuli. You did not hear as well. When you wanted to retreat from the world, you shut down on your hearing so that you were not distracted. The habit simply persisted, and you grasped upon it as the situation continued. Now. Because of some circumstances and conflicts with your husband in this life in the past, you did not want to hear what he had to say. You were finished listening to him, and therefore with him, particularly, you began to have trouble hearing.

To some extent this also is connected with your daughter Ruth and the other girl.

I want to tell you what I know about your days, and then I will tell you what you must do to change them, You are beginning to organize your life about your lack of hearing. You are beginning to make it a characteristic. You are beginning to force other people to relate to you in that regard. Now you are obviously doing this because you are getting something out of it, and you must discover what that something is and I will help you.

You need, first of all, to develop some of your abilities in a purposeful manner. You are not using them. You are playing with them, but not using them as you want to. The organizational part of yourself wants you to organize yourself, and so far you have not done this.

You made a remark when you came in here this evening about not being dressed at noon. Now my first piece of homely advice is you should get up at a decent time and immediately dress, and "dress." I do not mean a robe. This immediately lifts your own self-image, and prepares you for the day. It is a mental "set."

Now. As far as your fears are concerned, in your periods of depression, you feel that you have not used your abilities in a "responsible" way. You feel that therefore, you cannot "pat yourself on the back." You feel to some extent like a hypocrite because in, I believe, New Jersey, at least before you moved here, you spoke of your writing but you did not work with it in an organized fashion. You did not direct it.

In periods of depression you feel that your life, the main points, have passed, and that you have lost time—important time that you feel you cannot recover. All of these fears work together to cause the present difficulty. Now. There is no one who can change your life for you. But you can change it. And in that lies your hope and your salvation. And so you must begin to do so. You are now organizing your life about your hearing defect. In the main, you are forcing others again to relate to you in that regard. You mention it often. You bring it into the conversation. When I tell you now, "often," it would not otherwise be noticed, for you also exaggerate the extent of the hearing loss. I did not say there was not a loss. I am saying you are exaggerating the loss that there is.

There are several things that I will ask you to do. First, however, you must begin to love <u>sound</u>. You must not concentrate thinking: "I cannot hear." "What is there to hear?" "What are they saying?" "How bad is my hearing today?" You must instead sensually enjoy those sounds that come to you, and even imagine sounds when you are alone. Now this will automatically set your inner self toward the anticipation of further sound. You must take at least an hour a day during which you do not think of loss of hearing, and I will give you some hints as to how to do this.

But you must hive yourself some relaxation from the constant concentration upon negative aspects.

([Mary:] "This doesn't mean a sleeping time?")
It does not.
([Mary:] "Then you...then I take it you would not suggest an operation?)
I have not gotten to that part yet.
([Mary:] "Sorry.")
I will let you take a break, however.
([Mary:] "Thank you."

(During break—I think this break—I told Jane and Rob of when I was very young—ten or eleven. My bedroom window was only about 15 feet away from my parents' apt. house. The scandal at the time was the noisy and violent arguments of an Italian couple, Anna and Jimmy. If Anna didn't boil Jimmy's eggs just right, he'd curse her out, and she'd retaliate by throwing sore of Mom's dishes at him, both of them screaming. All thru my life I've thought "nice, civilized people" didn't raise their voices, get angry enough so that it showed, or display any kind of outbursts. Jim, I believe, feels the same way [or did]. The very few times early in our marriage when I would lose my temper, he would absolutely infuriate me by saying softly, with a smirk, "Temper, temper!" and so I would clam up.)

I am simply pointing out certain characteristics. You carry grudges, and you have carried one, several, concerning your husband for some time. In the meantime, he has changed.

([Mary:] "I'm realizing that.")
He is trying to get through to you.
([Mary:] "Yes, I know that.")

Since then, however, you began to "close down" and say: "I will listen no longer." You must learn, therefore, to be more forgiving, both to yourself and others. There are also some conflicts of a quite natural type between you and your daughter Ruth, who also has strong organizational qualities and artistic abilities, as you have. Now, on some occasions, you resent her manner toward you. And you resent it bitterly. At the same time, you allow your own actions to bring out this manner from her. You know when you are doing it that this reaction will result, and you do it, regardless, In that particular dilemma, your husband is between.

The other girl *(Mary—age 15)* I see figuratively, now "figuratively" standing by your husband's side; not as much like you as Ruth.

Regardless of your farm, you, in your own mind, feel "scattered"—that you are not doing enough in other directions, and you are not sure what those directions are. You feel blocked. You are doing two things with the ears, of course. You are telling yourself that you want to hear. The other part of you is saying: "I do not want to hear!" "I do not want to hear what you have to say." You are, therefore, sending contradictory messages. This accounts for the decrease in hearing.

Now, before your husband became more willing to communicate, before he made an effort, you had fallen into your own rut. You did not try to relate to him in any strong manner. You let the relationship stand at a surface level. For a long time this served you both. Then, however, when you moved a critical situation was set up, where you were thrown together. This immediately brought forth the conflicts that had been latent and largely left alone. He then tried to relate to you. He did try to make up for lost time,and he began to grow and to understand.

To some extent, this "threatened" you, for you were used to the old relationship. At least you felt safe with it. You had given up expecting from him, and you were afraid of being hurt once more.

([Mary:] "That's true.")

Now. As a result, you began this retreat. The inner problems can be faced and solved. Now, no problem is solved "forevermore". Situations are resolved, however, and grow and develop and change, <u>if you allow them to</u>.

Your ears, your hearing, will improve when you realize that the cause is an inner one and when you bring the problem out into the open, and when you use certain techniques that are simply aids. If you do this, you can improve without an operation.

([Mary:] "Good.")

If you do not do this, you will not improve even if you have the operation. Now, I am not saying that the operation may not temporarily help. But without changing your attitude, it will not help to any degree that will compensate you. But the decision, you see...

([Mary:] "What?")

But the decision...

([Mary:] "Yeah...?")

... must be your own.

([Mary:] "I'll have to decide if I want the operation or not. Is that right?")

You will indeed. I will not tell you.

([Mary:] "Uh-huh.")

I have told you what I think. The hearing, you see; the state of the hearing, is among other things a symbolic, physical statement of the lack of communication that <u>has</u> existed between you and your husband. Only now it is you who will not hear. That is not the only cause for the condition, however. The "habit" was set in the past when you "shut out" noise that you did not want to hear. You are in the habit of shutting out sound.

([Mary:] "Just in this life?")

In this is this life material. You are in the habit of shutting out sound. Now, you can even catch yourself if you are alert enough doing this by the feeling that you have. In a conversation—now listen to me—In a conversation that you now decide sounds boring when you enter it, you can catch yourself thinking: "This is boring. I will not bother to listen. It is too much trouble." Now you <u>think</u> those thoughts come to you because it is so difficult for you to <u>hear</u>. Instead, those thoughts were yours long before the disability showed itself. You thought that way <u>first</u>, before the condition, And whenever unpleasantness arose, you would make a series of decisions to shut out the sound until these decisions, one upon the other, finally "conditioned" you; you conditioned yourself not to hear. The problem is that after awhile, you see, you conditioned yourself so well that you no longer control the process that you began. And only then do you become frightened.

Now. You had a question.

([Mary:] "Do you think that the condition has changed for the better in say, the last couple of weeks, when my husband and I agreed, for instance, on the check-writing thing; not to write checks for cash and then... so that we could control the money.... I think this will help me to....")

The money was also a symbol of communication as far as both of you were concerned. It was not the money, but your <u>ideas</u> about the money. And clashes that resulted.

The point was...

([Mary:] "...Do you think....")

the communication,

([Mary:] "Hmm.")

not the money.

([Mary:] "Uh-huh. [Pause.] Do you think... I have a feeling; that things have started to chango for the better in the last couple of weeks—in that regard—communication.")

Every time you make a sincere effort—the two of you to communicate—then the situation will begin to improve.

([Mary:] "That's what I had a feeling.")

You must be willing, however, to accept whatever comes of the communication. The first time it becomes unpleasant, you cannot, therefore, the next time say: "This time I will not hear".

([Mary:] "... You have to hear it out....)

Or then you retract....

([Mary:] "You have to hear it out.")

Now, listen. You are not "hearing me out". As you behave with me, you behave with your husband and. others. You are not listening to me so much as thinking of your next question and what you want to say.

([Mary:] "Sorry.")

I mention it only to show you how you operate. It is obvious in this situation. It is a characteristic. You are sometimes so impatient to express your own ideas that you <u>do not listen</u> to others. Also, often, you do not care, quite frankly, what they think.

Now this does not necessarily refer to me, here. But if you do not care what they <u>think</u>, then, again, you will not listen. Observe yourself—in conversation. I do not mean to watch yourself so closely that you cannot think, but observe your own reactions and your thoughts. Honestly ask yourself in situations: "Do I want to hear? And if I do not, why don't I?"

Now I will let you take a break.

Now. Often, you use sound as a barrier. Also, you use monologs, and set up a barrier of sound to protect yourself from other people. And you do not realize that you do this. You erect barriers like walls—so that someone wanting to communicate with you cannot get through, cannot find a "hole" in your conversation to reach you. And the more nervous you are, the more frantically you erect this barrier of sound. You use sound as a barrier, therefore, and when you become doubly threatened, then you do not hear the sounds that come from without, but retreat from them. The entire "gestalt of sound" is therefore highly important to you in your "mechanism of survival". You have used it to protect yourself, either erecting sound yourself to protect you from communications coming from without, or, when this fails, by refusing—refusing to hear. You must, therefore, ask yourself where this charged attitude toward sound originated, and why you use it in such a way. And I will give you some clues.

You mentioned some yourself. To you, noise, from your early years, was to be avoided. Sound did not convey pleasure. You were not thinking in terms of the communication of pleasure. It became, to you, a method of conveying unpleasant information, and therefore to be shut off whenever possible. You will find that if you begin to cultivate the pleasure of sound, this will help you.

Begin to play music that you like. Listen to the rain. Do not "just listen," but allow yourself to be open to the different pattering sounds and sound patterns that the rain makes. Become fascinated with the behaviors of sound. Tell yourself that sound is like light; that it is easily available.

Now some people do not like to look at unpleasant objects or sights, but very few of them would stop using their vision and give up the good sights so that they would not see bad ones. Yet this is what you are doing in your present course. Give us a moment.

Try...

([Mary:] "Try?")

...yourself...to speak gently.

([Mary:] "Gently.")

Learn to speak easily and gently. You communicate easily and well in your writing because sound is not involved. The ability to communicate is yours, and you are highly gifted in that regard. You are simply dropping the communication on the sound level. Once you realize this and understand it, you can begin to relax in that regard.

You are denying yourself a certain joy in your own present femininity, and for several reasons. With some purpose, you see to it that you are not as attractive physically as you know you are. You play down your attributes, rather than dress them up. You have been worried about and afraid of the feminine aspects of your personality. Now some of this has to do with the situation that <u>did</u> exist between you and your husband, and to some extent with the situation as it <u>now</u> exists. There is a free and easy flow of communication that is wordless, that you block.

Now. To some extent you punish him for his past attitudes by not appearing as attractively as you could. You think: "It serves him right! What does he expect?" At the same time, you are afraid that if you do appear as attractively as you can, that you will be hurt again by him, and you are unwilling to take the chance.

(<u>Note</u>: In one of the breaks, I noticed two or three candles that were on Jane's coffee table. I said I was glad that candles were "in," because I loved to light them, and the few times I did so, at birthday parties or Christmas, Jim always got upset, mentioning the fire hazard—even when we had guests for dinner.)

The episode that you mentioned, for example, regarding the candle. In your mind, that is a romantic gesture, and when he makes a comment about fire, there are several unconscious implications that you make, and that in the past have been understood by both of you at an unconscious level. Now. You interpret his remark about the candle to mean that he is rejecting deep, romantic feelings of yours, and needs; and also that the fire means that these needs are dangerous—his fear of fire being a symbol for "Danger!". You think, unconsciously, he is saying to you: "These romantic needs are dangerous. They can cause a fire that we cannot control, fires being obviously destructive."

Now, this is you <u>interpretation</u>, at a deep level, of such a remark. This confirms your feeling that you <u>dare not</u> display strong emotions with him, and you feel all the more rejected. When you light the candle, you are testing him to see how far he will go with you, and when he makes the fire remark, you take it as a rejection of the entire romantic self, and the romantic situation. At the same time, this denial wounds you, because you also suffer from it.

He is much more open in that regard now than he was, and he understands his own emotional behavior better, as well as yours.

Now. You can be a very attractive woman, and you can fix your hair; you can play up your attributes, and you know it. This will automatically, you see, change the situation, for you will not change the physical aspects unless an inner recognition has first led you to do so. <u>You</u> will feel the richer for it, emotionally richer for it, regardless of your husband's reaction.

I want you to listen to this session well. I suggest, if you can, that you type it up, and also read it. And once a day, for some time. Now I will let you take a break.

(*Break.*)

You overeat, to compensate for the other joys that you do not allow yourself. If you began to paint for an hour a day, you would not need to eat so much. When you bring food and drink with you, you do two things. You bring along your own "security blanket", for one thing. You also show that you are insecure and frightened outside of the home environment, and must bring nourishment from there along with you. Now the joy that you experience when you are painting will be yours, and not desert you whether you stay in your house or go to someone else's. You will not have to worry about "carting it along" with you. As you probably suspect, the overeating is the one great indulgence that you allow yourself, and even then you surround it with all kinds of taboos. It is not the fact that you overeat, and that you are desperately frightened because you overeat—because of your sister's history. You do not overeat simply any food, but you surround eating itself with taboos, so that it must be "pure food," "good food," to your way of thinking. And there are foods that you will eat and foods that you will not eat, and you project moral implications upon the foods. Some foods are "good," to your way of thinking, and some foods are "bad." To you this does not necessarily or alone mean they are good for the body or bad for the body, but in themselves you give them moral characteristics as you would people. So that beneath the whole attitude is the idea: "This is an evil food," and be shunned as you would shun an evil person, within that framework of thought.

This is so that you will not enjoy your one indulgence overmuch!

Now. So far, you are denying a good portion of your hearing because sound can be unpleasant, and carrying this a bit further now, it can also be "bad." You know the three little monkeys who sit: "see no evil" and so forth. Now you have simply hit upon the "hear no evil." You have added to it the fact that you will not indulge yourself in joy, or in joyful pursuits, Unless you can rationalize to yourself by saying: "I am doing this for someone else," and that is the only reason you let yourself work with the necklaces that you made. You could say: "I am making these for class members" and therefore justify the pleasure.

What our friend here told you *(Rob)* is indeed true. You must realize that you are a unique and a blessed individual, and you must be as kind to yourself, and <u>kinder</u>, even, than you try to be to others. For they also bathe in the joy that you feel. It is most important that you understand this.

([Mary:] *"I'm beginning to."*)

The book that you bought, *Psycho-Cybernetics*, and the other one—both of these are good for you. But do not simply read them. Use them. Each book approaches various problems from different viewpoints. But together they will be of great help. Since you yourself began these reactions and originated them, you yourself can change them. And you can change them as of this moment.

Imagine for an experiment, now, a world in which there is no sound. Do not imagine that you are deaf. That is not what I am saying. But imagine that the world itself has no sound for anyone to hear. Do you see the difference?

You are imagining a situation in which there is no sound to be heard; whether or not you have ears, there is no sound. Then, imagine that, suddenly, a raindrop falls and makes a first sound... the first sound that can ever be heard. And imagine the impact and the beauty of that sound. Then slowly imagine other sounds appearing in the world, appearing in the same way that a flower might appear, so that sounds begin to be born in the universe. Imagine, then, the joy of hearing that sound in a world that had known none. Whatever sounds, then, that imaginatively come to you, feel the brilliance and miracle of them as they are born out of the silence. And then give thanks for a world of sound, and let yourself revel that you live in <u>this world</u> where sound is a part of your environment and surroundings. In all of this, do not think about your ears, but do the imaginative exercise exactly as I have suggested it. That alone, done once a day, will help arouse again within you the joy and wonder of that particular sense.

Now you can indeed progress, and you have progressed in many ways since you began Ruburt's class. And so has your husband. It has taken you some time to develop these habits with such <u>persistence</u>. And so you can change them, using that same persistence and determination.

Now you used the energy that your classmate *(Eleanor)* was sending you for other overall purposes. While you did not want to hear, her energy could not force you to hear. Indeed, you would automatically put up a defense, because you considered not hearing to be important to your survival. The exercise that I just suggested to you will, if followed, now, help you open up sufficiently so that energy sent to you can be utilized for that specific difficulty. But while you refused to hear, you would consider energy sent to you particularly to <u>make you</u> hear also a threat to your survival, and would be determined to block it. You must realize that your survival depends upon enjoying all of your senses fully. Reading the session alone should help you realize that.

([Mary:] "May I ask a question?")

You may, indeed.

([Mary:] "How long a day, each day, should I practice what you just suggested?")

As long as it is enjoyable. That is, no more than a half-hour, at the most.

([Mary:] "And an hour of painting every day?")

You should indeed.

([Mary:] "<u>That'll</u> be a pleasure!")

And enjoy it. And the exercise—do not strain at it. Now, you use your imagination well. So imagine these new sounds as they would appear, until you are really <u>dazzled</u>.

([Mary:] "Should I do anything specific to, like, go to the Old Ladies' Home and play the piano for them?")

If you do that, it is fine. But it is not as important as the painting. Doing things for other people is important, but doing things, as our friend *(Rob)* said, for yourself is imperative.

([Mary:] "Uh-huh.")

If you are joyful, you will help other people simply by being what you are. If you try to help others and you are despondent, you do not help them.

([Mary:] "I'm beginning to understand what you mean.")

All the suggestions that I gave you, however, follow including "dressing in the morning".

([Mary:] "What in the morning?"

([Seth and Rob:] "Dressing in the morning."

([Mary, laughing:] "All right. I'll do that.")

And getting out of the house.

([Mary:] "Yes. I should get out of the house more.")

Take your paints outside sometime. Think! How precious voices are! In your terms, they speak, and the sounds are gone and never recaptured. And who are you to say: "I will not listen, for this is trivial." These sounds are magic. Be thankful for them. You will never again be the personality that you are at this moment. Whatever self you will be, in your terms, or you were, each of those selves are unique, as you are unique. When you hear him *(Rob)* speak, his words are the magical signatures of the psyche, materialized in certain ways within this moment as you understand a time, and precious and a joy to hear. And so are the words of every man and woman, and the sound of every bird and every raindrop—precious beyond recall. So do not close yourselves to those sounds, and be thankful for them.

You have been afraid of displaying emotions. You think that tears are cowardly. You have not wanted to face your own emotions, therefore you are frightened of the emotions of others. You did not, habitually, display your emotions to your husband. Now he could more easily express some of his to you. He got out of the habit, however, You did not want to hear them. You consider tears "degrading." You considered, in the past, joy "evil." This did not leave you too many acceptable emotions.

([Mary, slight laugh:] "That's right.")

Now. There is nothing degrading in tears. Think of them, again, now, as being as natural as rain that falls out of the sky when the clouds are full. The rain refreshes the ground and tears can refresh the soul when depressions are freed to follow their natural course. Then, indeed, they flow away in tears and the soul is refreshed. It does not "hold onto its grudges". When you hold a grudge, you are like some angry, little black cloud that says: I will hold onto this moisture, and I will never let it go!" But clouds have better sense, and so easily they empty their contents and the rain refreshes the land. So can tears refresh the land of your psyche. And used in such a manner depressions fall away naturally and allow, if you will forgive me for a trite phrase, "the sun of joy to shine." Otherwise, the cloud becomes blacker, and blacker and blacker until the sun cannot be seen, and until the sun, when glimpsed, seems <u>wrong</u>, out of context, and does not appear in such a dark landscape. And so you try to hide it.

If you do not trust your emotions, then you can no longer trust your joy. And if you try to hide your fear, then, you automatically hide your joy. Once you begin to inhibit emotions, the practice spreads like a plague, until all emotion must be inhibited, lest the one thing that you fear show its face.

Now. The difficulty with the foot...did have a reincarnational setting, originally, as I mentioned. But there was no reason why that had to appear in

this life, particularly.
(*[Mary:] "The difficulty with the what?"*)
(*[Rob:] "Foot."*)
With the foot.
(*[Mary:] "Oh, the foot!"*)

It did originate in a past life, as mentioned, but it did not <u>have</u> to reassert itself, now. It served your purposes, however. And it was also another method of retreat. You did not have to go out into a strange enviroment, away from the home and hearth. Now, it predated the hearing difficulty in its strongest form, but the "habits" were always with you. You always "favored" one foot more than the other, and you built up muscular reaction. When you began to "clear" your foot—when you got the new shoes—your hearing gave you more difficulty. You needed more of a crutch, to make up for the symptom you had lost, simply because you did not understand the reasons behind the difficulties. And without understanding, you can medically rid yourself of one condition, only to make ready certain that you have another one planned to take over! You were finally driven to some kind of desperation, so you accepted the new shoes. You used the symbol. You could have been quite as comfortable without the new shoe, but the symbol was a good one, and you used it and took advantage of it.

But then you became frightened, and that is when the hearing difficulty, then, bothered you so deeply. You will not need to substitute symptoms in such a fashion, as you learn to look into yourself.

I've given you many clues this evening, and as you listen to the session, whatever remarks I have made, though they seem minute—take note of them.

(*[Mary:] "All right."*)

I am going to close our session. However, I want to tell you, again, that you have progressed. There is no reason why you cannot work things out, and why the relationship between you and your husband should not continue to improve. You are both doing well.

Ruburt's class is good for you. It is good for you both, not only because of the particular group here, and the subject matter, but also because it gives you contact with other people under a different context. It gets you out of your environment. It also brings the two of you together in a common experience.

Now I bid you a fond good evening. And you see, it was not so bad after all!

(*[Mary, laugh:] "No, it wasn't. Thank you very much."*)

You simply have some work to do.

([Mary:] "Thank you very much. And I'll try to do that work real hard."
(I kept tape open a bit for Rob.
([Rob:] "...the question would automatically answer itself—about your operation. Did you remember that?"
([Mary:] "I'm taping you."
([Rob:] "Seth said you could make up your own mind about the operation."
([Mary:] "Yeah. That I could...."

One small point. You have been punishing yourself quite often in the way in which you approach the medical experience. The idea of an operation, on the one hand, frightens you. On the other hand, you feel it is "just punishment for these ears of mine that will not work." The same applied to the mouth. In that case, again, the attitudes cause your reaction.

I am not telling you not to get treated medically when you believe that you need it. I am telling you that often you use medical treatment as a further punishment of the body. Often you use medical treatment as a reassurance. You are not quite certain, yet, that you form your own reality, and you want to make certain, in the meantime, that the medical profession can help you out!

([Mary:] "Yeah. I see. I don't know what to tell my doctor when I think he's going to suggest an operation. And I don't know what to tell him. Shall I say I'll think about it?")

I would leave it open, and leave yourself open. And try the experiments that I have suggested.

([Mary:] "Because I only have ten more days till I get the hearing test, and I have a feeling that he'll want this specialist to go in there and work.")

For now, I would forget the deadline. It will only make you nervous.

([Mary:] "Uh-huh.")

You are not to begin these experiments that I've suggested with the idea that "Well, I must hurry up."

([Mary:] "Yeah. I just didn't know what to tell the doctor. 'Cause he might want a statement of when I would get an operation, and I don't—I haven't made up my mind if I want one or not, yet.")

I would put it off, then, if you are asking my advice.

([Mary:] "Yes. Thank you.")

Do not make a decision until you are clearer in your own mind.

([Mary:] "Because I want to try to heal it without an operation.")

(Long Pause.) I think that you can. The delay, in any case, will not hurt you, in that particular area. And without changing your attitude, the operation will not help. Do you follow me?

([Mary:] "Yes, I do. That's what I thought you meant, too, before.")

Then, I bid you a fond good evening. And my heartiest regards to my friend over there *(Rob)*, who did not have to take any notes this evening.

([Mary:] "Thank you very much, Seth.")

Now. Wait for a moment. Wait for a moment. We will have a very brief Sumari healing song.

([Mary:] "All right."

(Sumari came through with a lovely song.)

(I showed Jane and Rob a little artwork, and my two Pennsylvania scrapbooks, and left a lettle before midnight with a great deal to think about!)

DELETED SESSION
JUNE 14, 1972   9:25 PM   WEDNESDAY

Now; give us a moment, and we will begin easily enough.

As you know, Ruburt concentrates his energy and focus. He does not spread it out. This applies to people as well as deep interests.

Once he became convinced of the validity of the psychic experience, and his abilities, then all playful attitudes deserted him. He grasped at it tenaciously, and added it to the then unchallenged work to which he had, until then, devoted his main attention.

The personality is such that it always looks inward.

It does not easily adopt what it considers frivolous hobbies or activities that would help divert and release the energies. He constantly worries about his work, then, and all it entails.

The search for truth in the beginning was carried on within the framework of the church. In a way he was rewarded for conventional thought, and punished for unconventional thought. His poetry was accepted and praised artistically, when the ideas agreed with dogma.

The church was a support in the household against his mother. When the poetry was thus criticized, Ruburt was afraid the support would be withdrawn. The thoughts were considered extremely dangerous. They were not treated lightly. To <u>some</u> extent Ruburt equates me with a more knowledgeable Father Traynor.

He therefore feels highly upset if he does not accept all of my views as he understands them, and makes it a point to repeat that rebellion now in a different way.

(9:34.) I suggest you close your window and turn on the fan....

The Catholic church, incidentally, as he knew it, while admitting the mystic experience, was highly suspicious of him in that regard. He was recognized as the too intent, emotional and mystical personality, and to some extent distrusted.

The search for truth and the fear of leading people astray are the primary points here. In the past any intuitive thoughts he felt but could not prove were put into his fiction. This protected him from censure, both from within and without.

(9:40.) Give us time.... The delivery of the material per se in our sessions, now, does not basically bother him. He is afraid of making people lose their faith. It was considered the sin of sins. He felt deeply betrayed particularly by Father Doran, and resolved never to betray others in such a way.

He is more upset than he realizes over the opinion of others, experts, in the field, that dabbling in psychic phenomena is dangerous for many people. This adds fuel to the fear that he is indeed leading them astray.

One letter from someone who wrote saying that *The Seth Material* contributed to a nervous breakdown is a case in point.

He takes too much responsibility upon his shoulders. He definitely does not like the religious connotation, and it is only here that problems arise.... We are giving what we can, to keep the channel open while we see what we can do.

(Pause at 9:46.)

What he wants to do is use his abilities to clear the pathways to clear understanding of the nature of the soul, although he would not use the term for so long.

He also knows that such channels lead other people away from, specifically, the Catholic church. He wondered if what he can give can make up for what they might lose. Before the material was public this bothered him, but not to that degree. It worried him when people seem to turn to the material in the same way that they might turn to a church, merely substituting one set of ideas for another, while never experiencing the concepts themselves.

The material you received from him was quite correct. At another level he feared that his relationship with me was the result of unconscious fraud, and trickery, that he had indeed become the false prophet, and conned you and everyone else, including himself.

This was because he had for one thing watched what he thought of as the two faces of Father Doran, who conned others in his preaching then showed quite opposing characteristics afterward. The quality of the material itself often kept him from admitting this feeling. The experience at the writer's convention also had an affect there, plus the young psychologist's remarks later—all of this accepted because of the inferiority feelings of childhood.

He was trying to go ahead and not go ahead at the same time.

He would not drop the psychic work. He never will. The public aspects of it alone brought up the false prophet. Now he has been doing penance in his terms: fasting, I believe it is called.

(10:00.) The feelings prevented him from going ahead far enough to allow his psychic experience to answer some of his doubts, yet he was too convinced of the validity to drop the work.

Some of my material is difficult to accept intuitively and intellectually at one time. You may intuitively grasp a point and intellectually not understand it, or the other way around. But Ruburt insists that he intellectually and intuitively understand each point, and agree with it, or it puts him in the position of publicizing ideas when he is not a hundred percent certain of their validity, and he considers this to some degree dishonest. If he is wrong and people follow him, where is he leading them?

So sometimes you see in such periods he will put off sessions. The three Christs material particularly affects him that way, for to deny the conventional idea of Christ is to antagonize not merely Catholicism but basic Christian belief. The same material presented fictionally would not bother him at all. He stands behind the idea, you see. He is afraid of being attacked, or he is afraid of the work being attacked, for that kind of reason, as his poetry was.

The difference is this: he was not presenting the poetry as truth for people to follow.

Many ideas are being presented in *Oversoul Seven* to get around that difficulty. He had been taught the dire consequences in church terms of losing your soul, and he was afraid of leading people astray whenever religious areas were approached. He believed enough however in his abilities and in his work to continue despite the deep dilemma.

(10:10.) The *ESP* book put him on record. The people that write to him as the result of his books often bothered him deeply, for he thinks that they look to him as you would to a prophet. And if he cannot help them then he <u>does</u> feel like a false prophet, offering hope and practically in a given situation being unable to give it.

When Venice's friend committed suicide some time ago, this affected him deeply, for a session had been held and it did not stop the suicide. His symptoms at that point deepened. He greatly enjoys the psychic and intuitive experience itself, the going ahead, but he becomes worried after that point as to how the ideas will be used and interpreted.

You may take your break.

(10:16—11:01. Oversoul Seven is Jane's sci-fi character.)

These areas have gone largely unexplored. He needs to be convinced, and to convince himself, that his work is indeed helping others, in that it is leading toward truth and away from distortion.

Ready arguments for the other side have been taken for granted by him emotionally. One strong portion of him knows well that Christian theology is far from any entire answer, that Christ was not the son of the only God; the other portion of Ruburt is still affected by those beliefs, and he did not realize it.

The emotional beliefs therefore could not be reached. A concerted effort should be made to gain the support of the part of him who understands. Your own reasonable arguments there will help. Point them out. Bring up arguments for that side. Part of this has to do also with the fact that his complete support in St. Vincent's Catholic orphanage was carried on by a religious order. *(For over two years.)*

Intellectually he changed his views. Intuitively he went ahead. The clash with the emotional aspects occurred only when a system of thought seemed formulated that would oppose the early emotional views.

The church itself has changed in that time. The feelings must be brought out into the open so that they <u>can</u> be handled in the light of his current intuitional and intellectual ideas. This is extremely important. You must help him counter them.

He is afraid of hurting people by upturning their views. At times he was told he would come to no good if he continued with independent thinking. Intellectually he did continue. He is frightened of setting up a new religion, afraid. In one of your own sessions at least encourage him to free associate, to say freely now what comes to mind regarding his feelings about the three Christs, and also ideas of the Anti-Christ. Let these <u>freely</u> come. <u>Then</u> go to work on them.

He is afraid of taking on Christendom, and expects some poison pen letters because of the three Christs reference.

In quite simple terms then he has felt deeply committed and frightened at the same time. The old Pandora's box. Once he opened the door of knowledge what would come through? I suggest also that on those occasions how when any frightening feelings begin to arise to call you, to feel free to free-associate with them and let them rise.

("Can I ask a question?")

You may indeed.

("How come these early emotional ideas haven't been influenced, at least some-

what modified by all the intuitive and intellectual activity, and new ideas, that have developed and taken place in the last few years?")

Because they were formed at a time before the intellectual and intuitive abilities developed, and were not a problem until the intellectual and intuitive abilities seemed to come upon a system of thought that was in opposition to the underlying emotional beliefs. Until then there was no conflict.

Keeping the church, he could always return to it. Setting up a new system of thought that he considered in opposition would make this impossible. You do have more to work with than you realize once this is understood though, for there are also strong emotional drives toward the desire for truth that can be allied with the early <u>released</u> ones—but these must be released and understood first.

Now that is the end of this evening's session.

(Good night, Seth."

(11:27. I don't think Seth fully answered the question I asked above on the previous page, but I chose not to press the point at this time.)

DELETED SESSION
JULY 17, 1972 9 PM MONDAY

Now—

("Good evening, Seth.")

Good evening. I have many things to say, and some will have to be continued, and barely begun this evening.

First, we will begin with Nebene. He was a man of the strongest purpose, high dedication, a severe perfectionist who drove himself and his students. He was a mystic, but a mystic given to great discipline, denial, restraint. He inhibited many of his strongest drives in order to focus them upon his search and the work to which he was committed.

He saw in his time how so-called mysticism and even dedication, without discipline, could divert energy, distort truths and pervert causes. He was well aware that high energy could be lost through dissipation. He dammed his own up, letting it out only in the deep but narrow channel of his interest. He had little use for spontaneity. He was afraid of it.

His methods worked very well in the transcription of his records, and purified his translations. He was afraid that spontaneity would cause him to color certain transcriptions from the past. His methods did not work nearly as

(My five-minute sketch of Nebene as I behan proofreading the session of July 17, 1972 for publication 31 years later.)

SESSION 7/17/72

(I studied this session to better grasp my Nebene characteristics then [and now] by painting his image, and then dr4awing him again, but now I'm appalled by my behavior in first-century Rome. Yet Seth's Nebene rings true—even including my relationship with Jane way back then.)

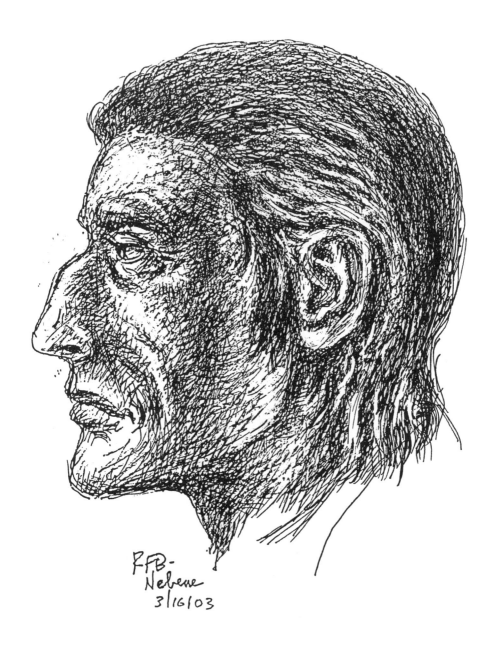

(And, of course, recording the thousands of pages of the Seth material in my meticulous way for over 20 years surely reflects a large portion of the Nebene psyche: keeping his own "purified" translations of ancient records.)

well in person-to-person contact with his students, however.

In dealing with these records he was suspicious of creativity, for he feared it could lead to original alterations where instead a literal interpretation was important. He was also however a creative man so there were personality conflicts, and he literally forced the creativity to take a weak secondary position.

The dilemma was, here now, between truth—a literal translation of ancient records—or a creative approach which could lead to falsification, so he was highly suspicious of the creativity in himself. Through discipline he thought that he had this suspicious creativity well in hand. He feared that his students would not have the same kind of integrity. He was therefore very severe in dealing with originality on the part of his students, considering it, again, a threat. He was indeed a taskmaster.

Now when you met Ruburt, and I will give you connecting points here, you recognized the strong creative abilities, and appreciated them, encouraged them. But within you also through association the remnants of Nebene roused themselves into action. The abilities were to be used. <u>You</u> knew that.

The Nebene within you however was quite certain that they must also be disciplined, kept within bounds and watched carefully. The same applied to your own creative abilities, where for some time a divergence from a literal pictorial illustration was felt to be wrong, or off. Some other personal information that I gave you concerning your relationship with your father this time also fits in here.

Now Nebene was aroused whenever the abilities showed themselves most spontaneously in Ruburt. Ruburt recognized the Nebene within you when first you met. Jane was dancing quite spontaneously, incidentally, and to boot somewhat tipsy. She felt you aloof and disapproving of the waste of energy, watching but not <u>swept along</u> as the other males were. A part of you enjoying the performance but a part, Nebene, critically wondering about the undisciplined use of such energy.

In this life Ruburt feared a laxness within himself because of his mother's remarks about his father. He knew his own abilities. He feared he did not have the wisdom to use them wisely. They must be <u>appreciated</u> but not spent foolishly. You appreciated them. The Nebene in you could be counted upon to see that they were not squandered.

You did know Ruburt in the past as Nebene, and she was then a dancing girl.

("When was that life?")

This is in your life as Nebene. Let us get to the details in our time. You died, I believe, shortly after the time of Christ—that is, somewhere between 35 and 50 AD.

You had a relationship of which Nebene did not approve, a sexual one. There were countless cults, and Ruburt as a woman was a prostitute priestess—the term is not a good one—of a particularly sensuous cult that had a connection with the land of Constantinople. *(Turkey.)*

It was emotional, unrestrained, given to orgies. You were unresistingly drawn to it, the power of your inhibited tendencies propelling you for release. So you had a secret life, unknown to your students for some time. It erupted suddenly at the age of 45 and ran for 10 years. You had no respect for yourself during that span.

Ruburt was 9 when this began, usual in those days incidentally. *(I was surprised at the age, etc.)* For some time in your relationship in this life, Nebene provided you with a framework to contain your own early emotions with your parents.

In this life you equated your own creativity with danger, now, to some degree. In the first place your father's creativity, his inventions, brought him no recognition, no money in your mother's terms. The creativity in your mother simply erupted in emotional tantrums, also dangerous and unproductive. You nicely channeled your creativity into comics, where it was socially acceptable and would also bring recognition in the terms of your society—cash.

Here Nebene within you rushed to your aid. He was appalled that your ability, while disciplined, lacked the intent and purpose, the search for truth and meaning, he felt being adulterated. Ruburt, with high youthful ideals, a strong sense of purpose, then came into the picture. He was accepted by you and by Nebene. Nebene felt the purpose would save your abilities.

He had already spoken within you, rousing you to dissatisfaction. Ruburt, who had led him astray in the past, would now lead you into high purpose and dedication. The two of you, Ruburt and Joseph, had already made agreements, as you know. Nebene however carried a grudge as Ruburt does, or rather now as Jane does. Ruburt does not carry grudges.

Nebene, while thankful to Jane, quickly let other aspects enter in once you had safely decided upon painting rather than comics, which were to him degrading. He was then afraid that Ruburt's spontaneity would divert you from the course that it had set you upon, so he began to take a stronger hand.

Part of the stronger hand also had to do with his attempts to help you with your family, to shut you off from too much distracting emotion, when for example you moved back to Sayre after New York. Ruburt however reacted most vehemently against this shutdown of emotional reaction. He felt then the force that was Nebene. Now at times his own overly-conscientious portions would agree quite heartily with Nebene's dictates. Because of his psychic abilities he picked up these qualities quite accurately. They would often seem so different from your own actions at a given time that he became highly confused, and distrusted his own reactions.

At a completely different level of course Nebene and Sharabena—do not ask for spelling now—understood each other quite well, and she would taunt him. Now regardless of what interpretations Ruburt wants to put upon what I am saying, whether or not he wants to accept the reincarnation influence, the fact is that what I am saying has a psychological reality that neither of you can deny, and one that acts constantly in your lives.

Now I must speak through Ruburt. I cannot therefore run willy-nilly without regard for his own psychological workings. On some occasions therefore his fears, and defense of you, would prevent excellent material, and at other times his fierce defense of himself would prevent it.

His fear of the truth of the material, you see, fit in very well with Nebene's tendencies, and so in certain ways they also joined in alliance. Take your break.

(9:44. I told Jane that I had been considering the role Nebene might play in our relationship in this life, for the last couple of days. I hadn't mentioned this to Jane though in any of our recent long talks. Resume at 9:56.)

Now, I have much more to say.

The Nebene characteristics came particularly to the fore in the transcription of my book of course, and with the encounter with your friend Sue. Nebene was furious that Ruburt would not speak for him. Nebene wanted to speak through Ruburt, knowing his abilities, and Ruburt refused.

With you, Nebene checked the details of the book. This put Ruburt under additional pressure, and he began to rebel more. You made some remark that the book was marred because of the great gaps in sessions, Ruburt's attitude, and so forth. Ruburt therefore felt that you were accusing him again of a poor performance, and for other reasons also felt that in your eyes these faults took precedence over the book's obvious merit. Because of the strain, and because he felt his spontaneity so hampered, he came up with *(Oversoul) Seven*, defiantly, where Nebene could not follow; pure creativity, he felt, with no factual details that he could be called upon.

A slap in the face to Nebene, saying "Aha, I am using my abilities as frivolously as I dare to, and you will get little more from me." At the same time he also felt guilty and the book, *Seven*, is filled with purpose regardless.

Seven himself is characterized by a dislike for details, and a grand disregard of formality. He is the epitome of Ruburt's spontaneous self, frivolous in a way of speaking but very definitely, quite of itself, filled with purpose but free-wheeling.

In the beginning it was you who mentioned the rest of the page to Tam—do you follow me?

("No...")

After Ruburt recited his first few sentences—

("Oh, yes." *The first page of* Seven.)

—but when Ruburt merrily began to write you spoke to him quite sharply, reminding him that he was dropping other projects to embark on a new one at Tam's enthusiasm. You implied his abjectness.

Nebene is quite jealous of Tam's influence, such as it is, but again, Nebene let it be known he disapproved. Now this had charge behind it later when you assured Ruburt you were delighted with the project. You had no such charge. The charge registered. A quick aside: your friend Sue's behavior: she was kicking her heels up at Nebene also.

Now Ruburt's own background this time, with ideas of truth and falsehood, tied in beautifully with Nebene. Nebene was as determined to get the correct reincarnational details because they were in his terms true, as Ruburt was determined to avoid them because in his terms they were not true.

Both of them have some qualities in common, therefore. Ruburt does not like to be held down by details. Nebene insists upon them. Ruburt feels that details often get in the way of intuition. Nebene feels that they are sturdy steps upon which intuition must climb steadily forward.

Now your (underlined) main failure in dealing with Ruburt is an emotional one. You cannot reason with the part of him who felt hurt deeply, or to the part that felt he was rejected. In your attempts to explain yourself in the main, now, you have tried to use logic and reason, when it was as I told you before a feeling of being deprived emotionally. He did not feel deprived intellectually.

You must reach him on the one level that you have been frightened of, through honest expressed emotional feeling, and again as I have told you often, through physical touch. I gave several sessions on that subject alone. The emotions and the physical body are so iterrelated that one automatically affects the other. Ruburt needs to be reassured on an emotional and physical level.

He felt insulted on those levels. You have quite carefully avoided them in your attempts to clear up the problems. The muscles themselves cry out to be soothed, and the physical touch, the relaxation of muscle, brings about an emotional release. An emotional release brings about a muscular one.

Now give us a moment. You can rest your hand.

All of this affected the sessions, and your reactions to the entire experience. I you think you will see many tie-ins. In the last months you have not had sessions. None of you were satisfied. Ruburt is quite deeply committed to them despite all of these colorations, and so are you.

He felt much time wasted, but held off, seeing if an absence from sessions would help his health. He had also resented the coercion that Nebene implied. Nebene was upset because of this own sense of purpose. Ruburt knew this but would no longer give sessions because he felt forced to.

Nebene has learned a thing or two. He was certain that given the chance Ruburt would throw the sessions over gladly. He did not trust Ruburt's overall consistency, you see. Part of the symptoms these last months have arisen and continued because of these ambiguities.

Therefore there was little consistent attempt made to reassure Ruburt's emotional nature, or reach it on an emotional or physical level. Instead you used reason. Secondly, the conflict over sessions: Ruburt himself felt he was wasting time on the one hand, and on the other was refusing to be coerced.

He also felt that you had already disapproved of *Seth Speaks*, not understanding the Nebene connection. Take your break. Incidentally, it is also Nebene who cannot understand why Ruburt's emotional nature cannot be reached intellectually.

(10:32—10:55.)

Now. Your ideas of personality and time dictated your question.

When you think of yourself simply as Robert Butts you limit your reality. Nebene characteristics represent a portion of your reality. It is up to you to use those characteristics as best you can, and they can be very handy in what is a present life existence.

<u>The lives are simultaneous</u>. In quite other terms Nebene wonders why he is bothered or hampered in <u>his</u> life situation, so devoted to detail and literal interpretation, by his strong leanings—temptations to him—toward creativity and spontaneity.

In whatever situation you find yourself, in whatever "life," (in quotes) there will be different focuses of abilities, conflicts of ability that are all challenges. You, as you are, have helped Nebene understand the importance of creativity, and so has Ruburt. And while there have been severe conflicts, understandings on all levels have occurred, and development.

Understanding then, you can use the abilities as you want. Before, they seemed to have an energy of their own, almost at times not a part of you, and Nebene experienced his own creativity as equally apart from him at times.

You quite gladly used those disciplinary abilities, and they served you well in early years as a framework in which you handle your parents' situation. It is up to you to become aware of them, realize their value, but not allow them to block other aspects of your personality.

The Nebene characteristics were also of help in the early days of the sessions in several ways, but I do not want to get off the subject. When you are using them well you think of them as quite your own.

("I'm just wondering when that is.")

Then you are not aware of them. They blend in with your purposes.

Now I will tell you that Ruburt's Josef, in *Seven*, is a very good approximation of another quite different life of yours, in which the emotions were given the fullest of sway—and you also have those characteristics to draw upon. They were warm, exuberant. Using them, and you do have them, you would have no difficulty in relating emotionally in the way I suggested. In helping Ruburt in this manner, you see, you automatically release portions of your own personality and abilities that have been repressed, and that is a portion of the whole situation.

For other reasons, for one because Josef was undisciplined, you have not spontaneously given expression to that portion of you. To help your wife you can do so. I want you to know therefore that such emotional behavior is a part of your nature. I am dealing with your end of the stick this evening because I had been blocked in the past from doing so, and the information is so pertinent.

The emotional qualities will also help your own work, of course. Both of you will be freer with your feelings, and in communicating them. Now this is enough for this evening. Do you have a particular question?

("I guess not.")

Then we will close.

("It's been very interesting.")

My heartiest good wishes. And I do the best for you that I can.

("Thank you very much. Good night, Seth.")

(11:15. Jane said she remembered little of the delivery, except that Josef was modeled after a life of mine. Then Seth returned:)

Tell Ruburt I said to think of these himself as simultaneous existences, and forget the word reincarnation if he wants. For that matter simultaneous existences is much closer to the truth of the matter. These personalities are alive in your now, as you are alive in them now. They are portions of your consciousness, your gestalt of being. They are individualized personalities. All of you draw your characteristics from the one entity that is the bank of your personality.

("Good night, Seth. Thank you." 11:19—11:25.)

Now, let me add several important points, covered earlier. First of all I have given you many sessions looking at the problem from different aspects. The suggestions given, <u>all</u> of them, followed consistently—and none of them were—would have led you through channels of understanding culminating in Ruburt's recovery. Added therefore to reasons given this evening are such issues given earlier, as a concentration upon negatives, and the methods given earlier to counter those will also be of help.

Ruburt's feeling of hopelessness added lately to his symptoms. Now. He personally utilizes programs and incentives. He needs his sense of purpose. In this particular situation, in the present, beginning sessions again is helpful in this context. The negative fears that he cannot perform however hypnotize the muscles. The positive suggestions are of great value with these necessary deeper changes of behavior. Do you follow me?

("Yes.")

The approach should be of loving encouragement: "You can. Try, and I will help you." Not, "You must."

I simply wanted to give you at least some idea of the entire picture. (Louder.

("Good night, Seth. Thank you.")

The session, to answer Ruburt's silent question, will work no magic by itself. It must be utilized.

("Yes. I understand." 11:33.)

DELETED SESSION
JULY 19, 1972 9:35 PM WEDNESDAY

Good evening.

("Good evening, Seth.")

Now we will have a relatively brief session, but I would like to give you some important immediate points to work on—not *(humorously)* that I did not give you enough the other evening.

Ruburt must see that the more he does physically the more physically agile he will become. His physical reassurance is necessary—that is, he needs to be reassured that physically he <u>can</u> improve, and perform.

Telling him that you are suddenly mad enough or angry enough to insist upon changes is obviously not the approach. He thought you were angry enough to begin with. Physical improvement, now, <u>in that context</u> (underlined), meant something else you were demanding, but did not expect.

Loving encouragement will work. Because of the material given the other evening, and Ruburt's own background, this is what happened in the past: he would manage to show some improvement as your attitude became more loving. He was still looking for signs that you <u>meant</u> the change—do you follow me?

("Yes.")

When you showed impatience with his progress it was sometimes a natural impatience, and sometimes Nebene's dissatisfaction with a student who should, with those abilities, do better. Ruburt would indeed perceive withering looks on such occasions. Neither of you properly understood your own reactions. But Ruburt would immediately panic.

After all, you <u>did</u> (underlined) disapprove. You were not pleased with his performance, he was not living up to your expectations. He equated then a normal physical performance, from the standpoint of his condition, as an impossible perfect performance, while feeling that nothing short of perfection would please you.

I am bringing this out so that you understand, both of you. You would insist he overreacted, that no one should be that suggestible. He would think of the abject label again, have no use for himself, and think the whole thing useless. If at the same time you seemed overly critical—to <u>him</u>, now—of a manuscript, say, or his missing sessions, then it seemed approval was denied him from the one person whose integrity he trusted.

In his own way of course he is also a perfectionist, and felt himself falling far short. Do not stress so much that he must go out, as much as things you go out <u>for</u>, to your bars, shopping or whatever.

The stimuli encountered outside will automatically meet response and bring up other reasons for going out. The stimuli now is very limited. Once he is in stores for example the urge to buy is renewed. The mind automatically turns to things it would like.

Having a drink together in the yard is different than going out because it is the spontaneity of going that is to be encouraged.

The difficulty showed itself in Ruburt in keeping with the style of life that you were both accustomed to. You did not go out without a reason. The idea was to avoid chores, time taken from work, ordinary mixing with neighbors. You never felt a responsibility to go out, but a responsibility to stay home and work.

To tell Ruburt he has a responsibility to go out is a new idea. Instead, reignite the normal spontaneous desires he had to go out, despite the responsibility he felt he had to stay in. He always felt guilty taking a sunbath, for instance.

Both of you had to acquiesce to some extent in the situation. He did not choose for example a way of action, even physically, that would go against your style of life or ideas, but cleverly wove these into ideas you both initially deeply believed in. when you were working particularly at Artistic, you could not say he was out gadding around and not using his abilities. There he was in his chair. He could not leave it.

Now give us a moment.... The insights he received yesterday were quite legitimate, and show why he went along so readily with your projections. Earlier his own spontaneous nature, his desire for social intercourse, his simple love of fun, were strong enough to overcome the inner feelings that made him shy away from people. When these were undermined the inferiorities arose and he began to avoid people.

You seemed to have no use for neighborliness, particularly. This went along with ideas of dedication to work. In here you need a note concerning Ruburt's insights of yesterday. *(When Jane burned her finger via steam from a baked potato.)*

He is not to be babied. I am not saying that, the emotional encouragement however is important. He felt earlier that you withheld it because you had little use for anyone who needed it, that to request it was impossible to begin with. You could not demand it.

In the main he felt that you would have even less use for him, that you valued individual independence, and the pride of making it alone too much.

The car lost, was lost—no coincidence any more than your behavior during the flood. You know you chose the situation. It is important that a new car be purchased as soon as possible. He felt that the last one was purchased by you in order to reach your parents, begrudgingly, that you would not have purchased a "new one" for him for example.

This has its roots with the Lincoln—you follow me—and later when you did not offer to pick him up at nursery school, and told him in the same situation you would have too much pride to accept a ride.

I am mentioning these. Some are details. They are important. If you or Nebene ever thought that objective details were important then see how important Ruburt thinks subjective ones area. You lit cigarettes for him, particularly when you were in public, but you did not open the car door unless he asked you, or reminded you when that hurt or humiliated him.

Lighting his own cigarette in public was the one wild gesture of independence he allowed himself because you made such a point of lighting it for him. He was saying "In big things where I need help you often refuse to help, and your help is a gesture as when you light my cigarette, when I can do that myself." So if Nebene is a stickler for details and carries grudges, so did our friend.

Now you may take a break. And do not let me keep you too long. *("I'm okay.")*

The whole thing boils down to the fact that he thought and felt you would not help him, but demand that he use his own abilities and help himself independently of you. You held his arm once as he crossed a busy street, in, I believe, Cobbleskill, and he never forgot it. At other times you would say "Be careful," impatiently, "Watch where you are going. Don't you see that car," when he simply could not turn that quickly, and was terrified. There were other occasions when you held his arm and helped him and he remembers each one.

His idea was to chart his course, hope he could reach the other side of the street, and that the cars could see him.

He is deeply ashamed to have you see him go down stairs, because he fears your disapproval. He is afraid you will see him as he is, then, and wash your hands of such imperfection. For you to offer to help him would be of great benefit on the stairs when no one is around.

("I thought he didn't want me to. He's told me that often.")

He is afraid to, but if you saw the worst, as he thinks of it, and accepted him as he is, then help him, he can be pleased to show you any improvement. The improvement will follow if my suggestions are followed, and if both of you understand the reasons as given.

(10:21—10:55.)

Now. Some of these extreme reactions on Ruburt's part were brought about by his psychic understanding of Nebene, so he could not adequately communicate with you. If you reacted as Nebene you would later rationalize the results to him—while he would know in that (underlined) instance he was not projecting so he could not trust his reactions toward you.

Your explanation of a Nebene reaction would be so reasonable, later. You could not understand his insistence that you gave him a withering (underlined) look, but he felt it with the vehemence behind it. Against that he became vehement himself, stubborn, and determined to fight in you a quality that on the other hand he did not honestly think you possessed.

This put him on guard so that he would then often misinterpret ordinary remarks that you made. Had the two of you not let your own communication lag, such misunderstandings would not have occurred.

Ruburt dispensed with our sessions on a regular basis with a vengeance after Nebene showed himself, toward the end of the book *(Seth Speaks)* in the living room.

Now all of this can be remedied by interaction on both of your parts, and the willingness on both of your parts to give-and-take and not be afraid. Both of you often try to hide in your work from normal daily intercourse with others, and to make your work carry the burden of your humanity. That can only dehumanize your art, when carried to the extremes.

I am not telling you that dedication to work is not good, as you know, but it cannot take the place of all other human interest and communication.

Now I bid you a good evening—and there are still other sessions that both of you can read to your advantage. *(Meaning deleted ones.)*

And some day you will not need me to interpret your feelings to each other. You will do it quite directly, and our sessions will be on other matters.

("Thank you, Seth. Good night." 11:07.)

DELETED SESSION
JULY 31, 1972 9:15 PM MONDAY

(Jane was ready for the session at 8:45, so we sat for it in our bedroom for extra privacy. Seth didn't appear; however, although Jane said she felt him around at various times. Finally at 9:15 she said "I've been set up. Instead of telling us about it, Seth's letting me feel the emotions of that young girl you were involved with when you were Nebene, at the time of Christ...." This was in or near Constantinople. The girl's name was Sharabena, and she was Jane in that life as I was Nebene.

(See the deleted session for July 19, 1972. Now Jane looked rather uncomfortable. She said little at first, though I could tell she was recalling material from that past relationship. Actually the relationship in question, while called a reincarnational one, is a parallel one to our own. It is happening <u>now</u>, not two thousand years ago. Whenever I mention a "past life," this is what I actually mean. Jane also endorses this idea.

(The following material is taken from notes I made at the time, and memory. It wasn't recorded because we weren't prepared. Jane spoke too rapidly much of the time for verbatim notes also. Consequently what is cited isn't in order, either, although this doesn't seem important in this case. "We were called Zaphorites then," Jane said. "I feel like yelling and kicking." She kicked my foot very lightly. I was prepared if she did go into a rage, but this didn't develop. "I was part of that cult Seth told you about last time...you know where it was. You really had no use for me or for yourself, while we were together," she said. "You hated yourself but you couldn't stay away from me."

("Why, I was <u>really</u> beautiful then...I used to pee on our robes—I ripped them

off us," she said, *"when we were alone. You wanted me to. But you wouldn't be seen in public with me, you kept the whole thing secret. You were ashamed to be seen with me—just like you got ashamed to be seen with me now, after I got my symptoms.... I even loved you then, too, like I do now."*

(Jane displayed mild symptoms of anger and resentment, which grew somewhat more vehement at times. She also smiled. *"Why, that's where Sumari came from. Don't you see? I sang and I danced."* In here she sang some Sumari songs. I thought them especially beautiful. They weren't loud but very melodious and softly-syllabled. In between the songs she spoke to me in Sumari. During these episodes I could follow the meanings quite easily; ritual was involved, as well as passion. Listening, I felt a marked regret, and wondered that this other life had seemingly assumed such a strong place in our "own" lives. I asked Jane about this later.

(*"I was so beautiful, then,"* she said, *"so perfect physically that I relied on that. I disdained anyone who wasn't physically perfect. I paid no attention to the beggars, or people who showed imperfection...I used to taunt you. I came to your school once: I sashayed around your classes and you just about hit the ceiling...."*

(*"I'm ready to quit getting even now if you are,"* Jane said in answer to a question of mine. *"Now, I get the messages and you have to write them down, whereas before you had the ancient records and made the copies yourself. I wasn't needed, in that way. But I was spontaneous, like I am now, and you needed that then just like you do now,"* she said with emphasis. *"You were very rigid in the way you made lines, in your work. It's like it was all black and white then. This time though you're adding to the lines, and I wanted to be here when you put flesh on them through your painting."*

(*"You chose your father in this life because in many ways you were like him as Nebene. And I chose my mother, who turned out crippled, for similar reasons, I guess. You also picked your father so you could watch a family situation under those terms, because you knew you weren't going to have any children in this life. And your father wasn't nearly as anxious to have children as you might have thought, either, this time...."*

(There was more, of course, that I didn't get down, or recall, but it would follow the same vein. It was very revealing. It served to make me think anew that when such memories are recalled consciously, then those involved are compelled to deal with them. I felt a strong depression and regret, as stated before; I could have asked more questions. I didn't feel like defending myself very often. In answer to a question, Jane said that although reincarnational data would remain buried in many cases, it would still have to be dealt with, worked out in the present life in present terms.

(We took a break at 10 PM. During this time we received a call from my brother Bill, in Rochester, New York. We then had a discussion that lasted until

10:25, when Seth came through.)

Now, good evening.

("Good evening, Seth.")

—and we will begin part two of this evening's session. To speak in terms of mastering a situation already phrases a situation in poor terms. *(A remark I made during discussion, etc.)* You choose situations in order to learn and understand. The two of you, now, chose that aspect of your lives together in this life, to help you understand the meaningful relationship between spontaneity as connected with the emotions and creativity, and discipline as connected with the intellectual: to feel and understand the creative tension that connects them both, to learn the personal aspects of emotional relationships as they affect others, and the reflection of the emotions into creative endeavor. You served to help Ruburt find in this life direction. He also helped spur your own sense of direction in your early days together, when you turned from commercial art.

The commercial art served your emotions quite simply. It allowed you to release your emotions in stereotyped impersonal ways. Some situations, drawn, might be of highly charged areas—the Spillane strips, for example—yet the release of the emotion was stereotyped. You knew that one of Ruburt's purposes would be to insist upon the expression of your emotions to him personally. Because of other life aspects you knew this.

You both knew the tension that would also result, for you would to some strong degree resist. He needed direction however, and he knew that you would help give it to him. You would help him mold and direct his own strong emotional nature. You would have gone to the most considerable lengths to help direct his energy. He would have gone, and has gone, to considerable lengths to allow you to freely begin to express your emotional reality to him.

All of these purposes and strains were apparent from the day you met. He quite rightly thought—in, now, a certain framework—"How sick do I have to get?"

Now you gave him great help in achieving direction, and could not understand why he did not understand this, and that naturally you were pleased with his progress. But in your <u>emotional</u> (underlined) reaction you did not show your pleasure. You have, now, begun to reach him emotionally. This is your goal as well as his.

You have always wanted, in this life, to express yourself emotionally in that fashion. You taught him how to direct his emotions in his work. Because of the tensions and the challenges, however, and for other reasons having to do with this existence, Ruburt became worried that you would not relate to him in the emotional way that his nature demanded. You asked me how you could relate to him emotionally. Do you remember, in a recent session?

("Yes.")

Now I tell you that you are doing so.

It is correct *(as Jane had remarked)* that you allowed your feelings to show when you were angry or annoyed.

We cannot have a session until dawn. I want to give you, therefore some more immediate suggestions. You have, you know, done well with Ruburt since our last sessions. He needed a while to be reassured that you were not going to change back. He does not want you to baby him, nor do I. He is worried that you will think he does.

The foot *(when Jane lost a large part of a callous)* is an excellent sign, and it also shows you both what suggestion can do. You mentioned the foot specifically, reminding him several times, and this reinforced the suggestions.

Now with Ruburt, not necessarily generally, specific suggestions work well, when they are not overdone for example, and the progress then serves as an extra reinforcement. Regardless of the reasons, there are habits of thought, specifically, regarding the symptoms, for example. *Psycho-Cybernetics* programs will help him there, dehypnotizing him. If he imagines himself easily and playfully, now, mounting the stairs or going down, this will help. He must not tell himself "The next time I will do it right," but do it as a game, imaginatively.

You must help him realize that physically he can do more than he realizes. Your emotional rapport now automatically helps. Many of your old sessions on that sort of thing specifically will be of benefit. Again, remark upon any improvements. Do not at this point judge him against your idea of perfect performance.

("I don't.")

Now. Give us a moment. *(Pause at 10:55.)*

With the emotional rapport, and following through on the suggestions given, there will be added improvements, and some quite startling. Money-wise you will be fine, and trust Ruburt in money matters. Your shelter (in quotes) "problem" will be taken care of. You will do well.

The main problem being the emotional rapport. Now while this has shown itself in Ruburt's symptoms, it also showed itself in your work. Yet it was not your problem alone, but a challenge for both of you, as stated earlier in the session. It is important that you see that clearly also, so if you have questions on it ask me when you read this over.

Now, I bid you a fond good evening—and the early part of the session was under my auspices.

("Yes. Thank you very much, Seth. It was very good, and much appreciated. Good night." 11:00 PM.)

DELETED SESSION
AUGUST 2, 1972 9:16 PM WEDNESDAY

("Come on," Jane said at 9:05, as she waited for Seth to come through. We'd sat for the session at 8:50, when Jane said she was ready. This was the first time I'd heard her express her impatience at Seth, as though <u>everyone</u> was supposed to be ready when we wanted a session.

(Finally at 9:15 Jane "felt Seth around." "I'm not blocking," she repeated several times, reiterating that she really wanted the session, no matter what it said.)

Now. Good evening.

("Good evening, Seth.")

I have a few more suggestions.

Without going into reincarnational information just now: from this life Ruburt got into the habit of not physically expressing emotion. Some of the reasons were given in other sessions. He was demonstrative, but not demonstrative.

Fears and deep worries were not given physical expression. When your own communications became somewhat limited, he did not express worries to you, and brooded inwardly. He needs to realize that he can indeed physically express himself.

Now give us a moment. I suggest therefore that he make an attempt to express his moods, both joyful and sorrowful, in physical terms through body motion. Encourage him in physical activities. Even small successes, as he sees definite improvements, will be of great inner value. Try a simple game of pitch and catch, for example, but some physical release in terms of playful activity. Even slow dancing, for example, until he can manage fast dancing, but the use of bodily rhythm.

Play your radio—another example—and the two of you dance to it at home if you want. The outside atmosphere is good, however. When his legs bother him, they do want activity. I am trying to give you, again, some immediate helpful methods.

The use of your apartment: he can rather easily inspire himself along that line, even in cleaning and fussing, where the body activity is secondary to another desired secondary end. Any ideas along these lines that you think of will be of benefit, even if only having him once or twice a day walk as well as he can up and down the hall.

The desire to go places and do things, or buy things, or see people—all of these things are good because they imply physical action. You sidestep many of the blocks to action when the stimulus is a good one. Do you follow me?

("Yes." This is an excellent point.)

Do not let the fear he told you of this evening go below the surface again.

(At the supper table Jane expressed a fear that, although both of us are well aware of it, she seldom mentions: that she won't be able to recover, that the symptoms have gone too far, have been around too long for full recovery, etc. This is indeed charged material.)

Many have been in far worse situations, and healed themselves. He should not overestimate the poor points of his condition. The fear can make him do this, so he seems even far worse physically that he is. It does not lead to a realistic picture, then. Instead to dire images of being for example, bedridden.

A sensible look at the picture therefore will show him that he is indeed far better than that feared image. Again, there <u>must</u> (underlined) be a concentration upon the health that he does have, and the freedoms he does enjoy, for these will lead to greater freedoms. This is his end of the picture right now, and what <u>he</u> should do.

Now. He is onto something with his theory of Aspects, but the theory is not as yet fully developed. What he has so far will lead even further. When he types up the material received so far he will make other new connections.

(Jane received the material on Aspects, as she calls it, during two days just before the disastrous flood that swept Elmira on June 21—23, 1972.)

Look over the notebook of last summer. The methods used then will work with far greater effectiveness now because of the other information you have received, and the necessary changes in your relationship that have occurred.

Do not wait for proof. Ruburt must act as if he has the resources, and then the resources show themselves. When he finds himself negatively imagining a situation, he must immediately realize this as a negative habit pattern. Then re-imagine the circumstances, seeing himself performing adequately, but without telling himself that he must be therefore perfectly all right on the next occasion. Do you follow me?

("Yes.")

You may take your break.

(9:35. At break I asked Jane some questions about her Aspect theories. She did very well, discussing them, and finished up being really enthused. She said she enjoyed talking about the ideas a great deal. Resume at 9:55.)

Now. The emphasis you see should be on doing things, without worrying about how they will be done. On the end, not the means. This is where Ruburt gets confused. That is extremely important.

(Yes. This is excellent material.)

A small example. If he wants new curtains or clothes, then the stimuli automatically activates the body to perform. Now you have seen that in operation. When he concentrates instead upon how he is going to get to the store, he is concentrating on the means.

Go out again to your establishments, where the environment itself is suggestive, you see. Do not worry if the first time our Ruburt does not perform; nor should he, but cultivate the environment in which this is normal, and he will react to the stimuli.

The idea of a ride will get him down the steps, while worrying about how he will get down the steps does not help. These are small but important points. I mentioned before the benefit of groups. Do you recall—the exchange of energy, and so forth.

("Yes.")

A concentration upon his work, and not upon the symptoms. It is extremely important that he understand this, and break that circle. We want a concentration outward now, away from the self, so that the self can heal itself. Again let him paint, and consistently. He will find himself standing up at an easel.

The concentration away from the self is the most important point I can give him now. The concentration should be on work and pleasure and activities. Have him read this; and I expect him to follow these suggestions as well as you followed the information I gave you. *(Emphatic.)*

The class activity is good for him now. Both classes, and the changes he has made are beneficial. He needs the relationship with people. Now give us a moment.

I am not going to tell him where Aspects will lead. I do not want to spoil the fun <u>for him</u>. I do want him to know that he is on the road to something, and that it will help him understand me far better.

I should also open up some further experiences with both Seth II, Cyprus, and *Oversoul Seven*. I am letting our book go for now, but we will be returning to it and with Ruburt's full consent. I would like to add here that had he taken my early suggestions, he would not have become involved with spiritualistic literature, or groups or individuals.

You may take another brief break.

(10:07—10:30.)

Now. Tell Ruburt I said this:

He is physically capable of performing now with much better flexibility than he does, and with comparative physical ease and comfort, at this time. He has therefore simply hypnotized himself into believing he cannot.

Ask him to take this for granted, to accept my statement as true. The methods given this evening will allow him to act and perform with far greater ease and effectiveness, therefore. His <u>physical</u> (underlined) condition is not as bad therefore as it appears. Do you follow me here?

("Yes.")

There is a distinction. Now. Using the body <u>as it is now</u>, with its abilities, will automatically help to readjust such physical problems as the bent legs. Do you see the difference?

("Yes.")

The muscles will cease fighting each other. Now I <u>do</u> expect all of this to be followed. I am laying down therefore definite suggestion. A program of sorts, and I will expect progress reports this time. In other words, tell him, I am not giving the session for my benefit but for his, and not to hear myself talk. And I know I have your cooperation.

If you will think of this, both of you now, and you must, as a creative challenge, this will be of great benefit. Now give us a moment.

I want to see his days filled with different kinds of activity, therefore. Not that he feel rushed, not that you begin running from place to place, but that the concentration be as directed.

And if this is done you will see results, You have seen some. Your compliments are always the frosting on the cake, and he responds to them more than you imagine. You respond to his compliments, you see, and have always basked in them.

He should not compare his physical condition with your own, however, but feel himself unfold and open. Do you have any questions?

("Not particularly." Because Seth had done a great job, etc.)

Then I will let this be our session for the evening.

("It's very good.")

We expect good results from it, and you are doing very well indeed, and should enjoy an opening in your own work. My heartiest regards, and a fond good evening.

("Thank you very much, Seth. The same to you, and good night." 10:40.)

DELETED SESSION
AUGUST 7, 1972 9:25 PM MONDAY

(Today we returned from a weekend visit with my brother Dick in Rochester, New York. My mother, who now lives with Dick and his wife and family, made the trip back with Jane and me as far as the parking lot at Enfield Glen, Ithaca, where we met my other brother, Loren. Mother was transferred to Loren's car during an

interlude in a driving rainstorm. She is to spend a couple of weeks with Loren and his wife Betts before returning to Rochester.

(While we were in Rochester I mentioned a question to Jane that I thought Seth ought to consider. According to the chronology of events that Jane made up from her old notebooks last year, the symptoms began <u>before</u> the psychic manifestation of her abilities. At the time this knowledge was a surprise to us, since we'd fallen into the habit of thinking the symptoms were an outgrowth of the psychic abilities.

(In a recent deleted session, Seth told us that Jane's symptoms deepened after she held a session for a friend of Venice McCullough's a few years ago. The friend committed suicide, and Jane regarded the session as a failure. My question simply wanted to explore the relationship between the onset of symptoms before the psychic work, and the fact that a psychic "failure" had the ability to deepen them. While I could make intuitive guesses as to connections here, I preferred to hear what Seth had to say.

(In our talk before the session, I had the feeling that Jane kept sliding away from the direct consideration of the question. She often went into detail concerning the suspected session, without saying anything about the fact that a psychic experience could make worse symptoms that had begun before the psychic work, per se, had become conscious knowledge to us.

(Once again we sat for the session before 9 PM, and once again it was slow in coming about. Even though Jane told me she felt Seth around at 9 PM. At 9:20, she told me about the "shuddering" feeling she'd experienced in her chest in Rochester, after I had first mentioned the above question to her. Jane said that when I brought up the question again tonight she felt the shuddering return, although it was located farther down her torso, in the stomach area, this time. At 9:25, though, just before the session began, she said the feeling was better.)

Now, good evening.

("Good evening, Seth.")

I want Ruburt to read his last session daily *(of August 2, 1972)*. He has not done so. He has made an attempt however to follow the suggestions, and this has given him some pointers about his subjective state of mind. Some improvements have indeed shown themselves. But the entire session is important, and each of the suggestions is geared for him.

He did not tell you the many times he used my suggestions with good results in Rochester, simply because when he had the time to talk to you other matters had arisen, and he forgot some of the instances.

On one occasion he did almost come very close to the feeling of freedom necessary, but all the suggestions need to be followed, not simply the ones he happens to remember at any given time. The suggestions are given in such a way that one makes the other easier to follow. They work as a group therefore also.

Give us a moment. Again, the session to be read daily for a while. It is very important that when he feels caught in a dilemma—to move because he wants something, or not to move because he thinks it will hurt—that he not prolong the dilemma, but move despite his mood at the time.

His idea of trying to help others was a good one. This involved physical motion in Rochester. He will tell you. I will have something to say regarding the affair you mentioned, but give us a few moments on that.

I am afraid I am holding him to the line with that particular session If he wants my help, therefore, he can no longer avoid following my advice—and tell him that I know he has been, but he must do so more completely, with that session.

I am repeating myself for a good reason. The concentration must be on projects, and the more concentration is placed upon projects, the less will feed the symptoms. Have him tell you of the Rochester incidents.

Now the affair with Venice's friend involved the false prophet idea again. It seemed to Ruburt, with his understanding, that if his information was coming from a paranormal source, and that source was good, then it must also prove itself to be infallible, or he was a false prophet. He also felt accused by you, believing that if he was using his abilities really fully, as you wanted him to, then there would have been a way provided so the woman would not die.

He felt that the burden rested upon him, which of course was hardly the case. He also felt that Venice needed the proof of that woman's complete recovery, and felt that perhaps his own doubts or fears prevented delivery of the particular information that might make the woman decide to live.

The whole class knew of the session. He was disappointed in me, also, thinking that I should have been able to save the woman. At the same time he resented being put in the position to begin with. His mother had attempted suicide several times. On a deeply unconscious level he worried that perhaps symbolically he did not want to save the woman—who was, incidentally a mother. He felt responsible for his own mother's suicide attempts, to <u>some</u> degree, and this added to the situation.

He felt he let you down also, you see. He had hoped to be a great psychic, in his terms, about then. But a great psychic, you see, should have been able to raise the dead and save the living. He completely forgot that personalities have their own choices to make. He had also been reading about the great percentage of successes with faith healers, for example, and he considered this a personal failure of an important magnitude.

At the same time he was feeling that he would not be a great writer either, you were telling him he was using only about a tenth of his abilities, and so in both areas he was not living up to his expectations or yours, to his way of seeing. There are other old tie-ins here, in that he was always considered very good or very bad, in that people always liked him instantly or disliked him instantly. You could not ignore him. But the contrasts were always stressed in early life, so that if you were not the one you were the other.

He was giving a good deal of time to our sessions. The woman's session, to him, was to some degree a test of the material's practical worth to someone in deep trouble. The woman's death obviously meant that it did not pass. Again, he forgot the integrity of the personality. It must make its own choices, and may accept or refuse help given. The woman did not want the session, and had made a decision she did not intend to change. Venice's will or anyone else's could not stand against that.

Now you may take your break.

(9:51—10:15. The subject matter of our discussion is spelled out in the following material.)

Now, I have been following your discussion, and to some good degree you are correct. Ruburt has allowed himself to become hypnotized by certain images and ideas, that he considered true.

In the picture of reality he has been accepting, for the reasons given in past sessions, he did not believe he could move capably. As matters progressed he did not believe it was possible for him to perform physically in a normal manner. You must act in accordance with your idea of reality. You cannot do something unreal.

Some important blockages would therefore come when he tried to tell himself he could do something, such as walk downstairs correctly, when at the same time he did not believe it possible. This was in my suggestions I emphasized the ends rather than the means. It is also why I want the session read so often, assuring him as it does that even in his present physical condition alone he can perform with much better flexibility—

("Yes, except that he doesn't believe it.")

—than he previously believed. If the suggestions in the session are followed, they will alter his picture of his own reality, and through action. Naturally the session must be followed and not just read, from the sketching or painting suggestions right on. If that session is followed faithfully for two months, you will see some nearly spectacular changes.

Now. The session contains more than is apparent, and there are developments that can arise from it as a direct result of concentration being directed elsewhere, a release of energy seeking new outlets in other words.

Try to adjust your own attitude as you hope Ruburt will adjust his. Encourage him therefore to follow the session, and assure him that you believe he can follow it. Do not tell him ahead of time that he will not succeed. Do you follow me?

("Yes.")

The emotional rapport, and your greater acceptance of him, expressed, helped in making this inroad possible. The dent in his armor, as you put it.

Now. Thoughts have their own energy. Your thoughts and everyone else's. Your own greater awareness now, with Ruburt, to him represents the first real break in your armor. It will also serve to release feelings of joy that you have inhibited. These feelings are released not only in paintings that you are working on, say, now, but on paintings that were completed earlier. Your emotional reality permeates everything with which you come in contact—across the board, regardless of the time element.

These feelings, this extra vitality, enriches then paintings that you did in the past earlier. These feelings were picked up by the people who have been buying your paintings of late, and the same feelings will radiate outward, you see, wherever the paintings may be. As the session is followed Ruburt's joy will be liberated through the body in the same way. Do you follow me?

("Yes."

(This is excellent material, well worth remembering. I want to keep it in mind especially re paintings and sales, of course. It's still working as I type this, on a class night; one of Jane's students bought another portrait. This one I'd finished but a couple of months ago. I didn't expect this sale. Even as I write this paragraph, another student asked the price on a still life I painted a couple of years ago....)

You are quite correct, that conscious involvement is necessary on Ruburt's part. But then the released energy can act on the images in the same way that the feelings acted on the paintings.

The feelings or emotions automatically reach out, therefore, altering all objects within your reality, but from the particular focus point of its emergence. In Ruburt's case the body, where the lack of joy showed, and in your case in the paintings, where the greater expressiveness will now add—and has—its own vitality.

As you help yourselves then you help the other, and as you help the other you help yourself.

(Again, this is excellent material.)

I did have some interesting comments to make concerning your visit, but it can wait if you would like to retire early.

("No, I'm all right.")

Then give us a moment... To some extent, in certain terms, you have upset both of your brothers, and your younger brother's comments concerning money were directly related to two events in your life.

(While taking a drive to the drugstore on Sunday, my brother Dick told me he felt he "didn't have much" as far as money was concerned. He was quite incensed over published reports that 10% of the population in this country controls something like 58% of the wealth, etc. He talked about owning more land, farms, etc., and that what he has, with his wife, represents a compromise as far as acreage, the house, commuting distance, etc., is concerned. To Jane and me, he is very well off indeed.)

One, the fact that you left your job, and two, the fact that you have a new car. If you had the recorder I could tell you more about it quicker.

("It's all right."

(This is all news to Jane and me. Of course I left the job at Artistic last February, but didn't tell Loren and Betts this officially until phone conversations after the June flood. Jane and I bought the car after the flood also.)

First of all, because you are the eldest, and because of your father's position, because you were making good money as a young man, Loren braced himself against your situation at that time. You were the one starting out making money. Both of them wanted to beat you at the game, simply because you were the eldest, but as they began you gave it up.

In the back of their minds they are suspicious that had you continued you would have beaten them, and now they can never know differently. They cannot understand, either of them, how you could leave your job, their own sense of worth is so bound in possessions. They are deeply insecure, but good men. For you to leave your job and have a new car is doubly mysterious. They respect you, for that matter, in a quite mysterious way to them, that they do not understand.

They suspect that you might end up financially well off while taking a route that to them is completely illogical. If you can get possessions while not having a worthwhile job, then they must work that much harder for more possessions, to prove their way correct, and yours lacking. This is not a malicious intent. They must have more to show for all their work, you see.

If you do well financially, then your well-doing puts a burden upon them, to understand the validity of your kind of life, and Ruburt's. This makes them question in ways that make them uncomfortable. Yet you do what you do for them, also. For certain portions of their personalities, under different circumstances, tempered differently, have leanings in those directions. But the core of their being does not.

To a lesser extent the same applies to Ruburt and the sister-in-laws. A woman choosing to have no children is not a woman they can understand, yet each wonders what other abilities of their own they might have nourished, or what they would have been. For Ruburt to make money, to become known, puts this same kind of burden upon them, you see, of understanding.

The two of you represent the loners, of course, who strike out for themselves. There is much more here, but I suggest that we wait. You can have the information whenever you want it, or request it. There are connections with the children, where you serve as counterpoints.

I bid you a fond good evening.

("Good evening, Seth. Thank you very much.")

(10:56. After the session I told Jane I thought Seth didn't finish dealing with the question I'd outlined before the session. As Jane herself had done in discussing it, Seth spent much time exploring the second part of the question, relating to Venice's friend, while not saying anything about the onset of symptoms before the psychic abilities showed themselves.)

DELETED SESSION
AUGUST 9, 1972 9:08 PM WEDNESDAY

Now—our session will begin.

("Good evening.")

I am following through, you see. And this is what I want, where I can comment as we go along on Ruburt's progress.

The entire program, all of the suggestions, must automatically become a part of Ruburt's life. The session in a nutshell contains my recommendations at his particular point. As I somewhat expected, he is trying too hard on some issues.

These, therefore, are further comments relating to how he is following the session, and adjustments for him to make.

It is somewhat natural, now that he has determined to get better, that he become aware of his own evasive actions, as he has. He is not to let them concern him now. Such concern merely brings them further into focus. Simply say "to hell with them, they will not last."

He is not to make an effort to get up correctly then, but instead to take it for granted that the program will automatically and is automatically allowing him to. His trust in his body will grow as the program is implemented, and you have barely begun to utilize it.

I want it read daily for its suggestive value, and also to acquaint Ruburt with its many aspects. Some physical activity, if only dancing by himself with the radio, should be a part of this program. I specifically suggested painting for several reasons. I want him to paint steadily at the easel, as mentioned, where he is standing, but with his attention directed elsewhere, and because of the particular refreshment painting gives him—the release from work and pressure.

It also involves subsidiary accomplishment that is not demanding, but that would always be a necessary part of any avocation of his. Now I suggest a different approach, also, that may help change the focus from physical symptoms to physical accomplishment. I suggest a game. I believe he will fall in with this idea easily. I want him to list his physical activities, so see how many new ones he can perform in a playful manner. These can be as simple activities or motions as he wants. He can pick any area he chooses, but he is to tell you about the accomplishments.

This is not putting you in the role of a taskmaster, now, but I want you to join with him: "Can you do this? Come on, it's only a game, see what you can do." He likes that kind of challenge as long as there is no stigma attached to nonachievement. And the idea is, quite simply, to reward him for achievement.

This can involve anything, and can start out at levels of achievement he knows he can reach, while gradually trying other levels. He knows for example, he can walk up—up, now—the first flight here from the landing, without as much difficulty as the other stairs.

He can begin by walking up that flight, seeing how many times he can do it without too much trouble, but paying no attention to the way he goes down, which has been much more difficult for him. Do you follow me?

("Yes.")

Seeing how fast he <u>can</u> walk—this is another example—in the house, say, away from pressure. The idea here is on accomplishment.

All of the rest of that session is important, even suggestions that do not seem emphasized. I mention this specifically since in the session itself I tell you that the concentration should be on work and activities, and <u>not</u> (underlined) on the condition you are trying to get rid of.

Finishing *Seven* itself will be of benefit. You should get out on weekends, both of you, or some other time. Now give us a moment. *(Pause at 9:30.)* I want it emphasized though that I will work with Ruburt on this basis. Pretend you are paying me several hundred dollars a week, tell him. Now. As I have told you, there is no real line between consciousness and unconsciousness. They are both aspects of something that you do not as yet understand. They are aspects of being.

I am bringing this up because of the discussion in class relating to nonevents. And give us some time with this material.

In your terms consciousness springs from unconsciousness, but the unconsciousness from which it springs is far more "conscious" in terms both of scope and intensity, than the consciousness you know.

There are events on what you would call the minus side of being. They would be nonevents to you, not only because you would not experience them but because, in your terms now, they would seem to rush back through the source of unconsciousness. They would be unhappening, unbecoming, again in your terms.

They would rush through being to unbeing, vanishing, it would seem to you, into extinction. On that other side of being however, where unbeing would seem to be, on the underside of existence as you think of it, is a phenomena that can hardly be translated into words. There is a nonevent within and surrounding each event.

From these nonevents all events are actualized. In the dilemma of what I can only call cosmic creativity, there are always potentials seeking for expression. No single event actualizes all of its possibilities.

I am not saying that nonevents are only potential events, however. Nonevents represent the tension, in your terms between being and nonbeing, the power and surge of unactualized being, <u>ever</u> (underlined) "present" (in quotes). There is no beginning or end therefore to nonevents. Every event is a portion of a nonevent. Now you may take your break.

(9:47—10:08.)

Now. You must keep up your communication, particularly in those areas where you do not understand each other. *(The material on nonevents should be read to class.)*

Another point I wanted to make about your painting. The sale of your faces should show you that these do have meaning for other people also, though they are not conventional portraits.

You and Ruburt have always done well expressing your intellectual ideas to each other. It was your emotional feelings that you did not express adequately, and again, do not neglect your intimate relationship.

Were your recorder set up again, I would simply chat with you in a give and take session that would allow you to ask more questions. You are both in a period of transition. You have particularly been doing well with Ruburt. A touch of the playful attitude however will help.

(Several pages in here were put in with the regular material, since they dealt

with the flood of June 21, 1972, etc. Session 611. The following excerpts were interspersed with the general material after the break at 10:31—10:44.)

Now. One remark. Simply tell him not to try so hard. Follow the session, trust it will help, and the other suggestions. Those not yet tried in the session will automatically take care of some of the initial reactions. Do you follow me?

("Yes."

(Then later: "How about reincarnational material about Ruburt?" In relation to symptoms, etc.)

That will be included as it is pertinent, and you may specifically request it at any given session....

(End at 10:54.)

DELETED SESSION
AUGUST 30, 1972 9:45 PM WEDNESDAY

(Richard Bach, the author of Jonathan Livingston Seagull, *left this morning after having been our guest since Monday, the 28th. He called Jane last Friday from his home in Bridgehampton, New York; he wanted some insights into his writing of* Seagull; *Richard attended ESP class last night, and heard Seth, Sumari, etc. Jane also gave an excellent reading for him.*

(Richard's editor at Macmillan wants to see whatever work Jane has available, that is uncommitted.)

Good evening.

("Good evening, Seth.")

Now. First of all, I have some comments. Again, I am sorry you have to write this down rather than simply listening. Because I am in a chatting mood, and I have goodies.

("Okay.")

The meeting with your Seagull friend was significant for many reasons. Symbolically, *Seven (Oversoul)* was important because the book showed Ruburt the wedding of psychic ability and creative ability, emerging as fiction and art form, and his baby.

The connection between the two was securely made. The meeting with your Seagull friend however also helped cement this realization on his part. The acceptance from another writer, simply on that level alone, was important: But the meeting with someone who also shared psychic and writing ability was vital.

Ruburt realized that he had held back psychically. We have discussed this. The dream book manuscript, again, represented that dilemma. At one point he tried to insist upon the dominance of the conscious mind, and became pedantic. Seeing that his own ability is greater than our Seagull's—in certain, now, important areas—he realizes what can be done when he does go ahead.

The last session for him—that is, the last key session I gave—is also connected here, for in following it he lifted himself enough above negative attitudes so that he could attract such a meeting. The psycho-cybernetics that he also began because I told him to do what he had done last summer also helped. So he opened himself up to influences that he needed.

I told you that financially he would do well. The same elements appear in your own painting and in their sales. Of course I want that session, and those immediately following, followed faithfully, and the routine as he has now developed it. He knows what that is. I also want you to read those sessions, and the key one particularly—once a week or so, though he is to read the one each day.

("I usually do read it," etc.)

His reading for Richard was also symbolic. It represented the acceptance by another writer of his psychic abilities as well as himself.

Now some connections between Ruburt and Nebene are obvious, though perhaps not apparent. Ruburt always knew from childhood unconsciously of the strength of his personality, its potential, and his ability to sway others.

He did therefore develop a strong conscientious self, so that these abilities would be put to good purposes, and not frittered away. Until he was absolutely certain that he was on the right track, he would hold back, as indeed he has—but only to a certain degree, as indeed he has.

There are reasons, reincarnationally, for this caution. Nevertheless, the point has now been reached where he does realize that the basic self is good, and the abilities are being put to good purpose. The realization has to do with results from the sessions mentioned, and the ensuing events.

Now your physical situation will change. Using Richard as a case in point, Ruburt sees what happens when full consent is given. He has now an example that suits his <u>sometimes</u> (underlined) literal mind; but his following of the session made that example possible.

The overconscientious self therefore equates, you see, with Nebene's overconscientious self in other areas. Do you follow me?

("Yes.")

It is therefore no coincidence that Richard was a student of Nebene's, and the material on the reincarnational aspects *(that Jane gave in ESP class last night)* is quite correct. In so helping Ruburt, he *(Richard)* is also paying back a service to Nebene, for he owed him much.

(In his radio and TV tours, Richard offered to mention The Seth Material

and Seth Speaks, *to help boost sales. This besides asking his editor to read Jane's material.)*

I will very shortly now be involved in our new book, and with Ruburt's consent: and Richard's visit, or one of other probable events like it, was to occur before the book continued.

As Nebene, while attracted by Ruburt, and in love with her, you considered her evil, and your attraction to her as a weakness on your part, a debasement: so now you find yourself in the position of helping Ruburt understand that his basic nature is good, that he is not leading people astray, as in that life you thought he was.

At the same time, the existence of the Nebene characteristics served to bring to your attention the Josef characteristics. Nebene to some extent then was a trigger of creativity. The realization of Nebene would automatically lead you to question, to bring to your conscious attention characteristics that otherwise you may not have recognized; blocks to your creativity, and yet strong drives toward the nature of truth, from which your creativity also springs.

For Nebene's being was deeply involved with the search for truth. Nebene's students are also coming back to say hello—

("I've noticed that.")

—and he can be pleased with their progress. His desire for truth inflamed them, and all of their aspects, even while his methods served as counterparts against which they rebelled.

Now give us a moment.

Ruburt's way has been different in many respects than your own. Before this, in those terms, he has chosen lives of great contrast and extravagance, with one or two characteristics relatively predominating, either for example extremely intellectual—genius—or idiocy. Dire poverty or great wealth.

He was at one time possessed of a great desire for power, and led, in those terms now, many astray. It is for that reason that he so fears the false prophet idea. Give us a moment. Is your hand tired?

("No.")

This was when he was a male in Turkey, as the country has been called, and you were his cohort, as in the dream he had. There were two Turkish lives, one after another. He was a great leader, driven by the desire for power, and by a sense of purpose, in the Ottoman Empire. He wanted to conquer, and bring the world under Ottoman sway.

He used the sword—another reason, incidentally, why he does not want to hurt anyone now—and the magic of words, and was involved in wars against Christendom. He knew Pete *(Stersky, a member of Jane's ESP class)* who was then a dancer, a woman.

The two of you were exceedingly close in male comradeship—far more intense than any known now in your time. In your terms he was—in your terms from this standpoint—he was a fanatic against the Christians for religious, political and economic reasons. He feared Rome and hated it. It was no coincidence that Father Traynor used to read *Don Juan of Austria (in the Catholic Church the young Jane attended)*, for they knew each other at that time.

Ruburt demanded utmost obedience. He lived for the cause. Many were killed upon his word. His sense of energy was boundless, and he was convinced of his purpose. Toward the end of a long life, however, he began to doubt. Life was cheap. Give us a moment.

(Pause at 10:25.) But he took a nationalistic glory in killing his enemies. Each death he saw as a triumph for the cause.

I am not sure, here, if the word is Tartar. You were with him, but because of personal loyalty to him and the brotherhood of male with male was considered sacred—but you became appalled that he was leading his people into destruction.

He died, and came back as the next leader—this leader being the one that saw the final dissolution of the Ottoman Empire. He felt that he had led, in the second existence, a whole people astray, for a cause in which he had once completely believed, and given entire allegiance.

He determined then to keep this power to sway people in line, until, if ever, he was sure of his cause. He led armies, then, and to what end, he thought. It was in that life also that he knew Sue as the personality that sometimes has emerged between them.

Now take your break.

(10:30. Jane remembered the material. She's also had images. At break she got a series of images of the first ruler, bloodthirsty and joyous as he killed, she said. A great sword, a shield, cries; white teeth and dark skin. "And absolutely convinced of his views. I must be getting him bigger than life, because now I see him bounding all over Europe with his great big shield." She had these images or impressions off to her left.

(Resume at 10:45.)

Now this is one of the reasons why he was so worried in this life, about leading people away from Christendom, for he did it before.

In the first of those two lives, both of you to some extent tried to enforce your ideas of truth <u>through</u> force, physically. The use of great physical force therefore was used purposely. You were involved with your ideas of truth in an entirely different context, as was much of Europe at that time, and some of the world now.

You were not that out of keeping with your times, then. The whole world, more or less, was experimenting with the use of brutal force as an accepted method of enforcing ideas. Anything else was the exception. There are other connections with this life, in which Ruburt chose a woman for his mother who was helpless. Not only could he not attack her, but he was in a position where he must serve her.

Now the woman who was his mother this time had a connection with another leader—I am trying not to get distortions in here; you may have to check some of this later—I believe Charlemagne, and Ruburt slew him in battle, after he was first crippled. The two were bitter adversaries. Ruburt put himself in a position therefore where violence could not be used.

The mother had been particularly given to the mutilation of prisoners, and hence chose the physical condition finally—not, now, as punishment, but to understand the experience—and to develop abilities under those conditions.

It was then, when Ruburt found himself at all close to a position of any importance, that he came into difficulties, because people would begin listening to him again, and he had to be sure his message was a true one.

The personality however, tell him, lived according to his lights, possessed a primitive love of nature, and did, now, inspire others with heroism under the conditions chosen In the second existence mentioned, he was again a leader, but had learned the two-tongued nature of power, and allowed the Christians to win. In a way he handed that burden over to them. They had to grapple with it, and for several centuries.

Had they not, the history of the world as you know it would have been quite different. The Ottoman Empire ended up stripped of its power then on purpose, where the deceiving nature of power was given to Christendom, and in this our friend saved his people from a probable future in which the unsavory aspects of power predominated for them.

He took the temptation away. I have a small point here, in that Hitler represented as a bleedthrough from a probable reality—extremely interesting. He was a personality who literally should have been born back in those eras, and was not. In one respect he was like a time projection, appearing out of place, a psychological warp brought into displacement by a phenomena that psychologically could be likened to a natural phenomena like a volcano.

The energy from that time, the disturbance between Christendom and the East, generated such energy—very simply put, now—that the physical times could not contain it and it erupted, in your terms, into the future.

As an analogy, most events are this high. *(Jane held up her cigarette lighter.)*

The events in the times of the Crusades, for example, were this high. *(Jane raised an arm over her head, full length.)* Following the analogy the times, the physical times in which they would ordinarily have occurred, would have ended, say, here—*(Jane indicated a spot six inches above the lighter)*—but the energy was so great that it catapulted some of these events, displacing what you think of as time, so that they appeared, as Hitler did, where theoretically, now, they should not have.

This kind of displacement can occur, but in practical terms, the terms by which you judge time, this is unusual. Hitler appeared therefore as a far more vicious character against your current world, than he would have had those other times contained him.

Yet his emergence was important, reminding the race of the perils into which it could indeed fall. In many respects however Hitler was not a complete personality in usual terms. Part of his vitality and what would have been his redeeming qualities, were sunken in the past in which he did not exist.

Now man, despite all appearances, is always dealing with the nature of reality, and his historical periods are simply areas in which different methods and ways are tried—all, as he learns to manipulate and use the energy of which he and his world are composed. And all of these, therefore, these searches, exist at once in greater terms.

All of those involved in the Ottoman Empire had their reasons therefore, tell Ruburt, and the victims acquiesced to the basic assumptions of the time, as much as you and Ruburt did. The energy released was fantastic. It also involved the opening of many channels through which sheer vitality was made accessible and served as an impetus against which man could judge his progress.

There was an unabashed joy with the splendor of the body, and sensuous delight, that Ruburt can now remind himself of, and that served to help regenerate at least portions of Christendom that were given to ideals of bodily denial.

The Ottoman Empire's death in its own way regenerated Europe, and its energy gave birth to the civilization that you know. The death of the Ottoman Empire enriched Europe. The pagan "Joy of life" in its own way sparked new blood. Christendom would have died out otherwise, for it was already tired. Unwittingly therefore Ruburt aided the growth of Christendom as it became known.

Now, you can take a break or end the session as you prefer.

("We'll take the break."

(11:17. *This was actually the end of the session. While talking Jane had images in trance that she couldn't describe now, concerning Hitler and displacements "shooting out" of their times, etc.*

(After the session she had more impressions off to her left of the Turkish leader—"the white teeth and dark skin. He loved fancy clothes. He had enormous vitality, bounding about, killing with a joyful childlike innocence, if you can put it that way. He seems like a giant to me." Jane said her body reacted in different ways—"with a thrill, a chill, an empty stomach all at once....")

DELETED SESSION
SEPTEMBER 4, 1972 9:05 PM MONDAY

(At 9:05 Jane said, "I'm getting some real weird stuff. I'll tell you about it in a minute...." We were sitting for the session, but as things developed Seth never did come through.

(To recap: after supper tonight Jane told me she felt "warm." Our apartment was quite chilly in actuality, as it has often been since the June flood; both of us had been cold all day. Now Jane was warm and more relaxed than usual. I went to work in the studio on the illustrations for Oversoul Seven. *Jane told me later that after I left she began to get very strong feelings that the phone was going to ring, with some exceptionally good news for us. Possibly Richard Bach and his editor, Eleanor Friede, were involved. These feelings became so strong that Jane wrote out a description of them.*

(Jane's predictions have been very good recently. At 8:45 she came over to the living room for a session; I was still working. She had the idea she should rub between her eyes in a circular motion— "You know, where the third eye would be," she said. At the same time she was waiting for the phone to ring. When it did ring a few minutes later she called to me to answer it. It stopped ringing however after three times, long before I could get over to answer it.

(While I was getting set to take notes, Jane said she felt her subjective legs "going around in circles." She had stopped rubbing her forehead by now. She also felt that hands were pulling her legs down, straightening them. She sat leaning back in her rocker, very relaxed, eyes closed; at last she told me she got a whole lot of stuff that time.

("Some of which was great and some that I didn't like ... The eye thing was like a tunnel and I went through it, through matter. It wasn't as great as the time I went through the house next door, but this tunnel was very long and I went into another universe. I was floating and flying among stars and lights. Then I came down and there was this big body there. I landed on its head or shoulder. It was naked; like a transparent body because I could see the veins and nerves in it...."

("I began to move it from the outside, slowly, like a marionette But then I did-

n't like it, because it seemed to be in a wheelchair. I went ahead with it, but I didn't know whether it had died, or what." Now the tenant in the apartment above our living room began to play rock music very loudly, but Jane seemed undisturbed as she talked to me. Her eyes through most of the conversation were slitted open, her voice usual. She seemed to come out of the state temporarily. "I followed the body... through a series of chutes and came out like a butterfly."

("I made some connection between that wheelchair and this rocker, thinking it was a wheelchair, and that big portrait you painted of the patient in a wheelchair in the county hospital where your father was," she said. "Then I came out. I got nervous when I saw the great big thing was in the wheelchair, but I decided to go through with it whether it was me or not. Then I came out of it."

(9:25. "I've been doing something else," she said after a lengthy pause. "Wait a minute... Then I was behind my head. I rushed down my own spinal cord, into my body. Then I saw a lot of little tiny men. This is hilarious. They were inside my knees, with hoses, washing out my knees with crystal clear, pure water. Then they went to the back of my neck... Now they're climbing up the bones of my spinal column and straightening them out and doing things..."

("Now I feel really big—like that figure. Oh, I'm getting really bigger... like I'm really big and light like a balloon." She smiled at 9:30. "And now these little men've got little things like trowels, and they're taking scoops of white stuff out of my body and throwing it away. They spray something on the part first, that makes this white stuff soft, then they scoop it out."

(Jane had laughed, but now she sobered. "They're real tiny; they're building what looks like scaffolds in the backs of both of my knees. Now they've got bushels of blood, fresh blood, and they're throwing it into my veins... And now they're changing electrical fixtures in the back of my spine; and now my knees are lighting up...."

(9:35. "Now they're pulling out some short muscles between my knees and feet," Jane said. She touched the sole of a foot. "A lot of it down here had to do with up here, the knees.... It's funny because all this makes me feel so big. The little men are up under my arm and it feels like its floating up and out; they're lifting it up, and using a heat lamp on it under the armpit. I feel real good and relaxed there now..."

("I feel giant-sized now, though, again... It feels like my left leg is up higher than my right one, though I can see that it isn't. And it's straight. They're lifting it up and out from the hip, and doing something underneath it."

(9:40. "This must be my astral leg; it's falling back and forth from the knee; the heel touches my spine, which I can't do.... Now the little men are doing it with my right leg, but they're having more trouble with it than with the left one. But now they've got it. I'm getting a funny feeling now, like I'm almost physically up off the *floor, in a sitting position—I know I'm not—but it's almost as though the chair wasn't there."*

(*Jane burst out laughing, her eyes still slitted.* "Now it's as if I'm going back into the chair, only through it, my legs going through it. Then I was racing up a flight of stairs. Then I was in the chair again, only now it was like a wheelchair. I saw a devil image walking away from me in one direction, and on the other side of me an angel image, walking away; and I knew I had both these images of myself. Then they walked into each other and blended, standing in front of me," *she said,* "and while I didn't see this as clearly, it's what I am."

("Next I was running like a kid. I threw myself down in the grass and lay there and relaxed, lying on my back.... And now, see, I'm talking and these little men are working on my hands, my astral fingers. Wait," *Jane said, after a pause,* "I'm getting some words—"

(*In the same average voice she began:* "In the shadow of the image organized religion [at the same time my hands want to fly up], after it has been set up, has always been afraid of revelationary knowledge; to protect itself; and the Catholic Church in particular cast it in the form of a devil, which I was taught: the sin of pride, wanting to learn."

(*Jane continued:* "But that devil image comes from a long pagan line of earth gods, and always represented the innate knowledge inherent even in the earth itself. All the ideas of the fear of the inner self come from the basic division that has for so long existed in the minds of man since the birth of organized religion... Religion tried to make the devil into a black shadow of God, His counterpoint and yet opposite, but man forgot what counterpoint meant. Personified, for example, the devil is the fury of a storm, but disconnected from a storm's great creativity."

(*9:52.* "I feel like my hands are doing all these weird things in the air while I'm getting this material," *Jane said. The music from above was louder than ever, but she seemed to be oblivious to it.* "Then I went up like in a spiral through that room upstairs with all that music and energy, and shot out above it. My hands were tied but then they were cut loose and flew out in all directions. I feel like I'm really giant-sized, pacing through this room and talking." *Pause.* "I forgot: my head went up through the roof and I guess I was a giant walking over the earth. Then I was walking slower, and finally I was walking under water...." *I guess I better come out of it."*

(*Pause at 10 PM.* "I got too conscious of what I was doing," *Jane said,* "and of the music upstairs. But my hands feel so nice and warm. It's the first time I've been warm in three days."

(*At 10:05 the music from up above stopped, and I heard people leaving. Jane sat slumped in her rocker, very relaxed, eyes closed. Then she began to talk again.* "I heard the people go out upstairs. I was giant-sized again. My flesh felt like dough, the *little men were kneading it like dough. It's a real funny feeling, I can't really describe the sensation. The little men were working on my knees when I heard the kids upstairs leave. Before that they'd worked on my shoulders real fast, shaking my astral shoulders around and around...."*

(Jane's head moved rhythmically from side to side very slightly as she sat slumped in her rocker, eyes closed. *"My skin was too tight and they worked all over it. Then one ovary had a little black spot on it, and they snipped it off—and lifted it up somehow—and I thought that's why I haven't had my periods... I feel like I'm a giant to those little people, with this method of self-perception I'm using; now they're back working under my knees."* Jane paused at 10:15. *"They dipped my head down and took the top of it off. Then they scooped out some stuff like they did before, this time from where the top vertebrae meet the skull, and they threw all this stuff away. Then they worked on my shoulders."*

(*"I think I got the wheelchair image about this rocker, too,"* Jane said, *"because we first got it for your back.... My feet still feel like they're resting on air, but I know they're not,"* she said, looking down.

(We took a break. There was a little more to the session after we thought it was over, and I made notes about what was said without using verbatim quotes. Jane had some very beautiful images, she said, of the muscles of her neck and back as they supported her head. She could see into her body. She saw the muscles named first as a series of snakes with many heads; the heads changed into hands that supported her head and rotated it about very flexibly. Then came images of the muscles and fibers of her arms.

(We were evidently done by 10:31. When Jane got up she didn't seem to move about the room any faster. Yet, she said, she felt an image walking just ahead of her; at the same time the feeling of warmth had left her. Residual feelings and images from the session did remain with her, though.

(*"The images with the snakes and hands was one of the most beautiful things I've ever seen,"* she said.

(A note: Jane received a <u>letter</u> from Richard Bach the next day. Dick and his editor want to visit us September 19. This is covered in Jane's predictions and material received before the session tonight.)

DELETED SESSION
SEPTEMBER 6, 1972 9:19 PM WEDNESDAY

(Loud rock music was playing in the apartments above and below us as we sat for the session in our living room. We were sandwiched in between. *"I vaguely have the pyramid effect," Jane said at 9:10. Seth Two didn't come through, but some very interesting effects developed later in the session. That portion is included under the 612th session in the records.)*

Now—

("Good evening, Seth.")

—your situation is indeed changing for the better. Hereto hampered energy is being released, and you are both more open. The changes within a 3-year period will be drastic in terms of abundance, and fame.

I want you *(speaking to me)* to purposely liberate more of your own exuberance. You have in the past not fully realized the abundance of energy personally open and available to you, the overflow that makes everything easy. There will be a book with Macmillan, and others. And there will be other developments out of our sessions, and other books of my own also.

Many of these developments were dependent upon understandings. Many of these Ruburt has now come to, and others he is nearly upon. Some of your own attitudes had to be changed. Tell Ruburt to think of health like money, and he will have much of it, for in that area he is clear now. That is a definite advance, you see.

Your own negative feelings in that area have subsided sufficiently. I want you to ride the energy, however, and recognize it. Feel it in yourself. I am speaking to you personally because you still do not draw upon it as freely as you can. Ruburt is aware of the feeling. His trouble has been directing it in various areas. You have directed it for example in health better, but you still need to get the feel of it. You feel it in your work when you are doing well, and that is the feeling I am speaking of.

It has begun to work newly for you in the sale of your paintings as you dropped barriers against their sale; but feel it surround you and surround both of you. It is working for you both now, and powerfully in the areas of work and abundance, in terms of inspiration and material. Feel that energy surround Ruburt also with health.

You are drawing people to you now, you see, in a different way than you were before. There will also be money coming to you from an unexpected area, but as an offshoot of your creativity.

I suggest that if possible you sit tight here for six months—unless however something comes to you. Other aspects of your work and our work will also be showing themselves. I do not want the two of you to forget or put off your intimate relations. Let your very deep relationship bubble over. Ruburt's condition <u>is</u> (underlined) no excuse for either of you. You each need that refreshment.

Now others are being drawn in your direction, people of merit and note.

Your financial needs are now being more than satisfied, and there will also be breakthroughs, so that you are contributing. You are contributing in any case, of course, not only in *Seth Speaks* but in the book to follow.

I am speaking beside that, of your own work. There are psychic insights that will become available, and are being available, in terms of your own work, that will open up new areas to you in it.

You will in the future rather unexpectedly find yourselves possessing some Florida property.

Ruburt is coming to new understanding that is definitely changing the health pattern. The affirmation from Murphy's book helped because this time he finally understood it emotionally. Our session, the August 2 one, helped lead him to that understanding.

In various existences you have led each other in various areas, and often at the same time. For example, Ruburt leading you in one, and you leading him in another area. So utilize those (underlined) characteristics creatively and openly and unashamed, by actively encouraging him to go out, as today.

In that area he can use your leadership. In terms of material abundance, now, follow his leadership. There you have a partnership, as in our sessions you are partners, and in your work. Do not withhold your leadership in that direction therefore, but give it gladly, as he can give it gladly in those areas where he is now growing proficient.

Your leadership in that area will vastly speed his own understanding, which is now growing, by leaps and bounds. But where he is tentative he can use your leadership, as where you are tentative you can use his.

Your potentials now in all areas are therefore excellent, and many of the problems that were meant to be solved, have been. Ruburt has finally established his part in all of this. He has learned enough creatively so that our important messages can de given in many ways.

The return of the check, for example. Had he not done so I would have suggested it, but the understanding had to be his. Some recommendations given in that one session still have not been followed, though an effort has been made to follow many suggestions. The others should not be forgotten. I suggest you give attention therefore to those still not tried with any perseverance.

I will have something to say concerning Ruburt's experience the other evening, but first I suggest your break.

(9:47. Jane said she must have changed. Before these days, she wouldn't let much of this kind of material through, being afraid of wishful thinking, distortion, and error. She remembered some of it.

(See the 612th session for the balance of the material obtained this evening. It's

quite unique. I typed up that portion of the session earlier, and it's already been read by Terry Jacobs, a physicist from IBM at San Jose, California. He was our guest from last Friday, September 8 to Sunday, September 10. He said the material was "fantastic." It is seemingly concerned with atomic structure. Terry has the material, and is copying it before returning it to us this week.)

(Re the sentence by Seth about a book for Macmillan Co.: Richard Bach, of Seagull *fame, and his editor from Macmillan, Eleanor Friede, are to visit us on Tuesday, September 19, according to a note Jane has received from him.)*

DELETED SESSION
SEPTEMBER 18, 1972   3:45 PM MONDAY

(This afternoon Jane received a royalty check from Prentice-Hall for $819.00, covering sales to June 30 of The Seth Material, *hard and soft cover, and the first copies of* Seth Speaks. *Both of us were amazed.*

(We mixed drinks to celebrate. As we sat talking in Jane's studio she eventually said that Seth was around. The notebook was handy, so I told her to go ahead if she wanted to let Seth come through. Our mood was exuberant.)

Now, congratulations.

("Thank you Seth.")

I have been telling you this all along, if you recall, that your financial situation was changing.

The change, while admittedly advantageous, reflects the fact that people are being helped, and that in our way we are able to help them change their picture of reality for the better, and to enlarge their understanding.

In my book—the next one—I am going to discuss more about the nature of personal beliefs. Your beliefs, that artists and writers were poor, were quite conscious. You accepted them. When you changed them your reality began to change.

These ideas were not inaccessible. You believed them, and you did not examine them, except when you brought to the surface of your mind arguments that reinforced them. Do you follow me?

("Yes.")

I have told you of Ruburt's energies. Released now in that direction, and convinced he is "right," you will be astounded at the financial benefits, and material ones. You will also be astounded at the amount of work that will be produced, and is now latently in production, now that he sees that he can be artistically creative in his terms, mix and match the psychic and the creative (dash)—designations. These are still somewhat (underlined) separate to him, yet his ideas of doing good, being right, creating artistically, are now combining.

He is on the verge of realizing that they were all one all the time.

The psychic work will also enlarge his personal creative endeavors. This is affecting you, releasing your own creative energies, for his holding back in the past reinforced your own tendencies in that direction. I have said this before: as he helps you by releasing, as he has, these energies in the directions mentioned, then help him by taking the initiative at times, as he has in those directions.

Your impulses and tendencies, physically speaking, your desires to go out to do things, are better developed now than his, now. So let your normality serve as a sounding board for him. When you play this down, thinking it either useless or at best not profitable, then you deny him the advantages of your better wisdoms in that area.

He is now at a point where he can use this kind of help, where admittedly in the past he was not (period).

(Which, of course, is just why I hadn't stressed such things for some time. I had grown used to seeing them fall on impervious ground.)

If you try simply to spontaneously express your own normal feelings in terms of going out, etc., he is now more able to follow your lead. That is, do not inhibit your own feelings. You do not help either of you when you do.

If a normal physical routine is followed in the household, naturally all else will follow.

The stress need not be on the physical or nonphysical. I mention this because there should be no divisions, and in trying to maintain balance, now, Ruburt has a tendency to think "Now I should try to be physical," or "Now I should work," where the two flow effortlessly together, and you can help him see this.

He is growing to new understanding, and he will, as my book progresses, make sure he does not concentrate upon what still needs to be done, but upon his successes and his recent physical improvements.

I hope you will still talk to me when you are rich.

("I'll be glad to.")

I counseled you not to move for six months. You will be much better equipped to do so at that time. Ruburt did put himself through what he considered a necessary period of stress and training. He does now realize that there were unfortunate side effects.

I want each of you to write a list, yourself—and this involves work—a list of your conscious ideas about yourself, your conscious beliefs. You will find that some of these conflict with others. I then want you to make a list of your conscious beliefs regarding each other, and you are then to discuss these. That will also be one of the exercises I will give in my book to others.

Ruburt has no intentions of being physically incapable of being able to enjoy his success. You have that to count upon.

(At once I found this to be a genuinely-hilarious statement. It fit Jane as I know her to a proverbial T.)

I want your ideas concerning sex and its part in your lives written down with the others, and honestly faced. I also want you each to consciously know what you think, secretly, about the ways in which Ruburt's symptoms keep you from doing certain things, both of you.

If you do not want to do these things, and you are sure you do not, then admit it, without relying upon the symptoms as a handy excuse.

Your own work is progressing, as you know, and by leaps and bounds. I will have more to say about this later on. If you would examine your own beliefs, you would realize why you waited this long, and I am talking about conscious beliefs.

Now I expect your joint and individual exuberance to spread in all areas of your life now—freely—but you must begin those lists and you must take what I have said this afternoon to heart, not bury it in the records.

Again, my congratulations, and I expect you to congratulate me.

("I do. Thank you, Seth.")

One small note: your physical touch in terms of massage is of value, as I have also mentioned.

("Yes.")

(4:09. Jane and I began a discussion about symptoms, then Seth returned.)

Now, you both (underlined) take it for granted that Ruburt cannot live a normal life. That is your belief at this time, and you had better change it—both of you—for he can—

("That's great.")

—so change your habits. Set up your life situation about a normal pattern, and because Ruburt has lost a clear idea of what this is you can help him here. Your financial situation is increasing beyond your early dreams, because of a change in belief—so begin acting as if the normal pattern exists. Set your life up in that way and it will be. Even you do not realize how it is restricted.

And now, again: I am not talking for my benefit, but yours.

("Good. It's appreciated. Thank you.")

(4:16. During break I mentioned two questions to Jane, without insisting upon getting answers this afternoon. One had to do with the meaning, or information available, concerning the portrait I had recently finished. I had just framed it,

and it sat on the bookcase behind me now. Jane could see it from her chair.

(The second question had to do with Seth's ideas about our appearing on the David Susskind show, TV, in New York City, should we be asked. The publicity department at Prentice-Hall told Jane last week that this program was thinking of asking us to be on the show, and that possibly we'd be contacted this week.

(A note: Publicity at Prentice-Hall also told Jane that Newsweek Magazine *might do a story or review re Seth, and that this might take place within two or three weeks, etc. Jane evidently wouldn't have anything to do with this venture.*

(Resume at 4:19.)

Now about your painting, I will speak later. And I am not telling you what to do. You do as you like about the show.

My <u>advice</u> is, stay away from it. There will be other shows, more advantageous. But do not use the symptoms as the reason for not going on the show.

("I don't think we did."

(The first day after Jane got the call, we thought of all the reasons we didn't want to do the show—including the material on the show and Susskind in Daniel Logan's book, The Reluctant Prophet. *The next morning, I arose with the thought that all our stewing was after all academic—Jane's symptoms would prevent us from being on the show to begin with —we couldn't see her physically negotiating airports, taxis, hotels, studios, New York City, etc.)*

That is a habit, one of the areas where the symptoms can be counted upon for an excuse. Do you follow me?

("Yes.")

—as a rock bottom answer, that both of you can use to escape doing what you do not want to do. So the answer would be simply that you do not feel the show would be advantageous at this time.

("I guess that's what we decided.")

Give us a moment...There will be other shows, and he will be in a physical position to handle them. But you must understand that in your mind—now, you, Joseph—have thought of the symptoms as the reason why the answer (in the negative) would be given—and that is using the symptoms as an excuse. Do you see the difference?

("Yes.")

Then I will let you rest.

(4:22—4:24)

Now. Beliefs: you felt that the discussion was needless because Ruburt could not make it anyway, physically. *(The TV show.)* Ruburt <u>could</u> make it physically—maybe not in the condition you would like, but he could appear on the show. Do you see the difference?

("Yes.")

(4:27. This proved to be the end of the session. I would like to add here that we did realize that it wasn't utterly impossible, physically, for Jane to negotiate an appearance on the TV show. But the difficulties involved made it unlikely that we would bother to try this.)

SESSION 617 (DELETED PORTION)
SEPTEMBER 25, 1972 10:45 PM MONDAY

(The following is the balance of the regular 617th session for September 25, 1972. Seth spent the first portion of the session dictating on Chapter 3 of his book, The Nature of Personal Reality.)

Now. I want to talk to you. We are near the end of this chapter. You may take notes or not, as you prefer. I have taken Ruburt to task many times. Now it is your turn.

("Okay.")

He is exhausted by the barrage of negative thoughts that you have recently exploded in the household. I know you have been busy, but you have not examined your beliefs as given in the book.

You are insisting that your negative ideas are reality. There is a deep love between you. For reasons that I will get to, and to some extent have told you, you got into the habit of inhibiting joy, and being a stranger to gaiety.

Now these episodes begin and follow a rhythmic pattern, and Ruburt recognizes it. You begin to concentrate upon the <u>negative</u> (underlined three times) aspects of the news in the paper. This initiates such an episode. You go from that to the neighbors, the environment, Ruburt's condition, and Prentice.

As you do, your behavior does change, and Ruburt <u>there</u> (underlined) is not projecting. You look at him on <u>some</u> (underlined) occasions—far less than in the past—with great impatience and disapproval, as far as his physical condition is concerned, so that he feels he would have greater dignity alone on his knees than trying to walk with you with that look in your eyes.

Now for some time he did not see that look, and you were doing very well, but you slid back just at a time when he was trying to put the advice in my book to use.

You do exaggerate the Prentice relationship negatively. There <u>are</u> negative aspects, but you concentrate upon them. You accuse Ruburt of never forgetting a thing that you said of a negative nature, but you hold all of Prentice's errors in your mind, and so far refuse to <u>concentrate</u> upon any good in that relationship.

You are <u>aware</u> (underlined) of the good, but you do not concentrate upon it. You <u>concentrate</u> (underlined) upon the negative aspects.

Now Ruburt worked against that concentration of yours in producing *Seven*. Now he is very much in love with you, so it is difficult to get some of this data through. He does not like you criticized. Your own ideas concerning the artist in society being poor, mistreated and at the mercy of others—now this is a core belief of yours that you consider a truth, and the nature of reality.

It severely limits you. You have projected it into contacts with publishers. Now do not say to me that is the way things are. Do you understand?

("Yes." I wasn't about to.)

That is the nature of an invisible belief. If you had been more intimately connected with Ruburt's classes, the same hassle would have resulted. Now Ruburt until recently has had the same sort of belief concerning his body and its abilities. The artist was not physical—simply put, a thumbnail description.

You can recognize the limitations. He is still in the process of trying to conquer that. His freedom, earned, has been bringing results financially and creatively in work areas. It has resulted in a greater freedom in our sessions because the two of you together discussed your conscious beliefs about sessions, and Ruburt learned that many of his previous beliefs here were limited.

Yours were freer, more constructive, and he finally understood this, so you helped him. You did not realize however that you projected <u>also</u> (underlined), that if he harbored resentments in one area you harbored them quite as stubbornly in another.

Last summer there were some important improvements physically, plus a rebirth of Ruburt's creative abilities. The reasons should be obvious. You each gave yourselves daily suggestions that are no more than the repetition of new conscious beliefs.

You tried to change your beliefs, and worked at it.

(About 4 pages of material followed this, but it was too fast to record. I considered it the best part of the session, but now do not have it to read. It is impossible for me to remember at this typing, of course. It was about spontaneity and joy, etc.—obvious things, really, which become self-evident once mentioned—and how Jane's symptoms represent our joint negative thoughts. My parents were also discussed. The session ended at 11:20.

(The material about a negative cycle being fueled by a reading of the papers was new to me, and legitimate. As a result I've stopped reading the New York City papers at least, and have noticed a definite improvement. Jane and I were discussing the session when Seth came through briefly at 11:35:)

Now: tell Ruburt there will be schools of thought built upon core beliefs.

Tell him that.

DELETED SESSION
OCTOBER 2, 1972 9:37 PM MONDAY

(A 9:20 PM we finished dusting our cat Willy with flea powder.)

Now—I want to have a quiet chat with both of you, even though I do most of the talking.

Generally speaking, it is better if book dictation is done alone, or with those with whom you are well acquainted and easy. This is simply because there are less psychic distractions, and it is easier to focus into one clear channel.

The needs and desires of others naturally enter in, and some energy must be used to close them out. That is why I did not have a full dictation for our Seagull and friend.

(Richard Bach and his editor, Eleanor Friede, who witnessed the 618th session for September 28, 1972. I was somewhat surprised at this data; upon reflection it seemed we should have anticipated this. It might be a good idea to include this portion of the session with the next regular session.)

The more interested and excited they are of course, the more their own needs and answers ring out. It is difficult for Ruburt to block out these additional psychic distractions.

It was for this reason also that I spoke to you the other evening. He was doing very well in having to deal with such distractions when you commented about the reincarnational material. He took this as a rebuke. You wanted the session to go more clearly in that direction, and he wondered if he had been blocking.

All Dick Bach needed that night after Robert Browning was another fancy tale. He needs that challenge, as I told you, so it was not Ruburt blocking.

(No rebuke was intended upon my part, to Jane, when I asked her, during a break in the 618th session, if she was going to give Dick more specific reincarnational data. I thought he wanted it at the time. The Robert Browning reference concerns a letter Dick received from someone [a medium?] who told him that he'd been Robert Browning in a previous life.

(Seth later said my question to Jane was Nebene speaking. I try to control this, and have succeeded often.)

With strangers the sessions often are personal, however, because their own needs and emotional reactions are initially so vibrant. Later, other material that does not necessarily concern them can very easily follow.

Ruburt did exceedingly well, considering: his reaction *(smiling)* to a new "big" (in quotes) editor. Now give me a moment, for some of this material I want you to have now.

The Seagull is above all your friend. He will continue to be a celebrity. He will also have some storms to weather. He is deeply loyal, even more to ideas than to people, particularly when his need for freedom is respected. He will be of great help to Ruburt, and in advancing our work.

You will of course also benefit. The repercussions have not yet really begun.

(Possibly here Seth refers to the results flowing from Dick's mentioning The Seth Material *on his TV and radio shows in the course of talking about his own book,* Jonathan Livingston Seagull, *etc.)*

Seagull also needs friendly assurance, and some help as he learns to go deeper personally into the nature of reality and his own reality, and we can help him there.

Now. As far as Aerofranz is concerned.

(Tam Mossman, Jane's editor at Prentice-Hall, is to visit us tomorrow.)

His bubbling enthusiasm was partially responsible for his contracting *The Seth Material.* He was looking for answers, and young: he looked in any direction. He was not particularly discriminating. He was also not rigid in his ideas, however, and sensed the importance of the material, and as a young editor impressed his (underlined) boss by his own enthusiasm. He learned as the book progressed, and he did stand up for the book to the best of his ability at the time.

He does look for miracles. He does listen hopefully to each voice, but he is no fool. He is going places. Ruburt is deeply loyal to him, and he is to Ruburt. Aerofranz is not (underlined) particularly businesslike in his approach. He has not had (underlined) to fight for a book in strong terms, but his energy and belief helped it greatly at Prentice, and was transmitted to the salesmen.

Ruburt's own ideas have also changed. Aerofranz did indeed pick them up at times. In his enthusiastic feeling for the book, the best he could do with his lack of training was to think of it in terms of the best in the occult market.

Ruburt's own ideas in the past were not clear enough to offset this. No matter what Ruburt said, he thought of himself as working in a highly specialized, misunderstood small field.

(A note: I read this session to Jane after it was over, which I seldom do. When I was through she surprised me by saying, "Good. Now I can get rid of my symptoms because I'm getting out of the occult field. Now I don't have to go on any of those shows as a psychic," etc.

(I for one had never thought of Jane's symptoms as having such a cause, but...I am still puzzled by the worsening of her symptoms when we got back home after

being on tour to publicize The Seth Material, *in September of 1970. Now we can see that she is getting into the regular trade-book market. Eleanor Friede and Dick Bach both stressed this. Tam Mossman is here as I write this. He too has agreed to do all advertising for Jane's books in the regular trade-book field, rather than the occult.)*

There are intuitive and very playful connections between Ruburt and Aerofranz that are highly creative. Ruburt will end up with another publisher, but he will also be with Aerofranz for some time. The two together, you see.

(At this writing, October 3, Tam has expressed his desire to contract Jane now for Adventures In Consciousness. *Jane has the manuscript half done, perhaps. Tam's statement was quite unexpected by us. Jane had no plans to show him the manuscript. Yet in the course of their discussion this afternoon about business affairs, the script came into focus. After supper Jane said to me, in effect: "I don't know how we do it. It goes on at some level between us, beneath consciousness—this thing of deciding what we're going to do next.")*

Aerofranz will also have a much better position. There is a strong benefit here, in that he has been in on the material, <u>relatively</u> (underlined), from the beginning. He has a feel for it. The sales alone will generate much better contracts.

(10:05.) I will have a few words to say to him on my own, that will set things straight.

(Tomorrow night in ESP class.)

Oversoul will be followed by another.

For <u>now</u> do not do shows. The books are selling well, and will be selling better. Your position as not being publicity seekers works strongly to your advantage now, as far as *Seth Speaks* and *The Seth Material* is concerned. This will not <u>necessarily</u> be the case with *Oversoul Seven*. Do you see the difference?

("Yes.")

We will discuss that later on. There is no need now.

Seagull is a different kind of a book. Console can freely speak about it in public, because it carries within itself its own lovely camouflage. A series of shows now however would mitigate against what we are trying to do. Do you see the difference?

("Yes."

(10:12.) When you do shows on occasion, later, your position will be assured. Seagull *(humorously)* will be our angel Gabriel.

I am trying to mention situations that you have to deal with practically, so that your way will be easier and you will not lose time over such issues.

There will be enough money so that the material can also be distributed in edited version from the earliest sessions. This is what you are supposed to do with money that you do not need. I am telling you ahead of time.

Now Seagull may be involved, but you will also handle your own end of the financial stick—that is, you will also be able to contribute financially.

The Seagull goes ahead for us, and in a way that you and Ruburt are not equipped to go. You are both too solitary for that particular kind of endeavor. Seagull whets the appetite. Its readers will find more where its author found more, so the Seagull flies truly.

Now he was a student of yours, as Nebene.

(During the 618th session, which Dick and Eleanor witnessed, and during which I manifested the Nebene characteristics by quizzing Jane about reincarnational data for Dick and Eleanor, Jane also "saw" Nebene by my chair—as she had on the previous occasion some months ago when Sue Watkins was present. This time, Jane said, Nebene had changed; his face was less pinched and narrow and demanding, more open, etc.)

There will be rather large changes for both of you, beginning shortly, and in two years your entire physical situation will be altered for the better You must remember however that the material is for all of the people, not for a few.

You may take your break.

(10:22—10:35.)

Now, I will make myself plainer.

You are witnessing the birth of a phenomenon. The books will sell beyond your wildest dreams.

There were many alternate probabilities. *Seagull* is the one that materialized in this reality. Dick's very open attitude has already helped Ruburt immensely—another writer, you see; the blending of the writer and psychic, highly important to Ruburt. Dick however did not know where to go after *Seagull*, until he came onto our material, and it (underlined) will help him.

Now there is a connection between *Oversoul 7*, and the young, sometimes bungling young soul—Ruburt's creative sparkling, spontaneous self and Aerofranz. Do you feel the connection?

("Yes.")

There is the same connection with Seagull. I am telling you that all of you were connected and are. Aerofranz knew, quite well, that Ruburt simply had to do some fiction. He also knew that the center of Ruburt's being was involved with our message. Ruburt knew this also.

Aerofranz knew the practicalities of publishing, in his reality. There was energy on both sides, but Seven was, and is, literally Ruburt's inner self flying quite as the Seagull flies—for fun, freely, without having to answer questions, and without having to be brought down to specifics.

The joyful parable. Aerofranz was involved in that, in that he recognized *Seven* instantly for what it was, and responded instantly to *Seven*'s enthusiasm. You, Ruburt, Aerofranz and Richard are then all connected.

Now Eleanor is also, and the sometimes delightful snobbery in Aerofranz finds its mirror in Eleanor's connections. There are no accidents. None of you are strangers. To some extent Aerofranz will also be caught up in this, considered therefore a better editor.

I told you once that Frederick Fell was an excellent publisher for Ruburt's book. You never directly questioned me about that, but Ruburt was not prepared for that book to sell in any great manner, and it was to his advantage that it <u>appear</u>, to give him a book, but also that it lie quietly for a while.

The paperback will do very well, however.

(The paperback is due this fall according to a letter Jane received from F. Fell some months ago.

(In <u>late October</u>, F. Fell refused a collect call from Jane. She wanted to ask him when the paperback would be out, etc.

(Note: In December, 1972, a fan sent Jane a letter he received from F. Fell re the ESP *paperback. It's been "postponed indefinitely". F. Fell didn't write to Jane, however.)*

Because of Dick, you will become involved with some people considered important, but it will be up to you to remind Dick of his roots. You will have no trouble remembering your own, so keep it simple.

Your paintings, in a few years, now, will be in some demand, and you will find yourself quite spontaneously doing multidimensional portraits.

Ruburt has been refreshed often by your support of him. He will never forget the flowers, and this has added to the sense of inner serenity that he is in the <u>process</u> (underlined) of achieving. You can trust him in business matters. I tell you this.

Continue your physical support and encouragement. Get him to go to public places, for here he is weakest, so that he builds up his conflict. He danced even at your friends', when the stimulus was presented. There he needs your <u>gentle</u> (underlined) <u>encouragement</u> (underlined).

Now I have not given dictation this evening, for we will proceed now as things become quieter, and I wanted this information for your benefit.

("It's very interesting.")

The alliance with Seagull, and any ensuing household excitement was highly creative and important. You will see more of him, but there will be good quiet periods of work between.

One of Aerofranz's purposes was to see that the material saw the light of day.

I bid you a fond good evening.

("Thank you very much, Seth. It's been a pleasure.")

(10:59. Jane didn't remember much of the material, so I read it to her. Both of us were surprised by the predictions, hesitant at taking them literally, I suppose; especially the parts about excellent sales, the beginning of a phenomenon, etc. Not that we're averse to these things, but to have them stated so baldly....

(Last Saturday Jane and I visited Cec and Jim Lord, at their trailer home in Westover Hills, Pine Valley. We saw their newborn daughter, Jacqueline Ann, about whose birth Jane had given Cec some accurate predictions. It was there that Jane and I danced; the first time, Jane said, since Marathon, Florida, last February.

(Add Data—October 11—call to Jane from Timothy Foote, of Time Magazine *—re cover story on Dick Bach. Timothy Foote to fly here Friday, October 13, etc., to call back re plane schedules. Telling me about it—we also reread this session—Jane said it would be more than a casual mention of* The Seth Material *in the article, and that now she could "feel a tremendous amount of energy gathering around" the fact of Dick Bach, us, Seth, etc.*

(See notes for deleted session of October 13, 1972, and session itself.

*(*Time *article appeared on Monday, November 6, 1972, issue for November 13, 1972.)*

SESSION 620 (DELETED PORTION)
OCTOBER 11, 1972 11 PM WEDNESDAY

(This material is taken from the regular 620th session for October 11, 1972)
Now. A personal supplement to our friend *(Jane)*. Give us a moment.

There are a series of beliefs, built up like blocks one upon the other, that of course form his experience. Now some of these are excellent. The ones that are less advantageous were used as methods of bringing about desired good ends—i.e., they were used in the service of "good beliefs." It is important that this be understood.

He had for example a strong positive belief in his own abilities, energy and power. He believed he could not only develop his abilities and bring them to fruition, but also help others.

He also had a belief, quite contradictory, in the unworthiness, now, of his being. This was accepted originally in this life, but also for other reasons from the past, from his mother.

The ideas obviously conflicted, and each collected subsidiary beliefs. He could go ahead but he must go slowly, with caution and safeguards to make sure the abilities were (underlined) fulfilled, not misused, because he did not trust himself.

The idea of money also had conflicting connotations. His father had money and was useless—according to early beliefs received from his mother. The father was also, with money now, sexually promiscuous, according to those beliefs.

To use his abilities freely and fully might therefore mean success, money, and sexual license. Your own ideas about money and success of course influenced his beliefs: your combined ideas now of virtuousness and thrift, as opposed to license. Ruburt therefore put himself in a position—as he knows, now—where he focused most of his spontaneity and attention on his work to insure its fulfillment, while cutting out all other distractions and possibilities of misuse or license.

So in their way the beliefs served each other. They began to change balance finally. His mother's death, the fact that you left your job, and his own growing understanding released him first in financial terms, because of an always latent knowledge and belief in the reality of abundance—his father did have abundance even while Ruburt believed in poverty as a child.

The idea reversed itself—highly important. It was always there.

That, plus the need for money when you left Artistic, and the release from the fear, the belief, that welfare would take what he made. The blocks to the positive belief disappeared, and the belief reversed itself, and quickly. Do you follow me?

("Yes.")

The belief in basic unworthiness was still present, however. Now give us time.

(11:20.) It is this that still keeps physical reins upon the body. The belief that the self must be kept in reins—a trust in the spontaneous self directed toward work, but a distrust of the spontaneous self when it is not so directed.

For a while there was a severe crisis, which passed, when he had difficulty writing, even, and we have discussed this, the conflict of images. When that was resolved the creative breakthrough was possible, and the resulting financial gains.

These in themselves however bring a feeling of abundance that will be translated physically as long as the initial negative belief is combated and reversed. Give us time.

It was never, except for the time mentioned, the writing self that Ruburt distrusted, but he feared for the worthiness of his being. The writing self was obviously a <u>part</u> of his being, and so justified it.

He still believes that he must hold himself in reins, because he will (in quotes) "run wild." This is the basic belief that is causing the physical condition. At times it does become invisible to him, so a part of experience that he does not consciously realize it as an idea about his reality, and not a statement of truth regarding his nature.

This is important, for to a large extent he has not realized it.

When he thinks he is consciously giving himself good advice, he if often speaking to himself with the voice of the usually unconscious belief. Some quotes for him to recognize in the future:

"I had better calm down. I am too excited."

"I better be cool and collected about this."

"I don't want anyone to think I am frivolous."

"I'll play down the sex angle so I'll look <u>respectable</u>."

"No one is to think I am a hysterical female."

"I move too fast."

You see, he was afraid that he moved too fast for his own good, that to move too fast was irresponsible. He must understand that the basic belief mentioned is a faulty belief, projected upon reality, and not a picture of it. That is one belief that he has not been able to separate himself from.

He has used it therefore as a counterpoint that he does not need. The belief was generated in his childhood, but it was always the underside of the opposite belief in his abilities. If he had not trusted his abilities so much in his particular way, he could not have felt the other freely-spontaneous portions so threatening. Do you follow me?

("Yes.")

Now. He trusts our work far more than he did, and this is to our advantage. He is also beginning to trust himself, as a person. The financial accomplishments add to his person-respect. He sees, for example, that he is also liked as a person who has certain abilities, and this is beginning to alter his beliefs about himself.

The invisibility of the belief however made it difficult for him to deal with it. His conscious resolution is activated, and this is very important. Now do you have any questions?

("No.")

It is in black and white, and can be dealt with. He is already benefiting, and has since our August session, but the final separation of the belief from the self is important. *(Louder:)* The prognosis is good, however. Do you have any questions?

("No.)
Then I bid you a fond good evening.
("Thank you.")
And smile.
("About what?" Pause. "Can I ask you a question?)
You may.
("Do you have anything to say about Mr. Foote coming here?"
(Timothy Foote, book editor of Time *Magazine, is due here tomorrow to interview Jane in connection with a cover story the magazine is doing about Dick Bach.)*
No more than I implied in the remarks I gave you. I want to leave you some surprises; and I repeat that Ruburt intends to enjoy his hard-earned success. And you can count upon that.

You have been invaluable to him, particularly of late, and I ask you to consider your own beliefs about his complete recovery. You react to each other's beliefs. And <u>now</u>, a fond good evening.

("Thank you. The same to you." 11:45)

DELETED SESSION
OCTOBER 13, 1972 8:50 PM FRIDAY

(Timothy Foote, senior editor in charge of the book review department for Time *Magazine, interviewed Jane and me today in connection with a cover story he is to write about Richard Bach and* Jonathan Livingston Seagull.

(Timothy Foote arrived by plane from New York City at about noon, and left at 4:30 PM, driving to Saratoga and Skidmore College to see his daughter. Timothy Foote, Jane and I got along very well; seemingly we all liked each other. Timothy Foote was very interested in Jane's abilities, and said he would like to return for a session with a recorder. He is to write to us.

(As it was, Seth spoke very briefly to Timothy Foote at about 3:00 PM, discussing some remarks all of us had been making about Freudian psychology. It wasn't recorded or noted. At the time I thought the brief appearance a little odd, but when it developed that Timothy Foote wouldn't be staying for supper, as we had planned, Seth's appearance made good sense.

(Some time later Jane told me she picked up that when Seth spoke Timothy was suspicious—"Seth <u>would</u> speak now, you see, in order to make an impression," etc.

(Timothy Foote told Jane he would review Seth Speaks *for the magazine. We*

didn't ask him to do this. He told us his review for Richard Bach wouldn't "be hostile;" he didn't particularly like the book. Jane, liking Timothy Foote, told me later that had he stayed for the evening she would have had a session for him; yet we feel there were reasons he <u>didn't</u> stay, and that things worked out for the best all around.

(*We did not expect a session this evening. While Jane and I discussed the events of the day, however, she said Seth was around, and that we could have a session if we so chose. The following data tells in the main what the three of us talked about today. The session was held in Jane's workroom.*)

Now—

("*Now.*")

—a fireside chat. (*Humorously.*

("*Okay.*")

Ruburt is beginning to get the picture, as the saying goes. And of course it is no coincidence that Timothy Foote, being the kind of man he is, came here, and is doing the Seagull's story.

For he is a kind, well-intentioned, intelligent man, searching to make sense of the nature of reality by using the yardstick of available beliefs. His kindly inner skepticism is the same as that that is within many of the magazine's readers. They will (in quotes) "want to believe" *Seagull* and its story, for example, but they will not come from any homogenous background of acceptance, necessarily. Do you follow me?

("*Yes.*")

An individual who completely accepted what was going on here, and *Seagull* without question, <u>could</u> (underlined) also possess a fervor that would, or could, overstate the case, rouse instead within people conflicting beliefs. So Timothy's approach is an excellent one. (*Note: November 7: Timothy's article bears this out very well.*)

For Timothy individually and personally what happened here, little as it was, is not only important to him, but in terms of continuity ties in with the earlier Lourdes interest, and picks up a thread that has run throughout his life. He is ready now to go ahead in certain areas.

(*Timothy Foote described his learning about the healings at Lourdes, France, while he was an overseas newspaper correspondent, etc.*)

He has always been deeply concerned with the nature of reality, both from an intellectual and emotional standpoint, and where *Seagull* did not reach him personally, he was fascinated by the phenomena of belief behind it, and then was fascinated by the phenomena of belief behind the Lourdes healings.

(*Pause at 9:00.*) His intellect however leads him to ask questions that are <u>basically</u> (underlined) intuitive. *Seagull* does not intellectually reach him—that is, it does not intellectually by itself inspire him, while the phenomena behind it does.

This has to do with his personal characteristics and inclinations. It is not meant as a reflection on *Seagull* therefore, but on the various ways in which different people will receive such information.

Our material will give Timothy something to sink his teeth into, in ways that suit his particular fashion. He is playing a part in bringing the message to the people initially in several aspects, in as undistorted a fashion as possible.

Do not overlook the Saratoga connections of Timothy or Eleanor *(Friede)*: for Ruburt this also provides a sense of continuity that had been lost, and a focus point in his life, a gathering-together point most necessary, that will serve to collect and even regenerate his energies. He will be known as an excellent writer in his own right, and as one who produces our material, which he will be in a position to give freely to the world.

(Oddly, at least temporarily, Jane and I had overlooked the Saratoga connections involving Jane, Eleanor and Timothy. Certainly it seemed more than coincidence that lots of the great things starting to develop involved people with this common denominator running through their lives—of Saratoga Springs, NY.)

Take your break.

(9:07—9:12.)

Now. Ruburt's psychic abilities, with my help, enable him to fulfill and develop his creative writing abilities. They never were intended to be dropped as far as his person is concerned.

Part of our message of course involves the use of all abilities, and Ruburt's own writing ones serve to make that point. His abilities were not to be merged or to disappear, perhaps, into psychic work in those terms.

It is true that all spring from the same source—creativity—but the divisions between his personality's use of those abilities, and my use of them, was not to be broken down. He had to be free to do both. There was a period while he learned to readjust, of course. He was learning.

Your positions are in the process of changing drastically, as mentioned. *(See the deleted session for October 2, 1972.)* My material and books, and Ruburt's, and your paintings, will affect the world as you know it. Through Ruburt there was never an in-between. His characteristics were such that his energy would carry him beyond in all areas, if they carried him at all.

This could not happen until all layers of his personality—

(We were interrupted by the phone ringing at 9:20. It was Tom Hartley, trying to get in touch with Peg Gallagher. Both work for the Elmira Star-Gazette. After the call I read Seth's last sentence to Jane. Seth then finished it:)

—were in line, with his activities, and developed so that he could handle the ensuing experiences, including the enlargement of your acquaintances.

(To me:) Your attitudes had something to do with it, but there is also an inner harmony, in that events happen when they are ready. Your leaving Artistic was also an element. Otherwise your attention would have been too divided. The message is now clear enough and securely enough established, so that it can ring out freely.

Eleanor's and Richard's acceptance of Ruburt, and of <u>all</u> his abilities, was important also. I told you that your own work would show greater development, and so it will. And in its own way it will also deliver the same message, and there will be a gallery connection for you.

(9:25.) Each of you are playing parts that you accepted. Richard, Eleanor, Tam, Timothy, and yourselves. Each taking the roles that you can do best, and developing your own potential in so doing.

And our book will really take off, and that is all I will tell you now. *(Emphatically.*

("Thank you.")

And our friend *(Timothy Foote)* will be back with a recorder.

(See Timothy's letter of Monday, October 16, 1972.

(Pause at 9:27.) Give us a moment. A postscript. It is for Timothy's daughter, or rather it is to Timothy about his daughter's request.

(Timothy told Jane that his 16-year-old daughter voiced two questions for Seth: "Is there a God? Does He know what's going on down here?" We hope we recalled them accurately.)

Let me begin humorously by saying, "Yes, Virginia, there is a Santa Claus."

(Jane told me after the session that this quote refers to a well-known newspaper story of some years ago.)

In the same way: yes, there is a God. The earth emerges. It is given like a gift to you at your birth. It is there, then, like Santa Claus's toys when you were a child. You ask, who is the giver?

The child accepts the Santa Claus answer for some years, and then becomes disillusioned, realizing that the Santa Claus of Christmas tales is a myth. So in many ways the stories of a God are myths, but you are still left with a bag of toys on one hand, and the luxurious earth on the other, so the question still remains.

My answer is that the myths in their own way try to hint at answers that are basically nonverbal, and at concepts that are themselves the fountainhead from which the earth and all existence springs.

(9:35.) Is there a God, or is there a being, or a source behind all reality? You know the answer as well as anyone else does. You are as alive and aware as anyone else, and the secrets of your being are also the <u>secrets of being</u>.

You must look within yourself then, for in the last analysis the beginning and the source of creativity and being reside in each individual consciousness, in the same way that each tree contains its own seed. So it is to the seed of your own knowing that you must look for such answers.

It is only because you tell yourself that you do not know the answers that they seem unavailable. This is very briefly the beginning of an answer to a question that of itself initiates other questions, and should in your own mind.

Your concern with it, the question, is quite practical, whether you know it or not, because your ideas about the nature of reality will color all of your actions within physical experience.

And that is the end.

("Thank you very much, Seth. That was very nice.")

Now. I will let our friend here take a rest.

(9:42. Actually, Seth's humorous reference to Jane marked the end of the rather short session.

(A copy of Seth's answer to Timothy's daughter will be sent to Timothy, probably after his article about Dick Bach has appeared in Time *Magazine. [Copy sent to Timothy Foote October 21, Saturday.]*

(Added Note: Timothy Foote also told Jane and me that he'd like to do a feature story on Jane, Seth and me for Time *Magazine, but that it probably wouldn't ever be done—the magazine being "too secular"—Timothy Foote's words. I don't know whether he meant cover story, a la Dick Bach.*

(Secular means worldly, temporal, not religious, etc., according to dictionary.

(See Timothy Foote's letter of October 16, Monday. Mailed two days later. We received it Friday, October 20.

(Richard Bach cover story: November 13, 1972.)

SESSION 621 (DELETED PORTION)
OCTOBER 16, 1972 11:35 PM MONDAY

(This material is taken from the regular 621st session.)

Now, a few remarks and then some dictation. *(On Seth's book.)* Have Ruburt mention the book copies in class. It will be taken care of.

("Okay." I believe Jane forgot to do this the next day.)

Now. He is beginning to utilize important knowledge physically. He needs

TIME INCORPORATED

Richard Bach Cover Story 1-212

LETTERS

VIA AIR MAIL

TIME & LIFE BUILDING
ROCKEFELLER CENTER
NEW YORK 10020
JUDSON 6-1212

Monday, Oct 16.

Dear Jane & Rob:

I'm sending back with thanks, the original log of Richard Bach's hearing with you and Seth. Many thanks!

And much gratitude, too, for taking me in on short notice and devoting the better part of a fine fall Friday to me and TIME.

I fear I've repaid you badly by leaving my raincoat in your closet. As soon as Jonathan Livingston Seagull is finished here, for good and all, I'll be in touch about ways and means of getting it back.

I'm reading in The Seth Material and naturally have questions, hopefully for another time.

Room 26-16

Sincerely,

Timothy Foote

Encl. 1

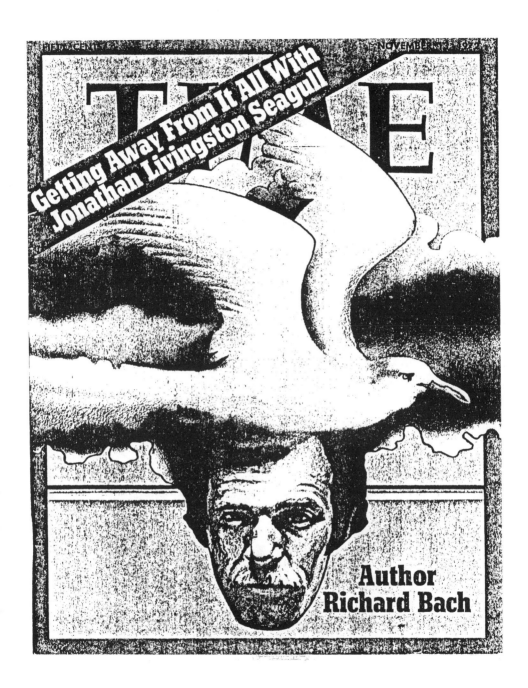

(Jane and I were most pleased to be included in Timothy Foote's story about Dick Bach in the issue of November 13, 1972. We wished all involved the very best—including ourselves.)

your enthusiasm, and you need to work on your beliefs concerning his condition.

You told Timothy what I told the Petries, about the importance of telepathy and ideas on Peg, yet often you do not realize those implications with Ruburt. His enthusiasm for a program is important. The program makes little difference. Do you see?

("Yes."

(Timothy is Timothy Foote, book editor of Time *Magazine, who interviewed Jane last Friday, October 13, concerning a cover story on Richard Bach, etc.)*

The physical breakthrough <u>is</u> (underlined) coming, and will be because of a shakeup in beliefs. In his value system, *Seagull*, etc., had to occur, or something like it. A fairly startling event may be connected here.

Things will break loose after the *Time* article. *(Next week.*

(Story appeared actually on November 6, 1972—Monday. Dated November 13.)

Ruburt accepted some beliefs from you because he looked up to you. No blame to you. The beliefs were necessary to his development. They tempered others, but now he should become aware of his own natural flow, and follow it.

Some sessions for example can be quite long, but the time is right.

He has inhibited physical aspects in terms of decorating, etc., going out—those areas, out of a sense of duty. But his own rhythm can now assert itself, and when he is puttering he is also psychically thinking and creating.

Now your <u>rhythms</u> of work may not always agree. That is for you both to work out at a conscious level.

Tomorrow for example let him without guilt let the day be used to putter in the bedroom, play with poetry, do what comes naturally without a sense of guilt.

("Okay, I'll tell him.")

He still feels freer alone physically, and more self-conscious getting up for example when you are there. If you will both remember to <u>playfully</u> change your beliefs, then this will not be the case. Do you follow me?

("Yes.")

Your sex life—and I have told you this countless times—is important. Your <u>emotional</u> (underlined) sex life, as last night shows; when you let down with each other and really show your feelings.

Now. Rest your hand and we will have a bit more dictation.

(11:47. Jane sat quiet briefly, still in trance, then resumed dictation on Seth's book.

(See regular 621st session, this date, for more re Timothy Foote, etc.

(Time article postponed a week, presumably to Monday, October 30, 1972. Eleanor Friede told Jane in call on Monday evening, October 23. A friend of Eleanor's saw part of Timothy Foote's story.)

SESSION 625 (DELETED PORTION)
NOVEMBER 1, 1972   11:05 PM WEDNESDAY

Now. End of dictation. The next block of material I want to give you at the beginning of the next session for the book.

I have some remarks for you two instead. Now I want you to make out a list of beliefs about yourself, and another list of beliefs about Ruburt. I want him to make out a list of his beliefs about you. I want him to concentrate, now, upon those beliefs that are working for him, to quite consciously build up the sense of his own worth by listing the uses to which he has put his abilities. I want him to then stress, this week, all of his good points, and as much as possible to ignore for that amount of time the negative ones.

Twice a day for 15 minutes at a time, to take the place of psycho-cybernetics, I want him to dwell upon these positive activities and characteristics. This will automatically help replace some of the negative beliefs concerning unworthiness, and is an effective way of avoiding pitfalls.

For a week I want you to concentrate on Ruburt's good points and abilities and accomplishments also when you think of him, until I get further in our book. You do not thoroughly understand the interaction of beliefs, the give and take of energy patterns.

Now the same exercise for readers will be a part of the book in a later chapter dealing with that subject partially. In simple terms you will be taking energy from one area and putting it in another. Now that is the end of the session. We will return to chapter five at our next session. *(Louder:)* My heartiest regards to you both.

("Thank you. Good night, Seth." 11:45.)

SESSION 627 (DELETED PORTION)
NOVEMBER 13, 1972   10:40 PM MONDAY

(This is the last part of the 627th session. Seth called for a break for Jane at 10:30 because she had been coughing rather steadily for some time. This was an interruption of the material on Chapter Six of Seth's book, but as long as a break had

occurred I suggested Seth say something about Jane's cold. She'd had it for perhaps six weeks—since, I thought, we had visited my mother and brother in Rochester, NY. I was puzzled that it was lingering so long.)

Now. Give us a moment. Some of the information we will give you this evening, and some following dictation at our next session. I am keeping his voice low.

Now. He is working with beliefs, juggling them. The cold symptoms began some time ago, and have been kept while he makes up his mind to dispense with the more familiar ones. The cold does not involved physical slow motion.

It brings to the surface some other physical feelings, however, that are connected with the usual symptoms. He is meant to see the connection. The sinuses are involved. The feeling of being full through the body—heavy—has a connection with the full-head feeling, initially, of sinus origin physically.

When he began clamping down on physical spontaneity, tensing of the head, neck and jaw areas was involved, leading to a sinus condition. The cold is meant to lead him backward mentally and physically through the group of beliefs that initially cause the entire condition.

It begins with the sense of unworthiness mentioned often, but it led to a pattern of behavior where he began to hold his breath, so to speak, tense the muscles in self-protection. To hold the breath however as in fright.

The cold symptoms however also lead to a certain feeling of fluidity rather than dryness, which is in itself evocative of motion.

The cold symptoms also have operated to increase his circulation. The body combating the (in quotes) "new" symptoms is also creating antibodies that affect the old symptoms. He has had a better appetite. The body has been calling for more food and nourishment, and quite unconsciously he has been consuming a larger amount of peanut butter, which is giving him several nutriments that he needs.

The fact is of course that he doesn't need any of the symptoms, but in the interrelationship of his beliefs the cold results as a method of understanding, and of bringing about certain necessary physical changes.

It began—the cold—after Eleanor *(Friede)* showed such pleasure with *(Jane's autobiography)* Rich Bed.

(Eleanor's letter about this is dated October 4, 1972. We were in Rochester October 6—8, 1972.) In Ruburt's past a cold was the one quite acceptable symptom in childhood of escape, for example.

Intuitively he began to understand the physical connections between that kind of cold and sinus involvement, and his condition. *(Gestures to include the whole body.)* A cold is something that comes and goes, and is not permanent, and he is to see his other symptoms in that same light—not as he saw them earlier, as a permanent-like situation.

He quite understands how in childhood he adopted colds and discarded them, and is to see then the other symptoms in the same light. For these reasons the cold was adopted. He needed to see how he himself in a <u>relatively harmless</u> (underlined) incident in miniature, so to speak, could create such conditions as the cold, and in growing out of it see how he can grow out of the other symptoms.

All, then, a lesson in the nature of beliefs as he applies them to his own body and behavior. A test case. "I will give myself this, and get rid of it, and then apply what I have learned to this other situation that has been bothering me."

And tell him these ideas have been very near ordinary consciousness.

The public, or the people, have also been involved in this test case. He needed to know that people saw and recognized the symptoms of a cold so that when he was rid of it he could see for himself that they no longer perceived those symptoms in him.

He was earlier afraid, you see, that his symptoms otherwise had become so real to others that they would continue to perceive them. In other words for a test case he produced a miniature symbolic situation physically materialized. Solving it is meant to give him the confidence that it can be done in this other area.

The cold, beyond that, is also symbolic in that his bout with the other symptoms had to do to some degree with being out in the cold—out of it.

Rich Bed is highly important to him personally and creatively. He would feel out in the cold no longer for several reasons, mainly because the book so beautifully combined the continuity of his earlier life with his later activities.

Now out in the cold also means that you are stiff. The antibodies produced by the cold symptoms result in a body activity that has produced some fever—but a benign one that warms him up and increases circulation.

(Long pause at 11:14.) The coughing has brought into activation the use of certain muscles also, particularly in the chest areas, and taken his attention way from other areas of the body that are being revitalized while his attention is elsewhere.

The cold for example is also bringing in particular an increased blood flow through the head and neck area, and also to the extremities. Certain stresses have been relieved physically. Bodily the cold creates a diversionary tactic—still a stress situation, but an impermanent one that changes momentarily the hormonal output.

It represents then alterations of beliefs toward a more beneficial condition. At one other time such a situation was set up. The cold's duration was far briefer, through very intense, but his overall condition was better then.

Then the cold did serve to drastically improve his health. Because he did not understand the nature of his beliefs however the improvement, while lasting for some time, deteriorated. This time the body's overall condition, using the method adopted, required a longer period of such stress-transformation, and so the cold condition has been of longer duration.

There is quite a bit I can say involving both of your attitudes toward those poor people not as level-headed as yourselves *(louder)*—your beliefs about them, but that can wait until after dictation at our next session.

Now I bid you a fond good evening, or you can take a break if you prefer. *("We'll take the break."*
(11:27—11:33.)

Now before I leave you then for the night I will make a recommendation. The telephone situation as it occurred on two occasions lately brings up in both of you a beautiful case of beliefs, conflicting beliefs, on both of your parts. Whenever such charged situations happen they are always the result of beliefs not consciously examined. These have to do on both of your parts with ideas of spontaneity and communication. I refer to the Cec Lord event and the man calling the other evening.

Behind the events therefore are highly charged beliefs <u>about</u> (underlined) reality, that you have not examined, either of you, and about your relationship with each other, your stance in regard to the outside world, as well as ideas about freedom, spontaneity and responsibility.

I want you then to make a list of your beliefs concerning those events. If you consider them as beliefs that you hold, both of you, then you should be able to discuss them calmly, and understand what happens. You have not understood your own beliefs, much less communicated them to the other, and your joint behavior in such cases has largely resulted because you each hold conflicting ideas yourselves.

It is not only that your joint ideas may conflict but that within yourselves you hold conflicting ideas regarding such situations. Such an exercise will also clear up other issues, and in areas that you do not suspect. Can I count on you both then to face the challenge, and do what I suggested?

("Yes.")

And not next month. I bid you then a fond good evening.

("The same to you, Seth. Thank you very much.")

Your penis position is also involved in some of the beliefs hidden and unrecognized, and will appear in such an examination.

("Good night.")

A fond good evening.

(11:43. A note added after Jane's death in 1984: she worked upon her most interesting autobiography, From This Rich Bed, *periodically over the years, but never did finish it. I still have the manuscript.)*

SESSION 628 (DELETED PORTION)
NOVEMBER 15, 1972 11:35 PM WEDNESDAY

(This is the last delivery in the 628th session. Before the session I asked if Seth would discuss the Time *Magazine cover story about Richard Bach in the November 13th issue, published November 6; and the various predictions made re sales, etc., in the recent deleted sessions.)*

I will continue with this fascinating subject at our next session. *(Louder. A reference to Augustus in Chapter 6 of* Personal Reality.*)*

Now. It seems you want immediate results, but it all takes time— *(humorously.*

("I get it.")

—underlined, in your time.

Some of the results mentioned earlier will come from conversations the Seagull has with people in California, who ask him about us. And *Seven (Oversoul 7)* will also be mentioned.

Timothy *(Foote)* will not forget you for his own reasons. His interest is aroused, and he will pursue it. *Rich Bed* will appear in the near future.

In *Dreams (recently)* Ruburt tried to assess his psychic experiences, and could not do it. In *Adventures* he will be able to do so.

The other information given still applies, but all of it unfolds in your terms of time. Your work with beliefs today was most beneficial and so were your evening lists. They generated enthusiasm. I have told you this before: there is much not yet given as yet in the book, that you do not understand.

Your loving encouragement will help Ruburt change his own beliefs, for you can (underline three times) help him trust his physical body. You cannot do it for him, but you can help or impede his progress.

He did better than usual (comma), lately, in the store today, and immediately found himself substituting a bad coughing spell *(in the store, P&C)*—highly illuminating. But in his scheme of beliefs a cough can be rather easily dispensed with, and he was aware of this.

Much will become clear as the book progresses, but your joint working with beliefs is of great value.

I will have some remarks to make concerning the I Ching, but remind me after our next dictation. It will be of great interest generally also. Only a certain level is reached, however, and great care is needed in interpreting symbols that have their origin in an entirely different civilization than your own.

The Murphy version is more applicable than the older version Ruburt referred to.

His list with the physical goals is excellent. I told you before that some physical gamelike period should be adopted, and suggest your rackets and birds—but activity that is considered fun.

Now I bid you a fond good evening—unless you are ready for more dictation. *(Louder.*

("Nope.")

My heartiest regards.

("Thank you, Seth, and good night." 11:51.)

DELETED SESSION
NOVEMBER 24, 1972 10:37 PM FRIDAY

Now: Much of the information, and the most pertinent part, is buried in your files—I tried to give the data in various ways, although it was quite definitely given also in terms of the physical relationship several times; and only at one particular period did you try to take advantage of it.

It is all there is black and white, including suggestions in the sexual area, why it would be advantageous, the various emotional points of resistance that would appear during such encounters, and their significance, and much more.

I initiated programs. The importance of some of these was that Ruburt would feel simply that you were taking an active intimate interest, and lending a <u>positive</u> (underlined) hand.

I suggest, if this will do me any good, that both of you take the work involved and find those sessions and finally put them to use. I told you that he felt emotionally deprived, whether or not this seemed logical—that he felt uncherished, whether or not that seemed logical.

In the face of this he threw even greater determination into his work and his "success" (in quotes), to make up for what he felt as other deficiencies. All areas became therefore more sensitive. Blame was projected by him upon other areas, because only when he allowed his thoughts to really surface would he blame you in <u>any</u> way. And when he did he felt guilty because he knew that you <u>did</u> (underlined) love him.

He felt emotionally deprived regardless. In your own background you learned to voice silent disapproval. It became a defense mechanism. He kept the symptoms for several reasons—and again, all given—to preserve what relationship you had, for one thing.

He felt that for all your talk you wanted him to discipline spontaneity in a way basically impossible for him, that to release it in physical terms would mean two dangers: You would find him unbearable; and his sexuality released, would then demand fulfillment. He feared he would look elsewhere. You schooled yourself not to display emotion of a warm, spontaneous, happy nature, and he needs that kind of display.

Self-protection kept you from doing so. Your love for him in the beginning was strong enough to release you to some degree, so he knew it was in you. He felt it, and he was furious after the taste of it to have it for any reason withheld.

As he told you, he fought for it. You had arguments and reconciliations. After a point his stubbornness was aroused, and he felt that you wanted him to beg for what should be his. Now all the connecting material has been given, and presented in different ways.

The symptoms were also a protection. He was trying to hold back, so as not to be rearroused by promises only to be turned off again as you withdrew. There is a connection of course with his mother's reaction, simply a habit pattern where she would tell Ruburt she loved him, and then in Ruburt's eyes be cruel.

The words meant little. On the other hand he almost would have settled for the words. The balance for him changed. Where you two had been emotionally allied, he felt you were on the other side. As he must watch himself before the world, he must watch himself before you.

You were the one who could really hurt him if he let go, by your rejection of his emotional dimensions, he felt. He felt you only accepted certain portions of him. Others would not be accepted, and you would run from them.

The body cried out to be touched. It said "I am not being nourished." He kept trying to get your attention with the symptoms while using them to protect himself at the same time, unless he saw signs of the particular warmth and acceptance he needed. He felt he could not afford to let the symptoms go unless he was willing to give you up entirely, and he would not do that.

All of this has been given, Joseph. He watched and waited to see if you would bring in his rackets when I suggested it—to him a symbol that you would tolerate frivolity in terms of such a game.

He did not think you wanted him to be free of symptoms, because he thought that then you would be faced with problems of emotionalism that you wished to avoid at all costs.

Whenever he began to improve some of these issues would become quite clear and obvious. On some ways the two apartments, he felt, were an honest symbol of your relationship. When he annoyed you by thrashing about in bed, this was of course what the thrashing about in bed was supposed to do—remind you of his presence there.

Your answer, "Get up, or go into the other room," he interpreted as the basic rejection.

There are definite points—and check the old sessions—where emotional resistances will be reached and he will want to cry during the sexual encounter. They should be worked through, and they are detailed, or this is detailed for you.

He felt you did not want him to get well, because you would then have these problems to consider, and they bothered you. On one hand then, he did not want you to have to contend with them, particularly if he could take the tension. There was however simultaneously great resentment: "How sick do I have to get before you will come back to me, and how can I be sure of it?"

This was still however you see quite selfish, in that you are the person he wants. He was willing to do it. He is not looking for an endless adolescent love affair, but in his terms (underlined) the simple emotional creature love, support, that he felt you must, because of your nature, largely withhold.

To compensate he realized that you gave all you could, that you were his partner in work, in seriousness and in important endeavors (underlined), but he wanted touches, and because of his nature reassurances.

He tried to show you his love, but finally he became ashamed of needing you, and felt even that you thought less of him because of it. It bothered and annoyed you, since it was a demand, and he did not believe in demands, and one that brought problems up within you.

The reincarnational material given in the bedroom over there one night was also a statement of that nature—the night in which Ruburt related to you as the priestess-prostitute you visited.

Your lack of verbal communication of your exact feelings, plus your learned facility for facially expressing disapproval, only allowed him to reinforce his ideas.

Your face does not as easily express your pleasure, so that did not physically show as often. But again, my dear friend, this has been given in these same terms.

One note: I will not keep you late. You may have a break now if you want. *("Okay.")*

(11:25. Jane's trance had been good. "I'm about as weak as water," she said. "Not only that, I feel like throwing up." She didn't, but she definitely felt sick. I told her it was because of the data in the session. We had asked for the session yesterday, in light of what had come to the surface regarding our problems in previous days this week. We felt we had learned much.

(The session ended here. We were tired. The session had started late because we'd had unannounced visitors from out of town who had heard of us—so they simply dropped in....)

(Already I have made emotional improvements, and Jane has made physical ones.)

DELETED SESSION
NOVEMBER 26, 1972 8:10 PM SUNDAY

(This session was quite unexpected and spontaneous. It grew out of the last deleted session for November 24, 1972. It very well answers the attempts Jane and I have been making to integrate the session for November 24, and the 367th session for October 1, 1967.

(Jane felt much better the last two days, etc.)

Now, good evening—

("Good evening, Seth.")

—and good thinking, in asking for the interpretation. *(Of the 367th.)*

The session contained information about vital aspects of Ruburt's personality, but given in your terms at a particular period of time. More intimate material concerning your own relationship could not be given then, of the kind given later. He would not allow it.

The point about success being a critical factor *(in the 367th)* also means that it was a potentially creative factor. It could bring various potentials to bear that could be used positively—or in your terms negatively.

What was not said is this: he felt that no one with whom he had been intimately involved believed in him as a person, or trusted his intrinsic value, except for yourself. Your meeting and love helped reinforce all of his own creative aspects and rearoused his faith in himself. While he had that strong faith in himself, the other tendencies, including the false prophet ideas, lost all but the most minute significance.

His mother, Father Ryan, Walter, some college friends, Mozet, Hays, all of those persons in one way or another implied strongly at times that he was either a saint or a devil, a creator or a destroyer. He held his faith in himself despite those odds, and because of the vitality of his youth.

You alone seemed to accept him as the person that he was. Love is a great reconciler, and the greatest healer, and so is trust. Some of this can be given later if you want specific connections. As your own complaints grew however, about your job, this place *(house)*, publishers, and his behavior, he began to feel that he did not have your trust, and therefore the old doubts, slowly at first, began to emerge.

He was afraid to make a decision for fear that it would be the wrong one, and sometimes literally afraid to move for fear of making the wrong move, and earning your displeasure of disapproval.

It is true that for some time he then projected portions of his own overly-conscientious portions upon you, and then reacted; but it is also true that you had schooled yourself to display displeasure through a heavy silence, and were afraid of displaying your happier, sunnier emotions.

When he was spontaneous, it seemed, you <u>did</u> (underlined) disapprove. At the time that session was given *(367th)* those elements were paramount. It was because of his great love for you and his knowledge of your great love for him, that your disapproval, by contrast, <u>was</u> (underlined) so chilling.

If <u>you</u>, who loved him so deeply, distrusted him, then you see he must seriously consider that he must indeed watch himself carefully.

(8:25.) Unfortunately your own illness brought up in you some buried characteristics that then for some time became the habit rather than, as earlier, the exception.

You do have strong perfectionist leanings. They <u>are</u>, whether <u>you know it or not</u>, also projected by you upon Ruburt, so that you do see his physical condition as an outrage, not only literally but symbolically. This is something quite beside your normal urge to see your wife in good health.

Ruburt has always known this. To some extent he had equated his recovery as almost impossible at times, since in those terms, now, and <u>when</u> (underlined) they operate, it puts him in the position of trying to be perfect. Do you follow me?

("Yes.")

There is material, buried in the files, that says clearly that our sessions began for many reasons—your joint desire to know, for example, and to probe together into the nature of reality. They also began because Ruburt most desperately wanted you to be well, and tuned into a greater source than usually available to that end.

Intuitively the personality knew its abilities also, so there was the creative urge to develop and grow. The two blended. His desire to forge ahead philosophically beyond any school or church also was involved, and his artistic endeavors—which bloom in my books, now, as well as in his own work.

The entire psychic situation then brought into your lives fantastic energy, and attempted to correlate diverse creative, personal and psychic goals. All for this was focused into a particular time, as you think of it.

It demanded growth, creativity. It was born of such diverse elements, in this life term, as your sign, "Make a galaxy, Jane," and also born because of those stresses that had deeply by then already made themselves known.

Now take a break, and if you are willing we will continue briefly.

(8:35—8:45.)

Now. Ruburt felt that his symptoms were, in your eyes, the concrete indications of his imperfections. They became a symbol to him. You would not accept him as he was unless he was perfect. You would not accept him with the symptoms as an imperfect being, and love him anyway. He felt that unless he became physically perfect <u>again</u> (underlined) you would not love him again in that way he wanted.

He had to be perfect for you in order to be physically perfect, and he felt it impossible to be perfect enough, so that this could be physically materialized. He felt you were rigid in your standards. Now much of this has to do with his own characteristics, as given, and ways of reacting. He was afraid you would become like your father in his treatment of your mother.

He felt unable to <u>freely</u> (underlined) express his fears to you, feeling they would only upset you. You did not express your fears often to him, so he began to hide his warm, vulnerable self from the person he loved most.

The sessions having to do with your sexual life are important, vitally so.

Now I know what questions you have, so give me a moment.

(We discussed the questions at last break to make sure Seth would cover them tonight: from her records Jane recently realized that coincident with the mailing of the manuscript for Seth Speaks *to the publisher, and the death of her father, near November 15, 1971, the condition of her legs took a decided turn for the worse. Also, in the 367th session, Seth made certain remarks that have bothered her ever since —mainly about the necessity of his presence.)*

Both events are important—the death of his father and the mailing of the book. He felt that you were strongly dissatisfied with the circumstances surrounding the book: you told him it was marred because of his missed sessions; the fact that it was accepted instead of another book *(Dreams, etc.)*. And the Nebene characteristics that came out strongly as you worked with the details toward the book's end.

Another marred performance, with you he felt as the judge.

His father's death reminded him that he was suddenly quite alone except then for his mother, and also brought up the question of age.

He could not satisfy either parent, or you, or apparently himself, and there seemed no place to turn. With you home, it seemed, you only noticed his imperfections more.

He felt—this is an answer to another question—that there was a veiled threat involved in my remark that I would not be dispensed with. There was none. He felt angry that often it seemed you trusted me but not him. He was never in danger of any severe emotional or mental difficulties. He would always cope—and in the main creatively, if unconventionally or bizarrely.

He did not feel safe however to go ahead fully if he did not feel he had a strong, loving, creature-type trust with you. Does that answer your main questions?

("Yes.")

He did feel accused in your eyes, and he was determined that your relationship live up to its potentials as much as was possible.

You may take a break or end the session as you prefer.

("Can I ask a question?")

You may indeed.

("It's nothing great. What do you think about the news he got about sales this week, because of the Time *Magazine article?")*

You already know what I told you, and it still applies.

("How about the Gallery *Magazine deal?")*

What about it?

("Should he consider it?")

It is already being considered. It can (underlined) work.

You do not as yet understand how your own attitudes affect such matters. It is dependent upon your own attitudes; how much publicity you want, and how you are jointly going to face the world.

It can work or it can be disastrous, then. You make your reality. There is no reason it cannot work, and well, with the proper attitudes. On your part, the relative greater importance of such a project to you over that of the writer *(for* Gallery*)* means that your attitudes will predominate. Do you follow me?

("I think so.")

Now you knew Ruburt's stubbornness. You knew he would insist upon drawing you out in precisely those ways that you desired and feared, so both of you were quite aware of what was going on.

You gave also creatively, and do not forget that. Age is involved, in that you knew Ruburt would go so far and no further, and so did he.

("With the symptoms, you mean.")

Indeed. He is too literal to let things remain hidden. He would have made changes, and insisted you face the symbolic situation in concrete terms, as in entirely separate apartments, or different bedrooms, until the physical situation mirrored the symbolic ones.

This would have frightened you enough so that you would have come to him freely, or in his eyes not cared enough to. Do you have other questions?

("I guess not.")

You may take break or end the session.

("We'll take the break."

(9:18. Jane had been way out. She remembered nothing, including the ringing of our phone across the hall. She was very relaxed. She also felt sick again, as she had at break during the last deleted session for November 24. She had a coughing spell. She walked better during break, though, and felt much better when the session resumed at 9:42.)

It is because you both <u>are</u> such loners basically, creatively and in normal physical life, that Ruburt realized that you must have a strong and vital, open and warm system of communication with each other. It also means that you alone in the main must meet each other's emotional needs. They do not find fulfillment from a large family in daily contact, for example, or from a large group of friends.

In his role as woman Ruburt would not want to appear in public with you unless he was gallantly and proudly escorted. He expected this always. For a while, now, the symptoms also represented a holding back because he feared you were jealous of his success, to save you embarrassment, as mentioned in the past.

In the main however he felt he did not live up to your expectations, that the two of you were not together emotionally.

He felt ashamed of what he thought you thought of as trivial unimportant matters, homey concerns. He became ashamed of them. Fear of childbirth was also involved. He feels you both can be more lenient now since the possibilities have dropped some: because of his age he is less likely to become pregnant, than when he was, say, 30.

He also felt sexually that what you wanted least was true spontaneity, for that could lead him to forget himself enough to forget proper birth control methods. You did not trust intercourse anymore than he did.

("Yes.")

A good deal for the leg contraction has to do with inhibited sexual impulse. There <u>will be</u> some resistance on his part *(touching leg)* as you resume a normal sexual pattern, simply because of the pent-up frightened energy.

You <u>can</u> get around this however, using methods given earlier, and reassurance. He will be afraid for a while that you will turn away from him again. It has never been what you said, so much as your unexpressed communications that bothered him. What is <u>said</u> you can face, work out, and encounter.

Before, in the past, you would each go so far, as given before *(louder)*, then let the whole thing go underground once more.

Ruburt would not allow that to happen any more, for both of your sakes. He would not hurt himself either beyond a certain point. Hence his just-surfacing thought last week about separate apartments. Beyond all this he also knew he had to consider the separate apartments while knowing they would not be necessary. Do you follow me?

("Yes. I'd just begun to wonder.")

He had to know he could do it, and that he would, while a portion of him knew quite well that it was not necessary.

Take a brief break. If you have questions, form them.

(10:00. During break we mentioned last February's vacation in Florida, and Jane's lack of improvement in spite of our efforts. Resume at 10:28.)

Now: I will not keep you, and if you are tired from note-taking, say so.

("I'm okay."

Several issues operated in Florida, and on the trip.

Your location. You gave it more negative ones than Ruburt, but each of you felt it was all you could afford, and poor at that. The contrast between your last stay there, and that one, and in your relationship, was too obvious for comfort.

You *(to me)* felt that your physical situation in the years between was not that much better—and on top of it you had quit your job. The two of you were in one room together, where Ruburt felt his imperfections could not be hidden.

You use the excuse of work, both of you, to isolate yourselves from other people while you did crossword puzzles, and little work. You isolated yourselves and did not put to advantage much—though some—of what I told you. You saw that when you did not rely on your work, you enjoyed few creature comforts. Do you follow me?

("Not exactly.")

You were not painting. Ruburt was not writing. You were faced with your relationship as it exists apart form your work together. Now do you follow me?

("Yes.")

The easy, spontaneous, daily, trivial, give-and-take was not there. Both of you knew it. You took approximately the same amount of time to do your puzzles as you usually spent working, to fill in the gap. Does that answer your question?

("Yes.")

Now though it may not seem so to you, the entire episode has been a creative endeavor, in which together you saw to it that various desired characteristics be brought out in each other. You particularly in the beginning, served as a strong impetus to Ruburt, freeing him for serious work.

You do not believe me now when I tell you that you have always exaggerated your situation and Ruburt's as far as its negative aspects are concerned—but you have, and this has been part of the difficulty.

You <u>will</u> see. Now I bid you a fond good evening, and my heartiest, freest regards for a joyful, spontaneous, and loving daily existence, in which all things have their place.

("Thank you very much, Seth. Good night."

(10:40. Jane's trance had been deep; she remembered nothing. I remarked about the excellence of the Florida data, and Seth returned.)

Now—I told you earlier something about that. He displayed his body wearing shorts and swimsuits, and that was also involved. Check the session.

(We thought the session was over, but began discussing Richard Bach's postcard of November 10, mentioning that he could accept a reincarnational hint or two. To ge some data for Dick, Jane went back into trance at 11:00.)

Now. A brief remark for our friend.

There was a previous relationship, in your terms, with your third child. Tell yourself you will have a dream that will tell you of the circumstances.

Tell our dear friend Eleanor to be less lovingly concerned—no one will take advantage of you unless you believe that they will. Look at the New York world and the California world with the eyes of the Seagull. Expect to find understanding and (in quotes) "real people," and you will.

For Richard the name Andrews *(spelled)* or Andrus is significant. There is a new book for you of course—I told you that earlier—and creature enterprises <u>will</u> (underlined) fly. There are two male relatives with whom you also had a relationship in another existence.

Console likes to invent new hemispheres to explore, and new vehicles with their own amazing controls. Richard then learns to operate the controls, and revels in the expertise. There will be more at a later time, and I appreciate my debut in <u>time</u>.

Richard sends you *(Jane and me)* postcards, and this is my private postcard to him, though my real address is difficult to find (period). I am keeping an eye out however for his affairs and Eleanor's, and I appreciate their endeavors on Ruburt's behalf. They are not needed, and yet on all of your behalves they are needed.

Now you cannot say that I always speak clearly. *(Humorously.)* And that is the end of our postcard.

("Okay. Thank you. Good night, Seth."

(11:12 PM. Again Jane's trance had been good.

(Notes: Richard Bach and Eleanor Friede called Jane Monday afternoon, November 27, from Bridgehampton, Long Island, before Dick flew back to Carmel, California, and I read this copy to them. Jane then mailed a typed copy of the data for Dick to his California address Tuesday morning, November 28.

(Checking his mail in California, Dick found a letter on White House stationery, written by Mr. Andrews. The brief letter commented favorably on Seagull, *and invited Dick to dinner in Washington, DC. Dick called Eleanor, who in turn called us at 9:08 PM Tuesday evening, November 28. Jane was in class so I took the call.*

(Eleanor said Mr. Andrews is on the White House staff, and the letter is President Nixon's way of inviting Dick to dinner with him.

(At the time I read the copy to Richard and Eleanor on the phone, the name Andrews had no meaning for them, etc.)

SESSION 629 (DELETED PORTION)
NOVEMBER 29, 1972 9:28 PM WEDNESDAY

(This is the first portion of the 629th session for November 29, 1972.)
Now, I bid you good evening—
("Good evening, Seth.")
—and I have a few remarks for you both.

I did remind Ruburt that the body, the body's condition, the negative aspects of the body's condition, that is not the problem.

(This afternoon while Jane was going down the front flight of stairs from our apartment, etc.)

The body is not the issue. As long as you consider the body's difficulties as the issue, then you miss the point, and again are tempted to deal with the result as if it were the cause.

(In quotes:) "We will be happier when Ruburt is better," or "We will feel more together when Ruburt is better," or "We will make love more often when Ruburt is better." All such ideas are not only beside the point, but lead you to use the symptoms or the result or hide the source.

I am to some extent oversimplifying to make my point, but the body is in the condition it is because you did not feel close enough together, et cetera. Do you follow me?

("Yes.")

Some information in the book will be of great value to you. It is not time for them to appear as yet in the book proper, but any material not handled in normal conscious life, not grappled with, if it becomes overcharged or lasts over a period of time, will be unconsciously expressed. The more you handle your conscious beliefs and daily problems and relationships then, the healthier you will be in all areas, even if you do not solve the problems. It is when you give up facing them on a normal daily level that you abdicate your responsibility, so to speak.

The belief that a given problem cannot be solved can cause much difficulty, unless you freely and consciously give it up; particularly when inner organs are affected, this point plays a strong part. A diseased organ that is then removed through an operation often represents an unfaced problem, or one that is considered beyond solving. It is then symbolically thrown away, you see. Since people only have so many organs to lose, that road can be dangerous indeed.

Ruburt spread his physical problem around more, bodywise; in such a way, he thought he could endure longer, you see, rather than attacking a critical organ.

You have made strides, and the gain is highly beneficial. I can only encourage you as you have begun. Now take a break unless you have questions on this material.

("No."

(9:41—9:51.)

Now. Still remarks—and be glad for them.

You have not come off scot free. You held back in your work, and in selling it, feeling that you must make up—not for Ruburt's symptoms, but because you felt you were not relating as emotionally as you could, and realizing that this same warmth was necessary to your work.

So if you did not give it as freely as you thought you should to Ruburt, then you would also keep it to the same degree (underlined) out of your work. This was not merely some self-punishing situation. You would be led to question why you were not pleased with your work as you thought you should be, and hence back to the original problem.

A good relationship between you frees repressed emotion on both of your parts, which then pours over into your work and illuminates all of your interi-

or and exterior landscapes both symbolically and literally.

The Speaker manuscripts are in your future, and will involve as I told you considerable work—a labor of love. Now give us a moment.

(9:59. This was the end of the personal material. Seth now resumed dictation on his book. During the above presentation, Jane was again aware of channels being available from Seth, about us, the speakers, the book, etc.; she could tune into any of these, etc.

DELETED SESSION
DECEMBER 4, 1972 9:30 PM MONDAY

Now. Good evening.

("Good evening, Seth.")

This is not dictation. Now. Contrary to most thought on such matters, no one is given a particular amount of talent that must then be used.

Talent does not come in quantities. Instead people have varying abilities to use any of an infinite number of channels, any one of which in your terms leads to an inexhaustible source. The channels by their nature will translate and shape creative energy with their unique dimensions.

You are not given 800 or 5,000 milligrams of talent. You are given your own nature, certain portions of it naturally tuning in to what in your case you could call the channel of art. You sense its great dimensions, the richness of its complexity. You are particularly attuned to it.

You have only to be open and receptive. When you think in terms of having (in quotes) "a certain amount of ability," then you become concerned that you use every portion of it, when in greater terms no such "it" exists.

You naturally express your nature through your use of the channel of art. Your ability to draw upon that channel is endless. The certain-amount-of-ability idea is highly limiting. It forces upon you a sense of responsibility to use what you have, while instead it should mean simply being what you are, and being what you are (underlined) will automatically produce excellent paintings.

You have to let yourself go and paint. In your early life you learned the discipline of form, most necessary. The knowledge of form is one that many never assimilate. You were giving yourself a thorough foundation. The framework, learning the form first, was adopted for several reasons, having to do with other existences, to some extent given.

Your knowledge of form now can work for you automatically, serving to give structure to those ideas which will come to you freely and clearly. Your own (in quotes) "psychic abilities" now give you easy (underlined) access to inspiration. You must forget the idea as you have it, that your painting must serve to work out problems. In that framework you set problems.

The paintings are to provide illuminations which are the result of questions and not of problems. You know enough technically to solve any such problems in those old limited terms.

We are onto you tonight. *(Humorously.)*

Forget the idea of man's work and what your paintings should (underlined) provide, and the idea of fame or success. Let yourself go with the joy of painting what you want to; but forgetting also, again, the idea that your paintings are working out problems, technical or not.

In doodles, in oils, in whatever suits you, and whatever suits you over a period of time, will find its own pattern. Do not harness yourself with the idea that you had (underlined) "so much" (in quotes) ability, and that you have not used it. That is not the case. You have instead an open channel. You chose to spend a good amount of time dealing with form.

You wanted to express ideas in paintings that do not come in youth, and to merge a particular kind of understanding with a particular kind of form. You had an existence in which your art matured early, as Josef in Ruburt's *Seven*. You dealt with emotion unrestrained by discipline, and with the feelings of a young man. Josef was not able to paint anything worthwhile past the age of 40, and he turned to a land-owner's province.

You wanted to express now the fuller inspirations that come later, and with an exquisite sense of form that Josef never learned. The sense of form incidentally will, mark my words, emerge in a new way for you, but even the information given that so upset you had its purpose in your whole plan.

(See the deleted session for November 29, 1972.)

You knew when you would be ready and your emotions, repressed until then, would then emerge as new to illuminate the forms and to fill them out.

You may take your break and I will continue.

(10:03—10:23.)

Now. Regardless of what you think, pure inspiration has nothing to do with time. Each artist has other overall concepts to work with besides those regarding his art.

Van Gogh, for your information, was (underlined) obsessed personally with ideas of self-mutilation, and underwent great inner torture. He chose those feelings however so that he could view the world and reality in a certain light. That light enabled him to do what he wanted to but could not fake: paint the world through that particular unique vision.

Wheat fields for example, filled not only with the vitality of sun and growth but bristling with creativity that (in quotes) "destroyed" each part of itself in death, that was transformed instantaneously into a new spectacular form in which the creativity and destruction were always apparent, and yet one in which violence was necessarily turned into life.

Personally then he took upon himself what you would say perhaps were great problems—too great for the personality to handle, but his inner tendencies for self-mutilation always kept his vision true to <u>his</u> main image of the world.

Your own great problem, the inhibition of emotion, fits in with your own designs as well as his did. He was not ever satisfied with his work and had far less satisfaction in general from his fellow beings than you have.

His "success" (in quotes) was no success to him. The illumination that makes great paintings, again, has nothing to do with time. A man may work for nearly a century and not attain it, or it may come tomorrow afternoon.

Van Gogh was true to his vision, which means he was true to the self he created for himself in that time, and so must you be. But you must also have faith in what you have done, for it was all done in faithful rendering of your view of reality (in quotes) "at any given time." And therefore the fact for example that you withheld certain kinds of emotion from it is not a failure.

The repression however was to remind you of freer patterns that would and could flow. A landscape is not lacking because it is not a portrait. They are two different kinds of things, but you would sense the different kind of thing. Now. The repressed emotion itself is apparent in your past paintings. It is something that you cannot try to put into them. You cannot fake it, and so you did not fake it.

The paintings therefore speak in themselves of the unspoken that wishes to speak, the hidden that wants to be revealed. One of your purposes has been to express just that.

You also wanted your work to show and express those mysterious moments when <u>the rivers begin to flow</u> (underlined), the heart learns to speak. The rain begins to form. You wanted to express in painting then the freeing of emotions—that could not be expressed unless first there had been repression, and those energies in full blossom that have nothing to do with age.

There are all kinds of other issues involved in which you and Ruburt acquiesced, and for your individual and joint purposes.

Now. Take a brief break. Ruburt will want his matches, and we will continue.

(10:45—10:58.)

Now you cannot regard your ability as something apart from yourself, which you must use. It is instead your own characteristic method of expressing reality, of perceiving inner data; the particular channel of your own understanding, learning and application, to which there are no limits.

Your ability is an expression of what you are. Considering it apart from yourself sets up a division that is unnecessary, and can be detrimental in that (underlined) regard.

You place too great a burden upon yourself when you consider your ability something that must (underlined) be used. It flows through you naturally. Many spontaneous ideas for paintings and sketches you automatically reject because of several reasons. They do not fit in with your ideas of work (underlined), or with your idea of what you think you ought (underlined) to do, or because you are being too ponderous, and hence shove away many spontaneously playful ideas.

Now give us a moment. You must recapture the feeling of painting for fun. The play of the gods: your natural expression. Instead you project ponderous ideas of success or failure, consider work as a series of problems to be solved, and forget the idea of spontaneously creating.

Do not think so in terms of stages of paintings and their execution. See the complete painting as you want it, and have the faith that it will look that way. Instead you are overly concerned with the stages it will go through, or must, and this is inhibiting.

Let the image in your mind flow imaginatively onto the board. You often think so in terms of the problems to be worked out that you concentrate upon those, in your terms. Do one of two things if there are distractions. Admit them and quite freely allow them to go into the painting freely, or firmly tell yourself that you will not allow them to divert you. But take one stand or the other.

Your form is ready. The ideas I have given you will bring that form to free life, however, if you use them. Your emotional life has already been enriched of late with the interactions with Ruburt. You are both doing well in following what I told you. Continue to do so.

All information given by me concerning the future and the books stands.

Your own giving is flowing into your work. Let your work have its way. Do not insist it be such and such. Allow it its flow; and now I bid you a fond good evening.

I will make a comment about the painting before I leave—and not one you particularly earlier expected. But there is the utterance beginning to speak, the face about to move, the eyes about to brim with feeling.

The image therefore of yourself standing with the knowledge of the unspoken, the unexpressed, on the verge of new expression. The painting on the verge then of coming alive.

And <u>now</u> I bid you a fond good evening.

("Good evening, Seth. Thank you very much.")

And then we will return next time to dictation. But you are both doing well.

("Yes. Thank you."

(11:22. The portrait discussed above is one I recently finished after many attempts. I nearly discarded it several times, and even now realize its shortcomings. I "saved it", and learned from it, but it of course bears the scars of the struggle. It's serving as the basis for new work and ideas also. The long-haired man facing the viewer's left.

(Larry from New York City wants to buy it.... December 5, 1972.

(Then Rick Stack—in April 1973.)

SESSION 630 (DELETED PORTION)
DECEMBER 11, 1972 10:47 PM MONDAY

(This material is from the regular session, 630, for December 11, 1972.)

Now. We have given you an idea for a book—Merry Christmas—and some dictation, beginning chapter seven. Now I have a few comments.

You are doing excellently, relating to Ruburt. The badminton is good for you both. The sexual encounters are also most valuable, <u>and</u> for you both from several viewpoints.

Ruburt often mentions schedules. Sometimes at certain periods in his life schedules are good, focusing his energies in certain directions. At other times he experiences them as limiting. Continuing your relationship as it is now is highly important, and the basis necessary for my next suggestion as to Ruburt's behavior.

This is for a definite schedule on his part for a while, that will channel his energy in creative goals, and also toward some physical goals—and incidentally away from the symptoms.

The badminton is to be a part of it, of course. Added is either a short walk per day, or going out with you. The four hours of writing and a half-hour devoted either to psy-time or out-of-body work. These periods can be extended as he progresses; that is, the psy-time.

Though he does not see the connection he has learned some important things this last weekend. Remind him that spontaneity does also include saying no at times. It is important that you discuss with him your ideas about our joint work, and the nature of my reality. The information given in past sessions applies.

The trust in the nature of his own being is important. When it seemed you were rejecting him this aggravated his own doubts. The program I outlined will be of great value, as will the book for you.

You should both, as Ruburt thought earlier, go out into the public at least one night within a two-week period. Ruburt is quite able physically to do so. It may be easier to go someplace where you are not known to begin.

Tell him immediately about my suggestion, for he has played around with the idea but not initiated it—the schedule is what I am speaking about here.

And now, dear author—I bid you a fond good evening. Unless you have questions I will end the session.

("No." 11:01.)

DELETED SESSION
DECEMBER 13, 1972 9:39 PM WEDNESDAY

(After supper this evening both Jane and I did a lot of griping and complaining about her symptoms, and our inability to solve the problems involved. We were very disappointed that all of our recent efforts, in line with Seth's suggestions, hadn't resulted in any improvement.

(We could only think that something, somewhere, somehow, had escaped our daily notice; yet to pin this down seemed beyond our means. We felt exhausted. I finally went back to the studio to relax a bit. Unknown to me Jane used her pendulum in her workroom. When we sat for the session around 9 PM, Jane said her pendulum told her that the symptoms were caused by the house we lived in, and, specifically, by the original owner. This individual, nameless to us, had built the elaborate shower in apartment five, which is one of the two apartments we have here.

(We used this shower for years. The only thing we knew about it was, after all, talk that the owner had installed it for therapeutic relief from arthritis. We had no idea if Jane's pendulum data was the magic we were looking for, but at least we hadn't considered this idea before. It sounded too simple to me at first, but still....

(Jane was so wrought up that at first she thought a session might not develop. Both of us were angry. "Boy, Seth, you better come up with some answers," she said. Much more talk followed; we speculated about ramifications stemming from the idea that the house was involved. Seth finally interrupted us.)

Now—

("Good evening.")

—if I may presume. *(Pause.)*

You always regarded this place as a place of transition. It was thought of in terms of social transition, or your place in society, and transition in terms of your work, particularly here on Ruburt's side—on his part. Money for example through books would allow you to move.

He is in a state of frozen waiting, and all of the elements given in the past have applied. The environment has gone down; the garden apartment here that he once thought of no longer exists. He thought of this place as highly desirable once in social terms—the best place you had ever lived in together. As the neighborhood deteriorated he became more and more irate, as did you.

Any thoughts of moving were always put off, until a tomorrow that has not come. Beyond the early years he did little improving. He is highly sensitive to environment, and needs—*(suddenly louder:)* and do not frown, and keep writing. I am angry at both of you this evening. More at Ruburt, but I cannot yell at him—

("I'm writing.")

(This was a real reaction from Seth. I felt the force of his momentary anger, I felt personally involved. I also thought that this might stem from Jane's expressed feelings of anger and resentment before the session, and her demands that Seth help. Perhaps this method had its merits?)

Now there were unfortunate aspects to which you both did react, but in the beginning there were compensating factors in the beauty of the environment, the whole view. I did encourage you to move at one time.

Now. It is the putting off of satisfactions that you want, always into the future. If you really do not care about the satisfactions they do not matter. If you constantly want them without making any conscious effort, then that involves a constant sense of stress.

Work is involved, in that Ruburt always expected you would move as soon as he made any amount of money at all. You have been also highly ambiguous in your own attitudes about your dwelling. He felt you would not do anything about it. He did nothing about it on his own, except finally to rent the other apartment, but he has been holding his breath quite literally, for some time.

In the past many of you here were of the same age group. Now with younger people about the thoughts are stronger that this is a place of transition. The fact that you have not moved does reflect a lack of initiative on both of your parts.

To some considerable degree you have not been willing to count on yourself. You have negatively assumed that you could find nothing suitable—no place, that is—and resented the time involved. The change, the added space, for a while did help, you see. Ruburt does feel closed in; to some extent you also do —not free for example in the summer to take advantage of the yard—one minute example. But you live with some constant aggravation.

(*It's true that Jane improved considerably when we took the second apartment across the hall the summer before last. Yet I, at least, didn't connect this with her improvement.*)

The two apartments helped, but in a way there is less privacy because of the public hall, you see. You have used your dwelling place as a symbol then, which is why it becomes important. Otherwise it would not be an issue. Ruburt has strongly held down any tendencies through the years to spend any money, small as it might be, in decorating, buying furniture, simply because of your joint attitudes, the feeling of transition.

These tendencies have been almost completely repressed. But, again, they are not unconscious. Ruburt felt disloyal thinking of them because such thoughts seemed to him to criticize your joint life style and purposes.

Many then of the things that you want, quite normal things, have been always (underlined) projected into the future, which no matter how he works never comes. This also applies to you. It is simply not that much of a problem to move—to act, to make a change—it is not all that dangerous.

The question, however brings up all of your attitudes—and you also have social attitudes—another apartment is no answer in that context. The thought of buying a house brings up strong feelings of inadequacy on your part. You feel that you should have been able to provide one for Ruburt by now.

He feels that you should have also, or you should have been satisfied with your work, regardless, one way or the other. So the issue is highly charged whenever you discuss it, and on the few occasions when you have looked around.

(*True. I always thought that my work made up for the lack of success in obtaining a dwelling we liked. I counted on the success of the work, so when the work seemed to be failing also I was caught.*)

The last episode, around the corner (*on Grove Street, in a flooded area*) did not apply, it was a token gesture. Each of you knew you would not live close to the river. Ruburt is also afraid of changing the status quo, however, as you are. So both of you have resented the other for not making a definite decision to move.

Now you may take your break.

(*10:05—10:28.*)

In many ways you are as stubborn as he is—and regardless of what you thought, you complained quite constantly, both about the job, your own work, and your dwelling. But once set upon a course, you would not change it either, and Ruburt would have done anything to see you happy in <u>that</u> (underlined) regard.

He felt finally that at least if you worked full time for yourself <u>that</u> (underlined) complaint would be taken care of. He considered it a practical move in the physical universe, one of the few actual changes that either of you had decided to make in all that time.

Now you are both creatures of habit, wanting feelings of security in which to work. Otherwise you would have moved a long time ago. Because you have no family you do respond with and to your environment strongly, and that response colors your health and your work.

Each person responds far more to the environment, that they also create, than is realized. The reason why moving often helps, and sometimes does not, is fairly obvious. A good move physically represents an inner change that then seeks a new environment in which it is materialized.

Without understanding however you can simply project all the problems. In your case a move would have such drastic connotations, and be so symbolic, that its beneficial nature is assured. Your <u>not</u> moving symbolically represents your not doing many things—your not facing many issues.

They will become apparent the minute you even <u>decide</u> to move. Your particular needs, for example. The parking for class. The feelings of privacy you enjoy, yet the need also for some neighborly encounters that you also require. *(Meaning me.)*

In your present dwelling there are many obvious issues. The two tiny kitchens show clearly that the nourishment of food has been given the last spot, in both of your lives. Ruburt simply carried it to the extreme, but the inclination is obvious in your dwelling.

<u>He is afraid to move</u> (underlined three times)—but he will also be excited. You are also afraid to move, and both of you are wary of fitting yourselves into a new environment, and in a small but significant way, of making a new personal world.

Ruburt is hardly able to do housework. He does not want to do it. It is his resentment against this apartment *(5)*. This room *(the living room)* is the only one he regularly enters.

He went like a squirrel, trying to satisfy his love of environment, changing this place about in a fury of frustration, and finally gave it up. Briefly, the new environment next door aroused him, but the apartment, while representing expansion, as I told you then, also carried a built-in boomerang—the public hall, the lack of coordination, a divided place. Of course it had advantages, or you would not, either of you, have considered it.

Both of you then have considered your dwelling place a symbol of not going ahead, of lack of initiative. Had you attempted better to coordinate the establishment, had you bought furniture, this would have made a difference. You never decided, you see, that this would be your home, for any (underlined) amount of time.

Now. Many of these characteristics are not particularly negative at all. For example, Ruburt never felt comfortable in the yard when *[the]* Spazianis and the neighborhood ladies gathered. Neither did you. The bushes at the side however, and the garden area, largely compensated, and the secret quality the corner had.

Your resentment of Spaziani when he sold was projected upon him. It was anger mainly at yourself. You felt forced to stay. Other elements were involved, but the strength of your resentment, its charge, had to do with your own feelings about yourself and this place, as did Ruburt's with Piper.

Leonard made a home here, and Ruburt for all of his disdain with Leonard's taste, was furious at taking Leonard's discard. Yet it always seemed impractical to do anything here, since surely you were both going to move.

Now all of these issues made him more and more susceptible to certain influences that were in the house. The influences were not dangerous unless you were in the mental mood to be affected by them.

There were a series of seemingly innocuous desires, but forever put off, it seemed. Now with people who have many other sources of amusement, occupation, family gatherings and social episodes, such things do not have such meaning. Most of your contacts are professional; you both work at home. The environment therefore becomes highly important, as the living medium in which you work. This is one reason why you were not as affected as Ruburt, because you were away from the environment part of the day. Do you follow me?

("How about the last year?"

(*Since I left Artistic last February, in other words. I also would like Seth to elaborate on the top paragraph on this page, about influences in the house. Is he saying that these influences were those indicated by Jane's pendulum this evening?*)

Up until that time. I am saying that the build-up of influences affected Ruburt more because this was his only environment through those years when you were away part time.

Now that you are here the relevance is important, but you do not have the built-up accumulation. At one time Ruburt could walk in the yard, you see, in privacy. He felt shielded. Now you do not understand how both of your attitudes were affected, as the house itself changed and as it changed hands.

You particularly felt threatened. It would be foolish to the extreme to stay here when you are both consciously and unconsciously waiting for the bridge to be built. You felt your territory threatened as soon as the parking lot was thought of, and earlier when Spaziani first thought of selling the place.

Some of the small, seemingly silly issues forever put off: a private backyard, shielding trees outside, a front and back door of your own, for Ruburt a dog, both of you a unit of your own; that is, a house over which you had control.

You have private rooms now in a public area that becomes more public all the time, as tenants, strangers, move in and out. For a while the whole house had feelings of privacy when the same tenants, for example Lucy, were here for some time. With a change in tenants the halls for example become anonymous, all of these feelings strongly operate, and on both of your parts. Ruburt reacts physically, he waits physically. You do not feel safe to work.

Now in this structure everything else is aggravated—the feelings between you and Ruburt mentioned so often for example. You both feel hampered in love-making. He does not feel he can let go. To raise your voice, to express aggression when you feel it, becomes a cautious endeavor. In the past you felt surrounded at least by relative good will… changing tenants alters those feelings, however. You both resented it.

I will let you take a break, and continue.

("Thank you."

(Louder): At least you are not frowning at me.

(11:10. When she came out of it, Jane said, "I'm afraid to move." She meant getting out of the rocker, going to the bathroom, etc., then said this was mixed up with moving out of this house, etc. Resume at 11:20.)

Now. The symptoms began to show when it seemed to Ruburt changes should be made.

In the beginning he was caught between sheer fury and desperation. His first hardcover was out, and instead of changing the situation for the better he was faced with a job after writing full time.

Your relationship at that time was very poor. I have given you material on it. It was a severe shock to him because of his earlier high dreams—and not to be smiled at. It frightened him.

("I'm not smiling, really."

(Rather, I thought at least that my expression was one of rueful recollection and regret….)

The Seth Material hardcover did not financially change the situation that much, but his classes began to bring in money. The dream book's failure was also important financially. The money itself meant little difference to him. Where he lives with you is <u>highly</u> important, and if you remember always has been.

When he decided to add to your establishment, his class did pick up, and has. He wanted to see if you could afford that much more rent, sure that if you realized it <u>you</u> (underlined) would see the light and decide to move. You were waiting for him to make such a decision. You both blamed circumstances, but also each other for the lack of initiative.

It seemed to him that you were always going to leave your job one day and paint, but that day never came and the two of you were going to move one day, but that day never came, so he forced the one issue. In Florida he thought seriously of living there to make a move, but nothing came of it. Your discussion this evening at the table about finances led him deeper into those feelings he tries so hard to avoid. Here he was doing better than ever, with more money in the offing, and to what purpose? Nothing would ever change. He could not keep up financially, much less think of moving, so put it ahead in the future again.

He often reads ads to you, testing your reaction. Only once did you take him up on this, so he felt you did not want to move. He is and has been terrified of making decisions where you are involved, because he feels you so resented your mother's treatment of your father.

Then he becomes angry when you say "Why don't you make a decision?" He felt you were afraid to, and if he made one and it was wrong, he did not want to take the blame. So he felt in an impossible situation: and quite consciously, when he allowed himself to become aware of his thoughts. He is afraid of hurting you, of making you move, or making you cry.

Now. Neither of you were ready to make such a physical change. Financially he could have, as you can now, but you were not willing to face the issues beneath. You would have moved out of resentment, feeling forced to, and not out of understanding.

Ruburt's own fear, and fear for you, kept the material hidden; as did incidentally, the flood. It was simply an excuse in a way, but on the other hand Ruburt recognized the difficulties during that time. Also you both felt some loyalty to the house, and would not leave it in that condition. Ruburt does not think of money, but he can produce it with great facility—when he wants it for something, so he has been enraged at this useless money, in those terms.

Now money for security he does want, but this he sees after the necessities are taken care of: a suitable environment. If he is not happy today, money in the bank is meaningless to him. He also felt that a house might interfere with your ideas of work—the added responsibility, and he kept that in mind.

Your mother's home would not have served your purposes, yours or Ruburt's. I tell you that so that you realize you did not make a mistake.

There is no doubt that it is easier for Ruburt to get clear information on others. This has to do with the mechanics of the mind. He is not involved in the same way with others. Even the information given to others, though it may be completely correct, will not be accepted unless they are ready for it. In this case the personality has to bypass itself as much as possible, and then hope for a clear-enough channel.

This evening for example, your after-dinner conversation aroused Ruburt's own fears, sent him into an emotional state in which he accepted them, used them, exaggerated even his desperation, hoping to force an answer.

The pendulum work and the ideas on the part of the intuitive self began the process, but then the emotional state had to be quieted from a peak condition in order for the session to proceed.

There has been deep resentment here, and on both of your parts, having to do with decision making, and misunderstandings. Now you may take a break or end the session as you prefer.

("We'll take the break. Thank you."

(11:45. After leaving trance Jane said, "I'm afraid to move," then explained that this time she was afraid only of moving away from this house. Getting up wasn't involved, etc. 12:00 midnight.)

Now. Through the years Ruburt has always been the one to watch the ads, at least in spurts, and watched your reaction.

It was never enthusiastic, and you never suggested checking on the places listed. When he did so he did it on his own, and you did not seem enthusiastic at all.

Trips *(vacations)* were meaningless in the context. They had nothing to do with moving. You knew you would return. Not only that but if you spent much money the possibility of moving diminished.

<u>You</u> *(me)* (underlined) have a tendency to think in terms of obstacles. Ruburt allowed this to add to <u>latent</u> (underlined) characteristics of his own. Your joint ideas then prevented you from ever thinking creatively. You never thought that moving could be fun—and that is your reality. No one else created it.

It is composed of a conglomeration of quite conscious but unexamined, or rather unassembled, beliefs about yourselves, some quite contradictory, and your "place" in the world.

You did not feel until recently that you were moving ahead in your work. The two ideas combined. The act of moving means leaving and beginning. While you were at Artistic you both used that as an excuse. All of your attitudes will come into focus as you decide to move, and when you move. That is, I think, enough for you both this evening, so I bid you a fond good night.

("Good night, Seth. Thank you very much.")

And do not be overly harsh on yourselves, as you both have an unfortunate tendency to do so.

(12:09 AM.)

SESSION 631 (DELETED PORTION)
DECEMBER 18, 1972 11:07 PM MONDAY

(The following material was delivered after book dictation in the 631st session. Break was at 10:55.)

Now. There is, as you know, a breakthrough in your work. The rest will flow from that. You both thought in terms of problems when you considered money, for example; you thought of the problems involved.

When you thought of the kind of painting you wanted to do you did the same thing. The concentration upon the problems in all instances contributed to them to a large degree. What I said about money applies. Had either of you really examined your conscious beliefs about this place, and put them together, you would have known that for yourselves.

I told you that you would be faced consciously with many attitudes that you had put into the background, when you decided to move, so Ruburt has been meeting some of his own. The holidays mean that the affair will be put of a while, so in capsule effect you have now the quintessence of the problem: now facing the issues that you earlier ignored.

Concentration in other areas, as you suggested, is the answer now while you made definite efforts in the moving direction. Ruburt is on the right track with his ideas today, particularly in concentrating upon the moment. This is highly important.

If that alone is kept in mind almost immediate improvement can be effected. Think however in terms of what you want as far as a house is concerned, and not on any imagined problems or obstacles in your way. Take it for granted you can find a house you want and can afford.

Form a clear picture in your mind. Place an ad in the paper stating your desires. If you want put such an ad in a Valley paper also. Use a box number, if that is your preference.

As you know, you (underlined) are getting back on a solid footing you have not felt for some time. Your response to my suggestions regarding Ruburt has been excellent. Everything I gave you last time applies, and it also shows him that you are willing to move in other areas also.

("Yes, but so far I don't think my encouragement has done any good.")

You have shown an important breakthrough in your work. Your brushes were straight and in good condition. Ruburt's will allow him to make his breakthrough. You must see how the problem acclimated responses leading to not moving, etc., on both your parts and continued Ruburt's condition. You focused, both of you, upon the problem.

("But I don't see any signs, really, that anything we've done has changed his condition in any way.")

I have not told you that there were physical signs as yet to see, any more than I have told you that you have already moved into another house, but both conditions do now exist.

A comparable attitude as the one you have would run this way: "I am sure I am going to move, but there is no house in front of me to move into, so obviously no such house exists." The answer is still your beliefs, and in your joint attitudes.

("I'm not projecting any of this into the future. I'm just saying that so far the beliefs leading to the symptoms have been impregnable.")

Many of them, particularly since the last session, are becoming fully conscious on his part, not invisible, where they can be dealt with, and that is all I can tell you.

There are invisible barriers in your understanding that you are moving through yourselves, so that what I am saying will become far clearer when you see the results that are already taking place.

I bid you then a fond good evening—

("Thank you. The same to you.")

—and remember, your beliefs are your beliefs about reality. That is the end of our session.

(11:30. After Jane was out of trance, I explained to her that I didn't understand the paragraph marked *. *Shortly after I began reading it to her Seth returned:)*

Now. You are tired. The analogy was a simple one. You painted a picture, showed great improvement in so doing, but you did not start out with crooked brushes. They were in excellent condition. Ruburt is trying to paint a new physical picture of his body from himself. In the analogy he does not start with your perfect brushes however, but with limbs not straight. His tools had to be adjusted first before he can make the same breakthrough, yet it is just as certain. I thought it was clear.

("I understand." True, I was very tired.)

Then I bid you a fond good evening.

("Thank you. Good night." 11:35.)

DELETED SESSION
JANUARY 1, 1973 8:30 PM MONDAY (A HOLIDAY)

(Late yesterday afternoon my pendulum told me that Jane's symptoms stemmed from her feeling that she had failed to become a successful "straight" writer—a novelist, poet, essayist, et al.; that she felt she had failed as the serious writer she had always dreamed of becoming, that the psychic work represented a turning down a wrong path; that actually, basically, the psychic work represented failure to her rather than success. I was very excited by these ideas, more excited than I had been in a long time. I intuitively felt them to be true. I discussed them for some little while with her before we went out to a New Year's Eve party at McClure's. Jane seemed to agree with the ideas.

(At a quick scan I thought the ideas answered all the questions we'd had about the symptoms over the years—explaining, for instance, their onset before the psychic developments, etc. They seemed to offer a unified theory to cover the years of our marriage, and even Jane's childhood. I saw at once that if valid they also meant Jane must shelve her projected book, Adventures in Consciousness, *and concentrate on things like* Rich Bed, *the* Dialogues *(poetry), and, perhaps, let Seth do his own thing in sessions. If this included writing books, okay. But crisis time was here, and something had to be done. I was somewhat puzzled that I hadn't asked my pendulum this specific set of questions before—or had I? If I had, perhaps I hadn't understood the answers, I thought; because certainly no action had been taken because of them, along the lines now contemplated....*

(The data in the session sums up our discussions following the pendulum session. It goes without saying that we were most eager for the session. I deeply hoped Seth would agree with us. We also had some questions, and these are adequately referred to in the session....)

Now—

("Good evening, Seth."

—we will begin easily enough, so bear with me.

I told you that as you considered moving your attitudes would suddenly become quite clear, and other issues would be deeply involved. *(In the deleted data for December 18, 1972. True.)* The idea of mobility in one direction, and of moving, would cause all of your other ideas to move.

I will mention some issues, and then come back to them.

For some time Ruburt felt he was a failure, as a wife and as a writer. He did not see you succeeding, either. Conditions mentioned far earlier made communication difficult, and he brooded. The mobility, the point of mobility, represented moving ahead in his work, or not moving ahead. The apartment became a symbol. It was quite all right for the aspiring writer. If however he could not achieve the kind of success he wanted, then he might as well have the trappings.

(I was quite surprised the other day when Jane told me that our two apartments were okay to her if she was a writer, but not all right for a psychic—especially one who was becoming well known and was visited by all kinds of people, etc. She also told me that to her the idea of stairs represented success and failure—up and down, etc.)

He is quite correct in saying *(today)* he denied to some extent an important aspect *(of himself)*. The problem was in consciously hiding the conflicts from himself, and in deciding upon a status quo. Status quos can never be maintained to begin with. Some of this should be clear, and is, I know, but we will put it together, and I will clear some issues for you.

The *ESP* book was meant to be a book—one book. In the beginning he did not want to publish the material, if you recall. Not because he did not like the material, but because then, at least, he understood that for him (underlined) assembling it during his creative hours was not fulfilling his kind of creative need.

(Yes, I recall clearly urging Jane to publish the material; most regrettable now, of course. A serious error, for at that time she instinctively knew what was best for her. I want her to go back to relying upon her instincts and intuitions.)

The creativity was in the sessions. Because he felt a responsibility to the work, and because of another publication—a hardcover book—he consented to *The Seth Material*. The "acclaim" (in quotes) of a tour helped revive him initially, and he began ideas of a novel.

It had a psychic basis. Tam wanted another psychic book. Ruburt objected enough to refuse to do a series like the Cayce books, but tried to compromise with the *Dream/Seth* book, which also involved him with the typing of records. You needed the money, he felt.

He tried to do a narrative, and use for example descriptive abilities—a valiant attempt to do two different things in one book. Before all of this, as the very first symptoms began, before the *ESP* book, he was already deeply frightened by the novel rejections, the *Playboy* rejections after they raised his hopes, the poetry book acceptance that fell through with Continental, and what he felt to be your joint deteriorating relationship.

There were also financial considerations. He had only lately freed himself from a part-time job. To refuse a psychic book that was definite, to try for another novel with no assurances, seemed foolhardy. At the same time his age bothered him. The young writer, aspiring, was no longer so young.

At the same time he began to doubt his writing abilities. Perhaps he had overjudged his talents. Following *The Seth Material*, requests came that showed quite clearly he was regarded as a psychic. Psychics helped people. I told him to stay away from spiritualistic groups. He has a strong sense of responsibility and loyalty. He avoided being a "psychic personality" (in quotes) in grand terms. I am digressing here to bring you another issue: the strong responsibility he always felt toward his writing ability, he naturally felt toward the psychic ability—but without the necessary sense of discrimination, since he didn't realize what such activities involved.

As a writer for example, alone, he does not feel a <u>responsibility</u> (underlined) to write <u>every kind</u> of book possible: gothics, mysteries, science fiction, poetry, essays, straight novels. There is no reason why he should, though he has the <u>ability</u> to write any of them well. So he need not feel that he has a responsibility to be a psychic healer, a clairvoyant, a medium, a psychic psychologist, and so forth, though he has the ability to be any of these.

He did however feel that responsibility. Conflicts arose because his responsibilities clashed. Other quite ordinary issues were involved, some fears he did not want to admit. At times he was convinced that he had made a failure of his life so far—with you and his work.

You were involved in his attitudes. He felt *(long pause at 9 PM)* that he had no right to try to do "creative" (in quotes) work that might not pay. He felt also that you were jealous of his own writing, but not of the psychic work, this being further in the past.

When you want a break let me know.

("Okay." A recent check with my pendulum shows no residue of jealousy in any area, etc.)

The dream book incidentally *(which Eleanor Friede now has)* in different form—far different—will be published. So will *Adventures*—and when he is in a better position to evaluate his *Adventures*. He did not want *Dreams* published. *Adventures* initially was a way of leading him back into "I" writing, and toward *Aspects* and *Rich Bed*.

It *(Adventures)* also served to regenerate his creative abilities, which had lagged in *Dreams*. *Seven* saved him from another *Dreams (book)* and also provided him with a contract.

My books will provide a different kind of accelerated creativity that can be achieved in no other way, and that will leave him freedom to pursue another kind of creativity that can come only from him, and <u>not</u> from me. This could not have developed in the beginning, however.

Do you want a break?

("Yes, I guess so.")

You do not have to take notes here. I am trying to bring you up to date consecutively, and interwind all events so that you can follow. *(Seth added by way of explanation, etc.*

(9:06. The session was going excellently, I told Jane. I mentioned three questions I hoped Seth would cover at least in part: Jane's projected call to Tam at Prentice-Hall tomorrow morning, re substituting Seth's new book for Adventures; Jane's planned letter to Eleanor Friede about Rich Bed*; and whether Jane should continue with ESP class.*

(Resume at 9:24.)

Now. Last summer, or rather the one before the flood *(in June 1972)* improvements were obvious *(in 1971)*. The reasons you should know. The pressure of the dream book was gone. He was not doing something he did not want to do. The move *(across the hall into our second apartment)* meant mobility. Your relationship began to improve to an important degree.

He was between books, just having money from *Seth Speaks*. There were several things <u>you</u> had still not learned, however, that you have now learned. The relationship would be very good, then, but some old characteristic responses of ours would occur now and then, and frighten him. He began to move toward a new contract, which meant *Adventures*, he felt, rather than *Rich Bed*.

Initially there was great enthusiasm with both, but *Rich Bed* was his baby and *Adventures* a method of learning and an initial way of releasing pent-up creative energy. It <u>had</u> a purpose, and has. It meant however more creative time spent in <u>examining</u> (underlined) the psychic experience. At the same time he hoped Tam would take *Rich Bed*, knowing he wouldn't. Unconsciously Tam sensed that dilemma, as he senses this one. *Seven* was the answer. In the meantime your being home also meant that he was face to face with you. You could see his condition, and as given earlier he tried to hide from you at times most of all.

After *Seth Speaks* was duly accepted, and while he was working on *Adventures* and *Rich Bed* initially, then he improved. The creative energy splashed over psychically in some poetry and in Sumari. Following that period he began to realize that *Adventures* <u>for the present</u> had served its purpose. Again he had another psychic book, and hopes of a contract, <u>and Tam did not want Rich Bed</u>.

Seven was the answer, but only if *Seven* led where it was supposed to lead. In the meantime there was the matter of a tour, or not, for *Seth Speaks*, and speaking engagements. He felt that if he accepted and became known as a psychic, in those terms, his chances of becoming known as a writer were lost, and beyond recovery. He would be pigeon-holed as a psychic. It was for those reasons that his improvement deteriorated.

Now, the stairs represent going up and down on a treadmill, and getting nowhere. He seemed unable to move in any direction. This had to do with your apartment, which actually suited him fine for some time. But other dissatisfactions not faced were projected there also, and exaggerated, while there seemed to be nothing he could do about it.

He also felt that if you were a success as an artist he could write what he damned pleased, hid that anger, and felt extremely disloyal.

He did not feel free then to take the chance, financially or creatively, to write (in quotes) a "literary" book. And yet whole foundations of his being in this life are devoted to that particular aspect of art.

Good theorists are not necessarily good practitioners, and good practitioners are not necessarily good theorists. Yet good theory <u>is</u> practical. Ruburt has provided himself with a small laboratory. Tell him to think of his class that way.

Seeing that group of people week after week, he is able to work with them, follow their progress and put theory into practice. That is sufficient. No one can be <u>adequately</u> (underlined) helped in one or two sessions, and it is not his responsibility, or mine, to answer personally the millions of people who need help, or even the relatively few who write him.

To some extent it is his responsibility to make the material accessible, <u>so that using it</u> others may learn how to help themselves. The class gives me the opportunity to speak directly to individuals, and that experience is automatically used in my books.

Ruburt's personality is not one that can be held down to specific instances, but *(is one)* to evolve theories that can be used by many.

Now give us a moment. A long one. *(Pause at 9:50.)*

As you suspect, there is no conflict between the psychic and creative with him, but he did fear from the beginning that his own work would be swallowed. This has not proven true, for many reasons, some having to do with development.

His own work was not focused upon as it should have been, to <u>his</u> way of seeing things. Now he must go ahead and take his chances. He speaks of success. What he means is the production of a work of his own in those terms that <u>he</u> considers art, an accomplishment whether or not it brings financial success.

He was angry that the psychic work was bringing financial success, to some extent, while wanting the money. The full development of his creative abilities however needed the psychic development. <u>Less</u> ability would not.

The full blossoming could <u>not</u> have come much earlier, but his rage did not take that into account.

Dialogues could not be written by anyone without Ruburt's experience. *Adventures* <u>would</u> have been an error <u>if</u> pursued further now. Later, with greater understanding and with a backlog of other work that contents him, it will be an excellent book.

Rest your fingers. Mobility seemed blocked in all directions, then.
(10:00—10:02.)

He well knew at times that *Adventures* was in part a ruse to content him, and assure him of a contract while I began my book, but he is afraid of taking the plunge on his own now. He was also afraid that you would be angry.

Bill Macdonnel, coming at this time of year, did remind him of the first sessions and the *ESP* book and the tooth incident, caused <u>physically</u> by the sinuses, was a message that the time was crucial, a crisis. He had to say no, now, and move ahead in his own area.

(A few notes for the record: Bill Macdonnel returned to Elmira over the holidays to visit his parents. He's visited us a couple of times. A week or so ago Jane had a dream in which she saw Bill with his mouth full of blood. Calling Bill a couple of days later to invite him to a New Year's eve party, Jane was told by Bill that he'd been to the dentist and had several teeth pulled the day of the call.

(Subsequently, Jane several times was seized with a strong ache in her lower right jaw. Her pendulum told her she was picking up on Bill. We haven't heard from him since the call. Monday, January 1, 1973, we decided to go for a ride, since it was a beautiful day. Unknown to me Jane's jaw began to bother her as she left the house.

(Discovering this on the way to Sayre, I pulled into the near empty parking lot of the shopping center on Elmira Street and gave Jane my own pendulum to use. We learned that her sinuses were involved in her jaw ache, and Bill Macdonnel, but also that she was strongly concerned about the acceptance of Rich Bed *by Eleanor Friede of Macmillan. Jane's jaw began to clear up as we drove through the countryside beyond East Athens.)*

I suggest then that he call Tam. There will be no difficulties.

I suggest immediately that you make symbolic changes in Ruburt's room, at once, and throughout your place as you desire. He knows you will be here for a while.

("What do you mean—a few weeks, a few months, or what?" I'd thought we would soon be moving.)

The mobility should begin here, now, while you begin looking about. Simply so you experience mobility immediately on two important levels: the work area through the phone call and decision, and your immediate present environment. Give us a moment.

Ruburt's condition deteriorated after the meeting with Eleanor. The situation brought into focus, you see, the entire problem. Seagull's middle-aged lady focused it further. *(Bach's description of Jane for* Time.*)* The middle-aged lady was mentioned as middle-aged, and as a psychic, poet and science fiction writer—a turning of the ways in that the psychic books were mentioned, but no books of poetry, which gave impetus to *Dialogues*.

Eleanor held out the bait of *Rich Bed*'s publication. Ruburt wanted to plunge into it, but was afraid to not take the money for *Adventures* instead—hence the same problem in new and more dangerous form.

Most of this was very conscious at various times, but your view of suburbia *(when we went house hunting with a realtor the other day)* helped to bring it into focus. Ruburt will use his creative ability in fiction yet, in a way that he could not have otherwise, to bring home the reality and dimension of human personality.

Our books will continue. He felt trapped and saw no way out. Even now he is afraid of turning down the money of letting that much work go, but he finally sees that that is his answer.

Now I have an important suggestion, to which I hope you will acquiesce, and it is important: You must really form a letter, a nice one, thanking people for their interest, explaining that for now private sessions are not given for individuals. These should be sent out to unanswered correspondence. Ruburt should devote himself to what he wants to write in his time. I will produce my books. There will be others (period).

For now let classes continue. Make the changes I suggested. Have Ruburt send *Dialogues* to those places he has in mind.

("Should he write to Eleanor?")

Write Eleanor, and explain the situation fully and honestly.

Each individual has within him guidelines <u>meant</u> to lead him in the ways best for him. You cannot compare yourselves with others. Ruburt's own feelings therefore <u>are</u> those guidelines. They may be <u>different</u> at various times, but they can be trusted. Ruburt's creative ability is his for a reason. It was meant to be used, as well as his psychic abilities were.

There are unknown dimensions then to his own work that will begin to materialize, and that would be buried had he continued to produce simply what he thought he should produce. And now do you have questions?

("Then we're still to think that all those reasons connected with the symptoms that you gave in the past still apply, along with these present ones given in this session? That all of those contributed something to the overall problems?")

They do indeed, but transformations in them would occur. Your lack of communication was important, and aggravated the problem.

("Is there anything now that you'd like to say that he won't let you say?"
(I asked this half as a joke.)

No there is not.

("I just mean, is he open now to what you may or can say?")

I believe I have answered your question.

("Okay.")

There are other elements not particularly mentioned in the background, but they are not crucial points. He felt he had lost his direction. Spontaneously feeling free to write what he wants to will also release him psychically.

("When I used the pendulum Sunday afternoon and found out about the reasons for Jane's symptoms, it seemed like I'd asked questions like that before; but nothing happened, there weren't any results—")

Because neither of you were willing to take the chance earlier, nor did you feel financially secure enough to do so. You were both willing to put up with the situation. The idea of physically moving automatically brought these issues into the light, and you helped Ruburt immensely. He would never have tried completely to write the book, but he could have struggled nearly halfway through—

("You mean Adventures.*")*

I do indeed. But both of you had to acquiesce, you see, or for him it would not have worked.

This time he believes you, because the suggestion came from you. *(To shelve* Adventures, *etc.)* He feels free to be a psychic only when he is not <u>labeled</u> (underlined) one exclusively.

Do you have any questions?

("I guess not.")

I suggest then that everything I have said be put into practice immediately. Then I bid you a fond good evening.

("Thank you very much, Seth. Good night."

(10:35. It is Wednesday, January 3 as I finish this session. Jane has already cleared the matter with Tam—who incidentally had a vivid dream Monday night, in which in distorted form he learned that Adventures *was to go by the board. Many elements in Tam's dream tallied with events depicted in this session, bearing out Seth's contention that Tam already sensed the conflicts over* Adventures, *etc. We are to send him what's done on Seth's new book.*

(Jane wrote Eleanor today; it will be mailed tomorrow. I have obtained the paint to do her workroom. Tomorrow Jane calls the paper to place our ad about a house. We have made a list of important items to carry out as soon as possible re these sessions, our ideas, etc.

(The galleys for Oversoul Seven *arrived yesterday. This has been most opportune—and in them Jane was delighted to see many hints and ideas for future work —many clear signs that she had already begun to feel her way toward the future; including poetry. Our opinions of the book have risen apace, though we liked it before also.)*

DELETED SESSION
JANUARY 3, 1973 9:45 PM WEDNESDAY

(It is January 4 as I begin to type this session from notes. As of now we have so far mailed the letter to Eleanor re Rich Bed; *phoned the ad about a house in to the Elmira paper; obtained the paint for Jane's workroom; put up new curtains in her room; begun inquiries about the duplication of the letter for readers who write to Jane; packaged the first six chapters of Seth's book to mail to Tam at Prentice-Hall tomorrow; begun to check the galleys for* Oversoul Seven—*all of these being items on the list we made out a couple of days ago. Another checklist will be included at the end of this session.*

(At about 9:40 PM, as we sat waiting for the session to start, Jane said she felt a bulky "something" off to her right, toward the bay windows in the living room. She didn't actually see anything, nor did the effect develop further.)

Now—

("Good evening, Seth.")

—Good evening. *(Pause.)* This is not dictation.

Most individuals dwell focused so rigidly in your particular area of space and time that the greater dimensionality of the entity is unknown to them at a conscious level. Any intrusions from other layers of actuality are promptly shut down.

They are considered as notself, dangerous or alien. Only in the dream state is any such communication allowed. The greater reality of the self is therefore largely unsuspected, and the great knowledge possessed by it remains unknown at a conscious level.

The conscious mind however is (underlined) evolving, in your terms. It is not the finished product. You may include this information in my book, but it is not book dictation. Creativity as it is generally known represents but a small portion of far more extensive capacities. Creativity as you understand it is the three-dimensional aspect then of greater abilities that belong to our consciousness innately, whether it is consciously materialized or not (period).

When it is so materialized much of the creativity is automatically expressed (pause), the individual being aware of only that ability that the mind can understand. Most individuals therefore do not contend with larger portions of their own reality. An individual sets for himself those challenges that lie within his realm at any given time. He does not tackle challenges that in his terms are too great to be solved.

Now. *(Slowly.)* Through the years *(pause)*, Ruburt has been more and more aware of other kinds of psychological realities and structures than those usually experienced. He was born with that capacity, having chosen the course. The capability was there then long before it showed itself.

Earlier he experienced high accelerations of creativity and consciousness *(pause)*. These accelerations and the capacity activated the thyroid gland, not the other way around. He sensed the energy, of course, and considered it one of his characteristics, but it frightened him. He had definite ideas of the ways in which energy should properly be used and channeled.

He was afraid of going too far too fast, and worse, of going alone. Controls were applied as he learned to experience and use his growing abilities. The fears about being an official psychic were to see that he did not fall into the temptation of allowing all the dogmas to be tacked upon the phenomena, so that he would not operate within old frameworks, and therefore tacitly give voice consent to them.

In all of this you also acquiesced. It was known that only by presenting the material in writing, and eventually in books, that his personality would accept it. He would also be driven to critically analyze the phenomena (hyphen)—and in books, because he is a writer—before he felt free enough to simply create (period).

The critical writing and the symptoms went hand in hand. They were both cautionary procedures, symbolic and literal, that he felt necessary. Until his own understanding of his nature and the nature of consciousness progressed, he needed those tactics.

You recognized them as signs of caution and acquiesced. The freedom of *Seven* was the first sign of release, but not accepted on all levels. *(Pause at 10:15.)* You understand, though imperfectly, what happens when you are between beliefs—sure that one is no longer adequate, unable to rely upon it as you once did, but not yet able to fully accept another.

Now until Ruburt's psychic experiences and the beginning of this expansion of consciousness and abilities, he was used to relying upon other levels of trust. He identified completely with his body. Afterward he could not identify with his body in the same way. A whole new orientation became necessary, and it did involve a time of stress.

The reasons given still apply, but all within this greater framework. The body's needs to some extent even have changed. Now much of this would have frightened you both in the past, and could not have been given until you reached a particular point of development, and achieved a new status both separately and in your relationship.

This is a significant session. I will let you take a break and continue.

(10:23. Jane's trance had been very deep. Her delivery had been very deep, especially on the last page. "He's still got a whole bunch of stuff," she said, "and I have a vague idea of what's going on.... I've got an awfully funny feeling, too—I'm waiting to see if you get it also."

(I didn't know exactly what Jane meant. Before the session she'd made remarks about it being significant. I agreed that it was but my interpretation of that significance wasn't as positive as Seth's, I'm afraid. I didn't ask Jane what *her interpretation of this significance was, by the way. But at first glance I thought a good case could be made for not opening the doors to psychic developments to begin with, going by the contents of this session so far.*

(Perhaps I was overly tired. I didn't consider any such development worth symptoms, for instance, even if they disappeared tomorrow. Eight years was much too much for such an experience....

(It also seemed that both of us had made the decision to confine the psychic work to sessions only, which I thought would at this time automatically shut down a lot of possible developments. I also felt there was a strong possibility the sessions themselves would go by the board unless Jane showed much improvement before too much more time passed. We believe we are committed to delivering Seth's new book, but after that....

(I thought at least that Jane could use the psychic awareness as intuition, etc., in her work, as everyone else did, do her "straight writing," and let it go at that. At this time, in view of our own experiences, I seriously doubted that very many indi-

viduals in our reality were truly ready or equipped to handle such developments without a great struggle—chosen or no. There was, I felt, a great chance the struggle would get the best of them.

(*This evening's material, session and notes, incidentally, answered somewhat frequent speculations of my own: why I had always stressed caution when speaking to others who asked advice about developing matters psychic.*

("In its own way tonight's session is as significant as the first session we had," Jane said. "It's like you've been through a training period you didn't even know you were going through—and now, in our terms," she said with surprise, "it's taken all that time. Like I've been scared as hell to move out of the old framework. I didn't know where the hell I was going...Take the Sumari, and when I hear the voices: what in hell am I supposed to do with those things?"

("Those attitudes are your own," I said, just before Seth returned. "Nobody else put those demands upon you; you chose them." I wanted to add that I had strong reservations about making some choices, even if we had the power to make them, but didn't have time. 10:36.)

Now. In your own way you have done the same thing, and for the same reasons, as far as your work is concerned. You have tried doggedly *(intently)* to interpret greater experience in old ways, using "old" (in quotes) channels that are adequate for usual creativity in art—but painfully restrictive as far as you are concerned. I will have much more to say to you regarding that.

You kept insisting on trying to portray new vision by using methods that could not contain it, and did not spontaneously allow your visions to flow into their own forms. I will return to this later this evening. Give us a moment.

The expansions of consciousness on Ruburt's part did involve some natural feelings of disorientation with his body and the world, that all in all were handled supremely well.

With the development of abilities however the importance of conscious thought became greater than before. The mind in one way was becoming more aware of reality, using greater energy and taking ever greater responsibility, which it did not bear to that degree before. The acceleration of mental creativity therefore meant that the creative energy of thoughts became ever greater in practical terms. Do you follow me?

("Yes.")

Old stray patterns of thought therefore, or depressions, became more readily materialized, as did more positive ones, to your way of thinking. Both positive and negative elements were more quickly creatively materialized. It is <u>almost</u> (underlined), at least symbolically, as if Ruburt were born at age 36 into a world with new rules, to which he had then to acclimate himself.

The expansion of consciousness is large enough to become a different kind of consciousness (dash)—if it as allowed freedom. He held back in the ways given. You held back from many of the experiences that you could yourself encounter, and you are now ready to begin an acceleration of our own that will be largely interpreted through your work, if you allow it.

You also felt that Ruburt needed you, particularly in the beginning, with both of your feet on the ground, so to speak; Ruburt is quite correct. In its way this session is as important as our initial ones.

When you want a break interrupt me. Otherwise I will continue for a while.

("Okay." Pause at 10:55.)

Ruburt's cautionary attitude was his way of maintaining balance. Usually his particular kind of development takes place in two lives, in your terms. Your own unswerving desire to paint is your impetus, as writing was Ruburt's and is, so that your knowledge would be interpreted in those terms—as, if you continue, it will be.

I am going to outline a program. The suggestions will not be given in order necessarily.

Ruburt must do his own creative work in his writing hours. He must for his health's sake take at least 15 minutes a day to relax in any fashion he chooses—but mental and physical relaxation. This is not diversion such as television, you follow me.

He is not to feel at the demand of letters, people, calls or otherwise. He is to feel free of those demands. They are not a part of his work. My book is geared specifically to people. When he realizes he need not be at their demand he can be freely grateful for his mail, and not resentful.

An honest, warm letter will be dictated by me *(louder)*, to be sent out. This absolves him from such responsibility neatly, and it is important that he be so absolved—not only for his own benefit but for other work, from which such demands detract.

For now class should be continued. Your social life should and must not be allowed to deteriorate. You both need that contact, but free you see of the demands he has felt from, say, correspondence. Nor need he feel at the beck and call of anyone who wants to come here for a session or otherwise.

Nor need he feel a responsibility to allow people to come to class from afar—but that might, generally speaking, represent his contact with others psychically. He should speak to Hugh, as he mentioned, and that is important.

Hugh will serve in your place in classes, unless you attend. Hugh can (underlined) serve in that capacity, but it is important now that someone does.

(11:08. "He isn't done, I can tell you that," Jane said after she'd come out of a deep trance. "I can sense other stuff coming—I don't know what I'm going to think when I read it." When Jane got up she could barely move about her chair. She sat down heavily, then said she had to get up to go to the john—which she did, slowly.

("The whole thing's unexpected by me," she said. I wondered why it should be, and also thought that this was a way the sessions would try to protect themselves. But then, there was Seth's book to be finished.... 11:20.)

Are you ready?

("Yes.")

There are to be some recommendations for diet. Some changes in his tastes have already occurred, to his surprise. He no longer enjoys raw steak as he used to, or even steak particularly, for example.

He finds himself naturally wanting grains such as rice and cereals, and has a yearning for potatoes, baked. His diet, and yours, should follow the following patterns: for him particularly, except for bacon which is dried, very little pork. Steak, if you will excuse me, only on rare occasions.

For him emphasis on potatoes in all forms except deep fried, and greens—spinach, turnip greens and the like. Citrus fruits for him should largely be avoided, particularly with milk together. All other fruits however should be better utilized in his diet. The pear and apricot juices particularly are good.

The peanut butter he instinctively seeks out, but he should get in the habit of eating other kinds of nuts—cashews particularly. And as he suspected lately, sunflower seeds are good. Cottage cheese with lettuce he likes, and both are good for him. Olives are an important corollary, and he likes them.

The commercial weight-gaining liquid is highly contaminated, and should be avoided. Malted milk is all right, good, but never more than two glasses a day. Fish, chicken, with some veal. Some beef is all right, but not as a steady diet. I definitely do recommend both the daily vitamin E plus an overall vitamin and mineral supplement.

All of this also applies to you, and cut down your own but not Ruburt's intake of salt. The food recommended has a stabilizing and nourishing effect on your (underlined) systems at their present stages of development. You can handle citrus, while Ruburt cannot.

Your salt intake is more than you need on the other hand, while Ruburt's is not. Give me a moment.

Later I will suggest that Ruburt cut down on both sugar and milk for coffee, but for now let it stand. The nuts should be kept on his desk however, and nibbled.

Now. The creative writing class has served its purpose, <u>provided</u> you keep up your social life. It should be dropped. He needs the time, and it has become a method of helping people.

All contacts with any spiritualistic groups must be avoided. The two of you, though I am speaking mainly to Ruburt, must combine your forces and cut out any <u>demands</u> (underlined) made upon you by others. I am speaking now of your working sphere of activity.

On the other hand you must at the <u>minimum</u> (underlined) work 4 and ½ hours a day at your own painting. Chores will be taken care of, and fall into their proper place. The same applies to Ruburt at his work. You can utilize your nap period to a far greater degree than you do. You are to consider yourselves pioneers. Ruburt in particular is now finally to forget other people's opinions of his activities, and forge ahead. Their opinions never affected you to that degree.

All of these suggestions will release both of you in important ways. He was never meant to give his entire conscious concentration to (in quotes) "psychic" work. The freedom of his own creative work will enhance those abilities, but also free him for some further expansions of consciousness that are meant to follow. The same applies to you, and in these endeavors you must work together.

My books are meant to give you some financial framework in which to operate in practical terms, besides their other purposes. There are roadways open that Ruburt has been afraid to follow for the reasons given this evening, to which he is now acquiescing.

The same applies to you in your work. Greater belief and trust in yourselves is necessary, and it is for this reason that you must ruthlessly cut out all other demands. These are also the roads Ruburt was afraid to go ahead in, and was holding back.

He now realizes that growth cannot be held back. Now later, but not in a distant future, your nap periods will be utilized for joint out-of-body work. The further developments latent since our sessions, are now ready to proceed. The feeling of accomplishment <u>and peace</u> will give you a feeling of greater time available within your daily framework. And as soon as the *(Xmas)* tree is removed, the badminton.

Now this is phase two, and you cannot regress, only go ahead—and Ruburt realizes it now. Give me and yourself a rest.

(11:50—11:51.)

Hugh, Marianne and Wade are to be given positions of responsibility. They will gladly accept them. Hugh's wife will mail out the form letters. She needs the feeling of helping and of being important. It will help her own situation.

Holding back from your own expansion of consciousness impedes energy through the body. When your own relationship was rocky, Ruburt therefore was twice as frightened as you were. These suggestions, if completely followed <u>consistently</u> (underlined) and wholeheartedly, will completely free the body. They could not have been given in this way earlier, for reasons that should now be apparent. You had to be within the framework of an excellent relationship with each other.

Ruburt had to understand his own creative necessities as a person, and accept the mobility of his own consciousness and those changes that it would involve. You also have to be free enough, and will be, to stand on your own position, and you must be free enough to cast aside the shackles that invisibly surround the field of painting, and even your own interpretation of it.

There are ways that Ruburt can be of invaluable assistance. Some incidents will occur in our sessions, and some in your coordinated nap periods, as well as in the dream state; and within a few months if these suggestions are followed.

Now the two of you are growing together in new ways, in which your individual aspects are enhanced. But through this, or because of it, a greater joint energy becomes possible in which all the abilities of your consciousnesses expand. It will be a most illuminating year. Give us a moment.

(Pause at 12:02 AM.) Your physical situation will change, and one day you will live closer to the sea, though not directly on its edge. Ruburt's grandfather was correct—you need a house open to the four winds.

Now I bid you a fond good evening, after a highly significant session—

("Thank you.")

—for you must go on in the way I have directed if you want to fulfill those abilities and purposes that you both have. And that is the end of the session.

("Good night, Seth, and thank you.")

The vitamins mentioned apply to you also, though not the extra one—just the complete capsule.

(12:07. Jane sat still in trance.)

You should make all efforts to move by spring. In the meantime Ruburt should "bless" (in quotes) the bed in whatever way he chooses, because of old aspects picked up when you were ill.

There are differences between the two halves of the house, having to do with subterranean waterways and old gas pockets. You had better let me continue with the information while it flows… The area since the flood is not as healthy as it was, having to do with mains that were flooded. Seek high water. It is purer. Do you follow me?

("I think so.")

That is the end. My best regards to you both.

("Thank you very much. Good night, Seth.")

(12:16. Again Jane's trance had been very deep. She told me she'd gotten the feeling from Seth that we'd have a significant dream tonight—of the kind he had talked about a long time ago. She had the feeling the session was "a big thing, significant." I seemed to be more reserved.)

DELETED SESSION
JANUARY 9, 1973 1:28 PM TUESDAY

(This brief session was held to help deal with Jane's recurring tooth symptoms. We knew they were related to Eleanor Friede and Rich Bed, *etc., as detailed before. But their increasing frequency alarmed us considerably today. We learned much with the pendulum today, and kept hoping we had finally unearthed the symptoms' cause. Each time the symptoms would return; today, after breakfast, then lunch, etc., so that we spent the whole day coping with them. I finally asked Jane after lunch if she could have a session regardless of whether she was bothered [as she was at the time of the session, to a lesser degree].*

(Even during the session Jane's voice was restricted, or quiet, as if she did not want to move her jaws and lips energetically.)

Now—

("Good afternoon, Seth.")

—and for now at least do not interrupt.

The aggravation of sinuses began before your trip to Rochester, when Eleanor spoke of *Rich Bed. (Eleanor wrote Jane about this October 4, 1972, praising* Rich Bed *extensively. See the deleted session of November 13, 1972, etc.)* I gave you some material on that—Ruburt taking on cold symptoms as given in that material.

It was to be a trial period. He was thinking of relinquishing the more general symptoms *(indicating the legs. This hasn't taken place yet.)*

The sinus became aggravated again Ruburt did the presentation for Eleanor, and to his way of thinking was, at least, immediately put off by Eleanor—no decision in official terms.

He felt hampered because of Eleanor's friendship. He wouldn't let another editor hold a book on such terms for such a time. When he decided not to do *Adventures (a week or two ago)* the book became more important in both literary and financial terms.

The last two days the legs and feet have been somewhat better. The jaw <u>is</u>

realigning itself. To some extent that, then, is therapeutic.

(A few days ago Jane told me, after she'd examined herself in the mirror, that her teeth were "straightening themselves out," etc.)

All of the fears are based of course on the belief that Ruburt must write to justify his existence. The basic insecurity, in other words.

Now. At this point proper suggestion given by you while he is in a light hypnotic state will help. These should be on the idea of his basic worth as a being, apart from what he does. A soothing loving voice will get through under those conditions.

(1:35—1:50.)

Now. Another tact necessary. Handle it as given above, building up inner security. Then make sure that Ruburt's fears are <u>vented</u>, that he acknowledges them consciously and does not attempt to intellectualize them away. They do have their own validity.

Once they are recognized then they can be met and dealt with, but they cannot be intellectualized away, and denied while smothering them and pretending that they do not exist.

You think such fears foolish; Ruburt does, so he tried to talk himself out of them while at the same time pretending that they do not exist. They are unvented, then. He is ashamed then to discuss them with you also.

It is important that you work from both ends. If Ruburt simply wrote down each day items that concerned him honestly, and discussed them with you, this would be of benefit. Then they could be met.

That is the end for now.

("Thank you, Seth." 2:00 PM. We thought it was the end but—)

Another note: He would be better off, you see, if he yelled and screamed in a quite undignified fashion. Your badminton has been dispensed with. It allowed for some unconscious translation of such feelings outward into action. And <u>that</u> is the end.

("Yes."

(Some interesting notes: We thought the session helped, and that the symptoms would vanish. In the middle of the afternoon Jane had a return of them to a lesser degree. We again used the pendulum, and learned a few new things. All of the reasons had to do with Eleanor and Rich Bed, *and* Adventures, Tam, *Jane's feelings of being cut off by Eleanor and Dick, etc. Seth's new book was exonerated.*

(I was too upset to give suggestions in the proper way after the session. Jane typed out a couple of pages. The last paragraph was new: she felt she <u>couldn't</u> pressure Eleanor because Dick was publicizing Jane's books. We hadn't asked the pendulum this question. I suggested a two-week deadline; then Jane would ask for the return of

Rich Bed *if she'd had no word from Eleanor. While Jane used the pendulum I gave some suggestions. Jane took a nap while I finished cleaning up the living room.*

(At about 6 PM, an hour before ESP class, the symptoms returned to a lesser degree. Both of us were once again alarmed. While Jane used her pendulum I gave suggestions, after reading this session to her. We went over what we had learned through Jane's pendulum about an innocent remark of mine, that Jane <u>didn't have</u> to ask Eleanor to return the script of Rich Bed *after a two-week period. By this I wanted to show Jane that I wasn't trying to tell her how to run things—but seemingly this remark instead rearoused Jane's fears that she couldn't insist upon action from Eleanor so quickly. <u>Jane wants action.</u>*

(Jane dressed for class, and the symptoms didn't worsen. She told me at a break in class that after the first few minutes she began to feel much better. During the evening as I worked in the kitchen, I heard her sing beautifully in Sumari several times; Seth spoke also, much more forcefully that he had this afternoon. Jane also told me that she liked class—we had discussed her dropping it soon—and that she intended to be "freer" in it from now on; and that the tooth thing would be conquered. It seems we learned a lot today. The fear we consciously experienced has been very instructive.)

DELETED SESSION
JANUARY 10, 1973 9:15 PM WEDNESDAY

(Jane had the "tooth bit" in a rather distant way, briefly after breakfast and after supper today. We talked over the causes, used some suggestions, and that seemed to take care of it. She feels much better. She is writing down her fears, angers, good points, etc., each day. This has been very revealing.

(I asked if Seth would discuss Tam's dream of January 1, 1973; her cold symptoms dating from last October; and the letter Seth has promised to dictate for correspondents. We played badminton today also. Both of us had many interruptions, and resolved to do something about this. We planned to get up much earlier tomorrow, for one thing.)

Now. Good evening—

("Good evening, Seth.")

—and let me go about this as usual in my own fashion.

For some time I have given you much advice, many suggestions, knowing full well that some would go by the board. Enough of them would be followed however to provide some kind of inner program, that would at least head you in the proper directions.

In reference to my book's theme now, the basic dilemma as well as its reasons and development, was quite available in Ruburt's conscious mind all of that time. He chose not to deal with it however because he was not ready to face the problem, he did not feel himself capable. He was not ready to make the move.

The trouble is that when you refuse to deal with such quite available conscious problems, you begin to organize other pertinent material about the problem, and it also becomes taboo. It is a game you play with yourself. Because you will not face the material, you cannot counter it with other conscious ideas, or generate other emotional feelings that would help you.

The unacceptable conscious problem therefore collects great charges of correlated emotional feelings that also go unexpressed. The summer that Ruburt was better, he began writing down his feelings and thoughts. That helped release some of them, did therefore release him consciously, and lead directly to his later writing.

They were not worked through, however, and he stopped the practice. Unknowingly you were working on the two levels given in my last session, through suggestion, building self-confidence while Ruburt wrote out his gripes and conscious thoughts. Until he produced *Seven*, however, he would not really consider facing the dilemma. *Seven* was the novel that showed him he could (underlined) write fiction.

Adventures served as the vehicle that brought to light many of his feelings against the psychic field, or rather his part as he saw it in it. It was necessary and served a purpose. One purpose was his realization that such a book, for now, even at his best, with personal orientation, was not his cup of tea. Much of the material in it later will be published.

The cold and the jaw difficulty—both of these were his physical interpretation of a growing crisis that had to be faced. He was ready to face the problem, to bring it out into the open, and the whole issue was finally brought out into the open through those symptoms. The critical period is over because of his recognition of the problem and his determination to face and solve it.

(*9:30.*) Certain ideas he has now are in a stage of transition still, a necessary stage. The tooth was meant to get his attention, to make him realize the importance of acting now. There will be no more great trouble with it. In a few days it will have completely disappeared. It is of great importance now however that he write down his thoughts as begun each day. It is not that he need concentrate on negative ideas. These are normal feelings and thoughts that gained such charge only because they were collected about the unfaced dilemma; whether or not he could make it on his own, or could afford the opportunity to try.

They must therefore be duly faced each day until they normally diminish into normal daily concern. Do not forget, in whatever way you choose to use it, the importance of reinforcing his sense of worth, <u>despite</u> what he does. The charge built up, <u>for him</u> (underlined) about time and work, is masking of course his fear of <u>not achieving</u> as he wants to. This is aside from normal practical considerations of time.

I suggest now, <u>for now</u> (underlined), that you each do arise at <u>6:30</u>, and take a good nap before dinner. I suggest this because it will help you both with your work. It is a simple method. It will also however give you freer psychic time in your nap.

This suggestion is for the present. The cold will also now be vanishing, as I tell you that following it will be the other symptoms. This only however if the writing habit is kept up, and the other suggestions.

(*A very important paragraph.*)

In two days Ruburt has become more aware of his problems consciously, and made connections that <u>had</u> (underlined) to be made. Future psychic work was also dependent upon a (in quotes) "correct" decision on his part.

Now give us a moment. *(Pause at 9:38. Fast pace.)*

Tam has great trust in me, in Ruburt's work, and basically in himself. He has always gone along with Ruburt. Their connections are good in waking life, but their relationship goes far deeper. Some of their waking reactions are incongruous. They are sometimes delighted with each other, and yet sometimes feel, in meeting, a conscious sense of disappointment while experiencing an inner sense of recognition and joyful enthusiasm.

This has to do in your terms with reincarnational relationships that I purposely have not given you.

As far as Tam's dream was concerned, I have a few things to say.

(*Tam wrote Jane on January 2, 1973, asking for some material on his dream of the night before. In distorted form he picked up that Jane and I had decided on January 2 that* Adventures in Consciousness *would not be written or contracted; that in daytime working hours Jane was to go full steam ahead on her own writing, etc. Jane called him on the morning of the second of January. [Copy sent to Tam on January 12, 1973, of this portion.]*)

There is a connection between Aerofranz and Ruburt, as well as a connection between Tam and Nebene. Tam knew the purposes of *Adventures* from the beginning—as did Ruburt, but neither of them could act on that knowledge consciously, for it did not serve as yet their conscious purposes.

The dream was not simply Tam's dramatization of a message sent by Ruburt, yet dramatization was involved. Ruburt acted out his ideas of a conventional medium for Tam, who in a dream state perceived Ruburt's dramatization.

Tam received the basic message, though in the morning. He made several distortions, substituting you *(RFB)* and the book I suggested *(Through My Eyes)* rather than Ruburt and *Adventures*. He did this to give himself time on a conscious level to deal with the situation. Some time ago, after *Seven*, he mentioned my book, my new book, to Ruburt, and Ruburt said he did not want to contract trance material ahead of time, so Tam let it rest.

Both of them knew on other levels that Ruburt needed a backlog of chapters, and the book well in progress, so Tam simply went along, as Ruburt did, until the time came when Ruburt realized he had full confidence, the book was good, and that *Adventures* had other purposes.

Again, in different fashion the material in *Adventures* will be published later, as will the dream material. Rest your hand.

(9:51. Still in trance, Seth/Jane said while pouring some wine: "I am giving you Tam's material together—it will be easier to type." Resume at 9:55.)

Now *Seven* will have its own following. It will become a mass product, however, and Tam will be involved as he has already been involved with *Seven*.

Tell him I am smiling, but I am telling him to trust himself and not look to others for readings. They will only confuse him. He will be connected with *Seven* and a movie. Some of his later writing will deal with me, with Ruburt's class, but in ways he does not suspect. I have great affection for him. His dream work will (underlined) show fruits, and he and Ruburt are involved in dreams together, though they do not recognize themselves in those dreams.

End to Tam.

Now you two are in the clear, with the basic dilemma out, being acted upon, worked through and faced; but the habits must also be combated by Ruburt writing out those thoughts and feelings daily. The badminton important as given, as trivial as that may seem.

Give us a moment. Or take your break if you prefer.

("Okay.")

(10:00. Jane's trance had been deep, her delivery rapid and intent. Seth was insistently present. "All right, all right," Jane said to the invisible Seth. I told her I was ready if she wanted to resume. 10:02.)

Now. I could not force Ruburt to face the dilemma until he felt he was ready to handle it—then he would see it as he does, now, as a challenge. All the other reasons given fit in. They were behind the reasons that he did not feel he could face the dilemma, but they partially masked it, also.

The fear then colored his other attitudes and reactions. His fear of the tooth pain was a physical interpretation of his fear of facing the dilemma, the pain of bringing it out into the open. Then he found it was not as bad as he thought—he could operate anyway, and amazingly well, as in class *(ESP)* last evening.

The class was important. *(As Jane said also.)* Because he now decided to do his own thing also, he was free to do his psychic thing also—hence today the out-of-body experiments conducted. *(Quite successfully.)* Once he saw himself simply (underlined) as a psychic, he became prey to all of the conventional psychic ideas, afraid of the sexual-demon characteristics connected with out-of-bodies, for example.

Seeing himself doing his own thing short-circuits such unnecessary reactions. The experiments conducted unconsciously also spread energy through the physical body where it was needed, and was therapeutic.

He had to realize his fear and his terrible dilemma in regard to Eleanor because it showed in concentrated form his own fear about his being able to succeed on his own, hence his dependence, that made him resent Eleanor. He had to work through that resentment.

Now you have also been afraid that you could not do your own thing on your (underlined) own, so you acquiesced to the situation. You understood, though you would not face your understanding. Ruburt's dilemma was quite clear to you. You felt you could not push him until he was ready.

(Almost with a laugh:) He resented that you did not push him in that particular matter. You understood however Adventure's meaning and significance, and helped him when you realized he was ready to accept it, by your suggestion. Do you follow me?

("You mean by my pendulum?" When I learned not long ago that Jane's symptoms were caused by her fear that her psychic work was not letting her do her own writing—that she was failing as a writer, that she wanted success as a writer first, not as a psychic, etc.)

I do indeed. The apartment situation was another symbol for moving—the physical one of impasse. It had to be faced on that level physically in your cases, before the other problem of mobility could come completely to light.

The physical changes however are supremely important, as physical materializations of inner ones. There are stresses now in terms of contracts and money, that Ruburt was not willing to face before. They are apparent now, and not masked. That is why the writing, as given, is important—that they be daily vented.

(Emphatically. Jane is still venting herself daily in the personal notes—with excellent results. She wrote: Middle Feb. 1973—I begin new Seven!*")*

Rich Bed will sell. There will be another, and another *Seven*. Ruburt was upset with the psychic reputation, not because it was psychic but because it was not the one he wanted. He is delighted with it as long as he is working toward what he wants. Then he can relax and enjoy it.

He felt it as a threat, rightly, while he was afraid to use his writing abilities in other forms, as he must. Only then will the true unity be apparent to him.

The *Gallery (magazine)* article will now be a great success. And so will Monroe's visit, as it would not have been earlier. I bid you a fond good evening.

("The same to you. Thank you.")

And my congratulations for getting through a hard time.

("Yes." Not that I consider we're through the hard time yet, by any means.

(10:21. Jane's trances had been deep all evening. Seth didn't get to the letter for correspondents. Robert Monroe is the author of Journeys Out of The Body, *Doubleday, 1971.)*

It is important that you feel free to move in all areas, and see the connection between all kinds of mobility, and face Ruburt's practical considerations about turning down one contract while thinking about purchasing a house—and that is it for this evening.

("Good night."

(Jane was yawning, again and again. She got more data as she yawned:)

Ruburt was quite conscious all the time about the reasons behind the symptoms. He just wasn't ready to face it. This makes my book extremely valid.

("All right, all right...." Jane said to Seth again, after reciting this passage to me.

(We talked about Bill Macdonnel, who stopped in late this afternoon to say goodbye before leaving for California. Jane said she had a lot of available material on Bill, also, but wouldn't give it. Then resume at 10:30.)

Now. You did not feel free to do your own thing until Ruburt felt free to do his, because you felt he was helping out so financially. This is at one level.

You were highly impatient, then. At the same time you knew that once you did commercial work for money as a young man, quite happily. It fulfilled definite needs. At any level of your artistic development thus far, you could have cashed in with some application, and been, you felt, betrayed by money and acclaim as a certain level of development.

You felt it would be <u>such</u> (underlined) a temptation that you might give in. All the time you realized that your proper way necessitated deeper understandings, and held out.

The money motive did help Ruburt in other areas, and led him to greater understanding while he always knew it had to be dispensed with. Do you follow me?

("I think so....")

There are intertwining purposes then that were met. There is other material I will give you later, that is involved here, and purposes in your art you are barely beginning to understand—and with that I bid you good night.

("Thank you. Good night.")

Let my freedom be your own. It is yours and Ruburt's..

(10:35. Again Jane's trance had been deep. She was very relaxed. "All I want to know is," she said, "how am I going to get from here [the living room] into there?" Meaning across the hall to the bedroom.

(It is Monday, January 15 as I finish typing this session. On the day it was held, January 10, Seth said there wouldn't be any more great trouble for Jane through the tooth symptoms. This hasn't proven out. The tooth symptoms have hung on, perhaps not as severely; they frighten Jane a good deal. Through the pendulum, suggestion, her writing, etc., we have learned a lot about their causes. Eliminating the symptoms though is like trying to pick up mercury at this writing. The latest wrinkle is that the teeth reflect her concern about money, eating, and my own success as an artist...)

SESSION 632 (DELETED PORTION)
JANUARY 15, 1973

(This material is from the 632nd session for January 15, 1973.

(10:45 PM.) Now. Ruburt never learned how to handle normal aggressive thoughts.

There was no <u>normal</u> (underlined) give and take in a family with siblings, where equals—children—could more or less safely express themselves between themselves.

Ruburt's feelings were largely directed against the parent. He was not encouraged, but discouraged from expressing normal anger. He was afraid of his mother's wrath. You know those conditions.

Normal angry feelings are natural methods of communication, ways of stabilizing situations. They serve to prevent <u>strong</u> (underlined) aggression or violence, both in animals and men. Coupled with a habit of <u>consciously</u> (underlined) repressing normal angry feelings, we have Ruburt's loyalty to you. The feelings mentioned at the *(supper)* table were conscious at times, but he refused to acknowledge them.

(They had to do with my painting, my lack of financial contributions this year, etc. Jane cried while telling me about them, and while we used the pendulum.

They also have to do with her teeth and jaw symptoms, and fear of eating recently, we've learned.)

When they began your attitude did not encourage him to express them.
("Do you mean tonight?")

In the past. I am speaking now of habitual ways of handling conscious angry thoughts. When you were ill they began, but he felt even less able to acknowledge them as his own. The background has largely been given of those times.

The Nebene characteristics, now creatively used, then also mitigated against Ruburt's easy expression of such feelings, and he did tie up some characteristics of Nebene with his mother's scorn. He is not worried so much that you have not made a great financial success of your art. He is ashamed of the following feelings:

He feels that you have not tried to make a success of your art, but have used excuses while blaming him for using excuses; that he tries desperately to sell his books, while you will not lift a finger to sell your paintings; that if he waited until he did his best work, he would never have sold a thing.

He feels that you are not satisfied with your work, and so will not try to sell it in the marketplace, while he must sell his work in the marketplace. There are several levels of feeling here. On one level he would not care, if only he felt you <u>were really</u> (underlined) painting what you wanted, and pleased with it; but you do not seem pleased.

(A few notes: I have always felt that my early life, being so different than Jane's, had a lot to do with my approach to painting, once I embarked upon it after meeting her when I was about 34. I didn't grow up with the consuming urge toward fine art that she developed about writing at an early age. I did commercial work for many years. I have always taken these differences for granted, and evidently assumed too much when I thought she understood them.

(Further, my urge toward doing my best work comes at an age when I feel that I <u>should</u> be doing my best work. When I started painting, I was appalled to discover my ignorance. I've spent years trying to learn. The urge to learn, perhaps overdone, may be one of the Nebene characteristics, [and as an aside I thoroughly wish the Nebene character did not exist.] But regardless of that, I didn't think my wish to excel in my chosen field necessarily a poor one. I was willing to spend the time necessary to master painting. Each one has been a trial. The last year has been very productive as far as learning goes, and I'm at the point where I expect it to begin paying rich dividends. It also seems that this point coincides with a time of trial for Jane and me, as witness these deleted sessions.

(I have for some time thought that Jane needed to sell her writings as a means

of justifying her life—whether these writings were her best work was, in that sense, immaterial; she couldn't possibly wait until her writing was a polished art before beginning to market it. So I don't believe comparisons between her selling her work, and me selling mine, mean much. I also have an attitude that is quite personal, whether it is a good one or not: I don't care too much what others think about my painting. Oddly enough, I am sure that my work will end up very successful, both as art and in the marketplace. So I can safely say that in my own way I am trying very hard to make a "success" of my work. Our methods differ markedly, however.

(I do believe that I haven't made enough of an effort to inform Jane of feelings and goals of mine that I seem to have taken for granted. I can only say that I thought she knew them, or many of them. They aren't all that mysterious. I hope I live in this reality long enough to get a few years' mileage out of what I think I have learned.

(Therefore I will make a harder effort to do both my art and to make it available to others and to get money with it, to broaden its communicative necessities—this I am perfectly willing to do once I understand its necessity. I do not seem to be the kind to dash off paintings to sell them and let it go at that. I want them to be transcendent. Perhaps erroneously, I didn't think I could <u>start out</u> with them being that—but I did feel sure that the state would be achieved.)

He feels highly disloyal facing any of these thoughts, mainly because he does not want to hurt someone he loves so deeply—the only person in fact he loves in the world.

We are going to get a good portion of this out, but you two have to face it on an emotional level, and you avoid it, both of you. These are not unconscious hidden things. Ruburt is faced with the fact that he is afraid to eat. He is ashamed because at one level he begrudges the food you eat, so <u>he</u> will not eat to punish himself.

We are bringing some beliefs out in to the open, yours as well as Ruburt's. You identified in many respects with your father, though often you felt forced to take your mother's part. You were, and to some extent are, resentful of women, and would not have married a woman who bore you children.

You would not be shunted aside as your mother shunted your father. You would not be forced to work as he did, and waste his creativity, so you chose a wife who would make no such demands—apart from other reasons. We are picking up one level here.

On the same level: With Ruburt's background he felt no man would support him, yet wanted to be supported. It would prove he was being cherished. The part-time job on your part was of course a compromise, but loving you, he felt it was at the expense of your creative output and purposes.

(A thought: I now realize that Jane put the same interpretation <u>on her own</u>

work—namely, the psychic work. It took me years to learn that she regarded her work in the psychic field—and the time and energy involved—as aside from her main creative goal, which is to write "straight" literature that is also art.)

There is no doubt that he began to feel that his every creative act had to pay off financially. Better that than have you tied to that job at Artistic for any longer a time. This put you directly on the spot. He wanted you to do your thing, at the same time that the financial pressure grows. Yet it was good that you left the job when you did.

(I told Jane after this session that I'd intended to leave the job in a year or so—in other words, at about this time, rather than when I did. I thought that by now we'd have a good financial backlog built up, and freedom of action. I didn't realize last year of course that she was so dissatisfied with the psychic image and the books; I blithely assumed that she felt she was doing good work, and that she accepted it, which doesn't mean that I had any thoughts of ever saying she shouldn't do any other kind of writing, ever. I had no idea of the bitterness or the depths of her resistance to, or feeling against, being sidetracked, as she sees it, from her main goals in life.)

He decided then, with your help, to drop *Adventures*, as was necessary at the time. The financial question was then brought to a head by your ideas also of moving. I knew of course this would be the case.

Now give us a moment and rest your hand.

(11:14—11:15.)

In his own way your father was saying "Since you do not trust my creativity I will deny you its benefits, even if I deny myself its benefits"—this to your mother; and you picked up a taboo: you could make money on art as long as you felt it was not <u>really</u> (underlined) creative—that is, commercial. But you would keep good work to yourself and not sell it. So Ruburt did not accept any of your answers.

Were you not selling your paintings to spite him or yourself or your mother? If you did not want to do portraits, why accept commissions? Say no. Give us a moment. *(Pause.)* His unspoken anger grew. He is pleased with my book. He was always deeply grateful for your part in *Seth Speaks*, and in the sessions. Your later, better communication and rapport made matters worse, for his unexpressed feelings seemed then completely unjustified, and his fear of hurting you grew stronger.

(I find the above sentence quite ironic.)

The more you spoke of prices of food going up, the worse the feelings about eating became *(and the tooth and jaw symptoms)*. Even our sessions would be contracted for in advance. Now this is fine with me. It makes no difference, and it will not to Ruburt when these connections are made clear.

He was also afraid that you would lose self-respect on your own and he could not bear that. Now you may take a break or end the session.

(11:26. I asked Seth for a break, but this proved to be the end of the session. Both of us were upset, of course. I told Jane that I had been having a change of mind, and that perhaps she shouldn't contract Seth's latest book in advance after all. I had become afraid a contract would reinforce the emphasis on psychic work that she wants to get out from under. I told her I would go along with whatever she decided on the contract, but did express my thoughts on it.

(I said I was willing to face whatever developed because of this action—that if I had to get a job on part-time basis, okay. After all, we do have money; money also is due from her father's estate, royalties, Rich Bed *eventually, and the sale of paperback rights by Prentice-Hall;* ESP *class also helps—Jane said she enjoys the class. I don't see her symptoms lessening, so feel that action must be taken.*

(Ideas of self-respect, or its lack, have never meant a thing to me... I am free of such burdens. When I left my job I thought it would please Jane, and of course I was glad to see it go, although I would have waited longer on my own. I must admit I don't understand why each thing we do seems to make matters worse. What is left in our lives to learn, to uncover? What do other people do? I pity them, I guess.)

SESSION 637 (DELETED PORTION)
JANUARY 31, 1973 9:05 PM WEDNESDAY

(This material is from the beginning of the 637th session. I asked if Seth could comment on the fact that F. Fell had canceled, or postponed, the appearance of the paperback edition of Jane's ESP Power. *We've learned this is the case through various people who have written to Jane—they had written the publisher. In the deleted session for October 2, 1972, Seth told us the "paperback will do very well, however." This was before the postponement happened. I thought our own attitudes might have caused it. Of course, we have not heard from F. Fell.*

(I also asked if Seth would comment upon the postponement by Gallery *magazine, this month, of their interview with Jane, scheduled for January 23, a class night. Jane received a telegram from Richard Kearns a few days before the 23rd. He promised a letter of explanation which still hasn't arrived as of this session. Even though Jane received a second telegram a few days ago, again promising the letter.*

(As it developed, Seth gave a partial explanation of the Fell affair, and the Gallery *material was not mentioned.)*

Good evening.

("Good evening, Seth.")

There are several issues involved with the Fell paperback. Ruburt did a double-take after I told you it would sell well. He thinks that my book—this one *(Personal Reality)*—should be read before people begin to dabble with the board and so forth. *(The Ouija board.)*

He suspects that others have some difficulty, that they do not understand themselves sufficiently, and add to their own problems through putting to use the methods in his first such book. He did not want it (in quotes) "flooding the market," used by people who would follow the techniques and then write for help.

There is a compassion, a jovial yet understanding one, that I can feel for such activities that is more difficult for you to experience, but in many cases the drama—the gods or devils who <u>seem</u> (underlined) to speak through the board, the sense of importance felt by the participators, the heightened emotional activity—all of these provide often, rich elements of experience otherwise lacking from a mundane daily existence.

A framework is also then self-provided in which deeper questions of personality, life and being are worked out at the specific level of the individual's experience. They are, such people, far better off than those who have no frameworks in which to see and experience their own greater experience in whatever terms. Even the (in quotes) "distortions" are necessary elements to their growth.

Distortions in many ways are simply truths appearing in ill-fitting clothes. That is the end of that.

("Thank you.")

Now, give us a moment for dictation.

(Pause at 9:20.

(Seth did not discuss the Gallery *affair after book work.*

(In mid-February, Richard Kearns finally called Jane, to tell her he'd been <u>fired</u> from Gallery. *He has her short story and a chapter of* Seven*—promised to return them—but not as of February 21....)*

SESSION 639 (DELETED PORTION)
FEBRUARY 12, 1973

(11:47 PM.) Tell Ruburt not to waste time crying over his mistakes. Remind him of the ways he has used his body well, and help him change his beliefs about it. Any physical gain, as badminton, physical achievement, should be stressed, and the movement that he does have encouraged.

His interpretation in *Dialogues* of Rooney's existence was excellent. Some ideas he has from William James *(Varieties of Religious Experience)*, the seemingly disconnected realizations about his body, dreams and dialogues, will altogether help him.

("You said you'd tell us about Rooney when we asked for it." Rooney died February 5, 1973.)

Give us a moment. The cat would have died that winter *(four years ago)*. In your terms it was a probable death. In a part of his reality he did die that winter. In your reality you kept him alive. He had been closed up in that house over there, and went wild and terrified.

Ruburt identified with him being closed up and running scared. He was afraid of the cat, considering him wild and caged originally, as his mother had been in his interpretation, so he felt forced to help the cat *(who did not have any love for him)*, as he felt before he had to help his mother—who would kill him if she had the chance.

The cat was aware in its terms of this. It became fat like Ruburt's mother, but no longer threatening. It was fixed. If Ruburt's mother had been fixed Ruburt would have had a different mother and different background, granting Ruburt had come <u>alive</u>.

The cat was male, called originally Katherine however, and identified as female. He got in scrapes as Ruburt's father did in bars. The cat knew of the identifications. He was willing however to trade these for several years of additional physical life, in which he also learned for the first time to relate to gentleness; even to be on terms with another cat, and Willy in his way served as a mentor.

Ruburt's mother hated cats, particularly black ones. He, Rooney, and Ruburt passed symptoms back and forth. He was not a passive receptor however, the cat, and he even learned from his encounters with Jack Wall. Many of Ruburt's feelings about his mother however are buried in Rooney's grave. *(Very important.)* Rooney however is free of a distrust that he had carried with him, having to do with his background in that house, this time, across the way, and was grateful for those additional years you gave him.

He was also however symbolic of evil to Ruburt, and to some extent then conquered simply through the natural passage of events. With the death of Ruburt's mother Rooney's purpose was done as far as Ruburt was concerned; and Rooney did a final service, for through his death Ruburt faced the nature of pain and creaturehood that his mother's <u>life</u> had so frightened him of.

(12:08—12:10.)

One small postscript. Ruburt must see his existence as arising from the natural cycle of his mother's reality and his own—two different things but connected. He did not cause his mother's illness by his birth. Her attitudes toward

Ruburt's birth belonged to his mother, and those attitudes of his mother were far more important than Ruburt's birth.

His mother chose a reality that seems incredibly tragic and painful from the outside looking in. In certain terms it was tragic and painful but it was <u>not</u> Ruburt's fault, and within it his mother achieved a different kind of knowledge and even triumphant experience.

She also helped provide a background that Ruburt wanted and chose. Ruburt's aunt was looking from without, and the consciousness of Ruburt's mother left the body as Rooney's did. There is no unbearable pain. Consciousness leaves first, though the body mechanism reacts, but without the "I" identity from which the (in quotes) "horror" comes. Do you follow me?

("Yes.")

Ruburt's mother wast turned in different directions, and her reality existed quite apart from any daughter. The end.

("Thank you very much, Seth." 12:21 AM.)

SESSION 640 (DELETED PORTION)
FEBRUARY 14, 1973

(This material is from the 640th session for February 14, 1973.

(11:46 PM.) Now: a brief note. Ruburt is working well with his beliefs, and seeing them reflected in all portions of his life as mentioned, *Dialogues*, some other thoughts he had only beginning to be expressed in Tim's *(Foote)* letters and his work, are working together in a therapeutic framework.

Now you know that part of his deep love for you is reflected in these sessions. The answers given symbolically are to your parents as well as his, and to all those who need help. The sessions among other things have always represented your combined love and trust in each other, and were generated by your experience as creatures, and your desire to look for personal answers; but more basically for answers asked by all of your race.

I bid you a fond good evening.

("Thank you." 11:50.)

SESSION 644 (DELETED PORTION)
FEBRUARY 28, 1973

(11:27 PM.) This is not dictation. Ruburt should continue expressing his

aggressive feelings—kicking as well as with the pillows and badminton. But this is leading him toward the beliefs behind the charged repressed aggressiveness, which is highly important.

Yes, have him read to you again what he wrote today, and discuss it.

He can now use that energy in normal physical motion. He has only to realize that he can, so help encourage him in aggressively going outward. There will now be a synthesis of dream and waking activity, and a greater physical release, but he must also work through his beliefs on *Rich Bed* and the material begun today. You can help him, but he must do the work. He must feel free to let himself go free of limiting concepts, but <u>he</u> must see, the self that he is now, that certain ideas that he considered important and basic collected limitations about them. He must work through the feelings and beliefs and today was an important breakthrough.

That is the end of our session. And congratulations on your portrait *(for Pat Bailey)* which is also a breakthrough. My heartiest regards to you both, and I bid you a fond good evening.

("Thank you, Seth. Good night." 11:34 PM.)

SESSION 647 (DELETED PORTION)
MARCH 12, 1973

(This material is deleted from the 647th session for March 12, 1973.

(9:37 PM.) A few notes, not dictation. A comment to both of you.

Your freedom, or the lack of it, exists within yourselves. In your situations and compared with others you can hardly complain of a lack, as far as impediments from <u>without</u> are concerned. So the impediments or the feeling of a lack of freedom comes from within.

The chores that both of you think of are nothing compared to the <u>chores</u> of others. Only because you think of them as chores are they bothersome. Your time is your own. You choose to use the freedom of your time in certain ways, and you are always free to choose. You have the freedom to add varieties to your schedules, to alter <u>some</u> of the time in which you work, but you do not take advantage of that freedom.

Thinking of the <u>idea</u> of freedom will make you more aware of freedom. You do not have to wait for example until this book is done. Even small changes in your habitual ways of doing things will initiate further feelings of freedom, and let you see that many of your taken-for-granted timely actions are highly ritualized.

There are many variations <u>now</u> possible with your present "work loads" that are not visible to you because you are not used to looking for them. I suggest that the two of you do just that. Such advantages do not exist for large groups of people. You force upon yourselves greater limitations that you do not need.

Because your work does involve you with both painting and writing inside, then any other variety you add to it can help make up for the varieties possible to others who have a daily change of environment as a matter of course. I expect you to put some of this material to use. Read over what I have said.

What you told Ruburt earlier of course does apply, but there are freedoms now of which you are unaware, so do not concentrate on the limitations, while at the same time do try to rid yourself of them by concentrating upon immediate possible freedoms.

Begin now, in other words.

(9:49.)

SESSION 648 (DELETED PORTION)
MARCH 14, 1973

(*This material is from the 648th session for March 14, 1973.*)

(*12:02 AM.*) A personal note before we close. Strong creative health-giving elements are surfacing. Ruburt was on the verge of realizing his freedom this evening in many areas beside the physical, and the strong therapeutic process is at work.

Peggy (*Gallagher*) was so surprised at Ruburt's ideas of the pictures that Ruburt saw clearly, though briefly, the projection involved on his part, but also on your own. The therapies begun are continuing in more concentrated fashion, and I want both of you to note improvements, to take it for granted they are occurring, and literally to say, as Ruburt did, "To hell with it, it is happening."

There are some things to happen that I am not telling you about along those lines, but you must both take it for granted that freedoms exist now to be expressed.

(*End. The photographs referred to are those sent to us a few days ago by John Eulenberg, from Michigan. He visited us a few weeks ago, in connection with Seth and linguistics, etc., and photographed us both in color.*)

SESSION 653 (DELETED PORTION)
APRIL 4, 1973

(The following material is from the 653rd session for April 4 1973.

(12:20 AM.) A few remarks—they are very simple and to the point: examine your beliefs jointly and individually. You both believe that Ruburt is sick physically in one particular fashion. A series of subsidiary beliefs followed, to which you both most heartily and concretely subscribe. You must alter those beliefs. As long as you hold them they will be most faithfully reproduced and objectively justified.

Ruburt will not navigate properly as long as each of you believe he cannot. As long as you belabor the physical condition you are not working at altering the beliefs. Regardless of their reasons, beliefs can be changed.

Altering the beliefs automatically changes the reasons. They exist simultaneously. You are each reinforcing them now. Pollyanna as it may sound, you must each imagine Ruburt able to navigate, and take it for granted that the rest physically will follow, without trying to force the issue.

That *is* the only way. There is no other way. These rules work for you as well as for everyone else. You both consistently in this particular regard operate from the outside, and become deluged, hypnotized by the exterior situation. That is all I have to say.

It is all I need to say, if you would for once, each of you, clearly understand. Amen and good night.

(Seth then returned to say something about a summer [which year?] when our tactics resulted in Jane's improvement.)

When you followed that procedure results appeared.

("When?"

(No answer.) But you fell back each time.

(12:30 AM.) Since you are talking to Ruburt from your outside, and telling him what to do, when you are not personally saddled in the same way that he is, then how often have you ever reassured him that he could indeed walk properly, get up easily, or joyfully tried to reinforce his confidence?

Your idea of helping him has been to remind him of the hopelessness of his condition, to impress upon him his dependence and dire straits. Now: If this is all you could do from the outside, then how difficult do you think it is for him to encourage himself from the inside?

One particular summer you each made joint effort at the kind of encouragement of which I am speaking, and you got definite results. You believed for a short time what I have been trying to tell you, and then dropped the experiment.

And now, I bid you a fond good night.

("Good night, Seth. Thank you.")

You allowed yourselves to be excited by hope and new beliefs. You allowed yourselves to feel enthusiasm and expectation, and you fired each other. That is what you must do now.

(12:38 AM.)

SESSION 654 (DELETED PORTION)
APRIL 9, 1973

(This material is from the 654th session for April 9, 1973.

(12:05 AM.) A few remarks for you both.

The material Ruburt thought was from me, was. I will give him more in the same way to keep you both on the right track.

Your brilliance (?) in your work, and Ruburt's in his, partially results from the fact that you ignored the mental reality, the psychic and spiritual reality you saw all about you. Do you follow me?

("Yes. I guess so." Although now I'm not so sure I do....)

Be courageous enough then to ignore some of the physical reality you see, as you were courageous enough to ignore the psychic and spiritual realities, and make your own. Now. By all means continue your sexual relationship. <u>If you can</u>, playfully, playfully together, imagine you and Ruburt chasing each other up and down the stairs, or dancing beautifully, or whatever comes into your mind, as long as it is not serious, and you do not expect instant results.

("Yes.")

Continue as you are with the papers in the morning, and I will add my two cents as promised. The last notes I gave you are extremely important, but he must not become overly concerned with results, but <u>know</u> that the new beliefs will bring results, as the old ones did, and as beautifully. Your encouragement is vastly important. I bid you another fond good evening.

("Thank you very much, Seth. The same to you. Good night.")

(12:15 AM.)

SESSION 656 (DELETED PORTION)
APRIL 16, 1973

(This material is from the 656th session for April 16, 1973.

(11:37.) Now: that is the end of *(book)* dictation, and give me a moment. I have a few remarks for you. My words for Ruburt are enclosed within the session. *(The point of power, etc.)*

Some for you are, also: but divest yourself of all your beliefs that you did not fully understand or use your painting abilities "in your youth." Forget thoughts like "It has taken me so long to learn." "Why couldn't I have known when I was a young man about my abilities, and how best to use them?" Think of yourself as a young man using them, and you will automatically be free of many hampering concepts in your work.

Such ideas, practically speaking anyhow, deny you the use of creative energy and vitality you think you had then, that you think you do not have now—the unbridled free energy and exuberance you have equated with youth. By equating it with youth in your mind you deny it to yourself in your present, and therefore deny yourself energy that is (underlined three times) available to be used.

This also denies you in subterranean ways from utilizing certain ideas and concepts. I will have more to say about that at another time, and I mean in terms of your work.

Have Ruburt read this session well. My heartiest regards to you both, and good night.

("Thank you, Seth." 11:45 PM.)

SESSION 657 (DELETED PORTION)
APRIL 18, 1973

(This material is from the 657th session for April 18, 1973.

(11:21.) Now, for both of you: this material *(the session)* was given so that you could use it to clear up many matters, and also because of course it will help others. Ruburt's exercise today however represented exactly what I spoke of, and in that way should be avoided—the paper that you read this afternoon, that he wrote—and when each of you review your joint past, do so looking for your accomplishments. There are many. Otherwise the past will seem like ashes.

Tonight's session should be read by you both and put into practice. The five minutes by each of you, plus the physical action as mentioned, and Ruburt encouraged to take action in the present.

There is material in the book that you have not had time to assimilate, but tonight's session, followed together, will be of great value.

Now I bid you a fond good evening—bugs and all.

("Thank you, Seth. Good night." 11:27. But Seth returned at 11:30.)

Specific suggestions for Ruburt.

1. Do the five minutes as suggested.

2. As far as possible, without pressing the point, make an effort to do what he would do if he were physically satisfactory. That is, write normal hours without taking time out as today, <u>unless</u> he is hit by inspiration to do so.

3. In one way or another, once a day have him do something to act upon the new beliefs. He need not take a walk every day for example, but on faith perform some kind of physical activity that he would if he were physically satisfactory. Take his coffee to the yard, for example. His idea of seeking out motion is a good one. No day should be spent concentrating on ways to get rid of the symptoms, as today.

4. As mentioned, go out together to public places, and begin acting in that regard.

5. Your suggestion of out-of-body activity is a good one, and diverts energy to a good goal.

These suggestions <u>can</u> effectively take the place of *Psycho-Cybernetics*, but only if they are followed.

Good evening.

("Good evening, Seth." 11:38 PM.)

SESSION 660 (DELETED PORTION)
MAY 2, 1973

(This material is from the 660th session for May 2, 1973.

(11:57 PM.) I have one small but important personal note for Ruburt. Writing in his journal daily with his notations of present programs always represents a conscious intent that serves a beneficial natural hypnotic suggestion of accomplishment. When he does not do so therefore, this is a sign of acquiescence to present conditions, or being hypnotized by the unpleasant current aspects.

Whatever program he works with for that time is important, for it is his manner of changing beliefs. He will understand what I mean. His positive successes are noted in his book. The negative aspects are usually not there—not because he omitted them: the book itself helps bring the positive experiences about, <u>because</u>, again, it represents conscious attempts to alter experience.

Alone then it is a positive suggestion. That is all.

("Thank you.")

My heartiest regards to you both, and a fond good evening.

("Good evening, Seth." 12:03 AM.)

SESSION 664 (DELETED PORTION)
MAY 21, 1973

(This material is from the 664th session for May 21, 1973.
(9:30 PM.)
Good evening.
("Good evening, Seth.")
Now: a few helpful notes, I hope, before dictation. The information will also be valuable in other areas. Give us a moment.

It is the ego of course that concentrates so intently upon physical reality and physical problems, as well as challenges. When Ruburt utilizes other focuses and turns his consciousness in other than directly-physical areas, when he turns several <u>angles</u> away, then to <u>some extent</u> (underlined) he frees himself to some degree from beliefs, but certainly from their effects. The mode of orientation is simply not the same.

It is true that his beliefs are also responsible for the fact that he <u>can</u> experience such alterations to begin with. While his beliefs are <u>partially</u> responsible for his astonishing facility, once in various altered states he is in a kind of freewheeling situation as far as physical reality is concerned. He is in it but not directly focused there.

As he knows, he switches on an easy gear. In certain stages of consciousness, beliefs can be changed more easily, but there must be of course an insertion from the normal egotistical level in <u>most</u> (underlined) instances.

Far from beliefs being embedded in the so-called unconscious, they are relatively speaking more plastic there. Beliefs are strongest at precisely the point of conscious impact upon the physical environment. The belief, any belief, is a conscious formation of ideas that are accepted as physical truth. The energy for the beliefs comes from other levels, of course. Without the energy the beliefs would wither.

(Long pause at 9:42.) In certain terms alterations of consciousness involved you in experiences of an <u>angular</u> nature, where perception uses physical reality as a basis, but forms <u>angles</u> from it. In certain terms the physical world <u>can</u> (underlined) be said to be opaquely perceived then, while other perceptions become clearer, but the normally conscious <u>attention</u> (underlined) is no longer so dominant, and even normal beliefs go into a momentary withdrawal.

They are activated again of course upon the next usual impact of ego consciousness with the environment. Ruburt believes in his inner agility. It is only with the impact of body and environment, of course, that he has difficulty. The free-wheeling states of consciousness can therefore be of help to him, the free-wheeling characteristic being primarily in relationship to physical reality. His intentness then is translated or transferred away from the normal environment.

(9:51.) The point of power exercise can be utilized from these other levels, where the inner mobility is then seen "rising upward". It would help if at those levels he imagined his body as plastoid, always in a state of change, as fluid as his thoughts, and not so much a physical thing. He often thinks of it as a thing to be moved, when it is instead an ever-changing, fleshy materialization of motion.

He does not have to move it. It can move quite well itself. We will have more, now or later this evening, but first dictation—or do you want a break?

("Yes."

(9:59. No more personal material was received. Plastoid is not in the dictionary. Seth created it as an adjective for plastic.)

SESSION 666 (DELETED PORTION)
MAY 28, 1973

(The following material is from the 666th Session for May 28, 1973.

(12:01 AM.) Have Ruburt read through the book he has begun *(Personal Reality)*. He is, now, working directly with beliefs. See that he does not concentrate on the old ones, while however recognizing them, and encourage him in his ability to insert the new ones. Do you follow me?

("Yes. I'll do it if I can."

(Louder:) You can. My heartiest wishes to you both, then, and a fond good evening.

(12:05 AM.)

SESSION 667 (DELETED PORTION)
MAY 30, 1973

(The following material is from the 667th session for May 30, 1973.

(Before the session I'd asked Jane if Seth could comment upon the reported drop in sales of Seth Speaks *recently as reported by Tam Mossman at Prentice-Hall. I wanted to know if our own attitudes had anything to do with this.*

(11:41.) Now—In answer to your question: of course you are both involved. You wanted time to figure out how you would handle the situation if sales continued as they began. The visitors, the letters, and the overall implications.

There were other reasons, in that the paperback *Seth Material* is <u>meant</u> to be read first, and lead readers into *Seth Speaks*. Overall the phenomena follows quite natural psychic laws. When the ESP book is reprinted *(Jane heard about this from F. Fell this week)*, readers will largely be already acquainted with my work, and bring that extra knowledge to that early book *(smile)*, hence enriching its potentials for them.

The situation is not negative unless you are thinking mainly in financial terms, and of great unusual wealth. You will be well provided for financially, as I have told you. Neither of you want to be millionaires. You can expect financial security beyond any dreams you had at marriage. And in the future great freedom, financially speaking.

There will be a foundation of sorts, and investments, for that is a part of Ruburt's particular nature, but this will come in time as you want it. The books are well established, and there will be an acceleration even with the hardcover *Seth Speaks* as the paperback is assimilated. You are not on a Dick Bach trip.

Financially, even now in embryo, your ideas are far different than they were. Ruburt knows how much he could make if he wanted to through classes; and even in choosing to have only one per week, a choice is involved that earlier did not exist. The same applies to what you could do in marketing the Seth material from manuscript.

You have, even now, a greater financial mobility therefore. As far as beliefs are concerned, Ruburt is working <u>directly</u> now with the proper ones, in the correct area.

Other material given by me was quite correct at the time as those beliefs were applied in the past to various levels of your lives, and as you each interacted. Until you realized that the point of power was in the present, I could only deal with those beliefs in the context of your understanding.

There is a significance in your dancing dilemma that neither of you have come to grips with—having to do with each of your natures and characteristics and ways of looking at a situation. Of course projection is involved, <u>on both of your parts</u>, and not therefore simply on Ruburt's . He <u>to some extent</u> (underlined twice) recognizes his projections, is consciously aware of them, and tries to deal with them, but in that particular situation you do not recognize yours, though you understand to some degree your different individual reactions.

Ruburt realizes the desperation behind his own sudden impetus to dance, and the effort behind it. He realizes you do not experience this, and does attempt to make adjustments on your behalf. He does this particularly since he realizes he cannot count upon his reactions. The next time out he might be willing to dance, and be relatively unable.

What neither of you realized is the acuteness with which you choose the situations. You have not gone to establishments where dancing is the usual thing, where a dance floor is available. Granted there are other reasons for it, nevertheless you choose to begin with a situation in which dancing is not the norm, where it requires on <u>anyone's</u> part particular effort, and a spotlighted situation.

Here Ruburt tries to force a situation, to set up on his part an incentive where he <u>will</u> be spotlighted, and therefore knows he will perform well, having chosen a "critical," dramatic framework.

Now it is this framework that you distrust. He interprets this to mean that you want him to be spontaneous as long as it is acceptable, as long as he blends with others, as long as he does not go too far. He is obviously in not the best physical condition, so the spotlight to you involves the illumination of weakness obviously apparent.

If you shy away from dramatic public exhibitions of emotionalism under the best circumstances, then here you are faced with a situation in which you see it <u>thrust</u> upon you by someone you love, and in your eyes under the poorest of circumstances. The physical conditions, the floor, the act of dancing when others are not, these circumstances are not to your liking. Beside that Ruburt, you feel, is not at his best physically speaking. The situation then is highly charged.

Ruburt feels if you love him you will make the effort, but you retreat. Other things are involved. He has had several drinks before he reaches that point of deciding to dance, or to ask you to. You project upon him the attributes of emotional extravagance that you fear in your mother. That is, what you interpreted as such. Quite simply to you it seemed not the place or the time, <u>precisely</u> because to Ruburt it did seem the place and the time. To him this meant that his emotional mobility could be expressed privately at home under conditions you both found acceptable, but not physically through the body. Yet both of you chose conditions that were not "proper" in those terms to begin with, and hence highlighted the situation so you could understand it. It is more difficult in a way for Ruburt without the highlighted situation, yet easier for you. The spotlight serves as an impetus for him, and as an impediment to some extent for you—so he was trying to use the spotlight as an impetus for action precisely because he doubted his abilities. Now: that is enough for this evening. My heartiest regards to you both, and a fond good evening.

("Good evening, Seth." 12:17 AM.)

SESSION 670 (DELETED PORTION)
JUNE 13, 1973

(This material is from the 670th session for June 13, 1973.
(10:08.) Now. Please do not interrupt. If you have questions I will answer them later this evening, and if you want you can have an extra session for book dictation.

Ruburt feels that he has a dragon by the tail. He is damned if he will let go and yet he is afraid to pull harder. You can specifically say that this has to do with what you call your psychic work, but even before "it" began he was aware of that energy of his, concerned about using it, focusing it, delighted with it, and afraid of it at the same time.

Even in his poetry, before our work, it always led him at certain times way beyond "himself." He tried to hold himself down because, he felt, that the energy was so strong that allowed freedom in almost any direction, it would bring him in conflict with the mores and ways of other people.

He is literally a great receiver of energy. He attracts it and it must therefore then go <u>through</u> him, translated into experience outward. He is himself. He cannot turn himself off, or his abilities off. It is only when you make a differentiation, and basically an artificial one, between other natural abilities and psychic ones, that you think of his psychic activities as a conflict.

In whatever level of activity he <u>focused</u> his energy, his activities would be strong, exaggerated in terms of <u>others</u> by comparison. He <u>is</u> a great mystic. Naturally, that is, a great mystic. And that is reflected through his poetry as well as our specific work. So that expression would come through poetry also with its "psychedelic" experience, regardless of our specific sessions.

Had he been for example a great actor, he would have met the same kind of problem in different form.

(10:22.) Greater recognition might help at a certain level, but this is not the answer. The fact that psychic books, so-called, do not give him what he thinks of as conventional literary praise is annoying but not basically pertinent.

He has been using the symptoms indeed as brakes. These brakes have been applied in what you <u>think</u> of as the psychic arena because that is the chosen situation. It is not physical mobility that worries him, but inner mobility. He is afraid to go ahead, feeling it not safe, yet he is damned if he will retreat, and for that matter he realizes that there is no retreat from your own knowledge and experience.

He has been afraid to use his abilities freely, and therefore set up physical conditions that remind him constantly of his body and objective physical life, for fear that he will go too far beyond it. He uses the radio often as physical noise to bring him back and serve as a guideline in altered states of consciousness.

He has been using the static of physical discordance in the same way. Now many creative people unfortunately do the same thing. On an entirely different level, one of your old favorites, Peggy Lee, has severe physical difficulties that are meant actually to contain her energy and force it along certain lines only.

Whenever Ruburt opens to the dream state, physically he is specifically worried about out-of-body travel. That was a challenge, and his own did not frighten him, but those of others did. His own _did_ bring him up short momentarily, but that he could have handled.

It is no use saying you wish no psychic development had occurred. It is like saying you wish a tree was a violet, or vice-versa. The experience _is_ his nature. This nature also required precise _and yet_ flexible and free manipulation. This is acquired naturally _through_ experience, through the experience of being himself. When he began to cut off his natural spontaneous expression in dream reality, out-of-body travel, etc., he denied himself the acquisition of that facility to _some_ degree.

Then he applied the brakes physically. The free flow of his experience goes rather easily, _and_ incidentally, safely and exuberantly from what you think of as objective and subjective experience, and his creative gifts then make subjective knowledge objective in terms of art.

It is then, again, the spontaneity of his own being that alternately delights and appalls him. I have said little about astrology, yet he chose to be born under that earth sign. _(Taurus.)_ It is one, for reasons incidentally that I will give you at a later time, that brings the flowering of ability in later years, and that also provides, _when_ strong talents are present, a conservative countering measure.

Now I told you that each day provides the answers to your problems, and each night. Ruburt's answer therefore is to go ahead with his own nature freely, practically. This does not involve our sessions. He is not afraid of them.

It _does_ involve his own private experience, opening up to himself, freeing the flow of his energy. There are several ways this can be done. It is his freely allowed subjective experience now that results in books—mine, and _Seven's_. He has set up barriers however against his own personal inner mobility. It is extremely important that he become more permissive, particularly in the dream state, and to change his attitude about dreaming, to go along with his experience and forget how he can make it understandable to others.

When he allows the experience, his creative abilities will translate it. He has been afraid of letting himself go and utilizing his energies fully, not objectively but subjectively.

He has nothing to be frightened of. His greatest achievements lie in that direction.

Now take your break, and I will have some specific recommendations.

(10:48—11:00.)

Now I am telling you facts. Do not put terms like fortunate or unfortunate onto them.

You however also expected Ruburt to put on brakes, and for some time acquiesced, as he did. You wanted what you thought of as adequate discipline maintained, and in other areas as well. The symptoms served secondary purposes afterward, and in all honesty for both of you.

(Intently:) You were not sure if you wanted to go on tours. The symptoms gave you breathing space. You each had an excuse ready-made. You were also worried about Ruburt's spontaneity in psychic matters, and for a while quite approved of the sudden brakes. Both of you to varying extents now were willing to put up with the disadvantages involved, and still to some extent you both feel the same way.

It is the effects you do not like, and that is all.

It is true that Ruburt's ideas predominate, that his reality is his, but yours is a part of it, as his is a part of yours. He felt therefore that you did approve of the overall idea, if not particularly the methods. And in the beginning you approved those in your own way.

You did not want Ruburt sick, but you did want brakes applied, and he chose the method. He chose the method for various reasons, from his experience. He had seen you drag your feet, applying brakes to a situation; and identifying with you, and not with his mother, his chose the same means.

Because of his own characteristic method he used them, the means, in his way differently than you did.

There is no doubt, regardless of what you think you think, that you also acquiesced, though thinking that Ruburt went too far. It is only when he goes too far that either of you get upset.

(11:10.) A less determined personality would have drawn back, shriveled, and denied its own abilities. Ruburt did not do that, and you would not have acquiesced to that, so your joint and private reality does not include it.

Now practically I am making some suggestions. They apply now, as the situation stands, taking your nature and Ruburt's into consideration.

He normally and naturally awakens often in the early hours, and does not get up because his body is too sore, in his terms, but he spontaneously feels an alliance with himself and those hours, and intuitively knows that his creative abilities are strong then, and his dream recall good.

I want him to come over here *(to the living room)*, make his coffee or whatever, be alone with himself and follow his impulses—to write or whatever, and to recall his dream experiences. You must let him know that you do trust him and his spontaneity, because before, no matter what you said, he knew that to some degree you wanted brakes applied.

(11:15.) A daily walk is imperative, and a symbol, you see, of walking inward. Also a nap in which subjective experience is freely suggested.

The inner challenges, faced, will be nothing. He will realize his safety and ability, but the challenge cannot be put off. Before he sleeps he should remind himself of his natural gift of inner mobility, and encourage dream experience and recall. This alone provides the meeting of inner and outer, and true mobility. You must let him know that you do trust his spontaneity, for it is also your own, as you know.

Let him know also you are there. In a strange manner, not to be given this evening, your own painting mobility is involved. I am not saying that his reality is not his own, that he does not have the joy and responsibility for it, but that you also share a joint reality.

Your confidence will increase his. Let him know therefore that you do trust him to go ahead spontaneously, regardless of where that might lead, knowing it will be beneficial and creative. The recommendations I gave to him should also be followed despite, and precisely because of any physical resistance. In the beginning for example he may not want to move.

Now tell him that I will look out for him in all of his dream and/or out-of-body journeys. His creative output will be vastly improved, particularly in quality. I will have other recommendations after these are followed for a week.

Now I will end our session. If you want an extra book session you may have it this weekend. If you have questions I will answer them whenever you want. Now *Seven* gave Ruburt the same information in a different way.

(I asked Seth a long series of questions, though many of them were repetitious. The main one concerned whether Jane's natural mystical nature had helped her in her times of need; I was most curious to know if this help had been given. Seth replied several times that "the answer has already been given in the early part of tonight's session, by inference. That is the best answer I can give at this time. Follow the recommendations." The session ended then at 11:35 PM.

(Both Jane and I felt considerably better. I'm going to ask her to add her own comments to these sessions as they are held. That way they'll actually be extensions of

the material, and a record of results obtained.)

DELETED SESSION
JUNE 24, 1973 9:08 PM SUNDAY

(This morning Jane and I embarked on a new program in an effort to track down the origin of her symptoms. They appear to be worse and we're vitally concerned. We wrote out a series of 14 questions for Seth, and planned for a session tonight. We also began a list of her beliefs. A list of my beliefs will be added. We want to have at least a session a week on personal matters, and two or three meetings a week for work on beliefs. As expected, some of Jane's beliefs at least partially answered some of the questions we had for Seth, but we still desire him to consider the questions.

(Jane's beliefs as listed already are very revealing, and much more is sure to come. Doing this work and having the session made us both feel much better. We slept well. Jane got up at 5 AM to do some work, and also went for a walk around the block before calling me for breakfast at 8.)

Good evening.

("Good evening, Seth.")

Now: We will start easily enough, with your question as to whether or not Ruburt considered your feelings in all of this.

(#12: Is Ruburt at all concerned with the effects of his present behavior on me—my feelings, etc.?)

He did of course care deeply, (and had) his interpretation of your feelings: he believed that the symptoms served you both, that you would on the one hand object, give lip service against his methods, but that underneath they provided you service.

We are working with <u>his</u> beliefs. He felt that you would find tours, etc., highly disruptive. There would be endless decisions to be made. The symptoms cut the need for decisions in that area.

We are starting at the surface and working downward.

As mentioned today, he felt they served you, helped you save face in your family, and in society at large. You were not to be given the second place. Ruburt obviously needed you. Some of this did have to do with old ideas that you were angry at him for any success if you had not achieved your own—and more, that the success might take you on tours and further away from your own work, which would make you angrier at him.

At the same time you encouraged him to success, but he felt only to a certain point, for the fruits of the success you might find disruptive. In the family to which he has always been sensitive he believed his success put you down, particularly with your mother and Loren. *(My younger brother.)*

Give us time, and we are still dealing with the same question.

His symptoms were meant, in a way, now, in regard to you, to make you feel better, for by contrast you became the success and he the failure. That failure was also meant to take your mind away from what he believed you believed was your own failure as an artist.

With others and strangers coming here, the symptoms put you, he believed, in a position of prominence, obviously the head of the family, having to take care of the frail woman—to compensate for the fact that he was financially making more. In this regard the illness was almost a gesture of defiance against any who would put you down.

All of this is still in answer to the same question.

At the same time he began to see what the symptoms turned you off to some degree, and this made him angry. Some late instances I have mentioned, having to do with <u>his</u> beliefs and interpretations now, of your actions in dance establishments.

He would purposely choose occasions in which dancing, to begin with, was at least not the thing—when no one else was dancing, when an ordinary person might have inhibitions against it. The very challenge was made because it, the challenge, aroused him to action in a situation in which he felt your natural inhibitions would meet up against his denied spontaneity.

I am making this as clear as I can.

When you refused to dance, he interpreted this to mean that he <u>was</u> right: he could be spontaneous only as long as it was socially approved, did not hassle you, and when he did not stand out from the crowd.

His sudden desire to dance and the freedom came fairly quickly after you started going out again. You stopped immediately, avoiding the situation. Ruburt's sudden desire to dance was also based upon desperation and defiance, which you recognized and reacted against.

There is more there, but it is a cameo situation involving many important ingredients, where he feels that letting go means he is too flamboyant for you. It is important because it involves both private and public circumstances, his attitude toward himself, you, and other people, spontaneity, and restraint.

He wanted to dance <u>precisely because</u> no one else was. Because you would stand out, because it was not the thing to do, and he felt and believed that those were precisely the reasons why you did not <u>want</u> him to do so.

You must understand I am answering a question. The symptoms as related to you are being discussed. This is a part of the picture.

The dancing situation is also important because bodily motion is involved. He always believed, now, that when you spoke to him in the past about walking faster than you, or not waiting for you to open doors, that you were saying to him "You are going too fast for me, and putting me in a poor social light."

He believed that you wanted sex, but that you were afraid of it, as he was, because of the possibility of pregnancy. Here the symptoms served also, and cut down the possibility of sexual activity.

He was afraid during the tour that you would feel put in second place, rather than as an artist being the star of your own show.

For some time he did not feel that you wanted him to get better, but only to keep the symptoms within bounds. Again, this is in reference to you, and not the whole picture. On one level he felt you were quite willing to have him do this, again, as long as he did not go too far.

Then he felt that you were accusing him of being stupid, but without trying to come up with any solutions of your own. Then he felt completely alone, with a problem he feared he could not solve. He looked to your reaction after any spontaneous behavior, and he believed, now, that your reaction was negative.

Very simply, the dancing episodes serve as an example. It seemed to him that if he spontaneously felt happy about a book that you would remind him of less favorable aspects. On the other hand he was convinced of your deep loyalty and love, and knew that you did want him to succeed and use his abilities.

He felt that you disapproved of class, of the spontaneity, and did not ever attend, while you were pleased with the money, and that if you attended you would be in second place. That is why when the two of you met as a unit, so to speak, with the Rochester group *(last week)* that he allowed himself greater freedom, and in that context he believed you approved. *(The Seth III episode, etc.)*

Again, on a very simple level, he believes that if he were better he would always be wanting to dance in improper conditions as far as you were concerned.

Now. As partners, to some extent consciously you agreed to varying attitudes at different times to the conditions, though the main elements of course are Ruburt's. You feel the necessity for some restraint in social encounters, and with the world at large. Ruburt is providing them, and also for his own reasons. He is showing the spontaneity in his work that you have denied yourself in many respects in yours. He is dealing with the world of markets that you have been unwilling to deal with. That is why you are so sensitive in that area.

You had better take a break.

(10:01 to 10:15.)

There are invaluable benefits that you each have that are invisible to you. You take them so for granted that you do not realize how extraordinary they are in comparison to other people's experience.

Your basic trust and loyalty to each other, for example. Many spend a lifetime searching for that recognition with another human being, or achieve it but briefly. You are blind to this, yet others are quite aware that you have it. Besides, you each have deep interests and drives that have always united you; and you, Joseph, in this life served as an impetus to organize Ruburt's abilities. He knew this. So did you. There <u>are</u> several time's simultaneous existences, and you are both interacting in several. This deep inner knowledge provides each of you, whether or not you realize it, with strong ties of creaturehood, and deep loyalties to "both worlds."

You did not want families, so your emotional ties with your mates were to be strong. In families several members at various times serve to objectify the whole family's particular attitudes in a given area.

The two of you in a more intensified framework portray your triumphs and challenges. You gave yourselves an intimate trust however with each other, and the sense of belonging that the majority of people simply lack.

(10:28.) Give us a moment.... To some extent it is a matter of some perfectly adequate beliefs not being tempered by others. Some of the beliefs Ruburt holds, that you think you disapprove of, you agree with—though not with his methods.

Give us time.... You have agreed that restraints should be used. Ruburt chose the method. The methods came from his own experience in this life. The things you both strongly agreed upon were allowed freedom within those limitations. Until recently you spoke to him against travel because you lost work time. He believed that you thought it a waste of time, so he did not believe his lack of physical mobility <u>that</u> way would hamper you.

He feared that left alone he would want to travel at the drop of a hat. Your deepest drives involve inner work. He thought he chose methods then that would annoy each of you the least.

You each have strong drives toward secrecy. Your idea was to isolate yourself on a mountaintop, where the world could not get at you. His idea was an arrangement where he could not go out into the world.

You may take your break

(10:37—10:46)

Now: you have asked for my help.

Until now you both got enough out of the situation so that you did not seriously challenge it. It was meeting both of your needs.

You have, Joseph, your own invisible beliefs. In a way Ruburt was doing precisely what you would do on one level—not leaving the house, avoiding tours, simply working, cutting out all distractions, and again you approved—not of methods, but of everything else.

You envied the concentration. On the one hand you said "Good girl," and on the other complained about the undesirable side effects. Ruburt was doing what you wanted to do, without the mountaintop. Only when the side effects became more and more obtrusive did either of you become frightened.

Ruburt took it for granted that the body could take so much, and that he could reverse the conditions. Then he became afraid that he could not reverse them, and only then did the two of you really become worried.

The idea of cutting down stimuli and concentrating on work was quite agreeable to both of you for some time, far beyond the time you think it was. *(Pause.)* You then had to do many of the chores, and go out into the world, in you must admit a small fashion, but Ruburt was afraid that otherwise you would retreat.

Only the physical effects frightened either of you for some time. Ruburt was afraid also you would retreat as he felt your father had. Therefore he put you in a position where retreat was impossible. To some extent you were afraid of the same thing.

Now all of this tonight is in response to one question, and would apply whether or not psychic work was involved. It is only lately that each of you have really become worried enough to want a real change.

A note: Ruburt's feelings toward this place *(apartment 5)* are significant and beneficial.

In line with invisible beliefs, there are many that are quite positive—ingredients in your lives that you simply do not appreciate, dimensions of activity that you take for granted.

Aspects is free, by the way.

Now you may end the session. We will have a good book session tomorrow. I will deal with all of your questions in private sessions.

("All right. Thank you, Seth, and good night." 11:05 PM.

(Seth's reference to Jane's book idea, Aspect Psychology, *touches on one of our other questions. Her editor, Tam Mossman, has offered her the prospect of a contract for a book on* Adventures in Consciousness *combined with* Aspects. *We've been wondering if it is a good idea for Jane to become involved with* Adventures, *in light of past problems. At this time we think it's probably okay for*

her to work on Aspects, *though.)*

SESSION 672 (DELETED PORTION)
JUNE 25, 1973

(This material is from the 672nd session for June 25, 1973.)

I will have our regular book session on Wednesday, and your next session when you prefer. Now give us a moment. In the meantime I have a few words.

These are beliefs of Ruburt's. He felt in the past that you did not consistently keep with him in any program of improvement, except for badminton. Because you were willing to go along now he believes in your complete sincerity at all levels, and in your willingness to help him.

There are things I have to say, saved for private sessions, having to do with his condition about the house. Tell him if possible to forget the symptoms as much as he can, and concentrate instead upon his work and our program. Encourage him to do so.

My heartiest regards to both of you and a fond good evening. Results will show.

("All right. Thank you, Seth.
(11:56 PM.)

DELETED SESSION
JUNE 30, 1973 9:45 PM SATURDAY

(Jane had obtained excellent material on her own today, working with beliefs about her writing, symptoms, and movement about the house. The idea was that physical restraints would keep her at her desk and remove temptations to do other things. We were anxious to hear what Seth would have to say about this material.

(We sat for the session at 9, but just then a neighbor began cutting his grass with a power mower. Our windows were open and the sound seemed especially bothersome. We waited for the job to be done, which took half an hour. By then we were both quite upset, although I think Jane's unease stemmed more from my reaction to the noise, than it did from any noise itself.)

Now good evening.

("Good evening, Seth.")

This small episode this evening is an excellent example of your joint behavior and beliefs. Noise to you personally is a symbol for all of life's distractions. You are then particularly sensitive in that area. Any discussion between you is at two levels, then, where sound of an unpleasant nature is involved.

Ruburt in his own way recognizes the charge behind what you say. Sound to him does not have the same meaning, though he may dislike the noise. He interprets your remarks therefore as aimed against distractions in general, recognizing your symbolism, and this makes him uneasy because in his own life he has taken the steps he has to cut down distractions.

He becomes more afraid of them as you speak in such a way, and through your attitude, as he interprets it, the distractions seem more threatening.

Now give us a moment.... Both papers he has done on beliefs *(this week)* apply <u>as beliefs</u>—the one involving you, and today's.

He is correct. The beliefs <u>behind</u> these were quite applicable and helpful to a youthful personality. His writing, as much as art does, sprang from periods of deep thinking, isolation, and involved strong tendencies to go inward more or less alone.

Creative people, if they succeed at all, often find themselves in a position where they <u>feel</u> that the precious inward isolation is threatened. Demands are then made by the outside world that were not made earlier. The inward work ends up causing them to relate to a physical world when they believed that their duty was to shut themselves <u>off</u> from that world.

Ruburt's set of beliefs for some time were so invisible, and he identified with them so completely, that it was extremely difficult for him to examine them in the light of the present and his now situation.

The paper written today should be discussed by both of you so that those ideas are brought completely into the open where <u>he</u> can consciously and intellectually examine them. Your emotions follow your beliefs. For many reasons then he was convinced that his course was correct. His methods <u>began</u> to alarm him, but even when they did, and he realized that he was making a bargain of a sort, he still believed in the premise that made a bargain necessary.

Because many of his ideas and beliefs were <u>also</u> bound up with you, your work, your ideas and his <u>interpretations</u> of them, then your relationship became entwined. Initially the beliefs were accepted because he had been taught to believe to fear his energy. On the other hand it was his pride. Now in another kind of life-style, with another kind of personality, the same belief might have been dispensed with easily. If energy flows in conventional accepted patterns it is not feared.

Give us a moment.... He had, as you mentioned, the inner knowledge of his own abilities that had, he felt, to be used. After his first marriage he determined, with the help of your love, to find a suitable framework. His natural abilities <u>are</u> unconventionally tuned, highly spontaneous, working through intuitive loops; in a certain way, now, from a <u>normally</u> conscious viewpoint, unpredictable.

(Intently, as above:) His nature then on other levels would follow the same pattern. He felt that this same quality, <u>physically translated</u>, led to a physical spontaneity that would make the inner spontaneity more difficult to achieve. Spontaneity and energy used in his work was one thing, but allowed physical translation, <u>he felt</u>, could mean bizarre, unreasonable physical complications.

If he were as spontaneous physically as he was mentally, then his living situation could become unstable. In your early relationship this could mean anything from sudden trips across country, an overactive social life, or even sexual attraction to men outside of marriage.

Before you moved here he felt that his energy had been too spontaneously used physically.

He was then just over 30, and felt that his abilities had not begun to show fruition. The beliefs gathered momentum then, coming from structures from childhood that he felt he could use, and from you ideas, which then, were very much like his.

There are other issues of which he has been lately somewhat aware, connected here for example. In the beginning the symptoms made certain that he would not have to get a job. That fear no longer operates. The belief as he wrote it alone was simply that to do his creative work he <u>had</u> to curtail other activities. In the beginning as an apprentice writer this was to allow him to develop.

When he found himself becoming at all known after the tour, the symptoms, after having lifted to a large degree, returned with a vengeance, because then he was suddenly, to his way of thinking, besieged by distractions of a different kind. Then he was also afraid that this spontaneity and unconventionally attuned energy could be misdirected, again physically away from work. He could become for example a television personality.

(My note added later: "I remember all of this well. How Jane got much worse as soon as we got back home from tour. RB, December 10, 1980.)"

He had greater temptations, so he applied more brakes.

Now: your attitude and his interpretation of it, <u>to him</u>, clearly jibed. Such courses would also represent distractions to you. He thought you hated distractions, and for a period of time he felt that you thought him one.

Since all of this made <u>such sense</u> to him, he did not change it. Nor could he see beyond it. Until yesterday he could not see himself <u>apart from</u> the system of beliefs.

His writing seemed dependent upon the curtailment of activities of other kinds. Give us a moment.... When the system was set up, for many reasons having to do with relative youth and lack of experience, he did not have any confidence in his conscious ability to say no, to hold to a "line of attack." He was afraid he would be swept willy-nilly. He was also afraid, particularly when he tried teaching, that he might be led to give up and settle for another occupation that would bring automatic respectability, money, and some prestige.

Give me a moment. I want to organize this so it makes sense to you... For other reasons, the fear of pregnancy for example, physical spontaneity was also suspect, and here again you were involved. Not that you consciously approved the methods used, but he had his situation and yours always in mind, and was convinced he was acting for both of your interest.

Now these are his interpretations, but whenever you rejected his spontaneous advances, for whatever reasons you may have had, this helped reinforce that idea. There was, my dear friend, little danger of Ruburt becoming pregnant, when spontaneous passionate moments on both of your parts were cut out.

You made love when it was safe to do so. Now this involved tricks on both of your parts, to which you both agreed. The conscious material was there. You simply ignored it. You made sure you had a good reason not to make love when Ruburt spontaneously wanted to, and the same applied to him.

In many areas then both of you controlled your spontaneity. For Ruburt this had greater dangers than it did for you because he is geared toward spontaneous action. Other issues would have subsidiary effects, all within the framework. For him the writing abilities had to be allowed freedom. The psychic initiation actually united them. The early novels, published, would have led to another kind of personal problem, since all involved were living. He would still have had to face the world, so to speak. To be free to write freely, he had also to make a certain financial success, or he would need a job.

With the dream book he tried to do something he did not consider artistic, and was unable to do it. He believed in the book's ideas, but the artistic framework for him was not right. When it was rejected my book was developing. Finances were mixed up with freedom to write, then.

Give us time.... He had schooled himself to believe that distractions of any kind had to be eliminated. This means that in writing a book he withdrew, and more and more, physically speaking. It was his idea of training. The issues were also operating between you, as his paper on belief indicates.

Do you want a break?

("No.")

He also felt that you reacted to his improvement by feeling threatened yourself, that you disapproved of it. Two particular beliefs here: The party at Bega's, and your "tirade" —his interpretation, about his dealing with Prentice on one particular occasion. For reference it is in his notebook.

These two events made him pull in his horns; or rather, his interpretation of them in the light of your relationship. He always <u>felt</u> now, and work this out yourselves, that you focused upon the most negative aspects of his condition, and ignored any improvement as minute. But more, that you almost disapproved of them, that you expected him to be in poor shape. So he would hide any he felt from you often for fear you would crush them, or make him lose whatever small confidence in himself physically he'd gained.

He then began to mistrust any improvements himself, and to think "So what? It has happened before, and to no overall advantage."

When he did not then get even those small improvements that generated even small hope, he became truly frightened.

Buying a house was in direct opposition to several other beliefs. The money from books gave him freedom to write more books, so to buy was a threat. At the same time he wanted to move, though he has been more satisfied than you.

The tooth difficulty arose because of the conflicts of wanting a new contract while thinking of spending money for a house. Also his great difficulty physically when you were looking at houses. He felt that you wanted one but that you were refusing to do what you <u>could</u> do—move to a rented place, and that did excite him.

The symptoms became intensified. The tooth symptoms however brought up a system of beliefs through his writing, and he faced some of them quite directly in a crisis situation. He saw what could happen when beliefs are allowed to run astray, and he attacked some then quite directly, and won out. The contract for my book, on a physical level, relieved him.

The beliefs had built up then to such an extent that highly ritualized behavior was involved. He <u>had</u> to be at his desk at certain times immediately. Now that has vanished. He worked that through out of sheer desperation.

<u>The reason that he could not get rid of the symptoms was simply that he believed them necessary requirements to his work</u>. The symptoms and curtailment of activities were invisibly combined, so that he did not realize you could consciously set up a system in which you could work freely without distractions, and be perfectly free to do whatever else you wanted otherwise.

Until that distinction was seen then <u>he felt his writing dependent upon the symptoms</u>. They were retained in order to maintain concentration, period. When a book was being produced, and afterward.

These ideas were a part of his youth, and therefore nostalgically connected with it also. Give us a moment, and rest your hand.

When you talk about people being insane, and point out the negative aspects of the race, Ruburt becomes highly uncomfortable because to him this means he has to protect himself against them, and justifies his behavior. On the other hand he becomes angry and frightened because it is precisely to protect himself against such "people, activities, and events" that he has tried to isolate himself.

Hearing you voice the same opinions, he becomes mad at them or at you, for he knows that those reactions of yours helped him form his fear of the world—helped, but are not responsible.

Take a break and we will continue if you are willing.

(11:15—11:28.)

Now. In one respect Ruburt is quite correct: you believe it is safer to express your doubts and negative aspects then to express your enthusiasms or hopes.

If you did not know that Ruburt <u>could</u> indeed manage to dance, though not in the wildest fashion, then you would not believe it when "faced" with the reality of his behavior around the house. You would think he could not do it.

Now if he said under those conditions "I want to go out and dance," you would say "I don't want to make you feel bad, but I don't think you can manage it now. Maybe later you can."

Now when Ruburt imaginatively saw the trailer, and so forth *(on our Sunday drive last weekend)* and experienced that mobility in imagination, your reaction was the same as the one used for my analogy above. In his way he was using an excellent procedure, and what you thought of as reminding him of the facts was instead inhibiting freedom.

A bicycle has all kinds of connotations for him. It seems unreasonable, watching him, to think that he could even begin to ride one. Watching him you would not think he could get to a dance floor, much less move. He mentioned adjusting the seat. You have been afraid to fix it, thinking he might hurt himself. That is another point however that is important.

Give us a moment.

You <u>are</u> to some degree, both of you, using the symptoms as excuses. Ruburt is afraid that if he can operate in a trailer, and he can, that you will find yourselves losing work time, running all over the country, and you are afraid of the same thing. Any project the two of you are attracted to but think will be distracting, you blame on the symptoms. Since this is never challenged you never know whether or not Ruburt can perform.

You say that when my book is finished you will move, yet each of you through the years has said "When this book is finished we will move." Move or not, you must be consciously aware of your beliefs and deal with them on that level. Now. Ruburt's coming back in here *(Apartment 5)* represented a willingness to face beliefs. To come out into the open, so to speak, with you and with the world.

Symbolic interpretations immediately became obvious, and yet brought out into the open, as in tonight's episode. I do not want to duplicate material, but Ruburt's seeing you working without symptoms was of great benefit. Your reaction then to the noise was upsetting, which is quite all right, because now your reactions there can be consciously assimilated. Your reaction is to yell about the condition, yet you do not move. His has been to say little and to withdraw. Though your particular <u>interpretations</u> of distractions may vary, to him the noise itself, for example, is not so charged. But quite rightly he recognizes the noise as your symbol for distraction.

Gradually his belief system led to more restrictive behavior, even to some extent impeding inner flow. The psychic was suspect in the beginning, as it seemed to conflict with his writing ideas. This was largely cleared through my books and *Seven*.

Letters and calls were interpreted as distractions mainly—as another pull upon his energies. He recognized the psychic source of his writing, which cleared the psychic area in <u>that</u> respect, finally. But he was afraid that the spontaneity denied in physical life would run rampant now in inner psychic experience.

The sex was denied on a physical level to a large extent, as he read so-called psychic books. Much of this is based on the youthful feeling he had to direct his energy toward his work. He found his physical age frightening for a while, and was therefore not able to use the experience gained with age. To give up the youthful ideas was to admit that he was no longer the young writer.

To let these ideas go was to let his youth go, and to admit that many of those ideas, believed in so strongly and so stubbornly, were not working any longer. Even your remarks about a black-haired wife meant the image of a woman in her 20's—the-younger-than-you obviously youthful, spontaneous and cute wife; not a 44-year-old woman with experience behind her, some sense, and who could stand on her own feet, but a much younger version, youthful enough to get into trouble, and to be humorously watched in that regard.

Give us a moment. You can see where in many regards your beliefs jibed, interacted, and yet you <u>have</u> lately both concentrated on the negative aspects, and this is one of your difficulties. Each of you.

When you do so the problem is all, and it blots out everything else. The more you concentrate on it as the problem in order to get rid of it, the more you blot out other aspects of experience that could help you solve it.

Now. From the rich bed of creative imagination springs the physical facts that appear within your lives. Ruburt's imaginative endeavor with the trailer for example represents the kind of activity that is far more productive than any attempt "to face" the terrible conditions that could result if the situation is not solved.

When he thinks in such terms he sees an old woman, crippled and alone, incapacitated, in a home, and the fear brings a feeling of powerlessness, not one of strength. The beliefs mentioned added up to beliefs on a physical level so that Ruburt believed that his arms and legs could not straighten out, that he could not <u>physically</u> walk well.

Finally it came to that, where earlier he believed he could reverse the process. Now he is at the point where he is beginning to believe he can indeed reverse the process. The point of power is in the present. You must believe it, regardless of what has happened in the past, in your terms. This applies most personally. Improvements <u>can</u> begin and continue in this present. The ideas in Ruburt's paper tonight are important.

Working nights or early mornings is a kind of solution, and a method of illumination in which he is forced to make conscious decisions. It is a way of consciously deciding to operate, to cut out distractions. It shows him there are alternatives, and will automatically make him think of others.

Seeing you work, as these last few days, instantly made him see other alternatives in which the same ends are met, but without cutting down on physical flexibility. The most seemingly impractical ideas, imaginatively considered, may be precisely the most practical in greater terms. Your expectations must be changed, and despite what so-called practical experience shows you. That is why a puny weakling who cannot lift a sack of groceries may suddenly find himself holding up a car so a child can escape.

Practically, in the light of the man's experience, such an activity would seem impossible. You have been looking, both of you, to see how bad Ruburt was, how much worse he would get, until each of you projected the situation into the future until he was nearly bedridden—all in a misguided attempt to get yourselves out of the situation.

In the light of that picture improvement was not reasonable, not to be expected. What <u>was</u> projected finally however was your complete statement that you no longer agreed with the methods, that you would no longer go along with them, and this was to the good.

Up until now Ruburt felt and believed that despite the unfortunate aspects you were willing to go along. He felt you were not willing on your own to face some issues on a conscious level, and as he grew more frightened he felt that you were willing to let him do this for both of you while you were accusing him because of the symptoms.

Now, that is enough for tonight. If you have questions I will answer them.

("No.")

My heartiest good wishes then.

("Thank you, Seth. Good night." 11:25 PM. Seth then returned at 11:27.)

As probabilities operate in each moment of your life there are minute improvements in Ruburt's condition, and minute backslidings; pulsations, really, of reactions. Now if you concentrate upon the improvements <u>with this understanding</u> that facts grow from that creativity, then you begin to structure your attention in the line of those improvements, minute as they appear. And they grow, sometimes slowly, or by leaps and bounds, and the backslidings begin to disappear, and become less and less apparent or meaningful.

If instead you structure your attention upon each backsliding, minute as it might appear, then the improvements seem to become meaningless and less apparent, until they seem to disappear. You have your choice. I believe you have the information to put it to use—and if it does you any good to know it, and it should, I am highly optimistic.

("Thank you." 11:35.

(Jane's handwritten notes: "Now the distractions are the symptoms—I have to get rid of them.

("I equated curtailment of activities with physical self-adopted limitations because when this started I didn't trust myself to curtail activities consciously. I saw no alternative.

("Why I Want To Get Rid Of Symptoms

("1. To write freely, with clear mind. Have more time. Slowness of motion cuts down writing time.

("I believed it was my duty to use my creative abilities each day, to concentrate fully there and to exclude everything else I could.")

DELETED SESSION
JULY 7, 1973 9:46 PM SATURDAY

(Before the session I read Jane two questions that I asked Seth to consider: 1. Why is she still losing weight? 2. Why does she move so slowly about the house, espe-

cially when getting up from chairs, etc.? We'd talked about items earlier in the week, without dwelling upon them. A rather acrimonious discussion followed my reading the questions tonight, but the session finally began.)

Now, good evening.

("Good evening, Seth.")

And I will get to your questions this evening. First, there are several points I want to make.

You forget Ruburt's literal-mindedness, and you overlook it. He can use it to advantage. His beliefs, for the reasons you are uncovering, led him to believe he was inferior in the physical arena, and so he withdrew from it.

The core beliefs and the resulting subsidiary beliefs are interrelated and work back to back, one to the other. The literal-mindedness applies. That is why the dancing is important. There is a difference between saying "we danced," to Ruburt, regardless of how well he danced, and the belief that he could not dance at all. True, that is a subsidiary issue, but it is one where he has insisted upon keeping <u>some</u> physical freedom open.

That freedom is then, and has been, applied in other areas that are not so apparent, and <u>has</u> helped both his attitude and health.

The dancing then each time is a positive issue, and acts to weaken the other beliefs, and stands as a contrast. It has been very important that that arena was left clear to some extent.

Now any other physical arena of that kind, opened, is highly beneficial because of that literal-mindedness, and each time this happens the predominating beliefs are to that extent weakened. Here is something else that he can do. He has proven it to himself, therefore. He <u>is</u> free to move in that regard.

The dancing <u>was</u> left open to some extent because it was not a daytime activity that conflicted with his other beliefs so directly.

Give us a moment. Use that power that you have, and it is multiplied. Use the freedom that you have, and it is multiplied. You are, Joseph, now, able to see many of Ruburt's negative concepts, but you are blind still to many of your own. The feeling and belief in freedom <u>must</u> come before its physical manifestation, and this regardless of any beliefs to the contrary.

If you act upon a belief in freedom <u>and exert it</u>, then it will automatically show you by contrast that the prior belief in lack of freedom was not in basic terms realistic. The prior belief will be chipped away to that extent. At the same time you must of course work at understanding the prior belief. But at the same time you must make efforts to act according to the new one that you want.

Your life is not—and I repeat—not as limited as you believe it is. You are not using the freedoms that you have. These freedoms used, particularly in view of Ruburt's literal-mindedness, would do much to weaken the beliefs in powerlessness that exist.

As a result then of other beliefs Ruburt withdrew from the challenges of physical activity. Simply deciding on a conscious level to reenter that arena, in his present state, shows in itself a change of belief, for before he did not want to try, and considered it a threat to his work.

To some extent he still does. But he is beginning to understand, and is willing to enter that arena. <u>He wants to</u> enter it, and there is the important change in belief that has occurred. He is still frightened, and will be worried lest he become too involved in it, but he is willing to handle that on a conscious level now, which is another important change in beliefs.

Before he did not believe he could handle that consciously, so it is important. Not that you go camping or not go camping, but that you realize the freedoms that you have; use them, encourage any physical ideas of that nature that he has, and do not make him feel inadequate to try.

He feels inadequate enough in that regard. Give us a moment. You, who do not have the physical difficulty, should now make an effort to initiate such things on your own. Ruburt realizes that he must no longer structure his life through his symptoms. You must realize that also, for there your ideas of limitation simply prolong them.

Before we get to your questions: if you want any more sessions from me on this matter, then each of you are to keep a list of any improvements you notice in Ruburt's condition. You may not notice the same things. Your lists do not have to coincide, but you are each to keep such a list. Is that agreed upon?

("Yes.")

(10:10.) You are both asking me for help, so I insist upon that list, and I also insist that each of you make an honest effort to stop structuring your present experience according to Ruburt's symptoms, and as much as possible leave them out of your plans.

Such structuring impedes your progress to a large degree, and prevents improvements that could occur. I have told you about the importance of imagination, both in building up and destroying beliefs, but you still do not understand completely.

With Ruburt's literal-mindedness, again, there is a big difference, a vital one, between freely imagining a trailer trip which then becomes a probable beneficial reality, and being told it will not work.

You do not understand the alterations in beliefs involved that even led him for example to think of that mobility, and how cleverly the idea of work and mobility were combined, or the attempt at correlation involved. The same applies to the karate body image, its significance escaping both of you largely, where Ruburt was seeing himself with a body image combining power, agility, and weight.

It is precisely the challenge of things like dancing when he is in poor shape, but coming through when others are watching, or a trailer trip, or riding a bicycle when it seems impossible, or climbing a tree, that has the imaginative literal qualities that inspires him to change beliefs, whether or not those issues in that way make sense to you.

In trying to show him his realistic condition in the face of such ideas you end up by making him believe also that they are unrealistic, stupid, and that he should not need challenges but only the simple joy of walking across the floor.

He went to an extreme *(intently)*, <u>cutting out physical distractions because he believed that he had to</u>. He was afraid that he would go to the extreme in the other direction. Now he is ready to open up. His beliefs are changing. But in the context of that change, the challenge of extremes still appeals to him. It is this that you have not understood. For that matter neither has he.

The karate image for him is a good one, far more evocative, intuitive, and powerful than his idea say of doing exercises, for it combines, <u>for him</u>, intuitive understanding with physical strength and agility.

Do you want a break before your questions?

("No.")

Number one also shows your own attitudes, for he is not continuing to lose weight. It stabilized. The karate image will now help him gain, and helps him correlate his ideas of creativity with a different kind of image than he has had before.

Your eating arrangement *(in Apartment 5)* occurred and in its way helped to stop the loss of weight. The dress was worn deliberately. He was ashamed to be seen in it, and yet it serves a beneficial purpose, for his own love of his body will automatically cause it to gain weight. His pride will do it for him. He was afraid it would make you feel worse. Yet the continuing cover-up physically denies the needed feedback that would be quite automatic as he looks into a mirror for example and knows well he needs to gain more weight.

This, you see, is connected with the trailer idea, and I am telling you because you still do not understand the importance of belief <u>and</u> imagination combined. He has gone ahead despite, in this case, your negative interpretation, and seen himself under certain conditions traveling in a trailer, writing, granted, but in front of strangers in a bathing suit or shorts, and he does not want to look like a bony witch. So already in his mind he is gaining weight, seeing himself fairly agile—but he felt this was in spite of your attitudes, not with your enthusiasm or understanding.

He felt that in your world and interpretation his ideas were Pollyanna, <u>but I tell you that is practical creativity</u>—and it can wipe out many negative beliefs, more in a moment than you can realize.

We will be getting into the second question which is much more difficult and detailed. Take a break or rest your hand and get him a beer while I leave him in trance. Take your choice.

("We'll take the break."
(10:35 to 10:55.)

You must not, either of you, concentrate on "the problem" in your good intentions as you try to solve it. It then becomes the prime reality of concentration. The more you can minimize it in your minds the quicker its solution.

The times that Ruburt managed rather considerable improvements even in the face of strong negative beliefs, were times when he managed to convince himself against all objective evidence that there was nothing wrong with him physically but habitual stiffness. That belief minimized the seeming impediments, allowed greater physical freedom that in its turn by contrast began to lessen the preliminary negative beliefs. That was the summer of which we have spoken, and the conditions did not continue for the reasons given.

When you imagine trips or any physical activity and carry them out, you are concentrating upon freedom, not limitations, and then you have those freedoms to build upon. Now with the tooth difficulty Ruburt did this, in his literal manner, while working with the preliminary beliefs at the same time.

Give us a moment. I mentioned and suggested his rising very early for several reasons, knowing full well a challenge and resistance would result. The morning stiffness has to do now with subsidiary beliefs and expectations, and also with the natural condition of the body in its present shape.

Give us time. His idea of work on one level is connected with the working day. His problem, the artificial dilemma that exists in the daylight hours as to how to spend the time, and the fear that ordinary distractions will take him from his work. The dilemma does not exist at night or very early in the morning.

He feels far freer and any work done before the ordinary day begins gives him a sense of physical freedom. Such a situation automatically provides no distractions and a resulting lack of stress. He is freer physically then to work at such times. Intuitively the connection between pleasurable creative activity and the mundane world of having to make money with it is to some extent broken.

When he gets up ahead of you he feels gleeful. He has put one over on you for a change, where usually he sees you as coming out ahead in that regard.

He is also relieved that you do not see him immediately, and this alone lessons the stress, for he is afraid that his condition bleakens your morning.

He could quite happily accept your early rising but he felt that you poked fun at him when he spoke of working at night or rising early—again not understanding how he could utilize extremes.

For some time until recently he was afraid, as mentioned, that his body could not recuperate. That is why any physical achievement or normal activity is to be encouraged. The belief behind all of this is simple, and you have it—that all of his energy, concentration, and attention had to be devoted to his work. Because he is so literal-minded this was his interpretation of it.

He did not believe he could consciously discipline himself as he thought you did. When this became entwined with your way of life and financial conditions, he dug in deeper. At the same time he did not want you to spend anymore time away from your own work. He cut out more and more stimuli toward distraction.

In the nighttime or early morning there is no distraction from the outside so at that level you lessen the stress, and Ruburt is freer. As long as you are working with primary beliefs this can be an excellent method of accelerating advances while reducing stress.

It would not be any solution if the beliefs were not faced, but with that understanding it can facilitate improvements. Enough sleep is important when beginning, however, or of course he will simply want to sleep through. In the ordinary schedule he becomes tired and blue toward the end of the afternoon if he feels that he has not done enough work.

Now some of this is connected with ideas of sex in earlier years, adolescence. If a male writer or artist had to work to develop his abilities, then a woman had to work twice as hard. You also picked of course a woman you knew would not want children, but Ruburt felt a division between his biological nature and his art back then.

He has felt a love for wherever you lived, and an abiding love for you, but also some conflicts involving the housewifely chores and the writing. You help often, and have always done so, but he felt that because of the male-female relationship any help you gave was something he should be thankful for, that you were doing it out of the extra goodness of your heart—that he should not have to be grateful.

(11:30.) Give us time. A strong impeding belief is the one that the body could not any longer perform no matter what he did, and this largely was the result of a concentration upon negative aspects.

That is why any physical achievements are important. You are correct, however. The badminton was dropped because it succeeded so well—but also because Ruburt was not able then to face the dilemma between the accelerated motion in the game and the slow motion otherwise.

It served a purpose, showing him what his body was capable of, and raises the question of why he was not using it. In all this I must tell you however that you both do still concentrate upon the negative element, and ignore the power of anticipation and its values in changing beliefs.

Ruburt must assure himself that he can perform adequately physically, that this is physically possible, and then that he can do it while using his full abilities as a writer, as a creative person.

Take your break.

(11:37 to 11:50.)

Now. The resistances are two. The most important one is that Ruburt must make a conscious effort not only to alter his habits but to handle what he thinks of now as distractions by conscious effort, the changing of a pattern, rather than by unconscious limitations on the body. So of course a dilemma is implied.

Beside this, when beginning such a venture, time must be allowed for the waking-sleep patterns to be adopted. The eating patterns also, and he will want to eat more. But such change represents at his level of behavior a definite attempt to substitute conscious alterations to seek the same ends.

Some resistance then can be expected. The method is important in that it is one alternate way, represents a conscious effort at solving the problem in a different way, and provides less stress while the preliminary beliefs are worked on. I will give you more on the preliminary beliefs. The important thing about them however is that Ruburt thought they were a proper method of achieving certain ends. He now realizes they were not; with your help other alternates can be used. Working together here *(in Apartment 5)* in the day is also one.

It also provides Ruburt however with constant stress, as he becomes consciously aware of other distractions, in his terms—physical wishes to do things that come in conflict with his staying at his table.

Before, he was even unaware of what he was blocking out—the desire to move, to wash a window, to go outdoors.

The procedure I suggested was simply meant as an intermediary, handy method that would allow him to realize he could handle the matter in other ways. The method of itself would also be illuminating enough in many areas to help release him from other beliefs. The effort required is considerable, in a way, yet the knowledge that he could make the effort would be important.

He does have a need for people, and for normal interactions, that is being inhibited. He is also still worried about you; should he suddenly decide he felt like going on a shopping expedition in the middle of the afternoon, what would your reaction be? You would not want to lose the time.

I will end the session, but I will have more, providing you two follow through.

("Okay.")

I bid you then a fond good evening.

("The same to you, Seth. Thank you, and good night." 2:06 AM.)

DELETED SESSION
AUGUST 27, 1973 9:00 PM MONDAY

Now, good evening.

("Good evening, Seth.")

And with this kind of session you must bear with us for a short while until we get at the proper levels.

We will begin with the material that is pertinent, and work through it to other data still more pertinent. A simple statement of fact, regardless of the reasons: Ruburt has a great but not neurotic need of expressions of love. A child does not always understand that concern for its welfare is the same thing as love. Sometimes it <u>may be</u>. Sometimes concern is a result of something else.

The parents who say "Brush your teeth because it is good for you, and I want you to be healthy," <u>may</u> mean "I love you," but the child would usually prefer a hug and a kiss. And if the hug and kiss is not given then the brush-your-teeth suggestion becomes an order to the child.

Ruburt is not a child, but you often do think that your concern automatically expresses your love, and take it for granted that to Ruburt that is clear. While he tells himself that your concern is based on love, and <u>knows</u> it, he felt that love for example last night through feel and touch.

(The phone rang at 9:10. It was Eleanor Friede. She and Jane talked until about 10:10.)

Now: While Ruburt is not a child he operates emotionally with a child's simplicity, and is at his best in direct personal encounter with you or with his friends, for example. With the same directness he does not want anything to do with people he dislikes, for whatever reason.

He was so direct emotionally that he idealized what he thought of as your relative detachment. This of course is old. At one time he felt his emotional spontaneity was indeed admired by you and encouraged, and he blossomed.

Then he felt it threatened you—that it would form a barrier between you. He felt that you thought he wanted more than you could give—or wanted to give, practically speaking.

He believed that emotional freedom would be construed as chaos, that while you said be spontaneous, you meant "Be spontaneous when it is convenient." Beside the personality differences, however, work was also involved. Spontaneous love-making for example would cut into the work schedule that both of you had evolved.

All of this _is_ old, yet the patterns began strongly then. He felt that his obvious femininity was almost a threat to both of your works, that he had no right to look sexy and tempt you both when spontaneous love play, for example, would not occur. He remembers you telling him not to kiss you or be sexually provocative unless he meant it.

By nature he deals directly with people or events. When he feels that this is impossible and tries to do otherwise, he runs into difficulty. Because you are only now learning to verbalize your feelings, this means that he felt, particularly in the past, that you dealt with him opaquely in an area in which he did not know how to cope.

He felt it unfair to keep at you for emotional expression of love through verbalization and touch when it was not natural to you. In self-protection he tried to become the same way, to inhibit his sexuality because of what he thought of as your temperamental differences, and also because of the work schedule interruptions.

Now. In the past, _not_ too distant, you often met his advances coldly whenever he did decide to try again. I can give you instances if you want them.

("No, it isn't necessary." Jane wrote upon reading this session: "How I often deal opaquely with Rob. Suppose now I wanted love in afternoon? Please let's discuss this w schedule."

These feelings were also based upon youthful feelings, that a woman's biology could be a threat to a writer, so there was a base there that made a certain sense to Ruburt.

Lately he was convinced that he was unattractive to you from the face down, that you considered him stupid, as he did, while having physical difficulty; that you were a perfectionist and did not want to see crooked legs—that _physically_, not mentally, he got in your way, and that physically you did not look upon him with approval, as he did not.

Now there are reasons—you have stated them well—for ambiguities of feeling on your part about Ruburt's condition. They are understandable. You make an effort to tell him he looks well on occasion, but stroking his body _tells_ him you love it—frowning at him does not.

If you both continue these sessions will continue. (?) If you let the personal sessions go then there are reasons why you each let them go. Again, it is because of the strength of your particular alliance, yours and Ruburt's, that your reactions to each other are so charged and interbound. There is only so much I can give you in an evening, but I have much in mind.

I will give you a break and I would like to continue. I am only giving certain aspects now, that are important.

(*10:37. Among other things, Jane wrote later: "I thought Rob was saying—when you're compl recovered, etc we'll take trips. Symbolism: When you're good enough." 10:52.*)

Now: Ruburt's work therefore became more and more important. It had to justify the lack of spontaneity in personal areas, and the same always applied to you. For a while at least he felt you met only in your work, and in the sessions.

Everything he does is literal and symbolic at the same time. He became relaxed and psychedelic one day fairly recently when he washed windows and you made a remark to the effect that you would not like to be at the mercy of such things. Do you follow me?

("*Yes.*")

To him it was a direct action taken against something that annoyed him—the dust—an act of independence since he did it, and a symbolic clearing away of inner debris. To completely redecorate and rearrange your apartment would represent a symbolic and literal statement. At least you would be perfecting what you have, and taking steps within that framework, freely redecorating creatively, changing your environment instead of squawking while staying. Yet he is sure you would consider it a vast annoying distraction, even though not as annoying as moving. But he has not felt free to go ahead in either direction.

Spontaneity, except in work, has been largely closed out of your lives, but it is to him unnatural. Spontaneous trips are in the same category, regardless now of the physical difficulty. Your way of life has been more natural to you than to Ruburt. The classes afford him some spontaneity.

At the same time he thinks of the two of you together. Anything you do as partners excites him. Any time you initiate a program to help him he is excited. When you do not continue it he is afraid that you are not willing to take the consequences, while you interpret the discontinuation to mean he does not want to improve.

In a way both interpretations are correct, though because of his position he is more apt to project negatives on you. Rest your hand.

(11:05. "I'm okay."

(Once again, Jane wrote upon reading the session: "If I've been afraid of letting R see me at my worst, don't be afraid of letting him see me at my best." And: "I didn't think R thought sugg. worked—any more—<u>either</u>!")

I want to give you some immediate suggestions. There are other issues involved but they surround the points given.

The information is all available but you are physically hampered in time, so I will clear up any points later and amplify. Because you are not in his position you are presently able to help him when he falters, to help him help himself. And you help—consistently—in a consistent program itself assures him that you do want him to be himself.

You are "above" some of his hassles, but familiar with them, so you can help by offering encouragement precisely when he is down. If his "downness" depresses you, as is natural, imagine how much more it depresses him, and try then to find your own footing.

Strangely enough, in encouraging his spontaneity you are encouraging your own, because often he acts for both of you. It is futile to say that life should not involve challenges. You have accepted them. They are accepted to be solved. You are seeing what happens when spontaneity becomes hampered through beliefs, and in your early life you believed you must hamper it in yourself. You are seeing what happened to your brothers. You are seeing what happened to your father.

You are seeing what <u>could</u> have happened to yourself. I am not just speaking physically, but you are seeing with growing understanding, and what you see will help others.

Ruburt is learning to understand the nature of the mind in a way he could <u>not</u> understand it second-handed, playing games, and in condensed form you are learning about the human condition. What you said today is true: You must learn to understand the creativity and responsibility of consciousness. Yet you yourself often said in the past that suggestion could not be <u>that</u> important. Suggestion causes your reality. The suggestions you give are given as a result of your <u>beliefs</u>.

The reasons why Ruburt improved to a large degree the summer you took this place *(Apartment 4)* were important. You worked together. You utilized suggestion together. You began the morning together, using suggestions consciously decided upon. You had a plan and you followed it. Besides, you took what were at times timely measures in physical terms—direct terms—to better your environment. *(Moving into Apartment 4.)*

SESSION 8/27/73

You took direct action. You communicated feelings. You roused yourselves, <u>believing</u> that suggestions meant something, and they worked. Good suggestions are not bandages to <u>cover up</u>, unless you believe they are. They represent the power of your conscious intent to change, and the <u>recognition</u> of that power and its <u>use</u> automatically displaces feelings of powerlessness.

Suggestions <u>can</u> change beliefs, for beliefs are only accepted habitual suggestions. When you use so-called positive suggestions you must implement them through action, but gently. You have each been structuring your experience largely through Ruburt's symptoms—both of you, so that when Ruburt might momentarily feel free you would remind him of his limitations, and when you might forget them Ruburt would remind you.

<u>Both</u> of you concentrate upon the symptoms and Ruburt's dire circumstances, which reinforces them. If you do this without feeling the symptoms, then at least understand how Ruburt so easily does the same thing.

1. For both of you, you must turn your concentration into other areas; and this applies to you for you are a part of it, as much as to Ruburt. I will give you directions to facilitate.

2. A definite approach <u>that I will initiate</u>, for you <u>both</u> to follow. You are in your own reality. You have chosen this one, even as Ruburt has. An ill wife in not inflicted upon you.

("I know it.")

3. Definite direct physical encounter with your environment. Presently, this will involve important but minute issues until the book is finished.

4. A minimum of one session a week privately.

Now. I want Ruburt to keep a pendulum by the bed. In the morning suggestions given with the pendulum, and both of you participating. He is not to feel ashamed of his body in your eyes, regardless of its condition. Again, in one night I can only give you so much, but he grew afraid, and you helped him today to combat that fear: He was frightened that the body could not change, and <u>your</u> belief that it could was of great help.

I would like to give you much more. Take a break or end it as you prefer.

(11:35. "Unfortunately, I guess we'll have to end it, then.")

There will be questions you have then that are not answered this evening. In the meantime follow the few suggestions given, and in whatever way you can, express your own spontaneous feelings toward Ruburt.... On his part, he must make an effort to rise above the reinforced feelings of despair, and to assure himself that his body can perform adequately <u>with</u> time, and following these suggestions.

The reasons for the intensified difficulty for the past two months are not as important <u>this evening</u> as the material I am giving you. Some traces have to be made in the material delivered, and "timely" reasons are still connected to these patterns.

If you want the specifics tonight you can have them. It is your decision.
(Both of us were bleary. "I'm afraid we'll have to wait.")
Then my heartiest regards to you both, and a fond good evening.
("Thank you, Seth. Good night." 11:45 PM.)

DELETED SESSION
AUGUST 29, 1973 9:13 PM WEDNESDAY

Good evening.
("Good evening, Seth.")
Now as usual with this kind of session, we will work into what we want to say. And your reasons *(for the symptoms of the last two months or so)* will be given this evening.

First I have some other necessary pertinent information that will make the reasons for the latest episodes clear when we get to them.

Ruburt is motivated quite simply and powerfully by his love for you and his work. Since he has known you these have been the two main directions out of which his being flows. Take into consideration the information given in our last session.

Now. When Ruburt had outside jobs he used encounters with others to take up the slack that existed between his emotional nature and your own. When he worked at home the differences in your temperaments became more noticeable. He was also extremely concerned that he learn to discipline himself—now that he had an entire day, and to prove to you his appreciation of the fact that you were still working out.

When the two of you could work together, he thought, all that would change. You would have time to work <u>and</u> play. You would be more emotionally demonstrative, freed from your job. His work would bear more and more the burden of his needs, and take up the emotional slack that was now apparent. It had to be everything, then. The more you two communicate <u>in the way</u> I mentioned, the less the pressure is in the work area.

This applies constantly, through all of the episodes.

The symptoms were obviously a result of inner attitudes, and also besides that a physical way of asking for physical action, attention, and emotional action and attention. Whenever he improved it was when the two of you embarked upon a program together.

Both of you were sure of your love, but each of you at various times were quite willing to let its personal aspects take second place, and I am not speaking alone of physical love-making. When Ruburt took this place *(Apartment 4)* he was about ready to say, "All right, we will be work partners." Then you responded with the display of love and devotion, plus a definite program, embarked upon together.

For reasons already given, both of you later fell down. Sumari, and even *Oversoul Seven*, sprang into being as a result of the emotional rapport that existed between you just prior. When *Seven* was finished *Dialogues* began, and our book was in process. Ruburt was encouraged to express his feeling, and emotionally. This gave him some freedom.

(Now in an aside Seth told me there were many "strings" to the material; that it seemed to come "sideways," but that it would all come together.)

I want to come back to this point in time, where we left off.

("All right." 9:36. Jane was taking many pauses throughout.)

Ruburt felt that you did not trust his relationship with Tam as far as the spontaneous handling of business was concerned, and that perhaps the dissatisfaction you expressed about Prentice had to do with a certain emotional sloppiness, where both he and Tam did not have the proper regard for detail, and lacked a kind of integrity that you valued.

Eleanor *(Friede)* represented a different kind of framework, in which business was business, while art was respected, and where after all matters of great money might be involved. Ruburt was rather proud of handling his own business affairs. Eleanor also represented on another level the establishment, the rich, literary, "in" crowd, and the great youthful specialized ideas of literary success.

Yet these people were coming to Ruburt because of his psychic work, and his psychically inspired writing. Eleanor, he discovered, was anything but his idealized concept of a literary editor. This was a shock. From the time Eleanor came she spoke with the words of Ruburt's past, glowingly presenting the possibility of purely literary success, prestige, and cash.

A cruel trick, Ruburt felt, offering promises unfulfilled. Yet at the same time Ruburt was able to catch an inner glimpse of that world, its emptiness and the obvious existence of important dilemmas, ignorance, and that finally—it was simply another field of human endeavor.

He felt he did not know much, but that he knew more in ways important to him than these people did. They were coming to him when he so desperately had wanted to join them, thinking that his idealized, youthful hopes would there find fruition.

Yet for the entire time he began to wonder, regardless, about his position at Prentice. Was he being taken for a fool? Should he have changed to another publisher? But this meant in his case: should he try to exclusively be the literary person again? Yet he found that these people wanted his psychic work most of all. And that while they appreciated his other work, his main value in their eyes lay precisely in the field that he thought would mean nothing to them.

In the meantime our books began to do well financially. These people, he felt, were not the romantic artists he had dreamed of, but sometimes very calculating, and would blemish an artistic product with what he believed to be moral incompetence.

The Seagull, while free, was not all that free. It is no coincidence that Tam is younger than Ruburt, for this to some extent helped water down the idea of Prentice as an authority figure. Eleanor, older and a woman, giving definite instructions, did represent an authority figure, both in literary terms and business-wise.

Ruburt saw Seagull, or Richard, as a child who followed Eleanor's advice, and in watching Richard's career, was able to see more clearly what that <u>kind</u> of career meant.

Dialogues represented a synthesis of literary and psychic endeavor. It also allowed Ruburt necessary emotional expression. Tim Foote represented literary recognition, yet he wrote to Ruburt to ask his psychic opinion on another psychic writer.

Seven represented the same kind of synthesis, and these were both Jane-type productions. <u>After</u> these Ruburt could not make up his mind. If you did not really approve of Prentice as a publisher, then he wondered seriously whether he should follow through with a new house, and with the hopes that Eleanor offered. You typed my book, and I appreciate the work and the reasons, but Ruburt felt it was also because you did not trust Prentice, and always that you thought another publisher would do a better job overall.

In the meantime—now, another string—he felt the need again to come closer to you, and you ended up eating over there *(Apartment 5)*. He had decided because of your more frequent demonstrations of love that he must try again for the emotional rapport with you that was so important.

This immediately brought certain aspects to light that had been hidden to some extent while you were more physically separated. Some of this has to do, again, with the fact that you thought your concern automatically expressed your love. You were together more. When you saw him try to get up he knew you loved him, but the frown was what he saw. He was always trying to hide from you. Part of it was his projection because he felt you thought he was so stupid for having anything wrong at all, so the more he saw you frown the stupider he felt, and the more guilty. And the more he tried to hide his condition.

Both of you have strong perfectionist tendencies, and they are used most constructively as a rule in your works. But you cannot apply them to people. Period.

Both of you at times do. In your particular personal relationship Ruburt began to feel that when you looked at him you were comparing him precisely with "that perfect physical self" that seemingly so eluded him, and in the face of that image, any improvement at all began to seem so insignificant as to be meaningless.

They were discarded as falsehoods. Regardless of your love, when you looked at him he often saw disapproval. By then this place *(Apartment 4)* represented isolation and retreat from your relationship's fulfillment in line with what it had meant earlier, and his decision to come out with you again *(into Apartment 5)*.

As he discovered today when he looked into a mirror, he was comparing his image now to what it had been several years ago literally—not only in terms of symptoms, you see. In an odd way he also thought, because of that, that you were constantly comparing him now with a 5-or-10-year earlier self.

Your own reactions since our last session are excellent. Ruburt felt, finally, that you saw him at his worst in the morning, and did not turn away from his as some crooked, broken, grotesque physical person. That was what he was afraid of in the light of your perfectionist tendencies. In a strange way he was relieved; seeing what he has been trying to hide, he feels, will give the both of you a basis from which you can operate, in which any improvements are appreciated.

He made the bed that day. Usually he would think of how slow and clumsy he was, and if you were waiting or watching how impatient you might be. That day, he thought "After Rob seeing how I really am in the morning—if he saw me now he would see how much better I am," and he felt proud of doing what he was doing as well as he could.

Another string: Because he hid from you for the reasons given, then he would become angry at you, perversely enough, when you did not understand his great joyful triumph when he felt like dancing. You expected it, from the standpoint of someone physically in good condition.

Since he felt that you judged his physical behavior from that "superior" position, then he felt that no improvement except complete recovery would get your approval. Anything else would always fall short.

In any suggestions used then, use the terms improvement, or better and better, for example. That gives him leeway. "I can walk with greater ease. I can get up easier and easier. I can be more physically vigorous." That sort of thing when you use physical suggestions, rather than the use of words that seem like absolutes, where comparisons are involved almost automatically between a given situation and a desired one.

"I can walk normally." Now that kind of a suggestion, automatically with Ruburt, brings up inner responses, arguments and contradictions with experience on a physical level. "I can walk easier," does not.

You said "I think you can perform 50% better than you are doing, if you realize it." That kind of suggestion is good. It arouses and stimulates activity without causing him to compare his experience with what is <u>to him</u> an ideal. Take your break.

(10:45. I read the material to Jane, then we had a snack. Resume at 11:37.)

Now: This is not as rambling as it may seem. I take it for granted that you understand the jumps in time. This was merely to remind you of certain continuities without going over events already mentioned—so going back to the point in time mentioned earlier in tonight's session: when *Dialogues* was finished Ruburt tried it out on Prentice, and felt briefly that Tam might take it. Even then there was talk from a time earlier about a paperback deal. This had excited Ruburt, as had the *Dialogues* possibility. Both fell through.

Eleanor, who professed such greater literary understanding and appreciation for *Dialogues*, in her turn refused it as well, and also *Rich Bed*. Ruburt never thought Tam had any great understanding of poetry; but what good did Eleanor's "superior" appreciation do if the book was refused after such compliments?

After Eleanor's refusal Ruburt was left with *Rich Bed*. Now this is his projection, and one he only realized at break: he felt that any incomplete manuscripts were indications of a waste of time, and that you thought he should publish everything he wrote, and that an unpublished manuscript was a blot of sorts. You often mentioned *Dreams* for example, when he was only too willing to forget it. So he felt guilty about *Rich Bed* even though it wasn't finished.

To him, *Dialogues* had to be published at once. When Eleanor came back onto the picture, the time before this last visit, there was also a trip to Rochester preceding it. Here was Eleanor again, saying, "Save me *Bed*," and even speaking of *Dialogues* while in no position to accept them. Here again, more strongly, were hints that Eleanor could do more than Prentice.

Later now, in the last period of time, when Eleanor heard that Ruburt had sent the outline of a new book, *Aspects*, to Tam, she astounded Ruburt by remarks of great regret, and implications that Ruburt had made an error. Ruburt was quite surprised, since Eleanor had not suggested before that a manuscript not be sent to Prentice.

Immediately the plans for the last trip here were made. In the meantime Ruburt heard of the Bantam deal, and Eleanor was saying "Hold off," without giving the reasons. Ruburt was frightened. Supposing he got Prentice to hold off and Eleanor's deal fell through? Physically he had never really forced a body image through athletics, for example. Feelings of any powerlessness, then, found easiest expression physically. He had felt <u>relatively</u> in control, business-wise, used to dealing directly, and this is one of the reason why he and Tam work together intuitively and business-wise so well.

All of a sudden he was told to hold off, and literally to him, not to act. In fact, what was specifically requested was nonaction. Now for the reasons given, and the developments earlier tonight, all of those issues met, since Eleanor's previous visit.

Ruburt began to feel powerless momentarily in the business area. At the same time the hiding-from-you issues that had developed, and are given tonight, had come into full force. Ruburt, as you know, does not like to say no, particularly to people like Dick, a friend. He knew however intuitively that he did not want to change alliance. H has simply hoped Eleanor would take what Prentice did not want.

The entire idea of changing houses involved treachery to him, as he interpreted it—Eleanor's remarks, that is, implied moral dishonesty, Yet still he was tempted, mainly because he wondered if Prentice <u>was</u> taking advantage of him.

All of the decisions he made, finally, were good ones from all viewpoints. In the meantime however, because of these issues all meeting, and his reactions as given, his condition worsened. The momentary feeling of powerlessness in the business area added to the physical sense of powerlessness. He was simply afraid that he could not improve.

Often he has inhibited physical feelings of love for you, for reasons given, but the other night he did not. You obvious love of him came through strongly, and rearroused him.

Remembering your past ideas toward Prentice, he wondered, regardless of what you said, if you thought he should stay with them. He was very afraid of losing a contract with Prentice for *Aspects*, and a Bantam contract, while waiting around for another arrangement. At the same time he was afraid of making demands at Prentice for fear he would discover that they didn't care if he stayed or not. Feeling that way he still went ahead on his own, and felt happily vindicated. The whole affair, with his reactions now, still had him at the point where he did not think he could physically recover, and he was caught in a panic that he tried to hide from you.

Before we finish tonight I want to speak about the responsibility for his consciousness, and at least mention the morning dilemma. Take a brief break.

(12:15 to 12:30.)

Ruburt took the responsibility for his consciousness in other areas far more than most people do. He had no strong background structure in which to build up a confidence in the body mechanisms. The youthful body was able to maintain an equilibrium.

Ruburt felt his consciousness more powerfully in almost any other area. It has been difficult for him to accept the fact that the mind literally controls the body. He now sees that he <u>must</u> exert his abilities in that direction, and your own understanding of the issue in that area will be of help to him.

It was not that he didn't accept the responsibility so much as that, in that weakest area, he did not realize the strength of his own conscious thoughts to alter the body mechanism. You can help him most by lovingly reminding him of that.

Once he completely understands it, he will accept the responsibility.

The morning episodes are directly related to the fact lately that he grew to doubt his ability to recover, and face each morning the prospect of a day in which he tried to hide those feelings from himself and from you. The hallway between the bedroom and the bath became, symbolically, the hallway to physical activity through which he was afraid he could not pass, and through whose portals he must go alone, since he did not want to burden you with his despondency over it.

Now that is the end of the session for tonight. Your own actions, plus the new insight Ruburt is gaining, will serve as your start. I bid you a fond good evening.

("Thank you, Seth. Good night." 12:43 AM.)

DELETED SESSION
SEPTEMBER 3, 1973 9:35 PM MONDAY

Good evening.

("Good evening, Seth.")

Now. First of all, our private session...You did an excellent job of recognizing the Nebene characteristics in yourself, and changing the nature of their direction. They <u>did</u> at one time operate in a perfectionist kind of demand that

Ruburt be perfect physically. That was different for example than an ordinary, less charged wish for his complete recovery.

We have not discussed the hidden Nebene-like characteristics of Ruburt's personality. They are, as Nebene's were, the result of a comparatively narrow, rigid focus, conscientiously embarked upon, and carried the same kind of restrictive "holy cause" charge.

They were meant to regulate creativity, as Nebene's characteristics were. In Ruburt's case that portion of the personality was to be a caretaker. These characteristics were also brought to activity in response to your own Nebene tendencies. The restrictions were thought to be ways of protecting creativity and ability.

You met these aspects in yourself and were able to identify the characteristics, and therefore deal with them. Ruburt has found that more difficult. This afternoon, and at various times, he has been able to isolate certain series of thoughts and feelings, and identify them as restrictive. <u>Before</u> he simply acquiesced to then, and was not able to perceive them as troublesome habitual patterns. These patterns lead quite predictably to moods of powerlessness and restriction.

In this life the early background meant that Ruburt's writing was done in the face of great distractions. He learned to turn them off. Now give us a moment.... *(9:55)*. It is important that when he recognizes such patterns now, as he is beginning to, that he communicate them to you *(as Jane did after supper tonight)*, until he gets used to handling them alone. He trusts your common sense, and such a measure will insure that the habitual mood reactions are cut short.

They were noticeable today precisely because he had enough peace of mind in the last few days so that comparisons could be made. I will give you more about the origin of these characteristics. For now I simply want Ruburt to learn to recognize them. They rose in this life at least in response to events that do not now exist. The possibility of his not using his creativity in this world no longer exists. The characteristics were meant to insure that he use his ability. Then, left alone, they would fall away. They have lasted because their nature was not understood, and Ruburt habitually kept them in consciousness.

He knew he had access to an amazing amount of energy, but pretended that he did not so that all the energy available would go into the effort to use his abilities properly. It was the correlation between the Nebene characteristics and Ruburt's Nebene-like characteristics that helped keep affairs stirred up for some time.

Each of you trusted the same kind of characteristics in the other, to keep you where you <u>thought</u> you should be. In this life Ruburt saw those same characteristics in Father Ryan, where repression was used to keep him in the church. These characteristics <u>were</u> necessary in the situation as given, until Ruburt learned the nature of the self, and could begin to trust it. With the belief that he can trust the self, the creative self, the other characteristics become unnecessary, for you cannot force creativity.

The set of habitual patterned thoughts, then, that he recognized today, ultimately work against creativity, for they destroy the sense of being peaceful and free within the moment.

(10:10.) Now, some other strings.

Apartment 4 then represents old beliefs, both literal and symbolic at once then. Ruburt, getting rid of old rugs, throws out old beliefs. In so doing he reinforces a sense of power over both inner habits and the physical environment.

Your own behavior with him has been excellent, and highly reinforcing. The love-making in particular must be encouraged, and it arouses your own spontaneity as well as his. Several advances have been made, all with your help. His inner self-image is changing. The morning mood is not nearly as glum. He has even smiled, and some physical improvements have been noticed.

You can help by encouraging him to remember that his body <u>does</u> have the capacity to do better <u>now</u>. He is beginning to realize it, but that should be reinforced in the suggestions given. I do recommend both morning and evening suggestions with the pendulum.

Your motorcycle suggestions on their own are worth a barrel of gold, for the change in image it infers, and for other reasons. When he begins to rouse, he comes of course into direct confrontation with impulses before hidden. He knows he wants to move furniture, to change the environment. Now some feelings because they have been inhibited, come out in exaggerated form—the hatred of the bathroom or the bedroom for example.

The rooms bear the brunt of beliefs also as mentioned earlier, but the inhibited anger against the conditions and against himself, for feeling powerless to change the conditions—these bring him face to face with issues he has hidden. The affair is much more out in the open—the conflict between work and other activity.

In that stage then, when he tackles a room for example, the fear that he will not be able to work, or want to, becomes conscious, with guilty feelings. Now this is to the good. Often a simple discussion with you of any such episode will clear the issue for him, where before in his secrecy he would hide it even from himself.

Such issues must be dealt with consciously now, and state your willingness to help. He can take walks. Tell him not to specify that he must walk a block or not go out at all.

We will be working toward a simple walk each day regardless of the distance, but as he becomes freer he himself will feel the impulse, as already he feels the impulse to change the rooms.

He is not feeling all of those impulses at once, but handling so much at a time consciously. Theoretically, he should feel free to work whenever he feels like it, for his own strong creativity will see that it is used.

Practically, at this stage of the game some system of time is a good policy, even while within it full freedom of thought, and day-dreaming, must be allowed. This should not be thought of as a bargaining with the self, or as an obsession, but instead as a practical method of dealing with a present set of conditions. When the time is come, there will be no conflicts with physical activity, for example, and/or work, for he will have put his priority where he wants it freely, consciously deciding to do so.

Take your break.

(10:33—11:10.)

In Ruburt's particular case, now, one set of beliefs led to a corollary set of physical beliefs about his body

The two sets collaborated each other quite automatically. Any lessening of beliefs in either area would be reflected in the other. Both sets have to be dealt with, therefore. Now you have other sets of quite positive beliefs also working for you, and luckily these will often help shake a harmful belief off balance. Ruburt's books are doing well. Financially he is doing well. Both of these areas help work against the sense of powerlessness that was tied up in the troublesome beliefs.

If a series of troublesome beliefs become so strong however, then the positive sets become less effective. In Ruburt's case however success in work does mitigate against the negative beliefs. In the past the balance of success versus failure in his eyes was so tipped at the failure end that he took but a mere breather of relief, then plunged ahead again with the same desperation. Hence, beginning each new book, he tightened his controls. Hardly any of what you both have learned, was <u>conscious</u> then, however. The same should not occur, now.

I want to make this clear because you will then be able to project such influences, and see how they can be used in other areas. For example, while he was convinced—and he was—that he looked more than his age, and was unattractive, then the time element made him push even harder for success. He <u>saw</u> himself older, and in the light of that his success was not enough.

I am not speaking merely in financial terms either, though since Ruburt is dealing directly with the world through his creative work, then money and reputation have become a symbol of success, that is basically creative. Feeling younger automatically made him more pleased with his success, then.

He is pleased with the latest business alliance with Tam. In the meantime however you have a group of body beliefs built up, and these have to be directly dealt with also. The physical confidence must be restored. Your little exercise this evening is an excellent example of reassurance, reinforcement, and practical learning. *(When Jane walked in her bare feet, etc.)*

Besides working with body belief, you are automatically working with the inner belief, showing him that physical activity can be mixed with creativity in the book and in our sessions, that you approve, yourself, and that he is physically capable.

While he was hiding much of this was relatively impossible. Now you are also being encouraged to develop your own spontaneity with Ruburt, in a cause in which you believe heartily. As mentioned, coming over here *(Apartment 5)* meant that he was finally willing to confront his feelings about your relationship. The other apartment now, then, represents isolation, where when he was running away it represented independence.

Working late at night, or rising in the middle of the night, still offers advantages in that there are no conflicts in terms of household chores, or even impulses. There is some conflict there now that did not exist earlier however, because he is afraid that means he is hiding from you again.

This requires alterations of patterns of sleep, that take time to change, but it can be done without completely changing from a day to night system. Some work before the ordinary day does give him valuable reassurance, for he knows nothing can undo it. <u>That</u> much is accomplished.

His physical condition had been so poor however that rising alone, he had that mood in any case to face. The anticipation of surprising you did help him conquer it to some degree. An alternate suggestion is for each of you to rise very early, well before the normal working day. While you are typing this would be workable. I am offering suggestions here, but overall I recommend that Ruburt maintain so many hours, and feel free after that to indulge in those impulses that he will now be more and more aware of.

When he gains confidence this will not be necessary and the hours should be used as a framework. He should discuss his feelings clearly with you about those hours, and if he finds himself scrambling to meet them and so forth.

Four hours should be a minimum; work this out with him. You will help him see more clearly. He will wonder if four is enough, if five should be mandatory, etc.

Now do you have questions about this personal session?
("No, let's take time to absorb this first.")
Then do you want some Jerusalem material now?
("Yes.")
Then you will have a break and we will begin.
(11:43 PM. The Jerusalem material will be found in the 678th session.)

DELETED SESSION
SEPTEMBER 10, 1973 9:35 PM MONDAY

(Just before the session Jane told me that Seth could give us what she called The Christ Book *at any time. In last Monday's deleted session Seth had included a section on Jerusalem, which I've included in the records as the 678th session for September 3, 1973. Seth told us we could have more on Jerusalem and related events whenever we want it, or have the time, so presumably the Christ Book idea stems from that. A good title.)*

Now: Good evening.
("Good evening, Seth.")
We will begin with personal material, and the continuation of your own sessions. Give us a moment.

Working on his book today *(Aspects)*, Ruburt made some important connections. I will put these into context, and add other information that he did not get on his own.

Now I told you that when issues are brought out into the open, there are certain conscious stresses and strains that earlier were not <u>apparent</u>, but hidden. The morning issue is finally rising into the significance that was buried before, and not dealt with. Your presence and help have been highly supportive, and also as I planned, your presence has made Ruburt more aware of his morning behavior and thoughts and sometimes he has tried to verbalize them.

Your efforts show clearly your intent to help; again, more important than you earlier realized. But in barely a week he has been forced to face that morning situation, to question it as he really did not before.

Today finally he made important headway. It was obvious to you both that he did not want to get up then, and the question "Why not?" was difficult to ignore. When you finally left to prepare breakfast for yourself, he immediately got up, and barefooted, carrying his shoes and other paraphernalia with him—something you usually do not see him do.

He was not walking properly by a long shot, but he wanted to get up, and he walked as well barefooted as with shoes. You were surprised, and voiced approval. He began to write notes for his book as soon as breakfast was over, and before the table was cleared. He felt suddenly comparatively free.

He worked an hour. You had lunch, and both returned after a short trip shopping. He took a shower instead of going directly to work, put food in the oven, worked another ½ hour, and yet found himself by dinner time with nearly ten pages of new material.

After dinner he wrote several more pages. Yet all in all he had worked a little over three hours. In the material he wrote there was information applied to himself, incomplete, but I will put it in order; and it has to do with the nature of creativity and his beliefs.

A good deal of what I will say explains the morning episodes. Since I am dealing with this particular area I will not include other issues. For the book he was exploring creativity and other ideas of work and play. Long ago you first used the word "work" in reference to your painting, and to Ruburt's writing. In the material given and given, the reasons are there as to why he latched onto some of your ideas—so I will not go into those here.

From now on he should forget the word "work" in reference to his own writing. Have him think of it simply as writing. Now this morning at the table he suddenly realized why he did not want to get up this morning, and why at other times he did not want to get up: he did not want to go to work, like a child who does to want to go to school. The connotations of the word crept into all areas of his life, tinged by unfortunate beliefs connected with the word.

<u>To his mind it is directly in opposition to creativity</u>.

This is highly important material, and one of those nights where you could save time with a recorder.

Some of the difficulty began when Ruburt started to connect writing with work. Remember his literal mind, and also that he does sometimes operate with extremes. Work was not play, then. It involved making money, definite hours, a routine and also adult status. He felt he needed that.

All of his ideas of responsibility became attached to the word "work." In the past as given, he wanted to prove to you that he was working at home while you worked outside. Later when money became involved, then for a while fun writing had to come after working hours.

Each day became a battle in which what he loved to do had to be transformed into work, with all of its unnatural connotations—<u>to him</u>. As soon as a workroom really became a workroom his creativity made him leave it, so that he could create outside of the work context.

Seven came precisely because it was free of all contract connotations, and so at the time did *Aspects*. My books so far were hidden creative goodies, inserted instead of books either contracted or to be contracted, and they were free of the work context.

Either take a break or get our friend a beer, or both, but the session is important....

When he felt you both needed money, the work aspects were magnified. He did not dare to drop them. He had seen your family's reaction to you as an artist. Work must bring money in that context.

Now with his financial success that pressure is somewhat removed, enabling those beliefs to come to light. He believed, for many reasons hinted at or given, that spontaneity did not mix with work. That work involved responsibility, discipline, material rewards, and also that it necessitated behavior that did not come naturally to him.

He tried desperately to schedule his highly creative productivity to fit that pattern. Whenever he had difficulty writing he would become more and more particular about his writing hours. He found that sometimes his so-called writing hours were not as productive as his after-hours writing. He loves to write at twilight, for example.

Sometimes after a full writing day, without too much actual creative production, he would do his best work in his free time after supper, when he did not have to work. So then he thought "I will schedule those hours into my writing day," and suddenly they became prosaic, and often lost their magic because then they became his working hours.

What he loved to do then was equated with work.

Work means conforming to Ruburt. Work meant working hours like other people have. They should be over at a certain time. You often said that other people could relax after supper. Their work was done while you and Ruburt were still busy.

Ruburt's normal "work periods" would often involve nonconventional hours, however, precisely because they were nonconventional. Each morning he felt it his duty to get up at a decent hour to go to work. At the same time <u>artistic</u> work had other connotations. Everything else was unimportant by contrast, so that other pursuits became taboo. If you went out in the day people knew you were not working. You early used the word "chores" for activities in which Ruburt took a childish delight. With his literal-mindedness, and for reasons given in the past, he also began to think of them as chores. Otherwise he would want to do them and not work.

In the meantime you had changed many of those ideas, and Ruburt felt betrayed and furious at you for leaving him to carry on these principles in which you had once so heartily agreed, in his eyes, you see.

Now I suggested the definite hours, knowing his position, knowing that he would begin to see that while any activity of course takes a certain amount of <u>time</u>, that his creative work will be judged not according to the hours spent on it but the <u>yield</u>.

This is what he is on the road to understanding. Anything that increases that yield is beneficial to his nature. Any given day a creative urge might span the day. At another time that creative surge might reach its peak in two hours, and deliver nuggets of creativity. His three-hour production today gave him more with a free attitude than five or six hours of determined application to "work."

When the work idea is carried to extremes than he is not even free in his so-called work time, because then he inhibits what he thinks of as nonwork ideas, and therefore much creativity. He has usually buried spontaneous desires to do other things, particularly in your apartment, so there were frequent dilemmas, finding of course physical expression in symptoms. There has been some improvement physically however since we began the latest group of sessions; but spasmodic.

You had better take a break.

(10:45 to 11:03.)

Now: When Ruburt's high level of creativity happened to be strong enough to easily include five or six hours a day he improved, since his inspiration took as many hours as he thought his work should.

Inspiration and creativity he felt he could trust, but never felt he could trust his working capacity in the way he thought of work. At the same time other activities became taboo as not-work, so it was "wrong" to putter about the house in his work hours, and equally wrong to work after hours, when people who worked should be free.

Each day became a battle to turn play into work, structure it, and make it personally and socially acceptable. Yet creativity kept escaping the work definition—in my books, *Seven* and Sumari; and he even felt guilty about Sumari poetry in work hours, for it might not fulfill work's requirements, produce money and so forth.

Your own speaking about distractions, chores contributed. Your habits are <u>fairly</u>, though not entirely, native to your nature. They were not to Ruburt's. He felt he did need discipline, however, as given in other session. The worries about money, age, all contributed so that he tried to <u>work</u> harder.

He was living with you, someone he loved who had a different temperament, and tried to make his align with your own because of his love, and also because he felt your ides were better. You were older, knew more, he felt; and you were also afraid of the spontaneous qualities that he possessed.

All of those reasons contributed to his course of action. He likes the unpredictable. He got up this morning because you did not expect him to, and he could act spontaneously—surprise you and delight himself. The very breakup of the pattern allowed him the fresh creativity even before the breakfast dishes were cleared.

He chose writing initially because of the spontaneity it offered, but his ideas of work directly conflicted with this. A writer could take a stroll anytime. Someone who worked had to keep at the job. A writer could make love in the afternoon. Someone who worked had to inhibit such impulses.

Now that is enough for this evening, but highly important. You can have more at our next session. You can have more material on Jerusalem or Christ now, or when you want it. You can have the Christ book when you want it. But the same applies for any other material you want from me.

("Well, we'd better stick to the subject matter for this session. It's more important.")

A note: in creativity play and work are invisibly entwined. In your society however work often implies something you have to do, a chore that must be performed for monetary reasons. With Ruburt the play-work elements that had once been together became separated; from play-work to work-play, and occasionally the combination simply became work.

<u>Both of you</u> must examine your beliefs, then, for some of them, Joseph, held you back creatively. You are far more a follower of the Protestant work ethic than you realize, and to some extent, for reasons given, Ruburt picked this up from you. That is, you are not to blame for this situation, bust I am dealing with that area this evening. Do you follow me?

("Yes.")

You followed the ethic to a larger degree than you realized, yet often in reverse fashion. You picked up the idea of work but frowned upon certain aspects of creativity as not safe or profitable—as your father's creative, inventive aspects did not produce financially in your family, and in terms of <u>work</u> did not pay off in social or family terms.

Your mother felt that his creativity was a threat to stability, so maintaining your own creativity stubbornly, you still felt to <u>some</u> degree that it was a threat, that it would not pay off, and so you tried to clothe it in the garb of <u>work</u>, effort, regular hours, and stability, and to deny or play down its playful aspects.

That is enough. You cannot keep up with me, but the correlations that exist, and the contrasts, between both of your fathers, are significant in how you handle your creativity.

Ruburt has always tried to adapt to your natural schedule. To some degree your own natural schedule is also the result of your own beliefs about your creativity. There is much more here, but I had better stop.

I wish you then a fond good evening.

("Thank you, Seth. Good night.")

You are, however, denying some aspects of your own spontaneity. Period, end of session.

("Thank you." 11:34. I was going to read the session to Jane, but she said, several times, that she was getting more material on me. Finally Seth returned at 11:40.)

Now: your own ideas of work also to <u>some</u> degree impede your progress. The faces that you alone can paint can leap into your mind no matter what you are doing, and they are not dependent upon good lighting, though your final rendition of them might be.

You have to some extent closed off your creativity by thinking of it in terms of the time you have to give to "your work." Again, while a certain time is required for any activity as far as artistic inspiration is concerned, there is little correlation, for artistic inspiration is independent of time.

Your creature feelings toward night, dawn and dusk, have much more to do with inspiration, though a painting, once inspired, may then take so many hours to execute. But your idea of specific work time automatically divides that time according to your beliefs from other times when you may be shopping, or doing something else far divorced from work.

The yard at 2 or 3 in the morning might amaze you, and ideas of paintings leap up. Your whole concept of work time brings about limitations also. You personally do not think of the dream state as work time, and therefore inhibit very definite inspirations. I want <u>you</u> then to also examine your ideas about work and creative activity.

I am pulling an Oversoul Seven on you, but I am gong to give you an idea for a painting, in the next three days, waking or sleeping—I will not tell you which—but I want you to be playfully alert to it. When you were doing commercial art you were utilizing some important aspects of creativity, though you were not matured enough to use them except in limited form.

You could work with nature despite what you think of as distractions, so examine your own beliefs about playful creativity and work.

I will give you more. And now I bid you a good evening, and hope you find what I have said helpful.

("I do, Seth. Thank you again, and good night." 11:55 PM.)

DELETED SESSION
SEPTEMBER 17, 1973 10:10 PM MONDAY

Good evening.

("Good evening, Seth.")

Now: when Ruburt worked out for money his ideas and beliefs concerning work were divorced from his ideas about creativity.

He does feel a strong responsibility to hold his own financially. Poverty in youth was counterbalanced by ideas of wealth because of the father's background. Ruburt hoped his talent would bring him some kind of magical translation of his father's supposed wealth. Working alone had a magic, yet while money came from someplace else—working out—the weight of financial desire did not rest upon creativity.

He wrote despite the fact that he had to work, and out of love of writing. When work in terms of making money was applied to writing, then divisions occurred in his attitude as to what might be salable and bring money, and therefore fall into the work category—and what might <u>not</u> be salable but highly creative regardless.

Sumari, particularly in the beginning, and poetry in general were dubious from a work-sales standpoint, and therefore suspect in writing time.

He has always had some kind of writing schedule. The confusion about it has to do with his interpretation of work and creativity. Often he tried to block out creative ideas he feared were not salable, or work.

Today he was afraid, for one thing, that if he left himself alone he would just write poetry that very well might not sell. He feels he is his own employer, and as an employer must see that he produces salable work. Creatively however he wants to go full blast regardless, and that is the way of course that he produces his best "work."

His attitude in its own way is the same as you mentioned earlier this evening, in that he believes he is lucky not to have to work out, and so must make what he is doing pay. Your talk about the time clock got through to him in the past only too well. The amount of time is not important, but his attitude toward it is.

You told him once he could not punch a time clock. He has been trying to show you that he can. He felt that with his natural spontaneity great discipline must be used, as given before. Working home meant working home, so he shut down impulses that might make him become distracted ,or want to go out when others were <u>working</u>.

Breaking schedule brought some of this to consciousness. It was carried to such an extreme finally that <u>often</u>, at least, his best creativity came after hours. The schedule became nearly an obsession. It had to be broken. If he chooses to work hourly again, it will be a new fresh conscious decision. For both of you however, you must understand that work was the rule for a long time.

Take your break.

(10:35—10:50.)

Give us a moment.

He feels that he has taken a chance that you have not taken, staking financial survival on creative work. But here also is one of the rubs, for both of you used to take it for granted that real creativity did not sell. So Ruburt became somewhat suspicious when he considered creativity of his own, and <u>afraid</u> that it would not sell because it was creative.

He felt therefore that he had to make his way of life pay. He used to feel that you were accusing him when you said that he did not know what it was to punch a time clock, meaning that he did not have the guts or the ability. At the same time you had not chosen that source either but very briefly. Creative work was his joy, but that creativity also had more and more connotations that applied to work and money.

It had to pay off. It had to be scheduled, and even the time within the writing hours was watched so that it was productive. At the same time distractions were minimized, impulses to move away from the desk cut down, and daydreaming, dream recall, and out-of-bodies became not business, not-work. Naps in the day meant laziness. If you were working out, Ruburt thought, you could not do this.

Now. There have been improvements of late. Do you agree with that statement?

("Yes.")

You considered them in a good light, and remembered what I said about absolutes. Ruburt however, sensing some improvement, wanted instant, complete recovery, and while he handled this better than in the past, tell him, nevertheless at his end he used absolutes again. Tell him to keep that in mind.

Your morning behavior, again, and behavior in general, has been of great help. His study of my book will be of greater help. His ideas concerning out-of-bodies are important. He is waiting for the Bantam check, which <u>will</u> come through. He is impatient because he likes me working on a book for him. *(Humorously.)*

The improvements do show that his beliefs are changing, and some of his anger today was simply energy that he has been withholding from himself for fear that it would not be correctly used. He is feeling impulses to go out for example for walks that he did not feel before, and be more physically active, while at the same time he does not <u>yet</u> feel able to perform to his <u>satisfaction</u>.

Also, dropping the schedule at my behest, the conflicts are more out in the open, so that anger is actually a recognition of impulse, frustration at not being able to follow through <u>adequately</u>, and the conflict between feeling the impulses and feeling that he should be at his schedule.

The schedule itself, with the beliefs he held, blinded him to the impulses because he would not allow them to emerge. I want him to continue with my book, and when he reaches the portions on point of power and natural hypnosis I will give him instructions so that both of you together spend five minutes a day at each exercise. This will double their effects.

Ruburt's insights, written in the margin of my book, about the correlations between his physical beliefs and his work beliefs, are correct, and important. Your affirmation that his body <u>can</u> perform better is also of great help, for those body beliefs also have to be tackled. He is beginning now with those.

(11:15.) <u>It is extremely important that he not concentrate upon the problem</u>—underline 10 times. Your idea about paintings and your list of correspondents is excellent. Ruburt's intuitions will also help you there. The books and *Seven* will do even better. Tell him he has no worries about *Aspects* that are justified.

If he thinks in terms of doing what he wants to do, even if he assigns time to the pursuits, he is better off than labeling anything work. Out-of-bodies, writing and spontaneous impressions are all things he likes to do, but some fell inside his work category and some did not. He likes challenges. Then have him "work" with them, and use them to his advantage. But do not overdo it, as is his inclination at times when he thinks in terms of absolutes.

For this week have him see how many times he can go out by himself or with you on a walk, but not a walk around the block or to the corner—a walk around the house will do. That is important. He is to continue my book, and make his moods known to you, as today, for you helped him.

This is bootleg material, so have him see how may times he can sit on the john, rather than have it that he must always do so every time, or not try at all. It is not a crisis if he tries a different pair of shoes and feels uncomfortable. Simply have him try again. It is important that he go with you shopping, as he has, but also that he walk outside even if he begins very slowly. If he cannot go around the block to start with, he feels despondent, but the habit of walking will grow as he gives it a chance.

Again, the concentration must not be on the problem.

The book is geared not only for Ruburt—and it is—but for many with beliefs like his, and incidentally yours, and so it will be of great benefit. He could not be consciously concerned with it, or use it properly, while producing it. This has to do with different areas of the brain being utilized.

(11:29.) Now a moment. When you use terms like arthritis you are using a belief system where names are given to states of mind, exteriorized. While you believe in the system you can find some help in it, but it is temporary, not permanent, and further binds you to a limiting system. Certain chemical changes do occur in any dis-ease. They are mentally produced. You can physically alter the imbalance sometimes, and gain relief, but another set of symptoms, physical or not, will materialize.

Changing beliefs will automatically correct any imbalance in the system, and certain foods for example will no longer "cause" a given condition. In most cases however it is the <u>belief</u> in the system that works, not the elimination of the foods.

Ruburt has a condition brought about my inhibiting physical impulses, and therefore body motion. The condition can be reversed by encouraging body motion. The beliefs behind the curtailment are now being laid bare, and the body beliefs themselves are also beginning to be tackled. The negative suggestions in such books as the ones Ruburt is considering buying would not help him.

I suggest, if he wants to, that he use the pendulum, which is utilizing his own body's knowledge, asking if any foods upset him. Refraining from those while working as I suggest with beliefs is all right, since he is using his own abilities. Do you see the difference?

("Yes.")

His suggestions should follow the lines of inspiration in his writing-requests for psychic and creative insight while avoiding absolutes. Again, physical suggestions such as "I can walk easier" are fine. Or "My legs and knees can support my weight." But avoid suggestions like "I can astonish myself," etc., of which he is so fond. I personally suggest, although he can do as he wishes, that he see himself rising at a decent hour to enjoy his day, and that he try two out-of-bodies a week during the day, as he used to. He <u>is</u> improving, however. The focus upon physical changes in your rooms is good. Continue it. Ruburt's ideas about out-of-bodies and death are highly important, and should be pursued.

I am seeing to your mother's comfort. Psychically she has met Daisy *(the deceased wife of my mother's brother Frank)*, and is in connection with Ruburt. You have friends because of your work and association with me, and your mother will be well cared for. She is psychically more a part of you than your father. He went in a different direction, as per material given at that time. Tell Ruburt that others helped his mother as he helps yours.

You can expect further improvements in Ruburt's physical condition as he follows this session and the book. You are doing a fine job with realities.

Now I will end the session or you may have a break and other material if you prefer. Or questions.

("Well, I guess we'd better end it, then.")

Then I wish you a fond good evening.

("Thank you, Seth, and good night." 11:50 PM.)

DELETED SESSION
SEPTEMBER 24, 1973 9:32 PM MONDAY

Good evening.

("Good evening, Seth.")

Now: Dr. Seth has a few preliminary remarks. Give us time as always with this kind of session.

Ruburt's *(very relaxed)* condition today was the result of Friday's news *(about the very good sales of all of Jane's books)*, and the body was ridding itself of a tension. Ruburt is aware that those purposes served by his physical condition are quickly vanishing. That is, he took on the symptoms because he believed that physical restraint was the best way to insure his concentration. I do not want to duplicate material given. For creative, financial and other present reasons, however, he felt that stern disciplinary measures had to be taken.

He took these for himself, and also in his own way for you, feeling that when he began to "make it" you would also be freer to do your thing.

He is now reassured enough to drop the disciplinary measures. He thought previously that Eleanor and Dick would be a means, and there was a period from the time when you met them, until now, when for him everything was critical. The carrot was out before the horse. The promise of where he wanted to be. These are just short phrases.

He believes now that he is in a pretty fair position, one he can happily accept creatively and financially. He has also learned along the way. It was not really great wealth, but some acceptable framework of financial security he was after, and some assurance that his books would bring him this, along with the freedom of creativity as he understood it.

There was some resentment against you, for he could not accept what he considered as a sacrifice on your part in jobs throughout your life, and yet he was angry because you would not do, he thought, what he had done—try to do your creative best, and then <u>force</u> the marketplace to take it. So if you had a job he felt you were sacrificing, but if you did not then he expected you to paint your best, and <u>make</u> the world take it, and pay for it.

Now on his part it was precisely that conflict that got him into difficulty, and that brought about the ideas of "work." He became angry, and still is, when you show normal criticism of Prentice and their dealings with our books, or his, because he feels that you do not really understand how difficult it is to market creative work, and since you do not sell your paintings you should not criticize his admittedly worrisome efforts. The fact that some of your criticisms are justified makes him worry the more, that he is not doing as good a job as he should.

He will not brook interference from anyone, including Richard Bach, in terms of dealing directly with the publisher of his own works. Your part in *Personal Reality* has been important, however, and the notes particularly, as they contribute. He wanted you both to be in a position where you could hold your heads up creatively and financially.

Now give us a moment.... He felt that in a way he was doing this for both of you: that despite what you said, if you wanted to paint for a living, or rather, simply to paint and thereby live, you would take those chances that he was taking, and whatever consequences that followed.

When you found what those consequences were, for Ruburt at least, you wanted no part of them. But in the old contract you had psychically made in this life, either of you would have done anything he felt, to paint and write and make the world accept what you did and pay for it.

So he was keeping the terms of the old contract. In the meantime you had learned so much, and so had he, but he still interpreted what he learned in the line of those old beliefs. He now realizes he has what he wanted—a creative framework in which to exist, with some financial independence. But he is now faced with body beliefs that have been built up as a result of the previous conflicts, and those are what you have to combat.

Today the body began to rid itself of tension. Ruburt is so <u>used</u> to body tensions that he felt disoriented and afraid. He does not need to go to a doctor, but he does need to pay attention to the physician within, and to heed the body's ancient wisdom.

Now I will give you a break, and then continue with some practical suggestions.

(10:05. Jane was still very relaxed. 10:25.)

Now: the original reasons for the condition are vanishing. In order to bring about those conditions however, Ruburt reactivated old body beliefs that now have to be dealt with.

He had healthy enough body concepts that had to be minimized to give him the symptoms, and this was done by reactivating beliefs he had "grown out of" before his symptoms. His mother gave him the idea that he was not graceful, for example, and this idea was reactivated. He was not allowed to take physical education because he was "not strong enough, and too high strung" when he was in high school. He was told not to run, but walk, to slow down because it was too dangerous to go fast, because he was too nervous. Now those beliefs, which he had dispensed with, <u>were reactivated as aids</u>, and they are the ones that now must be tackled.

<u>Your body can now perform better</u>—that should be used as a morning and evening suggestion, and anything you can say will be of help in that regard. It is highly important as a body belief. He must trust the relaxation period. There <u>are</u> periods where there is some disorientation, as the body rids itself of tensions, <u>at its own pace</u>, and they will be followed by periods of physical ambition.

He must trust the physician within. Concentration should not be on "work," but on aspects, poetry, his ideas. He is learning indeed the use of a different kind of inspirational time, which conflicts with his old ideas of so many hours.

While he is adjusting to this, let him take 3 hours a day, including Saturday, in which he is to be creatively free. He will do more "work" then than in 6 determined hours. Each day now, I want him to take his walk, <u>even</u> if it is only around the house. The corner is fine, but around the house is better than none; and to sit down for bowel movements.

He is to check with you when he feels blue, for your more objective attitude can help him. You are now left with the body beliefs, and <u>not</u> with the original ones <u>behind</u> them.

He lost confidence in the body as a result of his course, and lost trust in his conscious mind as it directs the body. My book will help him.

Now these are my week's suggestions, and I want, beside what I have just given you, a ten-minute badminton session daily, or pounding of the pillow for a lesser time—but one or the other. He must be encouraged to use the body, for he will see it respond, and the feedback is highly important for his confidence.

We are dealing now with body beliefs, then. Impress upon him that he is <u>not moving too fast</u>, that he is not so nervous that he must slow down, meaning slowing down the body.

Ruburt is left with the body image that he acquired. He is afraid that he cannot undo what he has done. He can indeed, but he needs to develop confidence in that belief, and each physical achievement is of great benefit.

To some extent he still projects his illness into the future. Any help you can be results in reinforcing his attractiveness, and <u>your</u> belief in his ability to improve physically. I will have other precise suggestions. They are geared to his progress, and later a change of environment will be important simply because of the break-up of conditioning.

I will have you both do the point of power exercise. But for now I <u>expect</u> this week's suggestions to be faithfully followed.

He wants to recover now. You must help him realize that he can. If at all possible go to an establishment at least once a week, where dancing is a possibility. If not, any kind of public endeavor is important. He can expect more relaxation periods now, so have him go along with them, and watch his moods then.

Give us a moment.... "Slow down because you are going to fast," *(was)* told him in his youth; he reactivated those ideas, interpreting them to mean that he must slow down in order to produce mature work. Naturally, left alone, his body and his mind both work fast, and there is nothing dangerous in that. He had been told he would burn himself out, so he came into his late 30's and tried to slow down. This has been covered in past sessions—many of them. He can trust himself and his own rhythms however.

You have working for you the fact that the beliefs <u>causing</u> the condition are quickly vanishing. You are left with subsidiary beliefs involving body motion that have to be directly encountered and challenged.

The vitamins do help combat the stress he places upon the body, but only while he works with these sessions and his beliefs. Your ages were involved, in that he felt you had only so much time. Remind him that the ideas he reactivated about the body may have had some application to a child, but none to a woman.

You have yourself obtained benefit from this last group of sessions, understanding the reasons for Ruburt's condition so that your gentle encouragement now can be highly advantageous.

He has been using his will to put his body down. He must realize—and he does <u>not</u> yet—that the will can be just as effective in releasing his body. In reminding him of this you can also be of help, for he was afraid that his will was powerless in that regard.

The guidelines for the work I have given are simple and not overtaxing. I want them clearly followed daily. Now—do you have questions?

("No, I guess not.")

You are both heading for financial ease. The books will again do better. This fact alone will help Ruburt's condition. Your own plans are unconsciously made. You will contribute creatively and financially. While you have been concerned with Ruburt, unconsciously in certain terms you have solved creative dilemmas, and soon opportunities will present themselves beside those you will make.

Ruburt's condition will improve. That is already established, but there is a great difference between improvement and the relatively complete physical freedom he can have, that will come as he realizes his conscious control over his body's condition.

Now I bid you a fond good evening. As per your article, a black hole was involved.

("Thank you. Good night, Seth.")

(11:31 PM. Seth's parting remark concerned a news story in the New York Times *today. It stated that a tiny black hole was responsible for the mysterious large-scale destruction in Siberia in 1908. Many theories have been advanced to explain the leveling of over 20 square miles of forest, with this one being the latest. We'll keep the article on file.)*

DELETED SESSION
OCTOBER 1, 1973 9:56 PM MONDAY

(During the past week Jane has made a spectacular improvement in the use of her right arm, with lesser but steady improvement in the left. There have been other good signs physically; she has also improved considerably in her daily walks, etc. The body changes for the better seem to be long-lasting—already they have existed for longer periods than any others in recent years. Needless to say we are both very pleased.)

Good evening.

("Good evening, Seth.")

As always give us a moment....

It is obvious not only that Ruburt is improving but that one important area of the body has begun to clear itself to a large degree. Do you agree with me?

("Yes.")

Then since we have that established, let me tell you that it is of course no coincidence, for the right arm was the area first affected. The body has its own patterns of behavior, connected with beliefs; but in this memory pattern there are tracings, and these are beginning to be erased in the order in which the condition was established. Do you follow me?

("Yes.")

The arm, by its sudden freedom, also serves as a model to Ruburt consciously, and also for the rest of the body to follow. He is aware of the feeling of freedom consciously, physically, as a portion now of daily experience and comparison. He did not have this before, and so it is highly important symbolically and literally that improvements will continue and be used as a model.

The feeling of warmth and identification with the legs, and sensations throughout the whole lower body, is also highly significant and necessary. Changes are occurring there physically, and circulation being increased to those areas. There are muscles and tendons that are thawing out, hence the body is acclimating itself to new conditions.

These improvements are happening in such a way that no undue stress is placed upon any particular group of muscles or tendons, and yet there <u>will</u> be some periods in which feelings of unaccustomed activity are present, and perhaps some tenderness, as muscles and tendons are gradually activated.

These feelings will also be accompanied by sensations of warmth however, and so should be accepted and recognized as new signs of mobility and action. He can begin to try to feel greater strength now in the right arm, and all improvements on the right side are being picked up by the left.

As I told you in our last session, the original beliefs behind the symptoms have largely vanished. Some are still coming to light. The body condition reflects subsidiary beliefs about the body that he mobilized for the other purposes that now no longer operate.

Some of these subsidiary beliefs are already beginning to melt, hence the improvements noted. Others await only physical proving-out in experience, and the time necessary in your terms for the body to readjust at an even rate—that is, an overall body of motion will be newly established.

While the condition reigned there was a characteristic overall body position and method of behavior that operated as a whole, and in line with his beliefs. It was organized, each portion of the body participating to give you the overall modus operandi.

Now that is changing. The changing entails adjustments at all body levels, so there are in-between periods, so to speak, physically in your terms, as all portions of the body react to any given improvement.

In the meantime Ruburt is aware of sensation that before was largely deadened. The old condition had its own balance. The improvements will follow their own rhythm as the body sets up a new balance in compensation. Some of this has to do with energy patterns and flows.

The hardest part, however, is over, for the sensation of freedom has been physically introduced through the arm into the system—and that message echoes throughout the system. Ruburt no longer believes he needs the symptoms. The condition therefore is beginning to fade. It will not take anything like the same amount of time to vanish as it did to establish itself. There will be sudden improvements on the physical level, as with the arm, but before that occurred there were changes in beliefs. There will be other almost unnoticed improvements that will not show until they "suddenly appear" as a major breakthrough—and these have <u>already begun</u>.

He has done well following my suggestions, particularly going outside. The squatting he performed *(last Friday night)* should be repeated once daily at least, for it reinforces the idea of letting go with the body.

Badminton or pounding the pillow should definitely be started this week. He <u>is</u> thinking in terms of improvements now, though, and this is an important development. Do not, in your case, over-remind him of what he is "supposed" to do, for he takes this to mean that you do not expect him to do it. He knows well now of your loving concern, and feels your love, and your love-making endeavors are extremely important to both of you.

Do you want a break?

("No." 10:30.)

The body can stand two more of the small vitamin C's a day now.

I want to say something about beliefs that became obvious to him today concerning time and "work." The ideas of work have been largely covered. His beliefs about time are important in relationship to his work ideas. As he noted, the belief was that he must be the young American poet, or the young American writer. Now we are dealing with an old belief system once shared to a large extent by you both.

In that system he saw you nearly ten years older than he, and in those terms unsatisfied; so he must work all the harder against time, and cut out everything else. In that system, as <u>he</u> developed it, there was no time for leisurely meals, showers, shopping trips or mundane enjoyments—only the work was important. Only it would survive. <u>The day in which it was produced would vanish and be nothing</u>—only the work would survive as a monument. The trivialities and moods, the feelings of morning and twilight would be extinguished—so he thought as you told him, and so against many of his natural instincts he tried to obey.

So the day became nothing more than a framework in which he must work, and in which all relationships had little value except as they were interpreted through work. He became pursued by time, <u>so that in his world</u> there literally was no time for anything else.

At the same "time" his body kept trying to assert its privileges and natural life, but he saw it as a tool to work. He understands now a good deal of this, but I want to put it in form for him. Even his writing time therefore became frenzied. He did not live in the moment, or know his body's present reality. Sensations and impulse were deadened, unless they could be translated into "work."

Now this did finally become so reflected that feeling shunted aside threatened his work, and he finally recognized this. He was afraid of out-of-bodies precisely because he did not have a good enough footing in the present. He did not have the needed support.

The body's weight was kept down for the same reasons, because he felt according to those old beliefs, that the body's sustenance and substance in physical reality was not important in regard to his work. These ideas are also vanishing now. The body with weight and substance might be unmanageable, filled with too much energy, and therefore want the physical activity he thought he must deny it for his work. It is not a matter of what he ate, but chemically what he did with the nourishment.

Any panic he now recognizes having to do with time represents left-over old obsessions about the necessity to work with a time limit. Even in those limited terms you see he realized that his achievements and production are in his terms now sufficient; but he must move out of those limiting ideas, and he is.

Take your break.

(10:50. Jane had been "really out." She was already aware of more from Seth waiting for her, she said. Now she was extremely relaxed; she has had many relaxation sessions since this series from Seth began a few weeks ago. Her body felt like water, and also warm. I described the good news in the session to her. "I'm going to light a cigarette, get myself together, and go back to the session...." 11:02.)

Now: all of Ruburt's presently-past beliefs added up to his physical condition—his beliefs in the nature of time, work, the body, his particular nature—they all tied in together perfectly.

Each person's personal reality has the same kind of unity. There is nothing that does not fit into the picture. There were achievements and joys along the way, and these should not be forgotten or minimized. They were all the result of beliefs also. Ruburt believed that they were only achieved by neglecting the body. He realizes now that the body's reality is the framework through which <u>all</u> must come in this life, and that limiting its vitality will eventually end up limiting all experience and all "work."

Now he is lucky, in those terms, for many never understand the pattern of their beliefs. His creative mobility <u>is</u> dependent upon his physical mobility now in this life—something he did not understand before.

You *(to me)* are also seeing what can happen when spontaneity is denied....The badminton or pillow-pounding allows for the expression of freedom, mobility and speed—the opportunity for it, and is therefore important.

He still does not completely understand the nature of what he calls Sumari time, in relationship with inspiration. This concept is extremely valuable however, in freeing him from old time ideas.

His idea of changing the present through altering pictures in the past is also pertinent and good. Have him continue the practice as he began it—it aids in understanding beliefs, and it does alter the past and therefore the present.

Give us a moment.... He should finish my book, then begin it again, this time following the exercises as he needs them. As mentioned, I will have you both do the point of power. Beer in any quantity should now be avoided. It is all right on your night out. These are aids only.

For now he is right to avoid citrus. The vitamin C makes up for that. Tell him to begin cutting down white sugar in coffee, or use brown sugar. Cutting down is better. Apricot is better than pear juice. These are simply aids that will later be unnecessary.

Fresh tomatoes are good. Instead of fresh *(so-called)* <u>commercial</u> tomatoes, however, use canned ones for him. But not tomato juice alone, canned.

Cottage cheese is excellent. Now bacon for him is good. In moderation that particular kind of fat is good as a lubricant. All greens.

That is all for this evening. The suggestions given last week, plus the badminton or pillow-beating to be continued, and the squatting.

The sitting down, whether on a chair or the toilet, has to do with the fear of letting the body go. Where the toilet is concerned the ideas of time enter in, where he did not want to take time out. Everything as given last week to be continued then, with the added suggestions. These are geared to his condition.

Make sure you "suitably" recognize his improvements. There will be more of them. But again, periods of readjustment which should be accepted as such. The mobility of the fingers is much better when typing—something he did not mention.

His dream recall will also improve, because he feels more secure in physical areas.

Now I bid you, my dear transcriber, a fond good evening.

("The same to you, Seth. Thank you. Good night." 11:27 PM.)

One brief remark: A rosé wine, rather than your Pisano.

("Okay." Jane's relaxation continued strongly; she went to bed. She confirmed that her fingers were much more flexible typing—something she'd forgotten to tell me.)

DELETED SESSION
OCTOBER 8, 1973 9:05 PM MONDAY

Now: Good evening.

("Good evening, Seth.")

We will begin slowly as usual with this kind of session.

Generally, with the conditions as given, your surroundings were well-chosen. The apartment house provided a structure in which Ruburt—

(The session was interrupted by a long-distance call for Jane from Cleveland. Resume at 9:19.)

Now: The framework provided an outside structure of nonchalant interactions with people, so that even when Ruburt was tempted to withdraw there was some exterior stimuli present. The surroundings also served other purposes. Not having children, you do not have that constant steady interrelationship with others in which you are brought back always to the immediacy of the moment. Your neighbors provided that stimuli also.

While Ruburt was in the framework of beliefs he held, the apartment house then did serve somewhat as a countermeasure. Sometimes he may have reacted negatively, but the relationships were important. He was not trustful enough of his own being to handle his daily life in more isolated circumstances.

Give us a moment... His beliefs have undergone their most significant changes, in that he finally believes that he forms his reality, and can change it. Because he is the person who delivers the message, he had to accept himself before he could fully accept the message.

When he did not then he questioned the message that came through him, and then could not use it properly. The body is in the process of balancing the right and left sides, and as noted improvements on the right side are being picked up by the left. In this case the right side is the teacher side. There will be periods of deep relaxation *(as today)*, and the opportunities must be allowed for so that gains during these periods can be utilized in action later.

All joints are being loosened. The feelings of unfamiliarity will only occur at certain stages. The warmth is continuing, the sign of energy distribution and increased circulation. Some realignment of course has already occurred, strengthening and loosening the left side so that he was finally able to mount the back stairs easier, and this will continue.

The badminton for 10 minutes daily is highly important, allowing a <u>short</u> period for the release of normal energy, motion, and activation of the joints as they are being loosened. 10 minutes a day is much better than 20 now and then. For now in fact 10 minutes a day is sufficient. Later we will add another 5 minutes.

The walking however is also important. There is no time limit set there. The walking will become easier, and as it does he can then walk further. For now let him continue as he has, but <u>daily</u>, walking to the corner when he feels the impetus.

Give us a moment… The inner beliefs <u>are</u> continually strengthening the ones of freedom, and the body is responding. It is precisely here that you run up against the body beliefs. They are in turn changing for the better. <u>I do not want him to think in terms of absolutes</u>. Yet at the same time all motions and actions reinforce the healthy body beliefs and dissolve the old ones.

Give us a moment here. The old body beliefs were adopted to serve the purposes of other beliefs about work that have now almost, but not entirely, completely dissolved. They have dissolved sufficiently enough to be inconsequential.

In time the body beliefs connected with them could dissolve by themselves, but the pattern of habit still operates, and some of the habits can be tackled much more easily than Ruburt realizes.

(9:45.) We will come back to this. Give us a moment. He is only now beginning to trust his body, and those suggestions should by all means be continued as given. He concentrated upon proofs of the body's "lack of dependability" in the past, and now is beginning to build up his faith in its dependability. Again, whenever he looks well tell him so, for your honest enjoyment of his person and body will now be of great value, since now he is open to that kind of appreciation. He can use it more constructively than in the past.

Remind him, and I know I am repeating myself, that concentration must not be upon the problem—which, remind him, has lessened. I want to get into some other issues here. Take a brief break and we will continue.

(9:52 to 10:03.)

Now, let us continue: Ruburt has been working with what he calls the inward order of events. Tell him that in that order of events he can walk so well at this point, now, that anyone would have to look twice to discover that he was not walking perfectly. That is the situation in the inner order of events now.

That inner order is being physically materialized. Your point is vital—that he separate the belief from himself, and recognize it as a belief: that he cannot walk properly *(at break)*. This alone will show excellent results. His legs and knees can bear his weight. This should be used as a morning and evening suggestion. It is true now. The belief that his legs and knees cannot support his weight is an old belief, and a <u>belief</u>, not a statement of fact in basic terms. Until now the belief, however, has resulted in a <u>condition of experience</u>—a falsehood perpetuated upon the body, to which it has then responded. The belief was the result of faulty perception and understanding, adopted because of those other beliefs about work that no longer apply.

The man who was bothered by epilepsy did Ruburt a service and Ruburt definitely helped him; but there in dramatic fashion Ruburt saw how beliefs operated, and through helping the individual also saw the best ways he could help himself <u>and</u> others as well. The man had his reassuring rituals.

Now: while Ruburt acquiesced to his condition, his own rituals <u>were</u> reassuring. He believed he should not get up. The rituals are more obvious now, and to some extent he becomes more impatient. Recognizing rituals as rituals will be of benefit.

All is progressing at its own rate, however, and tell Ruburt to trust this. The rituals will be abandoned, but gradually, slipping away. The inner self knows what it is doing. Ruburt is being released. There is no doubt of it—but in a safe, natural, and ever-accelerating rate both for his body and development.

I do not mean this will be a long drawn-out process either, but one in which he tastes freedom gradually, is not frightened but steadily encouraged, and in which there will be no backslidings, but understandings at all levels of body-mind relationships.

There will be sudden, <u>sometimes</u> spectacular new improvements in comparison with others, and these again will be the result of other less noticeable improvements constantly occurring.

Give us a moment.... The shoes are one of the rituals. The corns have been caused in part by poor circulation in the feet. That is being remedied. They were also caused by improper balance, so that pressure was constantly applied in the same places due to the underaction of certain leg muscles, and the stress upon others. This is also being remedied.

Ruburt believed he could wear only one pair of shoes. This was highly symbolic, meaning that he could walk only in one way. He purposely chose shoes that did not fit, in line with his past belief that he should not be physically active. There was then a built-in excuse also.

As his posture changes the corns will vanish. Now <u>undue</u> concentration upon shoes is not a help. He should however either go barefooted or change shoes for some short period during each day. The getting up and down each time brings him in direct conflict with the old body beliefs, and ideas of motion, that he used to repress. I will have more to say about that issue in particular at our next session.

Aspects is extremely important, for it represents the reorganization of his ideas, and in a highly creative framework. Continue the program precisely as I have outlined it. I have an addition of sorts to add. He has not begun squatting. I want this begun. He may even hold on to something if he wants to, but I want him to feel the sensation of letting go once a day at least, in a squatting position. As he progresses three such movements at one time will be of great benefit.

He will find himself <u>wanting</u> to get up earlier, finding he is enthusiastic both about his writing and wanting to have time left over for physical activities. For the first time in some time by then, he will actively look forward to getting up. Now it is no hassle to the degree that it was. Before that he did not want to.

He is more embarrassed now by his walking because of a healthy impatience that is understandable, but this must be kept under control so that it does not hamper him. When you are with him others do not offer to help—they see that he is taken care of. When he is alone and trying to be independent then people offer and he becomes dismayed. He used the last episode *(on the back stairs)* to trigger an important development in walking up the stairs, but he is not to imagine that everyone else is perfect because they look all right; then he deals with absolutes, becomes frightened, and exaggerates his condition, thinking in physical terms alone and forgetting those inner abilities of his, of creativity, that are indeed so important.

Do you have questions?

("Well, you've covered everything on his list except the bit about his teeth and gums.")

They will be improved as his overall condition improves. He should use baking soda, and brush twice a day as he does not do. Tension caused the condition, and the gums were weakened The vitamins are of a help.

("Can the teeth straighten out?")

The teeth can straighten out. I have a bit more to say here. Will you get Ruburt matches?

(10:50.) Do you want a break?

("No.")

A dentist would shudder, and often surgical methods are used to correct such a condition, when, if left alone, and with changes in a person's living situation, the condition would right itself. Often of course it would not, because of beliefs and conditioning. In this case however the condition will right itself as the tension is being released. The vitamin E does help, and Ruburt's idea of his own self-image is involved, also.

The brush for stimulation of the gums however is an important adjunct. It should be followed by washing the mouth out each time with a mild solution of salt and water, which stimulates and toughens the tissues. This should be done before bed. The other time is inconsequential—that is it can be done at any time.

At our next session I will discuss weight and food. This is also connected with the gums.

That is enough for tonight. Have him use it well. I bid you a fond good evening.

("Thank you very much. He's doing well, Seth. Good night." 10:56 PM.)

DELETED SESSION
OCTOBER 15, 1973 9:05 PM MONDAY

(During the last week Jane has had several long periods of relaxation, plus other signs of continuing physical improvement. In fact, she was still feeling the effects of a relaxation as this session began. It had started in mid-afternoon after she had received an OK from Tam Mossman re the publication of her book of poetry, Dialogues — *at least as far as Tam is concerned. The book will be published after* Personal Reality, *but before* Aspects.*)*

Now: good evening.

("Good evening, Seth.")

And give us a moment.... everything as given in the latest session to this date.

The session, the late one, dealing with "work" attitudes, should be read at least twice a week now. A new synthesis is taking place concerning Ruburt's ideas about his writing and life, so that particular session will simply insure that the old ideas are sufficiently broken up so that the new synthesis can form.

Ruburt received ideas about his on his own this week, and wrote them down. That synthesis allowed the new book idea to come to the forefront. Otherwise it might have been merely a probability. And of course *Aspects* applies here, and my own book, in that they both served as turning points for such a new synthesis and reorganization of beliefs.

I have some words to say first of all about the body's condition and method of healing operation. I will have more suggestions for the week that are important.

The relaxation periods bring about a necessary situation in which the muscles become more pliable, and are then gradually released. The amount of release varies according to the given muscle system and its interaction with others. During the <u>time</u> of relaxation then there often may be a less reliable overall posture. *(Which Jane has mentioned.)*

The relaxation continues longer to ensure that undue strain is not placed upon the releasing muscles until they are acclimated. They rest themselves, in other words, after each such treatment. This is <u>followed</u> by the desire to move. The inclination toward muscular activity then somewhat later appears as increased strength or pliability.

The right and left sides are out of balance. The relaxation episodes <u>naturally</u> provide in their own way, more easily and without discomfort, the same sort of benefit that theoretically would be received, say, in a chiropractic treatment. This is but one part of the process, however. The release of muscles takes place in such a way that the tendons around joints are gradually loosened, and then the body works on the joints themselves. Ruburt has experienced the <u>slight</u> soreness as rigidity in those areas begins to loosen. There is also the repair of tissue about the joints.

There <u>is</u> some swelling, very slight sometimes, when the joints are involved and this merely provides a cushioning process as circulation is quickened and pressure is taken away. There is repair in all areas. Because the procedure <u>is</u> a natural one, the heat sensations can neatly show you the areas directly involved at any time.

Give us a moment.... There <u>is</u> an ingredient in wine that the blood can use at this point in its building process. Also as mentioned the bacon. He is <u>at this point</u> in a better position than someone with an overweight problem, in that the joints do not have much weight bearing upon them, or fat to smother their mobility.

The vitamins do serve to help in the extra work being done by the body, of repair, although without the change in beliefs they would not be effective. The body is using what it gets now efficiently, then. Some weight gain can be expected shortly. Now nutriments are being utilized in repair work. After the short period and slight gain in weight, the weight will then normally return.

During the relaxation episodes there are also hormonal alterations. These are vital and they are rather swiftly occurring as Ruburt's habitual thoughts begin to change.

The suggestions on trusting the body must be continued, for the body's healing process now follows those beliefs. Before he was hampered by the initial beliefs, now nearly dissolved, that caused the disbelief in the body. Those body beliefs are now in the process of changing. As they change, bringing about improvements, you find them in reality as you understand it. The result you see is the materialization of the new beliefs, as before you saw the materialization of the old.

Now balance has changed, so that the new beliefs outweigh the old ones and allow the body to respond.

Ruburt is quite right in avoiding <u>your</u> cookies. His system does not need that white sugar, and yours would be better off without so <u>much</u> of it.

This week both of you read for yourselves the portions of my book dealing with the point of power and natural hypnosis. Next week I would like you to begin certain short exercises with them. First I want to be sure that Ruburt understands how to use them properly.

While certain stages are occurring there may be an uneven quality, but not necessarily, where he walks much better one day and not another, until the entire system is aligned, when of course the improvements will be held. This simply has to do with various muscular systems. I mentioned this only so that he understands, and is not disappointed if one day he does exceptionally well, and the next day does not seem to do as well. This may not occur, the unevenness, but it could as a natural situation as balance is restored.

He is doing well. The badminton again, however, should be established, and the squatting exercises. When there is a lengthy relaxation period he will know instinctively when to let the badminton go, for instance, but it should be established as a practice. For again it allows the new resiliency an opportunity to show in motion. Again, the ten minutes are sufficient.

As long as he trusts the body's improvement, he is better off to concentrate upon his poetry, *Aspects*, and other areas of his life, and to enjoy increasing physical activity. The body can repair itself now quite well if he lets it go its way. Once the beliefs are changed the rest follows.

The improvements themselves then give you additional beneficial feedback. Contact with the public is important for his confidence. Now take your break.

(9:50 to 10:02.)

Now: This will be a short session.

Ruburt must still go on to some deeper realizations, and he is on the way. Repression of motion cannot lead to anything but further repression. He understands this now. He is allowing himself freedom by degrees, letting down repressions one by one.

He realizes that freedom is within him. He did not understand that before. He realizes he does not need the symptoms, and is in the process of losing them. He must want freedom as strongly as before he wanted to repress it, and this is in the direction in which he is now moving.

He believes that freedom is possible, meaning physical freedom. Before, he did not. But freedom should not be thought of as an absolute, but as a process of fulfillment that will take place naturally because he wants it to, and believes that it will. All suggestions as given last week stand.

Your love-making continues to be important, for there he experiences letting go without effort, and that will carry over into other areas. This will be all. It is all that is needed if the suggestions given are followed through. He has plenty to work with.

My heartiest regards. Good evening—and you have good times to look forward to.

("Thank you, Seth. Good night." 10:12 PM.)

DELETED SESSION
OCTOBER 22, 1973 9:17 PM MONDAY

(Jane was very relaxed after supper, but she wanted to have the session. The period of ease had begun this afternoon, and was still in effect at session time. Jane has had quite a few such relaxations in the past week—nearly on a daily basis, I think. They have been accompanied by sensations of heat, sweating, and soreness, though not all of these symptoms were present in each relaxation. Signs seem very encouraging. Jane now gets over to the breakfast table in perhaps half the time it took her when we began this series of sessions....)

Good evening.

("Good evening, Seth.")

The week in its own way has been quite successful, and went rather as I expected. Several important breakthroughs were made concerning beliefs.

Ruburt saw how being away from his desk and the house worked creatively to his advantage, as per the ride to your mother's *(in Centerville)*, and the earlier walk around the block. There is no doubt of the many improvements, made up of a series of inner improvements that do not show as yet, except as the time element presents itself—i.e., he gets over here *(apartment 5)* quicker and easier.

The legs do not appear straighter as yet, however *(which Jane has been concerned about)*, but the change of tempo there reflects greater inner coordination. The soreness in the knees I mentioned as a possibility last week, but it discouraged him nevertheless.

Those joints are definitely being loosened, and the unevenness sometimes presented in walking is the result of new balances being set up gradually as the knees are released. Care is being taken that the release <u>is</u> fairly well balanced, but at the same time one joint may be more released than another in a given moment, causing the feelings of unfamiliarity.

As he knows the same is happening with the arms, but he is not walking on them, as indeed he has told himself. The dreams were meant to encourage him and to show him that the inner order of events does assure his improvements.

The promise in the dream made by you, that the events *(of Jane's great flexibility)* <u>were</u> indeed happening, represented your inner knowledge that he would make it now, and his own realization of the fact, as well as the body's acknowledgment. The first part of the dream involved excellent physical release and manipulability. The second part concerned new rooms, all rich avenues open to him, both as a result of the release and yet bringing forth the release. The rooms represented exploration, new areas of creativity in which he is even now involved.

The suggestions I gave *(in recent sessions)* amounted to a "schedule of activities," calculated to give room to creative and physical expression. Common sense applies. If he dances or cleans the apartment, then his natural impulses are being <u>physically</u> directed in those fashions. He does not have to feel that he <u>must</u> go for his walk when physically he feels like cleaning, for example. The badminton, unless he is in a relaxation period, is excellent, however, and should be maintained because of the opportunity for speed. Now it is the only way he can experience some, except for the swinging of the arms.

The "schedule" was meant to insure some physical activity each day; those days particularly when he does not go out with you shopping or for a ride, then the walk <u>is</u> paramount. But he has been going out each day.

(9:36.) Give us a moment.... The soreness in the joints will now begin to diminish simply because the first activation was bound to present some friction as the joints began to move from a state of relative rigidity. The heat cushions that effect, hence the frequent inner heat treatments. *(Jane was experiencing these effects today and tonight, etc.)*

The squatting exercise <u>was</u> difficult for two reasons—one having to do with beliefs, and the second to do with the soreness about the joints. The belief has to do with letting down, of course, and I will have more to say about this. That same belief has to do with sitting on the toilet.

Now. He has done well dealing with body beliefs as he was presented with them in periods of passive relaxation. <u>What we want to get across is the idea that motion is spontaneous.</u> To let go is to <u>go</u>.

In his belief system it seemed to him that to let go was to stop. Therefore relaxation became a dirty word, where nothing was done. In relaxation periods then he is apt to worry. Things will not get done. He feels guilty. He wonders how far along with the relaxation he should go.

The body's mobility, its freedom, its agility and its creativity, is dependent upon its ability to relax, to give itself up to itself, and therefore to the source of its being, to let go, in which case it is supportive, agile, and unhampered. *(Forcefully)*.

These sentences should <u>now</u> clear up that seeming contradiction between relaxation and doing that he has felt for so long. Relaxation is the springboard from which physical actions come.

Now—do you want a break?

("We might as well."

(9:50. Jane's excellent relaxation period continued during break. She didn't know if she could get to her feet. "I'm really out," she kept repeating. She said that she knew Seth had a "whole bunch of stuff there about parents." She was so relaxed that we decided to resume the session, lest she find herself unable to if she waited too long. She said she was determined to get the material. Resume at 9:55.)

Now: each person chooses his parents, accepting in terms of environment and heredity a bank of various characteristics, attitudes and abilities from which he draws in physical life.

There is always a reason, and so each parent will represent to each child an unspeakable symbol, and often the two parents will represent glaring contrasts and different probabilities, so that the child can compare and contrast divergent realities.

Ruburt's father, to Ruburt, meant laxness, relaxation to the extreme, without drive or fire, responsibility or control. Ruburt's mother meant <u>will</u>, drive, power, for she had power over the household and over Ruburt. But that power went nowhere, for Ruburt's father was physically free while his mother was not. <u>Ruburt thought he had to make a choice</u> *(louder)*. If will and power meant relative immobility but <u>purpose</u>—and purpose was what he had—then in the past he chose that above what he thought of as laxness, relaxation, and physical freedom that might mean frittering away ability, a relaxation in which nothing was accomplished.

His parents represented two extremes. His mother represented will untempered by spontaneity or relaxation, quite frankly a will for power over others. She made other people supply her wants, and was a despot. She was filled with energy however, <u>and</u> purpose.

Ruburt's father represented the other extreme, with no firm purpose, seemingly driven willy-nilly, and accomplishing nothing. Both parents could be highly destructive, however—Ruburt's father when he was drunk, and Ruburt's mother generally.

Ruburt chose the parents to see the contrast and learn the best way for him in which purpose could be combined with spontaneity, the will with the spirit. He had to see what both extremes <u>were</u> extremes—not practical or idealistic. All of this applied to his mental, psychic, spiritual, <u>and</u> physical life, and his overall purpose.

Now he is free to appreciate and use the energy shown to him by his mother in condensed dramatic fashion, tempered and freed by the free-flowing air of the father, and the physical mobility and sense of exploration that he represented.

The Christian-Science background with the father was also important, for it was this inner belief of the father that <u>did</u> sustain him, and that inclination of the father and <u>his</u> mother *(Mattie)* that Ruburt chose in his background to temper his own mother's beliefs and lead him in our direction. The daughter triumphs for the parent, then. The same applies in its own way to each individual, where the conditions and challenges and <u>solutions</u> as well are given in the chosen background. So the way applies in its own way to you.

Your father represented what you thought of as the secret, isolated creative self—more or less at odds with the world, unappreciated by it in family or financial terms; the alone, artistic self you thought unable to communicate, inarticulate and dumb, locked away from close communication with others, and indeed barraged by misunderstandings because of its very creativity—emotionally frozen, afraid to show itself.

Your mother represented the opposite in your mind—the emotionally explosive, suffocating immediacy, a female life and earthly ties, social commitment, homey chores and distractions that seemed to be directly opposed to solitary creativity.

We come back to will and freedom, discipline and purpose. Ruburt's background with his mother and his beliefs in will then merged with your feelings for isolation from your father. Ruburt blocked out emotional spontaneity, feeling that his father was lax. You blocked out emotional spontaneity, feeling that your mother's was detrimental to creative isolation. At the same time you admired <u>Ruburt's</u> spontaneity. You trusted it however <u>only</u> because it was merged with creative purpose. He therefore used it only for such purpose, <u>not wanting to frighten you with it</u> otherwise because he loved you so.

He was also afraid of spontaneity not related to creativity because of his feeling that his father went willy-nilly and produced nothing. In solving his dilemma, which was the creative one, the both of you triumph for yourselves and _for_ your parents.

Only by self-examination can you see how these issues merge in all areas of your living, and then project the ideas outward for others. Ruburt going out walking goes for both of you. You, relating far better than you even did with others, go out for both of your parents. Your mother knows that.

Encouraging Ruburt's physical spontaneity now, you symbolically encourage your own inner spontaneity, and both of you recognize that. Give us a moment.... There are reasons set by you because of the nature of your purpose, so that your best work will come later in your lives. Your mother realizes how she is opening avenues through which you understand more than you did, and she knows that you follow her on journeys of which other family members are ignorant.

Loren and Dick also chose the situation. Each parent also represented opposites to them—but different ones, and so they saw your parents differently. Do not lose contact with Dick. He is more like a son to you and Ruburt than a brother or brother-in-law.... I want you to see that all of this makes more sense in many areas than you may have realized. Ruburt's physical state is assured. Forget the day-by-day patterns. He will be free of them so that nothing is noticed at the worst. At the best he will establish a condition of <u>extraordinary flexibility</u>—which is still up to him. But the beliefs have changed enough so that the improvements will come and the walking will be remedied.

He may go beyond this to achieve an unusual flexibility. That however is a probability as of now.

For the week, take this session and the remarks given, then the point of power as given in my book, done by each of you daily without fail. Ruburt is to read more of my book this week. The understanding from this session will be of great benefit. I bid you then a fond good evening.

(*10:40 PM. "Thank you, Seth. Good night." As I type this the next evening—while class is in progress—Jane is enjoying another lengthy relaxation.... Both of us have done the point of power. Loren and Dick are my young brothers.*)

DELETED SESSION
NOVEMBER 5, 1973 9:29 PM MONDAY

(*Last Monday's session, for October 29, was held for Sue Watkins and George Rhodes. There was but little said about Jane's progress in it, except for a footnote at the end. Jane's progress has been steady for the past two weeks, however, and is in keeping with that described in earlier sessions.)*

Now, Good evening.

("Good evening, Seth.")

The walking progress is already assured because of inner physical events now occurring. These are following their own course, but some exterior improvement in that area should very shortly be showing.

Other adjustments are being made first to insure overall balance and coordination, as work is being done on the knees, leg muscles and feet. Otherwise too much strain is thrown upon other areas of the body, which then must compensate.

Ruburt should try, again, not to concentrate on the walking area. To take it for granted it is being taken care of. The soreness that sometimes occurs in joints *is* due to their activation, will not last, and should be accepted in that light. The few minutes for badminton are important, and gently familiarize Ruburt with the sense of quicker motion.

Give us a moment.... His remark following receipt of the check brought up the final clarification of beliefs. The connections were given as stated also.

(Here Seth refers to the check for $7,500 that Jane recently received from Prentice-Hall as half her payment for the paperback rights of Seth Speaks. *Jane wrote on the check's envelope that the money represented a "final payment" to me, etc.)*

The area of concentration now however should be not upon the body but upon daily living, his writing and your plans. *(The Nature of) Personal Reality* quite assures your financial situation for some time to come. One point I want to mention: Ruburt's mother tried to escape poverty through the calculated unrelenting use of her beauty, and it did not work. Ruburt in his own way tried to escape poverty through the use of his brains, and he was afraid that <u>that</u> was not going to work either. Ruburt's brains however gave him much more leeway than his mother's beauty gave her, and his intellect came with a counterpart—an intuitional and psychic counterpart that enriched it and kept it from becoming bitter or even ingrown.

At the same time the early beliefs were there, and were mentioned to some extent along with other issues. These also had to do with the unremitting purpose of work. In the meantime his intellect and intuitive abilities both discovered that the daily joy of living was important—as important as "work" or money.

For a time however a conglomeration of beliefs merged, so that he felt that he had to drive himself unremittingly: and this meant, to him, imposing disciplines as given earlier. The fears of time, the early fears that made him want to escape poverty, the feeling that all eggs must be put in one basket, and his reaction to you and your circumstances—these were all connected.

In his twenties he could well combine the idea of little money with his writing because he realized it might be that kind of profession, but he became frightened as the years passed. I am simply putting this in consecutive fashion, emphasizing certain points for convenience's sake now. The check, even in those terms, you see, was important. It is being assimilated along those lines. Then he will be able to feel completely free from that particular kind of long-term charged reaction.

He realizes well <u>now</u> that money is not all that important, yet the old beliefs were so entangled that he had to prove to himself that it was <u>not</u> so important after he achieved it. Otherwise he would always tell himself that he believed money basically unimportant because he was <u>not able</u> to achieve it.

I want it understood that money was not the primary goal, that his early drive to escape his environment was based on the false idea that worth was dependent upon your status. Being a writer would give him status even if he did not make money, though he hoped to.

The development of his psychic abilities frightened him, for the very simple reason that in his mind a psychic did not have the same kind of status. The writing abilities were always one manifestation of his own strong psychic nature, however, and his growth as a personality required the merging of both if even the writer was to succeed. All of this has been happening. *(Intently.)* His improvements are the natural result of a synthesis of personality and abilities and a reorganization of beliefs.

Rest your hand or take a break.

(10:00 to 10:14.)

Now: you had built-in status in Ruburt's eyes, simply because you were an artist. Status did not imply so much a place in society <u>as a place of self</u>. It held one to some extent aloof from society, being by nature an inbuilt superiority. Carried too far, such an idea can lead to an isolationism in which only work is important, and the daily joys experienced by others become unimportant and trivial. The very intuitive feelings behind the writer image were based upon the mysticism of nature, the joy of creaturehood; and yet pursued with too much literal-mindedness, the determination to write, once equated with work, led to important denials in those precise areas.

A concentration upon your plans, daily life, writing, and free psychic activity, will best now allow the body to continue its improvements without being watched at every moment. All suggestions as given should be continued. I will not give you definite recommendations as to what you should do now.

There should be some alterations however, changes simply to mark the end of one era and the beginning of another, even if it is but a brief vacation, or series of small trips.

By all means both of you should rejoice in the improvements as they occur. The feeling of trust, emphasized, will help Ruburt so that he does not become too impatient. When you go out in public he immediately thinks in terms of absolutes, and feels himself inadequate as a result, and his improvements seem trivial in comparison to what he wants.

A clear understanding of the point of porter will clear that up, that seeming discrepancy between what he wants and what he has. The improvements constantly show him that what he has is changing for the better and ever-approaching the flexibility he wants. I suggest your bars, and I bid you a fond good evening. Unless you have questions.

("No, I guess not.")

I still have a session next week then, once more. Remember the badminton.

("Okay. Good night, Seth, and thank you."

(10:32 PM. Jane is too concerned with bodily improvements, as Seth suggests, and we are still lax in playing badminton daily.)

DELETED SESSION
NOVEMBER 12, 1973 9:38 PM MONDAY

Now: good evening.

("Good evening, Seth.")

I will start simply enough.... As I told you, the reasons behind the body beliefs have largely vanished. You are left with beliefs about the body. These, denied the core beliefs that gave them birth, would naturally begin to weaken but could linger for some time, generally speaking, unless they were recognized <u>as</u> beliefs.

So beliefs about Ruburt's body on both of your parts, but of course primarily on Ruburt's part, must be understood <u>as</u> beliefs that then cause physical experience. Some of these have already begun to vanish, but both of you to some extent project them into the future, treat them as conditions in fact, and not as beliefs that cause conditions.

You become hypnotized then, both of you, by the effects. Each physical breakthrough manages to dilute that picture some, but often in spite of Ruburt's habits and to some extent your own.

There is a brief session that I gave some while back that points this out clearly. Both of you believe quite effectively that he cannot perform in certain areas. Now using the point of power as suggested you can break out of that circle.

I told you about the importance of imagination and the various characteristic methods that people have in utilizing suggestion through imagination. I mentioned also Ruburt and dancing, and the way he utilized challenge there, a way that would not be characteristic for you.

Now he is frightened to some extent of making the trip *(on vacation)*. At the same time he uses the challenge to activate his imagination constructively and to arouse his enthusiasm. Then in his way, with his reactions he tries to fire you with that enthusiasm, so hard won, and meets of course with your own kind of reaction.

Some of this has to do with the fact that both of you think in terms of absolutes, but often in different ways. Ruburt feels free enough to go to Florida, if he feels he does not have to face what he thinks of as your idea of absolute freedom, in which he is performing as normally as anyone else, or nearly so. If that is expected of him in line with both of your current beliefs in the body's poor performance then he does not feel free to go at all.

The fact that he plans a trip means to him that he is free to go, and that there are some gradations of freedom physically in which he can operate and use as a vehicle. Now: your idea that you are not going freely, with freedom, is in those terms an absolute. It means that within the gradations offered you will not have a good time, but will compare what you have with a "perfect" freedom that Ruburt now does not possess. All of this because of your beliefs about Ruburt's body—again, primarily Ruburt's beliefs, but yours also. Often I use "you" to refer to each of you.

Within Ruburt's present physical situation there is a degree of freedom for the trip and for enjoyment—an opportunity for manipulation, and understanding this will add to that freedom. You are each concentrating on negatives when you ignore the freedom that does exist, and denying yourselves pleasures that could help enlarge that freedom. This does not apply to the trip alone. Give us a moment.... If you both understood all I have said about the point of power, you would not compare the present physical situation with what is desired, and set the present situation in an unfavorable light, but as a progressive series of stepping stones toward the desired state.

You have many of the beliefs of your culture, though you have broken apart from many. You still allow your imagination to follow your negative beliefs, thus you *(me, RFB)* are often unable to encourage Ruburt actively, as he is often unable to encourage himself.

The body is responding despite this, however. The improvements can and will accelerate as you really believe that they can, and as you actively explore the freedoms that are now available.

A note about the curb incident Ruburt mentioned *(the other day while shopping at Centertown)*: it was precisely because each of you are still so hypnotized by effects that such incidents are charged to each of you. Your worrying about Ruburt 85% of the time does him no good and you less. You can see this quite clearly when Ruburt displays his side of the same picture, concentrating on symptoms.

A third of that energy on either of your parts spent on the realization that the effects are caused by beliefs, and an effort to change the beliefs, will work wonders. Ruburt did this with the shoe episode, and with the arm to an important degree. You cannot encourage him, saying "I know you can do it, honey, don't worry about it, you'll do better next time," when you are quite firmly convinced of the opposite.

Now: the walking most clearly shows Ruburt's beliefs and yours. The inner conditions are being righted, but Ruburt must see himself in his mind walking <u>better</u>—not perfectly but better for now, and he has begun in point of power to learn how to do that.

Your imaginations and emotions must be utilized constructively, and not to prolong the effects. Now take your break.

(10:12—10:28.)

In other words you have each been to a large extent concentrating upon the problem you want to be rid of, so that you see your entire existence only in that light, and you should each know better.

(Much louder and forcefully:) As far as your trip is concerned, concentrate upon the pleasures that are possible within it, so that neither of you manage to overstrain yourselves and forget the condition for one minute. I should not need to tell you this: see yourselves enjoying yourselves, having a good time, even within the horrendous conditions as they exist. You should each be ashamed of yourselves for ignoring the abilities, the freedoms and the pleasures that you have, and instead concentrating on the one area in which lacks are apparent, while at the same time not utilizing the methods I have given you to fully help yourselves in that area—and instead focusing your imagination to continue the situation.

In such a situation all enthusiasm becomes taboo, unrealistic, and only fear is realistic or logical. You allow yourselves little freedom in which to operate by ignoring, belittling, and denying the freedoms that <u>are</u> available.

Give us a moment.... In such circumstances you do not encourage each other, but each add to the problem. There is no reason why such a journey cannot be enjoyable, creative, healing, and bring you each great pleasure. If you each structure that experience ahead of time, however, and see it focused entirely on and through negative beliefs, then it simply becomes another hassle.

Ruburt's body <u>can</u> perform far better, and is in the process of so doing. You would each do it a great service if you would simply leave it alone, stop negative projections upon it, if you cannot manage to send it positive help through being willing to change your beliefs about it.

Your personal worrying, now, is <u>partially</u> the result of old cultural beliefs: you worry about someone you love, and this somehow helps them, and shows them your concern even while it may make you miserable. It also fills you with feelings of being a martyr, and this drains you of your own energy. It is the opposite way, unfortunately ingrained through cultural upbringing—the opposite of the way that should be followed if you want to help a loved one or yourself. For worrying is the prolongation of fearful, negative thoughts directed against another.

Now it does no good to say that the other person should have more sense then to be affected, for usually the other person has their problem because of the same kind of reaction. This applies not only to you two, but in many family situations.

Here imagination is negatively applied. Turned around however, with even a quarter of that energy used in the opposite direction, you can have a very helpful secondary support for the person in difficulty. You can tell yourself even that the person might after all take the opposite course than the one that you are imagining, and for a moment reverse the direction of your imagination. Done correctly this will automatically begin to relieve you of the pressures of responsibility felt earlier, and telepathically the other person will pick up feelings of support.

Now. Earlier Ruburt's beliefs behind the body beliefs causing the difficulty affected him in such a way that he picked up from others those moods and feelings that agreed with him, so often constructive body messages could not get through. Now however you are left with body beliefs that no longer have a foundation in other personal beliefs, so they will secede much more quickly in the face of encouragement, enthusiasm, and projects that are otherwise personally desired. These can be used therefore to activate the body now far better than before.

The means and methods should not be stressed however, for these will automatically follow. That is, in whatever way you can, see yourselves having a productive, enjoyable, creative journey. Ruburt should not <u>wonder</u>, for example, how he is going to manage in the morning, but overall see himself as enjoying himself, and the rest will follow.

You do not need to imagine him arising with your flexibility, nor should he at this point, but you should each expect continued improvement, and gradations of ever-growing freedom of mobility. Above all, <u>you are from this point to stop structuring your lives</u> upon the bedrock reality of Ruburt's condition. For that "condition" is not a permanent thing, but a changing reality, an improving condition.

You said earlier yourself that you probably hardly realized how your own viewpoint has altered. You said it passively. That viewpoint should be considered as part of the past. You can no longer use it as an excuse any more than Ruburt can use his symptoms as an excuse any more. <u>You</u> form your reality. If you want to sit back and say "My worry prevents me from enjoyment, creativity and fulfillment," then do so. It would be better if you said that entire sentence and then put it in the past, and added, "I shall no longer do so."

Then you will be free to release your own energy for yourself, and to actively and joyfully encourage Ruburt to do the same. There are many things, including this trip, that you both can actively enjoy—but not while you are insisting upon absolute freedom, while at the same time concentrating upon those elements in your experience that <u>seem</u> to keep you from it. Then your main concentration is not upon freedom at all but upon the lack of it, so that the freedoms that are available, even physically to Ruburt in his condition now, become minimized, and both of you suffer.

Now you are getting a session that many would give their eyeteeth for, so use it. Give me a moment.

(11:03.) Ruburt to some extent has also concentrated upon the condition again in an effort to get rid of it. You have done the same thing. In that light your other separate and joint accomplishments seem almost to vanish. Concentrate upon your love for each other. Concentrate upon your abilities, and on the methods you have now available that, used, will automatically dissolve the problem.

<u>Do not</u> hit yourselves over the head because of this session, wondering how you could be so stupid, for example. You know little, regardless of the mail, about the personal situation of others and the emotional climate in which they live.

You do not realize often the extent of your own triumphs or the models that you are for others, or the light that you are to them. Therefore your accomplishments are considerable, and will be greater. These challenges were chosen, and you <u>are</u> in the process of triumphing over them. If I am forceful this evening it is only because I want you to understand exactly in what areas work is needed. The results are, I tell you now, assured, as given in our late sessions—which means of course that your understanding of this session has already been taken for granted. So I bid you then a fond good evening, knowing already from my viewpoint that it <u>was followed long ago</u> in your time.

Some night later when this is over, I will give you some important information that will catch up with you, so to speak. So do not be downhearted. See yourselves in a future in which this session has long ago been given and followed with excellent results.

("Thank you, Seth. Good night."

(11:14. Jane said that the "information" Seth had for us concerned Atlantis. She was quite surprised, since Atlantis is a subject sort of suspect to her because of the Edgar Cayce connotations, etc.)

DELETED SESSION
NOVEMBER 19, 1973

(The first four pages are missing, and have been for many years.)

Earlier, when this latest group of sessions began, he could <u>not</u> have played badminton, much less taken that trip. At the same time this expansion <u>did</u> put him in situations that he had avoided before, and so the contrast between his physical situation and that of others was apparent—and to him, frightening. This in itself however was an advance, and it served to bring up the fact that these were body beliefs.

Psycho-Cybernetics worked well for a time, because at that stage the book served to break up body beliefs, though he hadn't tackled the reasons behind them. He has already planned to reinstate suggestions I have given—he knows the ones, and this should be done immediately. They were dropped for several reasons, but mainly because he still did not understand that body beliefs <u>were</u> involved, and that these like the others could be changed.

Now: he is to do the point of power exactly as he decided yesterday. Working with body beliefs. I suggest that you hear his morning as well as evening suggestions, and that you take a few moments, perhaps no more than 5 a day, to impress upon him the fact that these new beliefs can be inserted in place of the old, and <u>will</u> bear results. This is for your benefit also, and your joint benefits. For the speediest overall improvement can be expected as each of you realize together and separately that the condition can be, and is being, changed for the better.

There is a feel to this. You can tell when it is taking hold, and your joint belief is necessary. In the inner order of events it has occurred, and Tam, not knowing I have said so, has picked it up. *(See Tam's recent letter, in which he described his dream in which he saw Jane fully recovered, etc.)* But still in your time and terms I tell you to follow faithfully what I have suggested.

Give us a moment. Rest your hand.

(10:26.) When you tackle these body beliefs directly you will, literally, be surprised at the results. I suggest you speak with Ruburt for a few moments daily because of the combined nature of your energies, so for that period, however brief, concentrate upon the fact that the new beliefs are, even in those moments, taking hold.

Above all however do not concentrate upon this as a problem, but as a challenge you are even now overcoming, and let the rest of your day flow with other creativity.

The book will do far better. *(I should have asked which book.)* The questions that you have jointly because of your experience in this life so far will lead you to answers that will help many as well as yourselves. I have said this to many: but if you, Joseph, trust yourself and throw yourself onto the graces of yourself, then from you will flow all that you need or desire. The same applies to Ruburt. Do you have questions?

("No.")

Then I bid you a fond good evening. Some definite overall changes in your environment are important, however. Their nature is not. One part of your lives is over, with the death of both of your parents. This applies to each of you. You have chosen your heritage. What will come of it you still barely suspect consciously. Either your entire living arrangements here must be incorporated into a new unity or you must go someplace else, for you need a symbol of change. But in a working framework, even if a vacation is involved.

Now, I bid you a fond good evening.

("Thank you, Seth, and good night." 10:37.)

DELETED SESSION
NOVEMBER 26, 1973 9:31 PM MONDAY

Good evening.

("Good evening, Seth.")

In your terms and in your probability, your parents' lives are over, completed, and when in your reality you paint a picture it is finished, completed;

and yet even in that context it outlives your completion of it, and endures. Surely lives are as important as paintings, and as such multidimensional creations far outlast the paintings that are representations of the life you know.

When you have completed a life then it is as if you have finished a living portrait of yourself, using the mediums of space and time. Then you have the painting to examine. The memories and realities within that portrait are yours to learn from and to use as a model for other such living portraits in time and space.

Some are more proficient in using the mediums than others. Some deal with large stormy soulscapes and tumultuous endeavors. Some paint living portraits of themselves in peaceful times and places. Each living self-artist however tries to create the inner self in the material world, and each such portrait is indeed unique.

There are masters in living as there are the Old Masters of painting. Some of the Old Masters were adept at painting scenes of violence, warfare, sagas, with dark and dreary atmospheres, yet each so filled at the same time with life and vitality that the canvases themselves seemed alive. Even paintings of great destruction spoke of the great creative energy behind the talent that vitalized the very medium, and by its very creativity denied the very strength of the destruction so cleverly depicted.

The greatest Old Masters felt the inner self's great integrity, and its connection with All That Is, and each in his own way through painting tried to represent that energy and show it to others. The energy is behind all. When you look at the great world picture before you in space and time, look at it as you would a multidimensional worldscape, painted by some artist who was all of the great masters in one; and behind the scenes of destruction and conflict, feel the great energy that in itself denies the destruction that is in that case so cleverly depicted.

Now there are progressions, so to speak, of understanding, and when you reach the level currently experienced by yourself and Ruburt, then you will be driven because of the seeming conflict into the kind of synthesis that I have just spoken of allegorically. This applies to your understanding of private lives as well as world conditions.

You want to be an excellent painter. At least you want to paint your own unique vision, and Ruburt wants to write his. Those particular aspirations will lead you, and are leading you, to the realization that life itself is an art, composed of the same ingredients of inner inspiration, spontaneity and conscious organization and discrimination.

You still do not really understand. This does not apply to the two of you alone, but to your world at large: you make your own reality through your beliefs. You want to keep your beliefs yet change your reality—I am not referring to you personally here now—but this is impossible.

If you believe that you are pulled in all directions you will be. Your experience will prove it out. If you believe there is no peace in your world, in your private world, there will be none. If you want peace you must insert the belief in it and then your experience will justify it.

You cannot say to yourself twenty times a day "There is no peace," and at the same time expect to find some, with any possibility of achieving anything but conflict. There is no other way. Keep your cherished beliefs in conflict, but you will not find peace.

You can be alone in the silence, fairly isolated, and yet filled with conflict if it is within you. You can be surrounded by some noise *(as Seth, Jane pointed to the ceiling; someone was moving into the apartment above us)* or traffic, and feel its great synthesis with the vitality of life, and it can be conducive to peace. This does not mean that silence at times is not preferable to noise. It means that you make your own reality.

It means that the belief in discordant conditions initiates it. I am not saying that others are not involved, but that discordant thoughts bring about discordant reactions in others, to which they will react according to their own beliefs. But no one creates your private reality but you.

It is easy for you to say that your parents did not appreciate what they had, that they looked at the "bad" side of things all the time, but not quite so easy to see those same attitudes in yourselves.

When you consistently concentrate upon negative aspects you seek them out from your experience and all the available stimuli, until reality certainly does seem to justify your attitudes. Using the power point of the present, you seek backward into the past, reorganizing data to those ends, and project them into the future. You feel closed in. Depression sets in. If this is the kind of painting you want then at least be aware of it. If it is not, realize that you can at any point in the present begin to alter it and your experience.

Take a break.

(10:07. This turned out to be the end of the session. A long discussion between Jane and me followed, though not to much avail.)

DELETED SESSION
NOVEMBER 27, 1973 9:27 PM TUESDAY

(Tonight's session was an effort to complete the truncated session of last night.)

Good evening.

("Good evening, Seth.")

Now: we will begin again. There is an excellent book, called *The Nature of Personal Reality*. It will help many. It will help the two of you particularly, because your personal realities are so involved in it. That is, it will if you read it.

We are starting anew, and again this time I will not hold another session for you unless you follow what I say this evening.

You are to begin the book together, making notations as what I say applies personally, and <u>together</u> each of you following through with the exercises given. You want results, so, at the very least a ½ hour a day is to be used for this purpose, and when you have the time an hour. Before any time-consuming exercises are given however, read the book together and discuss it as it applies.

Earlier this evening you were discussing your beliefs, and beliefs is the name of the game. The exercises will serve you as well as Ruburt. In this situation two are involved, and "therapy" must involve each of you. Your own creativity will be vastly improved, and the exercises dealing with feelings will be invaluable to both of you.

You live in private yet joint realities. Ruburt has chosen his, and you have chosen that his reality be involved with yours. Ruburt is not simply stuck with a bunch of symptoms, and you are not stuck just with a wife who has problems.

The work with the book is to supercede any other suggestions I have given in the past for you. It has prime priority. Reading it and following the exercises will initiate your own inner and outer motion.

Now give us a moment. *(Pause.)* You <u>are</u> financially secure. Ruburt's classes will not suffer despite appearances *(the energy crisis)*. Much of what I said last evening applied to you, Joseph. Ruburt, so sensitive to your moods, and being self-conditioned to some extent himself negatively, reacted. He wanted to help you, and felt powerless to a large extent.

Your decision not to go to Florida had little to do with the energy crisis. You were both loath to leave your work behind and to allow yourselves the "lax" freedom. You wanted to get on with your own work, and to wait for the proofs of my book. You felt guilty at the thought of enjoying yourself so soon after your mother's death. You felt some self-punishment, denying yourself the trip to make up for what you felt you might have done for her in the past.

Ruburt was already leery of putting his physical condition to the test of the trip, and so easily acquiesced, worried also that perhaps he would lose out on *Aspects*, that was already contracted for.

Both of you have kept yourselves uneasy in your environment lest you become too comfortable. You concentrate upon the annoyances of your neighbors lest you become too close to them and emotionally involved and touched. You have lived here some years yet purposely avoided thinking of it, this apartment, as anything but transitory lest you put down roots and become involved in ways that might distract you from your work and purposes. Give us a moment.... You do not buy much furniture so that the idea of being transitory is more convincing. At the same time you stay where you are so you can work, while denying yourselves the sense of ease that you could otherwise enjoy.

(*To me:*) You imagine a quiet home in the country—the dream in that regard in your mind, knowing full well you have no intentions of using "valuable time" to mow grass, fix pipes or tend to furnaces. So you laugh at Leonard, who does so here.

At the same time you think, for several reasons, that at your age you <u>should</u> have a house, privacy to work, a way even of proving to your brothers that you have as much as they. Ruburt instead sees a trailer by the ocean, with each of you writing and painting—his vision, because <u>that</u> establishment requires no housekeeping and a small cash outlay.

You have done neither because in your present situation you have some contact with people, minimum upkeep, and all of this represents a kissing acquaintance with the world at large. You are in the establishment and yet not in it.

(9:55.) Give us a moment.... You both are so afraid of being tied down however that even in the apartment you did not allow yourselves really to feel at home—to buy your furniture, cheap or expensive. You love and hate family, precisely as Ruburt does. He because he never really had one, and you because you did.

A house in town reminds you each of family living, and you of your neighborhood. At the same time for all <u>your</u> protest, the *(to me)* apartment noises are comforting. You interpret them as conflicts. They remind you of the noises in your family home, conflicting and yet comforting. You rail at them, railing at your parents' arguments. To Ruburt the sounds are reassuring. He is not alone with his mother any more.

Each of you sees buying a house now as a threat, though you are at times tempted. You have always seen family life yourself as a threat to artistic production, and the first thing you would do if you had a house would be to build a studio outside of it. You did not want children. Whatever methods Ruburt chose to insure that you were childless you proclaimed with joy, glad that you were not the woman.

<u>Some</u> of the symptoms then were indeed to insure your joint work integrity. You identified as a child whose presence betrayed its father, your father being

forced to support you, particularly in the Depression. Ruburt as you know had his own reasons. Ruburt's relative immobility kept him childless. You were turned off physically often, or he was not able to perform when you were not turned off.

Your father was inventive, his creativity in that line you felt dwarfed by family responsibility. Your creativity would not be. You chose a woman (beside reincarnational reasons which you will finally be given one day) who would not bear children and who would have as strong a commitment as your own.

You would not be tempted toward conventionality, for your woman was not conventional. She would keep you from whatever leanings you might have had in that direction. She could be counted upon not to press you toward the world's ways.

Now: the other side of the picture. Ruburt sought you out for much the same reasons, with reincarnational background to be given. But Ruburt was the female: you would not bear any child, so the effort had to be strong on his part. Thoughts of buying a house throw both of you into a quandary because they directly come in conflict with your private ideas about your work and purposes, and your places in the world.

Give us a moment.... Your ideas of rustic simplicity do not match your feelings about dedication to work. Ruburt's ideas of owning a house do not match his ideas of dedication to work. That is why his interpretation is a trailer. Both ideas <u>are</u> idealized, sentimentalized and distorted in your minds, and either could be incorporated in your ideas of work if you were aware of the conflicts.

You have never allowed yourselves creative decorating freedom here, for example, and thus denied yourselves considerable satisfaction. Now the walking is directly involved with all of this. With the ideas of either buying a house or going to Florida, and what these issues involve in line with your current beliefs as given. Your mother's death makes Ruburt want to go further inward for more answers. At the same time he is trying to make outer decisions.

Now: we can only get so much through in an evening. I will continue this at your earliest convenience—but begin at once as given with the book, and the understanding, I hope, you will achieve from this session. I bid you a fond good evening, but unless you do what I have said, and until you do, we will not have another private session, for you will not be ready for it.

(With a smile:) I know you will be.

("I hope so." 10:25 PM.)

THE SETH AUDIO COLLECTION

RARE RECORDINGS OF SETH SPEAKING through Jane Roberts are now available on audiocassette and CD. These Seth sessions were recorded by Jane's student, Rick Stack, during Jane's classes in Elmira, New York, in the 1970's. The majority of these selections have never been published in any form. Volume I, described below, is a collection of some of the best of Seth's comments gleaned from over 120 Seth Sessions. Additional selections from The Seth Audio Collection are also available. For information ask for our free catalogue.

Volume I of The Seth Audio Collection consists of six (1-hour) cassettes plus a 34-page booklet of Seth transcripts. Topics covered in Volume I include:

- Creating your own reality – How to free yourself from limiting beliefs and create the life you want.
- Dreams and out-of-body experiences.
- Reincarnation and Simultaneous Time.
- Connecting with your inner self.
- Spontaneity–Letting yourself go with the flow of your being.
- Creating abundance in every area of your life.
- Parallel (probable) universes and exploring other dimensions of reality.
- Spiritual healing, how to handle emotions, overcoming depression and much more.

FOR A FREE CATALOGUE of Seth related products including a detailed description of The Seth Audio Collection, please send your request to the address below.

ORDER INFORMATION:
If you would like to order a copy of The Seth Audio Collection Volume I, please send your name and address, with a check or money order payable to New Awareness Network, Inc. for $60 (Tapes), or $70 (CD's) plus shipping charges. United States residents in NY, NJ, CT, PA, & TX must add sales tax.

Shipping charges: U.S.—$6.00, Canada—$7, Europe—$17, Australia & Asia—$19
Rates are UPS for U.S. & Airmail for International—Allow 2 weeks for delivery
Alternate Shipping—Surface—$9.00 to anywhere in the world—Allow 5-8 weeks

Mail to: NEW AWARENESS NETWORK INC.
P.O. BOX 192,
Manhasset, New York 11030
(516) 869-9108 between 9:00-5:00 p.m. Monday-Friday EST
Visit us on the Internet—www.sethcenter.com

Books by Jane Roberts from Amber-Allen Publishing

Seth Speaks: The Eternal Validity of the Soul. This essential guide to conscious living clearly and powerfully articulates the furthest reaches of human potential, and the concept that each of us creates our own reality.

The Nature of Personal Reality: Specific, Practical Techniques for Solving Everyday Problems and Enriching the Life You Know.. In this perennial bestseller, Seth challenges our assumptions about the nature of reality and stresses the individual's capacity for conscious action.

The Individual and the Nature of Mass Events. Seth explores the connection between personal beliefs and world events, how our realities merge and combine "to form mass reactions such as the overthrow of governments, the birth of a new religion, wars, epidemics, earthquakes, and new periods of art, architecture, and technology."

The Magical Approach: Seth Speaks About the Art of Creative Living. Seth reveals the true, magical nature of our deepest levels of being, and explains how to live our lives spontaneously, creatively, and according to our own natural rhythms.

The Oversoul Seven Trilogy (The Education of Oversoul Seven, The Further Education of Oversoul Seven, Oversoul Seven and the Museum of Time). Inspired by Jane's own experiences with the Seth Material, the adventures of Oversoul Seven are an intriguing fantasy, a mind-altering exploration of our inner being, and a vibrant celebration of life.

The Nature of the Psyche. Seth reveals a startling new concept of self, answering questions about the inner reality that exists apart from time, the origins and powers of dreams, human sexuality, and how we choose our physical death.

The "Unknown" Reality, Volumes One and Two. Seth reveals the multidimensional nature of the human soul, the dazzling labyrinths of unseen probabilities involved in any decision, and how probable realities combine to create the waking life we know.

Dreams, "Evolution," and Value Fulfillment, Volumes One and Two. Seth discusses the material world as an ongoing self-creation—the product of a conscious, self-aware and thoroughly animate universe, where virtually every possibility not only exists, but is constantly encouraged to achieve its highest potential.

The Way Toward Health. Woven through the poignant story of Jane Roberts' final days are Seth's teachings about self-healing and the mind's effect upon physical health.

Available in bookstores everywhere.